Getting Played

Getting Played

*African American Girls,
Urban Inequality, and
Gendered Violence*

Jody Miller

Foreword by Ruth D. Peterson

NEW YORK UNIVERSITY PRESS
New York and London

NEW YORK UNIVERSITY PRESS
New York and London
www.nyupress.org

Library of Congress Cataloging-in-Publication Data
Miller, Jody, 1966–
Getting played : African American girls, urban inequality, and
gendered violence / Jody Miller ; foreword by Ruth D. Peterson.
p.   cm. — (New perspectives in crime, deviance, and law series)
Includes bibliographical references and index.
ISBN 978-0-8147-5697-3 (alk. paper : cloth)
ISBN 978-0-8147-5698-0 (alk. paper : pbk.)
1. African American young women—Violence against. 2. African
American young women—Abuse of. 3. African American young
women—Crimes against. 4. African American teenage girls—
Violence against. 5. African American teenage girls—Abuse of.
6. African American teenage girls—Crimes against. 7. Victims of
violent crimes—United States—Psychology.   I. Title.
HV6250.4.W65M522 2008
362.76—dc22   2007037275

New York University Press books are printed on acid-free paper,
and their binding materials are chosen for strength and durability.

Manufactured in the United States of America
10 9 8 7 6 5 4 3 2 1

To my parents,
Linda and Jerry Miller
—for a lifetime of encouragement

Contents

	Foreword by Ruth D. Peterson	ix
	Preface	xv
	Acknowledgments	xix
1	Perspectives on Gender and Urban Violence	1
2	Gender 'n the 'Hood: Neighborhood Violence against Women and Girls	32
3	Playin' Too Much: Sexual Harassment in School	67
4	Respect Yourself, Protect Yourself: Sexual Coercion and Violence	114
5	The Playa' and the Cool Pose: Gender and Relationship Violence	151
6	Conclusions and Recommendations	191
	Appendix: Study Participants	223
	Notes	225
	References	265
	Index	285
	About the Author	292

Foreword

Ruth D. Peterson

In *Getting Played,* Jody Miller has once again offered up an eye-opening investigation of young women's lives and vulnerabilities. In her earlier book, *One of the Guys,* she enlightened us about fundamental processes related to girls' entry into and participation in gangs. This time, the subjects of Miller's research are perhaps the most understudied population in the field of criminology: African American girls, more specifically African American girls who reside in one of the poorest sections of St. Louis, Missouri. When such girls are the focus of criminological research, it is usually from the point of view of explaining their participation in delinquency or other problematic behaviors. *Getting Played* takes a decidedly different approach. Here, Miller focuses on girls' victimization and the embeddedness of such victimization in the everyday lives of these youths, with all that this means for discovering and bringing the reader face to face with a host of unpleasant realities. These critical choices (of topic and population) take us to a story of how intersections of gender, race, class, and place are at the center of girls' lives and experiences.

First, and most notably, Miller grabs readers' attention with the stark reality of the widespread occurrence of violent victimization among the girls she studies. Such violence ranges from what some would regard as mild forms of harassment (sexual and gender-based) to striking and heart-wrenching incidents of gang rape and repeated violent assaults. Indeed, one is hard-pressed at times to contain tears and felt-rage in the wake of descriptions of the worst cases of the violence perpetrated against young women. Such victimizations seem even sadder because they come at the hands of boys (and men) who are "friends" and family

Ruth D. Peterson is Distinguished Professor of Social and Behavioral Science at The Ohio State University, Columbus, Ohio.

members and who themselves bear the scars of subordinate racial status and disadvantage. This is not an unexpected finding, but the thick descriptions of incidents give a face and intimate quality to the violence that is chronicled in *Getting Played,* its male perpetrators (who strike poses of bravado and "play" girls to gain status and prestige among their peers), and, its female victims (whose own sexualized poses belie the everyday dangers to body and reputation that they face).

Second, through Miller's analysis, we see first hand the very real isolation of girls in their victimization as many incidents occur in situational contexts that are public (schools, parties, etc.), but where witnesses do not intervene to stop or redress the harassment or violence. Witnesses are often peers (female and male) who do not intervene because they believe "it is a private matter," "she deserved it," or for fear of retaliation. But adults such as school officials and neighborhood residents also witness these events without taking action. Indeed, some of the *offenders* are adult men in the neighborhood, even police officers. The reasons for the adults' behaviors are beyond the scope of Miller's analysis. However, it is clear that when certain adults (school officials, police officers) ignore ongoing victimizations, they also violate their obligations to protect young people and undermine their positions of trust with youth, who then cannot call on them for help. Hence, as the stories unfold, and in the wake of the failure of peers and officials to act, we come to see the substantial isolation of poor African American girls, despite the fact that much victimization occurs in social and public settings.

Third, Miller also brings us face to face with the negative consequences of girls' (and boys') own interpretations and explanations of the everyday victimization to which they are exposed. Indeed, an important feature of *Getting Played* is lending youths' own voices to their experiences. In doing so, two things become abundantly clear: (1) the extensiveness to which young women and young men view girls' victimization (as well as boys' violence) as problems of individual character rather than as products of structural and situational contexts that are shared by the young victims and perpetrators alike; and (2) how grounded youths' explanations are in gender-based stereotypes about how girls carry themselves and how "boys will be boys." Yet, the individualistic and gendered explanations are belied by the structural solutions (e.g., employment opportunities, educational and recreational programming) that they pose to address their problems and those of their communities.

Fourth, Miller's assessment brings home the point that youths' (and others') victim-blaming views have very real consequences for how violence and its aftermath are handled, often including increased danger for girls. As seen, the views are, in part, responsible for the failure of peers to intervene when a young woman is attacked. They also mean that victimized girls' primary response to violence and its aftermath is self-help in the form of changing one's style of dress, staying inside, walking with company, having male relatives retaliate, and the like. Because they do not reflect underlying structural causes, none of these strategies eliminates the violence or its threats. To the contrary, self-help strategies often put girls at risk for additional victimization, as well as reputational degradation. Self-blaming and victim-blaming is not the exclusive reason that girls engage mainly in self-help. They also do so because their experiences with school officials, police, social services agencies, and the like lead them to lack trust in these systems as sources of help. Unfortunately, as I read *Getting Played*, the young women's skepticism seems warranted. In reading, I wondered aloud about the long-term consequences for girls of relying solely (or mainly) on self-help for redress. For which girls would this approach mean a continuing pattern of being abused far into adulthood? Conversely, for which ones would handling such problems on their own mean becoming independent and resourceful adults whose choices lend themselves to violence-free lives?

Getting Played's central contributions are not alone in the very vivid picture painted of the victimization (and aftermath) that African American girls from disadvantaged neighborhoods face. Rather, the book offers broad contributions to criminology as it speaks to theoretical issues in areas of gender, race/ethnicity, and neighborhood crime. One way in which Miller characterizes her work is as a gendered ecological approach. This is certainly an appropriate representation, as the study is unquestionably oriented to assessing how the continuum of violent victimizations are gendered within a particular type of ecological context. Miller explicates the gender dynamics of violence against women and locates the degree and type of violence in a combination of (1) deeply embedded gender stereotypes and gender inequality that relates to control of public spaces and (2) the spaces that young women navigate on a daily basis, with schools being ripe contexts for sexual and gender harassment and the neighborhood being the setting for more serious violence.

Miller is successful in explicating the gender dynamics of young women's victimization, in part, because she is insightful enough to *not* limit her analysis to girls. Rather, she interviews boys alongside girls, thereby allowing the comparative gendered story to emerge in full. We see where girls' and boys' lives and points of view converge in ways that rationalize aggressive actions and justify nonintervention in disputes. And we also learn how the positioning of girls and boys diverges with respect to the meaning of violence, the control of public space, and aspects of power and circumstances that make girls vulnerable to victimization and put boys at risk for offending. In my view, the richness of the insights of Miller's study is largely due to the quality of assessments that can only come from a comparative approach. As such, her strategy is one to be emulated.

For feminist scholars, elucidating the gender dynamics that underlie girls' victimization may be the core contribution of *Getting Played*. My own vantage point on the book is as a scholar interested in the linkages among race/ethnicity, crime, and justice. In fact, one of my mantras over the past few years has been a call for researchers to embed analyses of criminal victimization and offending in a broad understanding of the overall ethnoracial structure of society. This is not a primary focus of Miller's book because her analyses are based on a single racial group (African Americans) in a single economic context (highly disadvantaged and predominantly Black neighborhoods in St. Louis). Nonetheless, *Getting Played* speaks to my concern in significant ways. First, because she uses a comparative approach vis-à-vis males and females, Miller is able to demonstrate variability *within* a racial group where members are seemingly similarly situated. This, in itself, is an aspect of understanding how broad racial structures affect crime. The contextualized nature of race makes the girls and boys vulnerable to involvement, albeit in different ways due to the intersection of race with gender. Second, and more fundamentally, is how Miller draws on the larger body of knowledge on race and neighborhood crime to set up her problem, determine where to focus her attention, set the meaning of the work in context, and interpret the patterns that she observes. The result is an extremely textured account of victimization that is embedded in the established findings and conclusions of existing quantitative and qualitative literature on race and crime and on neighborhood crime. There is no question that *Getting Played* sheds light on how girls' victimization reflects the racial structure of U.S. society.

However one sees the main substantive contributions of *Getting Played*, in the final analysis, it is a story about the social worlds of an important and understudied segment of adolescent society. It teaches us that where girls go, with whom they interact and in what contexts, and how they and their male counterparts interpret their everyday behaviors matters in fundamental ways for their well-being. Miller is to be commended for her nuanced presentation and for bringing us face to face with this social world.

Preface

In the summer of 1998, I was writing my monograph *One of the Guys* and also teaching a photography class to youths at a local community agency in North St. Louis. I have spent most of my career examining how gender inequality shapes young women's participation in crime, focusing both on structural and situational inequalities and on how ideologies about gender often place young women in the precarious position of upholding such inequalities, even as they stake out interpersonal spaces in which they work to exempt themselves from the broad ideologies that they, their peers, and the broader culture reinforce. But my research on young women's gang involvement had also sharpened my concern about the gendered victimization risks that girls face in disadvantaged community contexts, risks heightened by their participation in gangs and friendships with delinquent peers.

I sent youths out into their communities with cameras to document their daily lives. And week after week, I was struck and saddened by the portraits they produced, which barely resembled the kids I was interacting with. Young men struck poses intended to project an image of street bravado. Occasionally throwing up gang signs, they sent hardened stares into the camera lenses, mimicking the depictions of young Black manhood we see all too often in the media in America. Photographs of their homes and neighborhoods showed signs of the physical decay we have come to know as the contemporary nature of urban poverty. But it was the girls' photos that really stuck with me. Nearly every young woman in my class, solo or in pairs, came away from the course with a portrait of themselves, back turned from the camera, head turned to face it, and bent over, showing their backsides in a sexualized pose. Is this a celebration of female sexuality? Of Black female sexuality specifically? Or do we continue to teach young women that their value lies in their sexual objectification?

We live in a time of *Girls Gone Wild,* in what some have called a postfeminist era, where young women's newfound right to sexual desire has been too easily coopted and conflated with their sexual desirability, with their participation in the male gaze. And we know that women's sexual desire, and any of their behaviors that—correctly or not—can be read as sexually suggestive, still means they are held accountable for sexual violence against them. "No means no," but only when there is no evidence, however obscure or misleading, that can be read as an indication of "perhaps," "maybe," or "yes." We know this from social science research, from research on the character and functions of criminal law, and from the media—nearly every time a rape case makes headlines.

Boys will be boys, so women must stand up for themselves and be clear on their sexual intentions. Were you friendly to a young man? Sexual intent. Did you agree to go to a party with him? Sexual intent. To drink? Sexual intent. Did you wear tight clothes, a short skirt, a low-cut blouse? Sexual intent. Of course, not all men, young or old, adhere to such a belief system, and certainly not all would act on such beliefs even when they adhere to them. But in a court of law, let alone the court of public opinion, young women are not victims of sexual violence but culpable participants in sexual encounters they themselves are responsible for.

So what of our young photographers, many of whom were interviewed for this book? As I argue in the pages that follow, we as a society, as scholars, as criminologists have turned our backs on them. Don't get me wrong. Many researchers are dedicated to addressing and ameliorating the problems associated with urban disadvantage: violence, the decimation of communities caused by drugs and incarceration, and societal neglect and entrenched poverty, including the poverty of opportunities. In addition, feminist scholars have made tremendous inroads in recent decades in advancing our understanding of violence against women and improving the services available to the many victims of such violence. But urban African American girls have fallen through the cracks. They don't come to mind as the prototypical victim. They don't garner public sympathy. The roots of these ideologies are as old as the legacy of slavery. Certainly, they were found even in early feminist treatises on sexual violence, and they continue today.

But given the widespread nature of violence against women in American society, why wouldn't such violence be prevalent as well—and in particular—in impoverished community contexts where we know that violence is endemic, community and personal resources are limited, and the all too available opportunities for boys to become men rely on heightened definitions of masculinity that focus on interpersonal violence, respect, and a willing-to-do-anything persona of toughness and independence? When women aren't spared from gendered violence in the best of social and economic circumstances, why would they be spared in the worst? As I'll document in *Getting Played,* they certainly are not.

This book should not be read as an indictment of young Black men and their treatment of their female peers. My intent is not to further perpetuate the myth of the Black rapist. As feminist scholarship has consistently shown, violence against women is prevalent across all social strata in the United States. It is tied to the persistent nature of gender inequality endemic to our society. However, the particular forms it takes are also structurally and situationally dependent. And we, as a society, have created the circumstances that place young Black women at such heightened risk for gendered victimization. We've perpetuated the structural conditions that lead to the cultural adaptations and situational contexts that shape urban African American young women's risks. The indictment is of all of us.

Acknowledgments

The research I present here was funded by the National Consortium on Violence Research. In addition to consortium members, I thank Norm White, co-principal investigator on the grant, as well as Ruth Peterson, Darnell Hawkins, and Linda Sharpe-Taylor, who served as project consultants. I also appreciate the hard work of our research assistants, Toya Like, Iris Foster, Dennis Mares, and Jenna St. Cyr. I owe Toya a special debt of thanks. She was the heart and soul of this project. She cared deeply about the young people she interviewed and connected with them in ways that benefited the research tremendously. I alone bear responsibility for the analyses that follow, but none of it would have been possible without Toya's commitment to the project.

A number of additional individuals contributed to the production of this research. Olivia Quarles served as youth advocate for the project and was generous with her time and insights. She ran Project Respond (PREPP), the program where my photography course was taught, and provided her kids with an amazing amount of love and support. It's disheartening to report that during the course of our research, PREPP lost its funding and its doors were closed. The youths we spoke to lamented their loss of the safe haven they attributed to keeping them off the streets and daily contact with the mentor they relied on and loved dearly. Likewise, I thank Constance White and Beverly Humphrey at the now defunct King and Madison Tri-A schools, who coordinated interviews for us at their institutions. I am appreciative of Cathy McNeal, Jessie Bridges, Emily Byrne, Brenda Stutte, and Virginia Schodroski at the University of Missouri–St. Louis for their administrative expertise and support. And thanks to Ilene Kalish at New York University Press, both for her patience and her editorial guidance, and Despina Papazoglou Gimbel for expertly guiding the book through production.

Writing a book is a painstaking and time-consuming process. It wouldn't be possible without the support of great friends and colleagues.

Thanks especially to Rod Brunson, who was willing to talk through ideas with me at all hours of the day and night, and who read drafts and offered insightful feedback though all stages of the writing process. Marty Schwartz, Deborah Cohen, and students in my seminar on gender, crime, and justice (Jamie Fields, Dottie Kenoyer, Stacey Rinehart, Brenda Wirthlin) have also read and given me feedback on chapter drafts, Jessica Johnston read the entire work, giving feedback and checking for consistencies within and across chapters, and Jennifer Cobbina assisted with proofreading and created the index. Thanks also to my colleagues at the University of Missouri–St. Louis, for fostering an environment conducive to my research. Bob Bursik, Dave Curry, Scott Decker, and Eric Stewart, in particular, have been great friends, and their support has encouraged and inspired me. It takes a village, and my village at UMSL also includes Eric Baumer, Finn Esbensen, Beth Huebner, David Klinger, Janet Lauritsen, Callie Rennison, Rick Rosenfeld, and Richard Wright.

Thanks as well to my family and friends, for their enthusiasm and encouragement: Marilyn Morton, who's the best friend a gal could ever ask for, Nilu Abeyaratne, Rajivi Gunawardena, Gina Boteju, Greg Stiers and Debbie Nicodemus, Sarah Morton, Jennifer Bursik, Prasad Jayawardena, John Taylor, Guy Rhoades, Janet Holmes, my mother-in-law and father-in-law Janaki and Ranjit Gunawardena, Linda and Jim Fairchild, and, of course, my parents. Special thanks to my husband Puny Gunawardena, for keeping me well fed and not minding the countless hours I abandoned him for my computer screen. Finally, I owe a debt of gratitude to all of the young women and young men who shared their stories with us. I only hope this research can contribute something meaningful in return.

1

Perspectives on Gender and Urban Violence

In his bestselling autobiography *Makes Me Wanna Holler: A Young Black Man in America,* Nathan McCall describes the routine adolescent practice in his neighborhood of running "trains" on girls—what "white boys call . . . gang-banging"[1] and scholars now call gang rape. He explains:

> Although everybody knew it could lead to trouble with the law, I think few guys thought of it as rape. It was viewed as a social thing among hanging partners, like passing a joint. The dude who set up the train got pats on the back. He was considered a real player whose rap game was strong. . . . Even though it involved sex, it didn't seem to be about sex at all. Like almost everything we did, it was a macho thing. Using a member of one of the most vulnerable groups of human beings on the face of the earth—Black females—it was another way for a guy to show the other fellas how cold and hard he was.[2]

In another award-winning book, *Always Running: La Vida Loca—Gang Days in L.A.,* Luis Rodriguez recounts that rape was "a common circumstance" among his peers.[3] Both authors provide searing analyses of racial and class inequalities, urban violence, and their devastating effects on the psyches and behaviors of young men of color. They also describe violence against young women in their communities as routine. Yet, while many scholars of urban crime recognize the connections between racial inequality, neighborhood disadvantage, and violence, the gender-based violence so readily recounted by McCall, Rodriguez, and others is largely absent from the discussion. In the end, violence against young women is a ubiquitous but too often invisible feature of the urban landscape, and it remains largely underexamined and thus undertheorized.[4]

The reasons for this neglect are manifold. Mainstream criminology has long been criticized for its insufficient attention to both women and gender.[5] Androcentric perspectives continue to guide much criminological research and theorizing, leading to both an exclusive or implicit focus on men and boys and a failure to seek explanations for crime and victimization that take gender seriously as a structural, interactional, and symbolic source of inequality. This is the case in many contemporary studies of urban disadvantage and crime and is even found in recent work on violence against women.[6]

Not surprisingly, scholars of women's and gender studies—both within criminology and across disciplinary boundaries—have long studied violence against women, grounding the understanding of this expansive social problem in the context of gender inequality.[7] But even those of us who are committed to the field have been slow on the uptake when it comes to efforts to understand and theorize the problem of violence against women in urban settings. Here again, the reasons are complex. The early efforts of feminist researchers and activists politicized violence against women; the goal was to make an invisible social problem a visible one. Scholars have studied and theorized marital rape, date rape, and acquaintance rape, as well as intimate partner violence, documenting their existence across all social strata within society. A consistent goal has been to make it evident that violence against women is *every* woman's problem—and every *man's* problem—that, in fact, it has its roots in societal organization and culture.

An important component of this work has been to insist that our understanding of violence against women no longer be relegated to the cultural "boogeyman"—the archetypal image of the dangerous (Black) male stranger, lurking in the shadows, targeting the stereotypic innocent (white) female victim. On this count, feminists have certainly been successful. All of us now have a much more complex understanding of violence against women, and tremendous policy inroads have been made as well.[8] However, while systematic research has debunked the myth of the ravenous Black rapist rooted in historical legacies of slavery, economic, gender, and racial oppression,[9] we have been less successful in seeing and addressing violence against African American women and girls.

Though dramatic improvements have been made, white feminist scholarship has long been critiqued for not sufficiently addressing the interlocking nature of race, class, and gender oppression and for assuming or implying uniformity in the inequalities faced by women.[10] This has led to insufficient attention to the unique experiences of urban African American women and girls.[11] However, an additional complication—and one I have struggled with in this research—is some reticence in addressing violence committed by African American males against Black females. We do not need another reason to demonize poor minority young men. But since we know that most violence, including violence against women, is both intraracial and involves similarly situated individuals often known to one another, this reticence has meant that we have neglected to understand the unique experiences and risks faced by African American women and girls, particularly those in disadvantaged urban communities.

Given that criminologists focus on offending, one area in which gender scholars have made significant contributions is in documenting and theorizing the overlapping relationship between young women's criminal involvement and their experiences with victimization.[12] Some of this scholarship has examined victimization as a precursor to offending, while other works have emphasized the contemporaneous nature of victimization and offending by examining the impact of gender inequality on street and offender networks. Feminist criminologists have become increasingly interested in investigating how race and class inequalities, in conjunction with urban space, shape women's and girls' experiences of gender-based violence. But few studies have systematically investigated the relationships between poor urban communities, youth street culture, and violence against young women.

Thus, my goal here is to bring together these significant strands of criminological research, to investigate how the structural inequalities that create extreme—and racialized—urban poverty facilitate both cultural adaptations and social contexts that heighten and shape the tremendous gender-based violence faced by urban African American girls. Such violence is a critical social problem in need of careful theoretical and policy attention. And though violence against women is systematic throughout the United States, I argue here that it is particularly acute for adolescent girls in neighborhoods characterized by intense disadvantage. Young women do their best to navigate these dangerous terrains, but they encounter vastly inadequate social and institutional supports. Moreover, these are structural and ecological problems. They require policy solutions that simultaneously address the nature, function, and meanings of gender inequality and offer productive strategies for ameliorating the multifaceted and interconnected problems created by the structural inequalities faced by the urban poor.

Gender, Social Context, and Violence against Women

In a pivotal article, anthropologist Peggy Reeves Sanday demonstrated that sexual violence emerges as a consequence of structural and cultural features of societies. Using a cross-cultural sample of 156 societies, she used a comparative case study approach to examine what factors distinguish "rape-prone" from "rape-free" societies—that is, those societies in which rape is both widespread and allowable, versus those in which rape is both uncommon and penalized. Across disparate societies meeting the designation of "rape prone," she found consistent organizational properties that distinguished them from societies with minimal sexual violence. These included the institutionalization of male dominance (including, for example, women's treatment as property and their exclusion from decision-making), hierarchical gender separation (men as a social group being defined as both distinct from and superior to women), and generally high rates of interpersonal violence.[13] In contrast, rape-free societies were characterized by greater gender equality or complementarity, prestige and respect granted to women's productive and reproductive roles, and consistently low rates of interpersonal violence.[14]

Since Sanday's investigation, numerous scholars have examined the linkages between rape culture, structural gender inequality, and sexual violence against women.[15] Rape culture, typically conceptualized as "a set of values and beliefs that promote an environment conducive to rape," has been found as an important causal explanation of both rape and the treatment of rape victims. And researchers have found that structural gender inequality, including economic inequality, is correlated with rates of rape.[16] In addition, and especially important for our investigation here, researchers have begun to specify the characteristics of particular social contexts in which the risk for sexual violence is especially heightened.

Much of this work has focused on college populations generally, and fraternities specifically.[17] Sociologists Patricia Yancey Martin and Robert A. Hummer, for example, highlight three overriding features that make college fraternities particularly high risk: organizational characteristics, the types of behaviors that bring status and social reward to members, and "a virtual absence of university or community oversight."[18] They conclude that the roots of sexual aggression in fraternities lie in their organization as male-dominated settings, with valorization of narrow conceptualizations of masculinity—those that reward aggression, competition, and the devaluation and mistreatment of women. Group loyalty, distrust of outsiders, and limited community scrutiny or intervention create conditions that both foster sexually coercive behaviors and reduce the likelihood that such events will come to public light or be penalized. More recent research challenges these relatively broad generalizations about college fraternities but nonetheless suggests that it is those fraternities with the characteristics Martin and Hummer identify that are at heightened risk for the sexual mistreatment of young women.[19] Moreover, research on other male-dominated organizational settings—for instance, sports teams and military groups—has also found similar normative constructions of masculinity, as well as heightened male peer support for sexual coercion, and higher risks for sexual violence.[20]

Clearly, as privileged social locations, there is much that distinguishes college fraternities from the peer groups of urban African American young men. And just as contemporary research distinguishes between "high-risk" and "low-risk" fraternities, it is also the case that not all male peer settings and not all young men in urban communities participate in or condone violence against girls or the masculine norms that facilitate it. However, we do see important organizational, normative, and status parallels, particularly in what sociologist Elijah Anderson conceptualizes as the "code of the streets": behavioral expectations for young men in disadvantaged communities that emphasize masculine reputation and respect, achieved through presentations of self that emphasize toughness and independence, a willingness to use violence, and heterosexual prowess demonstrated by means of sexual conquest.[21]

Anderson and others trace the dominance of this presentational and behavioral style to structural dislocation. It has become a highly visible means of performing masculinity specifically because alternative forms of status and prestige are denied to young men living in disadvantaged communities.[22] Given "the unique history of racial oppression and persistent denial of access to legitimate avenues of mainstream masculinity construction . . . street reputation, pose, and associated violence become central to [some young] Black men's identities."[23] With this, I argue, comes cultural support for violence against women and its ubiquitous presence in the lives of urban African American young women.[24]

Criminologists have certainly documented that violence against women is heightened in the urban street world. For instance, ethnographic investigations of street gangs, drug networks, and prostitution have documented the intense degradation of women and the widespread violence against them.[25] These have been tied to the organizational characteristics of such criminal networks, as well as the reproduction of gender inequality and dominant constructions of masculinity within them. In addition, there is some evidence that broader structural characteristics in urban communities, such as unbalanced gender ratios, increase cultural support for violence against women.[26] This setting, where the victimization and exploitation of women is both widespread and highly visible, is the social context in which urban African American young women must negotiate their daily lives and personal safety.

Recent research also reveals that intimate partner violence is heightened in disadvantaged urban communities.[27] Thus far, I have primarily discussed research on the social contexts that heighten risks for sexual violence. Researchers have also found that male peer support and norms favoring gender inequality—including rigid gender expectations of women's and men's roles and responsibilities in relationships, perceptions of male entitlement, and the desire for power and control in relationships—heighten risks for partner violence against women.[28] However, much research has focused on individual-level correlates and motives for partner violence, and most contextual research has focused specifically on power dynamics within families and relationships. Because intimate partner violence—to a greater extent than sexual violence—is recognized as private behavior that occurs behind closed doors, limited research has examined the broader structural patterns that affect both social support for and interventions on such violence.

However, criminologist Michael Benson and his colleagues recently found that "the odds that a woman will experience intimate violence are over one-third higher in disadvantaged compared to non-disadvantaged neighborhoods."[29] As with other forms of violence in distressed urban communities, they link these rates of partner violence to both the social isolation present in such communities and the difficulties residents have in developing collective efficacy. Benson and his colleagues explain:

Even if most residents of disadvantaged neighborhoods personally disapprove of spouse abuse, they may not openly express their disapproval to the offender, because in these neighborhoods people are expected to mind their own business and to stay out of the personal affairs of others. In neighborhoods low on collective efficacy it is not customary for residents to take action for the common good. Hence, no one feels responsible to intervene on behalf of victimized women. Additionally, residents may hesitate to intervene in these situations because they fear that they will become targets of violence themselves.[30]

Thus, they point to important contextual features of urban disadvantaged neighborhoods that heighten women's risks for abuse.

There is one final issue of critical importance for our examination, and that is age, and specifically the role of adolescence in shaping youths' risks for such gendered violence. The social world of adolescence is highly gendered. It is a period in which peer relationships increase in significance for youths, and this is magnified, especially for girls, with increased self-consciousness and sensitivity to others' perceptions of them. In addition, it is characterized by a "shift from the relatively asexual gender system of childhood to the overtly sexualized gender systems of adolescence and adulthood."[31] Young women find themselves in contradictory positions. Increasingly, they receive status from their peers as a result of their associations with and attractiveness to young men, but they are also denigrated for behaviors defined as sexually precocious.[32] In addition, research suggests that adolescent dating violence often occurs in public spaces in view of peers and that the gendered contexts of adolescence make it especially difficult to intervene in abusive dating relationships.[33] Research also shows that adolescents are generally more likely to hold attitudes favorable to violence against women than adults. This is especially the case for young men.[34]

Once again, these gendered age dynamics overlay with contextual features associated with the racial and class inequalities present in urban disadvantaged communities. As psychologist Jewelle Taylor Gibbs explains:

As [African American youths] perceive barriers to their full participation in American society, they simultaneously are gaining greater exposure to the effects of poverty, drugs, and crime in their neighborhoods. These experiences foster feelings of cynicism, anger, alienation, and despair in many youths, increasing their risk for involvement in anti-social or self-destructive activities such as drug abuse, unwed teenage pregnancy, homicide and suicide.[35]

Youths in disadvantaged communities have few opportunities for socializing with their peers—a normal facet of adolescent development—that do not include some exposure to delinquent peer groups. As discussed in this book, drugs, gangs, and the congregation of young men in public spaces are an omnipresent feature of youths' neighborhood and community action spaces, and unsupervised parties and get-togethers are a primary means of spending time with other adolescents. Participation in such activities, particularly when combined with delinquency, heightens young women's risk for victimization, including the types of gendered victimization I examine here.[36]

In fact, such social ecological factors have been linked to the exceptionally high rates of victimization of African American girls. In recent analyses of the National Crime Victimization Survey, criminologist Janet Lauritsen reveals this stark reality. African American girls' risks for violent victimization are dramatically higher than for adolescent girls from other racial groups. In fact, their risks for nonfatal violence are nearly equal those for African American boys. These findings counter the conventional wisdom in criminology that women's risks for victimization are consistently lower than men's. Indeed, Lauritsen reports that African American girls' risk for non-stranger violence, including in their neighborhoods, is *higher* than that of any other group, including their African American male counterparts. Importantly, her analyses reveal that the relationship between race and victimization is accounted for, in large part, by factors associated with highly distressed urban communities.[37] Thus, it is acute poverty and its associated social contexts that structure urban African American young women's high risk for gendered victimization.[38]

The Study

My interest in violence against urban African American girls emerged from a long-standing concern with the experiences of young women in high-risk settings. In the late 1990s and early 2000s, criminologists devoted considerable attention to the problem of girls' violence, and the result was a proliferation of studies that attempt to explain and contextualize this phenomenon.[39] In fact, my last major study was an examination of young women's participation in street gangs. What I learned from that investigation, however, was that girls' delinquency and violence are but a small part of their experiences within gangs. Feminist researchers have routinely focused on the "blurred boundaries" between young women's victimization and offending, particularly by focusing on victimization as an important risk factor for girls' delinquency.[40] My research on girls in gangs also revealed the significant victimization risks prevalent in the *foreground* of young women's gang participation and the ways that these are tied to gender inequalities within the gang setting.[41]

The current study evolved directly from these insights and from my broader interest in the situational contexts of violence. I wanted to know, given the victimization risks young women face in gangs, what other facets of urban disadvantage shape girls' risks for victimization? John Hagan and Bill McCarthy have suggested that one limitation of much criminological research is the "tendency to discount foreground causal factors theoretically and instead focus on background and developmental variables."[42] I took their insight to heart when developing this research, and thus my specific interest was to investigate the social contexts in which violence against young women in disadvantaged communities emerges, with an emphasis on the situations that produce and shape such events. Specifically, I focus on neighborhood, school, and peer dynamics that structure girls' victimization risks, as well as the gender ideologies youths draw from in order to account for and interpret such violence.

My goal for the book is to provide a nuanced analysis of violence against young women in urban communities, and one that takes seriously youths'—and especially girls'—perspectives on these events. This is not necessarily the easiest of tasks. It means documenting the circumstances and patterns of sometimes-brutal behaviors, but doing so in a way that does not simply demonize the young men involved. It also means making theoretical sense of accompanying ideologies—espoused by both girls and boys—that often explain these behaviors by holding their female victims accountable. Despite the difficulties, our only hope for ameliorating violence against young women lies in understanding its place and meanings in youths' lives. My hope is that such an understanding will also expand the ways we think about neighborhood disadvantage, urban crime, and gender.

To accomplish the study goals, our team first needed to locate young people who were willing to share sensitive life experiences with us, and we had to design the research in a way that would capture the complexities of their lives.[43] We accomplished this by incorporating a number of research strategies, including the use of multiple methodologies and a comparative study design. The work is based on in-depth interviews with African American young women and young men in disadvantaged St. Louis neighborhoods but also includes surveys with these youths, as well as supplemental information on the characteristics of the neighborhoods they called home. About one-half of the youths we interviewed met the academic designation of "serious, violent or chronic offenders,"[44] while the remainder could best be characterized as "at risk": all had participated in some lifetime delinquency, and lived in community contexts that placed them at significant risk for exposure to problem behaviors.[45]

Thus, the study design was comparative in two important ways. First, we interviewed both young women and young men about their perceptions of and exposure to violence against young women. Second, we included youths—both female and male—who were engaged in ongoing serious delinquency, as well as youths from the same communities who were not. Interviews with females and males allow for gender-based comparisons, providing the opportunity to examine similarities and divergences across gender in youths' ideologies about gender and their interpretations of incidents of violence against women. In her landmark study of convicted rapists, sociologist Diana Scully notes that one of the limitations of research on violence against women is that we seldom collect information from the perpetrators themselves. This is problematic because we fail to garner insights from the very people whose behaviors we hope to intervene upon, and, when focusing most of our energy on studying the victims of such violence, we inadvertently perpetuate the idea that violence against women is a *women's* problem.[46] By interviewing both young women and young men, we were able to bring a broader gendered lens to our analysis of the phenomenon.

As noted, the second way in which this study is explicitly comparative is by including youths with different levels of involvement in delinquency. Participation in delinquency is consistently found to be the strongest individual-level predictor of adolescents' risk for general victimization.[47] Nevertheless, researchers caution that this individual measure "may actually represent an effect due to social context," and thus it is important that scholars "pay explicit attention to ecological context" when examining the causes of victimization.[48] In fact, "ecological proximity to violence is an important structural determinant of victimization," unmediated by individual activities such as delinquency.[49] Thus, our inclusion in the sample of both delinquent and "at-risk" youth from the same communities allows me to explore the ecological contexts of violence against young women, as well as how these are related to situational factors such as young women's and young men's participation in delinquent and other risky behaviors.[50]

The study did not allow for comparisons across race and ethnicity, however. We chose to limit our sample exclusively to African American youths, and our reasons for doing so were twofold. First, as I noted earlier, scholarly knowledge is particularly limited with regard to violence against adolescent girls generally and African American young women specifically, especially those "living in highly distressed urban neighborhoods."[51] This is despite the fact that recent evidence confirms that these young women face higher risks for victimization than do young women in other racial groups and ecological settings.[52] Thus, we have a pressing need for better information about violence against urban African American girls, including an improved understanding of how disadvantaged neighborhood contexts place them at higher risk for victimization.

Second, there is a long-standing tendency among criminologists to study urban minority youth in terms of problem behaviors such as gang participation, drug sales, and violence, rather than being attentive to harms such as victimization. This is exacerbated by a general bias within American culture to assign greater importance to the victimization of whites than people of color and to take race into account when evaluating the seriousness of violence against women and the presumed culpability of its victims.[53] By focusing specifically on the experiences of urban African American girls, this study fills an important research niche and brings attention to an issue that is too often ignored. Nonetheless, future research will benefit from the inclusion of samples that also allow for comparisons across race and ethnicity, as well as social class.

Sampling

Sampling was purposive in nature. We sought to identify youths both at risk and involved in delinquent activities who resided in disadvantaged St. Louis neighborhoods.[54] As I detail below, St. Louis was the ideal site for such an investigation, because it typifies the highly distressed urban community: youth were drawn from neighborhoods characterized by intense racial segregation, social isolation, limited resources, concentrated poverty, and high rates of crime. They were recruited to participate in the study with the cooperation of several organizations working with at-risk and delinquent youth in St. Louis. These included a local community agency and two alternative public high schools. Approximately equal ratios of young women and young men were drawn from each location.[55]

I drew on contacts from my previous research on girls in gangs to facilitate reentry into sites that would provide us with access to youth that fit our sampling criteria. The community agency was a neighborhood-based drop-in center in north St. Louis where youths from the neighborhood were free to congregate and socialize. I had conducted several interviews at this site for my previous project and also taught a photography class the summer before we began data collection for the study reported in this volume. My involvement in the center meant I was familiar with youths who regularly spent time there, and they were included in the sample. The two alternative schools drew youths from the St. Louis public school catchment area and were specifically designated to serve youths expelled from St. Louis public schools for a variety of infractions, including disruptive behavior and violence. The school counselors, with whom I had worked during my previous study, were asked to identify youths for participation in the study when they were known to reside in disadvantaged neighborhoods in the city.

In all, 75 youths were interviewed for the project, including 35 young women and 40 young men. They ranged in age from 12 to 19, with a mean age of around 16 for both groups.[56] Interviewing began in the spring of 1999 and was completed in the spring of 2000. The interviews were voluntary, youths were paid $20 for their participation, and were promised strict confidentiality.[57] Data collection began with the administration of a detailed survey, and youths were then asked to participate in an audiotaped in-depth interview that was typically completed on the same day.[58]

There are several limitations to my study resulting from our sampling. As noted, our sampling strategy was purposive in nature, and thus we did not attempt to draw a sample that would yield findings that are broadly generalizable. In fact, it is important to keep in mind that most of the youths we interviewed for the study had been expelled from school and were interviewed at the alternative schools considered the last resort before termination of their participation in the St. Louis public school district.[59] Despite considerable effort, we were unable to gain access to a comparative group of youths in the same neighborhood contexts who were thriving academically and socially. This is not to say such youths are not present in these communities. Instead, our networks as criminologists allowed us to gain access to at-risk and delinquent youths fairly easily, while the gatekeepers at churches and mainstream schools were much more reticent, and ultimately refused, to expose these youth to our research.

In addition, all of the youths we interviewed were currently attending school. This means that our sampling did not capture school dropouts or youths who were incarcerated. In fact, zero-tolerance policies in St. Louis city schools meant that some of the youths who ended up at the alternative school were placed there for a single fight or for bringing a weapon to school, in some cases for self-defense. This was evidenced by some youths' descriptions of their placement in the alternative school, as well as by the substantial minority of youths interviewed at these schools who reported a very limited history of delinquency. Thus, our sample includes youths who were neither wholly successful nor wholly unsuccessful in their navigation of the difficult terrain of adolescent life in the inner city. While I make no claim that our sample is representative, it does provide a meaningful cross section of at-risk and delinquent African American youth in the city, and the richness of our data allows for a thorough analysis of the nature and context of violence against these young women and the interpretive lenses young women and young men brought to bear on such events.

Data Collection and Analysis

Each interview began with the completion of an extensive survey, which collected general demographic and descriptive information and included questions about youths' friends and their social activities, their own and their peers' attitudes toward violence against women, their knowledge of peers' experiences with gender-based violence as victims or perpetrators, their participation in delinquency, their contacts and interactions with the police, their victimization experiences, and their involvement with violence against women, as both victims and perpetrators.[60] In the survey, we focused on three specific types of gender-based aggression: sexual harassment, sexual coercion and assault, and dating violence. We asked young women whether they had experienced forms of gender and sexual harassment, and young men whether they and their friends had engaged in such activities.[61] Regarding sexual violence, we asked about a range of sexually coercive and violent behaviors.[62] To contextualize dating violence, we asked youths about their sexual and dating histories, and we gathered detailed information about their current relationships. To measure dating violence, we used a modified version of the Conflict Tactics Scale, which included incidents of verbal abuse, physical abuse, and, for girls, sexual abuse.[63] Finally, youths were asked their own attitudes about dating violence, and whether they had friends who were victims or perpetrators of such violence. To examine peer effects, we also asked youths, both male and female, whether any of their friends engaged in or condoned the use of violence toward young women.[64]

The survey provides supplemental information for the data collected in the in-depth interviews, and we drew from youths' survey responses to guide the conversation during the in-depth interview.[65] These interviews are the primary data I drew from for this book to provide a rich, contextual examination of violence against urban African American young women. Our goal was to gather detailed information about the nature, meanings, and consequences of gender violence, in order to provide a relatively holistic assessment of how such violence is situated in the wider contexts of youths' neighborhoods and in their peer and dating relationships.

The in-depth interviews were semistructured, with open-ended questions that allowed for considerable probing. Youths were first asked to describe and provide recent examples of conflicts occurring in school, including incidents of sexual harassment and other male/female fights.[66] When youths reported being perpetrators or victims of sexual harassment, they were asked to provide further details about these incidents. They also provided accounts of incidents they had witnessed or heard about. We collected contextual information on those incidents described, including where it happened, who was present, and how teachers and other youth responded. Youths were then asked to provide a general description of the neighborhood, including its problems, and their reactions to neighborhood dangers. They also discussed the nature of male/female relations in the neighborhood, including incidents of violence.

We next moved to questions about youths' romantic relationships. They first provided general descriptions of their relationships, then spoke about any fights or conflicts. If youths had reported dating violence during the survey, they were asked to elaborate on these incidents and describe what happened, why and how it happened, and the consequences. We also asked young women who were victims of dating violence whether they had talked with family, friends, or others about the incidents, why or why not, and the outcome of such disclosures. We asked youths whether they talked about their dating relationships with their peers and to describe the nature of these discussions. We also asked whether they had friends who had been perpetrators or victims of dating violence, to describe incidents they had witnessed or heard about, and their own and others' reactions to these events. Finally, we asked youths to expand on their beliefs about dating violence, drawing from their survey responses to these questions.

The interview then shifted to a discussion of sexual violence. Young women who reported being victims of sexual coercion or assault, and young men who reported engaging in such behavior, were asked to discuss the incident(s) in greater detail. In addition, youths who said they had witnessed or heard about incidents of sexual violence were asked to describe these events or what they heard about them. As with dating violence, youths provided detailed information about the contexts, consequences, and meanings of such violence. We concluded the in-depth interview by asking youths for their suggestions about what could be done to reduce violence against women, as well as their knowledge of and beliefs about services available for the victims of such violence. This basic guideline was followed for each interview, although when additional topics arose in the course of the conversation, we often deviated from the interview schedule to pursue them.

The in-depth interviews resulted in a large, rich dataset on the nature, contexts, and meanings of violence against young women in urban settings. This methodological approach provided us with necessary tools for understanding violence against young women from the points of view of our research participants.[67] Rigorous examination of such accounts offers a means of "arriving at meanings or culturally embedded normative explanations [for behavior, because they] represent the ways in which people organize views of themselves, of others, and of their social worlds."[68]

In fact, the in-depth interviews provided two intertwined sets of findings: evidence of the nature of violence against young women, including the contexts and situations in which it emerges, along with insights into the cultural frames that young women and young men use to make sense of these events.[69] Juxtaposing these facets of youths' accounts—even when they appear incongruous—provides an important basis for developing theoretical insights into the place of such violence in youths' lives.[70] The analysis process required teasing apart and weaving back together facets of the data that yielded information about the realities of youths' social worlds and the belief systems they brought to bear on their experiences.[71] I hope the result provides richly textured insights into the nature and meanings of violence against urban African American young women.

Study Setting

All of the youths interviewed for this project lived in the city of St. Louis. The vast majority lived in neighborhoods that fit the academic designation "highly distressed": neighborhoods characterized by intense racial segregation; disproportionate rates of poverty, unemployment, and female-headed families; and high rates of crime.[72] In fact, St. Louis was an ideal site in which to conduct this research, because it typifies the highly distressed urban city and includes large concentrations of extreme disadvantage that result in social isolation, limited resources, and high levels of violence. We hear these descriptions again and again in scholarship on neighborhoods and crime, but how do young people in disadvantaged communities—both female and male—describe and experience their neighborhoods? What is it like to grow up and live in such communities, and to navigate daily adolescent life in this terrain? An exploration of these questions can provide a more vivid portrait of the study setting, which helps situate the subsequent examination of how such social contexts are associated with violence against young women.

Let's begin, though, with some numbers. Table 1-1 provides a comparison of demographic and socioeconomic indicators for the youths'

TABLE 1-1
Select Neighborhood Characteristics

	Respondents' Neighborhoods	St. Louis City	St. Louis County
Median family income ($)	24,806	32,585	61,680
African Americans (%)	82.6	51.2	18.9
Female-headed families with children (%)	43.1	28.8	10.7
Poverty (%)	33.8	24.6	6.9
Unemployment (%)	18.0	11.3	4.6

Source: U.S. Census, 2000.

neighborhoods, St. Louis City, and St. Louis County.[73] The St. Louis metropolitan area is home to a large population of African Americans, including more than one-half of the city's residents. One thing that's obvious from table 1-1 is that there is a much larger concentration of African Americans in St. Louis City than in the surrounding suburban communities. There is both a history to and consequences from this population distribution. One of the problems facing cities like St. Louis is the flight of the middle classes from central city areas. Such residents take their social, economic and political capital with them, leaving the poor —who are disproportionately minorities—even more socially isolated, and their communities even further depleted of resources.

St. Louis, for instance, was once one of the largest cities in the United States. As the region grew, however, large numbers of city residents relocated to areas outside of the city limits. In the 1950s, the city population was more than 850,000. By 1990, this number had dropped by more than half, to less than 400,000. These declines continued in the decade that followed, with the city losing nearly 50,000 additional residents (or 12 percent of its population) by the year 2000.[74] This population decline is significant, because it has changed both the resources available to city residents and their composition. As table 1-1 demonstrates, St. Louis City residents are in poor economic shape within the region. In fact, there have been continual disinvestments in the city since the shift from an industrial to a service-based economy in the region.[75] While deindustrialization and concomitant disinvestments have hurt the city overall, the effects have been strongest felt among its African American residents.

In conjunction with decades of population decline, racial segregation in St. Louis has intensified, making it one of the most racially segregated cities in the United States.[76] Though African Americans are among the middle classes also moving to the suburbs, the rate of departure for whites has been greater, such that African Americans went from 47.5 percent of the city's population in 1990 to 51.2 percent in 2000.[77] In fact, while African American's proportion of St. Louis County residents jumped from 13.9 percent to 18.9 percent during that decade, this is accounted for both by the movement of African Americans into the county and as a result of continued white flight, in this case out of St. Louis County and into even more distant suburbs of the city.[78]

Despite St. Louis City's nearly equal distribution of African Americans and whites,[79] table 1-1 also demonstrates that large parts of the city—including the neighborhoods of most of our respondents—remain highly segregated by race. On average, the young people we spoke with were from neighborhoods that were more than 80 percent African American. In fact, this figure conceals some important variation. One of the trends in St. Louis since the mid 1990s has been the movement of some African Americans from north St. Louis to the near south of the city, a section previously dominated by working-class whites.[80] These changes are reflected in our sample: approximately one-quarter of the young people we spoke with lived in more racially integrated neighborhoods than this average indicates.[81] I discuss some important facets of this variation below. However, the variation also means that the average figure reported in table 1-1 actually underestimates the racial segregation in the vast majority of our respondents' neighborhoods. In fact, approximately 70 percent of the youths we interviewed lived in neighborhoods that were more than 90 percent African American.[82]

Table 1-1 also reveals many of the additional economic harms associated with the problem of racial segregation in U.S. cities. The disadvantage found in the poorest urban Black neighborhoods is ecologically unmatched. Thus, sociologists Robert Sampson and William Julius Wilson point out that "the *worst* urban contexts in which whites reside are considerably better than the *average* context of Black communities."[83] This is reflected in table 1-1 by the low median family incomes, high rates of poverty and unemployment, and very large proportions of female-headed families in respondents' neighborhoods. Again, there was variation within the sample, with some youths living with even more extreme levels of neighborhood poverty. Notably, though 11 youths lived in neighborhoods in which the median income was at or above the city's average, data on the poverty and unemployment rates in these neighborhoods indicates they were economically bifurcated. In fact, not a single youth in our sample came from a neighborhood that was consistently comparable to the citywide averages.

Given this general overview of what the statistics reveal about youths' neighborhoods, it's time to contextualize these figures with youths' own accounts of what their neighborhoods were like to live and grow up in. I begin with girls' and boys' general descriptions of their neighborhoods, noting variations across gender and across neighborhood context. In chapter 2, I turn the attention more explicitly to the nature of violence against women in these communities, focusing on how gender structures neighborhood risks and the strategies young women employ to maintain their safety and security while going about their daily lives.

Living in the 'Hood

Asked to describe her neighborhood, Kristy summed it up in one word: "slum." For Cleshay, that word was "ghetto." Kristy elaborated, "I mean, broken bottles everywhere, people standing on the corner, everybody's momma out on this, everybody's daddy out on this, don't do nuttin,' you know. Police harassing you constantly." Cleshay's elaboration was similarly bleak:

Terrible. Every man for theyself. Ghetto in the sense of raggedy, people uncool to people, just outside, street light never come on, police don't come in after four o'clock. . . . Heavy drug dealing. They loud, they don't care about, you know, the old people in the neighborhood or nuttin'. It's been like, females, it was a ten year old girl who got raped recently and kilt and didn't nobody—our walls in our neighborhood thin, so I know somebody hear her screaming—[but] didn't nobody, you know, even try to help the girl or nuttin' like that.

Jackie complained that her neighborhood was "noisy, a lot of noise. It's dogs barking, people on the street late at night, neighbors loud, radio playin' loud, can't go to sleep. It's just a lot of stuff. One day this lil' girl got killed over there. Right down the street. . . . It be too many shootings over there and I don't like that." Maurice provided a comparable account:

A lot of gangs, lot of drugs, uh dirt. Dirty, like the streets are polluted. That's it. A lot of abandoned houses, lot of burned up houses. [That's] 'cause of the drugs and the gangs I guess. . . . Vandalism, they get into a lot of fights, bring property value down, you know, people don't take care of they houses. And you know, don't nobody really wanna live there no more so everybody starts to move. That's why [there's] a lot of abandoned houses. Then, when it's a lot of abandoned houses that means the block cold, that mean not that many police around. So that's when dope people move in on that block, you know what I'm saying, go open they shop there. And whenever they go do that, then, you know what I'm saying, lots of crackheads start moving in, lot of gangs, you know what I'm saying, lot of shoot-outs because people, you know, taking other people's things.

Several important themes are present in these descriptions. Each makes note of physical deterioration in the neighborhoods. Complaints against the police include both widespread harassment and under-policing.[84] Too many residents are described as unconcerned with their neighbors' well-being and as unwilling to intervene when someone is in danger. And the neighborhoods appear dominated by criminal networks that hinder the daily lives of residents. Crime and violence—including gender-specific violence—appear ubiquitous. As Maurice deftly points out, these facets of the neighborhood are interconnected. Though scholars have only recently linked such neighborhood conditions to violence against women, a substantial body of research documents how community processes like those described by Maurice and Cleshay evolve from structural inequalities and translate into high rates of community violence.

Specifically, scholars use the terms "social capital" and "collective efficacy" to refer to a neighborhood's ability to generate social ties and protective mechanisms among its residents. In order to facilitate the development of "mutual trust and shared expectations among residents," neighborhoods must have institutional, political, and economic resources available. Without these, neighborhood processes—like the willingness to intervene on behalf of neighbors and monitor the behavior of young people—cannot thrive.[85] Because youths' neighborhoods were often lacking in these requisite resources, residents had a limited ability to develop the social ties necessary for collective efficacy and thus were unable to control community crime. Moreover, because there was tremendous distrust of the police and their behaviors toward neighborhood residents, they were seldom viewed as a positive resource in combating neighborhood problems.[86]

It is also significant that many youths in our study did not see their neighborhoods as unusually or uniquely dangerous but, instead, as *typical* of the surrounding community. Asked how her neighborhood compared with others nearby, Tisha surmised, "it's not different at all. They all do the same thing. The neighborhood is the neighborhood [*laughs*]. It's all the same, all the way through." Raymond noted, "in every neighborhood there's drug activity and gang activity." Likewise, Tami explained, "it's mostly every neighborhood got drug dealers in they neighborhood. Or people that be shootin' and stuff." Rennesha concurred: "On the north side . . . it's all the same. The same stuff go on everywhere I guess. I mean, it's probably just a different [gang] color they going against, but it is the same thing." Consequently, Dawanna explained, "I don't feel safe nowhere for real. Anywhere you go you gonna hear a gun shot or something."

These descriptions illustrate another important structural feature of many disadvantaged neighborhoods: their ecological proximity to similarly situated areas. Sociologists Lauren Krivo and Ruth Peterson were among the first to examine the spatial clustering of extremely disadvantaged neighborhoods and the strong association between such concentrations and violent crime. Not surprisingly, these scholars found that such ecological clustering was more prevalent in disadvantaged African American neighborhoods than in similarly disadvantaged white neighborhoods. What this means is that, unlike poor white neighborhoods, poor African American neighborhoods do not gain from the spillover of "institutional benefits and resources of socioeconomically more advantaged" neighbors.[87] Because many of our respondents' neighborhoods were embedded within larger pockets of extreme disadvantage, their neighborhoods were even further hindered in their ability to generate the collective efficacy necessary to protect youths from such neighborhood risks. The internal vulnerability of their neighborhoods was layered within a broader spatial vulnerability.[88]

Gangs, Drugs, and Violence

When youths were asked to describe their neighborhood or elaborate on its problems, three interrelated themes came up repeatedly: drug dealing, street gangs, and associated gun violence.[89] Katie explained, "I don't think it's a good neighborhood 'cause it's a lot of gang violence goin' around, lot of drugs around there, lot of robberies over there. . . . Almost every day, arguing, fighting, just lots of violence and stuff." And Kenisha said, "it's shooting every other night, gangs, people selling drugs over there, it's real bad." LaSondra concurred: "I don't like that neighborhood, it's just too much happening. Crackheads roaming around, drug dealers, everything. . . . They shoot, rob, kill."

Tisha said drug sales took place in her neighborhood "every day, all day long." She explained, "it's people standing all around outside, people sellin' drugs, all that kinda stuff. They'll even come sit on yo' front [porch]. . . . When you not there, they'll come sit on yo' front and be sit[ting] like they stay there. You could come sit on yo' front, they'll come over there and try to talk to you." Tami described the disruptions caused by a neighbor's drug dealing. "[He] use to live next door to me and he was sellin' dope out his house. . . . They use to knock 24-7, early in the mornin'. And they bust his window out, shot at him and everything. Almost everyday."

An additional concern related to the drug trade was being harassed by drug addicts. Frank complained, "man, every day I see crackheads. They run up to me, like I sit there, like, 'Dude, have anything?' [I respond,] 'Don't come up to me. I do not do that, don't come up to me.' Always [the] same ones: 'Do you have anything?' Make me wanna punch 'em in they mouth." Likewise, Lisa explained: "Crackheads are over there 24-7. . . . I mean, they not causin' too big of a problem, but it's just, look at that, look at that type of environment, you know. Go outside and you gotta see these crackheads walk up the street like this, late at night, all times of the night. Then if you outside too, you gon' get approached and it's a crackhead. I don't like that."

Gangs brought their own problems, most notably fights and gun violence that emerged from intergang rivalries. Shauntell described the wide range of problems associated with gang activities in her neighborhood:

> It's a lot of gang bangin', gamblin', shootin', fightin', killin', cars, I mean, stuff getting stole. . . . Every day when I go home it's action waitin' for me, every day, it never fail. I mean, I can't say that it's always the people on my block fault, but most of the time it be. They'll hit somebody for lookin' at them the wrong way. They'll hit somebody

because they gay. Stuff like that, I mean, it's stupid. Just 'cause they gay you gon' fight 'em. Just 'cause they lookin' at you the wrong way, they gon' fight 'em. Just 'cause they wearin' the wrong colors, you gon' fight 'em. Say you from Herbert [Street] and we stay on Penrose.[90] You walk down Penrose, you fina [going to] hafta fight 'cause you stay on Herbert and you walkin' down Penrose. Shootin', I mean, we ain't had one of those since like three months ago. . . . But every weekend you gon' hear gunshots. Stealin'—every day. Every day boys come on our block with a different stolen car that they done went over there in East St. Louis and took and bringin' back down on our block. So they doing that, then the police chasin' them.

One striking feature of youths' neighborhood descriptions was a subtle variation that emerged across gender. While not uniformly the case, young men were more likely to describe their neighborhoods in ways that indicated their active engagement in neighborhood life, including its more dangerous facets. For instance, most young men used the pronouns "we" and "I" in their descriptions, while nearly all of the young women described what "they" do in the neighborhood. Young men were also more likely to emphasize territoriality in their descriptions and name their own and other gangs when describing their neighborhoods. This variation occurred despite the fact that both boys and girls were asked the same initial question: "Can you tell me what your neighborhood is like?"

Asked this question, Tyrell said, "everybody over there real tight. It's like Six Deuces, One Niners, Crips, and the people from Penrose. But like a couple blocks over, probably 'bout a mile away it's like other gangs or whatever. . . . If we all go over there messing with them, they come over messing with us." Carlos likewise situated himself in the thick of neighborhood conflicts. Asked to characterize his neighborhood, he replied, "call it the damn ghetto." Asked how he felt about living in the "damn ghetto," he elaborated:

I feel like niggas can't fuck with me. I feel like that's why I walk around with me a gun all the time. So a nigga come to me, talk shit, I'm just gonna shoot they ass. . . . Niggas be trippin'. In our neighborhood, niggas trippin' from the Bloods and "dookie" set and stuff. Niggas come from the other side of Jefferson [Avenue], trippin'. . . . My gang Six-O, blue and gold. We wear blue and gold. Somebody say, I mean, "sissy," we gonna get on 'em. We gonna shoot 'em, we gonna kill 'em, we gonna kick 'em and beat 'em or something.

Ricky, on the other hand, was critical of his neighborhood. Nonetheless, his description indicated his embeddedness in neighborhood networks:

It's a peaceful neighborhood if the police didn't bother people so much. I mean people only act the way they act in our neighborhood based on the police. I mean the police will ride up on a group of guys, I mean don't nobody have to be sellin' drugs or nothing. But just because we a group of guys, they'll get out [and harass us]. . . . I mean, I wouldn't say it just like it's all the police, 'cause you got them guys that's still out there that's tryin' to sell drugs—30 and 40 years old, 29, 30. They still out there trying to sell drugs. Then they makin' it bad for us 'cause this all we seen'. I mean, basically, if we had positive role models in our neighborhood it'll be alright. It's just no positive role models at all, dawg. I mean it's just everybody sell dope.

Lamont also complained of the problems caused by a lack of community role models:

[The neighborhood's] bad. A lot of drugs. They influence the kids. We see them with these fancy cars and all this money, riding around in these cars. And that's what we want, that's what we thinking in our heads: that's what we want. And the only way we can get that either two choices: go to school, get a good job; or sell drugs. . . . Most of the kids in my neighborhood dropped out so only way they can get it is by selling drugs. And most of they momma's on drugs. . . . What you see, what you want, what influence you, what your eyes see, that's what you pick up and keep 'til your grave, so that's what you learn, that's what you remember, that's what you know.

As these examples illustrate, when young men described their neighborhoods, they actively situated themselves within neighborhood street activities. This was the case even—as with Ricky and Lamont—when they were critical of what takes place. Such framing was rarely present in girls' accounts.[91] In fact, only one girl, Nicole, made similar comments: "It's cool 'cause when people come over there starting stuff everybody just come outside and be ready to jump that other street.

'Cause we don't like that, you comin' in our neighborhood makin' it bad for people that you don't even know."

Part of what makes these differences so striking is that our sampling strategy targeted high-risk and delinquent youths across gender. Youths' self-reports indicate that fairly similar numbers of males and females were involved in both serious delinquency and drug sales. Based on re- ports of lifetime prevalence, 58 percent of boys and 43 percent of girls had sold drugs; while about 25 percent of both groups reported having sold drugs in the past six months. Likewise, 60 percent of the boys and 51 percent of the girls reported having engaged in serious delinquency, with 30 percent and 34 percent, respectively, having done so in the past six months.[92] Thus, youths' self-reports of delinquency would suggest that males and females were similarly engaged in such activities, and thus we might expect them to exhibit comparable levels of neighbor- hood engagement. Nonetheless, young men clearly appeared more em- bedded in their neighborhood street networks than did the vast majority of young women.[93] This has important consequences, as examined in chapter 2.

Proximity to Crime and Danger

Not all of the youths we spoke with described uniformly dangerous neighborhoods. One notable variation was the proximity of drugs and gangs to their homes. For instance, a number of youths described their immediate block as relatively problem-free but nonetheless noted that problems with gangs, violence, and drugs were not far away. Walter de- scribed his neighborhood as "a good neighborhood then again it be a bad neighborhood at the same time." He explained this by delineating variations across blocks: "You got this whole section, and then like say this is a block right here and this the good block. But then there'll be these blocks over here that a whole different kind of gang color and then there'll be these blocks over here. So we just right in the middle of 'em and they shooting at each other."

Anishika also described her own block as "quiet" but said the sur- rounding streets were "loud. It's just too many gangs and all that stuff." She avoided those parts of her neighborhood, and favorably compared her own street to the surrounding ones: "Mines, I mean, it's more peaceful over there, it's just quiet and stuff. Like if I stayed on them streets and stuff, I'd probably be seeing something going on every day."

Likewise, Shaun said his was "a better neighborhood, 'cause we live on a one-way street so it ain't too much happening in the street. It mostly, you know what I'm saying, on the next street, down the corner." And Destiny said her own block was "cool" but the next block over, "everybody be out and it just be a lot of commotion goin' on down there."

"Quiet" neighborhoods were often explicitly attributed to the composition of their block—for instance, a disproportionate number of older residents or young children, and a lack of adolescents and young adults. Janelle explained:

> It really depends on where you're at. Like, where my parents live at it's a decent neighborhood. But like as soon as I go on the other side of the park, you know, where I grew up at, it's different. It's like where my parents are at it's decent, there's not too many kids. On the other side there are a lot of kids. They're always having their differences. And that's where most of the action [gang fights, gun violence] will take place.

Likewise, Robert said he "stay on a block with all old people. . . . It's cool, it's nice." However, the neighborhood surrounding his block was a "gang area, [and] they slang, slangin' drugs." Lisa said her neighborhood was "quiet [because] it's a whole buncha older folks." Asked if this was the case generally in her neighborhood, she quickly clarified, "no, just my street. 'Cause other streets, I mean, okay, the police officer got killed over there [recently], then turn around Friday, two people got killed at the liquor store."

Thus, even when youths described their immediate surroundings as comparatively safe, this was nearly always contextualized by the dangers present in adjacent neighborhoods or blocks. Sociologist Mary Pattillo found this to be the case even in middle-class Black neighborhoods, in which very few of the youths here resided. Though her research suggests that the residential stability found in such middle-class neighborhoods fosters "dense social networks [that] facilitate the informal supervision of neighborhood youth," it is still the case that the close presence of crime can provide both opportunities and an element of attraction for some neighborhood youths, as well as increased exposure to the risks associated with such crime.[94] Again, this is evidence of the spatial vulnerabilities that result from the clustering of urban African American neighborhoods in large pockets of disadvantage.

Racially Heterogenous Neighborhoods

Finally, as noted earlier, a minority of youths lived in racially mixed neighborhoods, and they often described these as different from predominantly Black neighborhoods. Alicia had lived in a racially heterogenous neighborhood for about five months and said, "it's good, it's fine. Ain't nobody be shooting or whatever, nobody be fighting for real. Little kids be outside playing, there don't be no drive-bys or nothing like that." Likewise, Bridget described her racially mixed neighborhood as "a decent neighborhood, it's clean basically. . . . It's a nice neighborhood, and its police and stuff around. There's not too many gangs and stuff around." Arthur said, "I stay on the southside. Quiet. It's not too much going on over there. We play football every Sunday, that's about it. Play basketball together. That's the only time it's a lot of people out."

Yvonne provided a detailed account of how she believed her neighborhood differed from others, focusing specifically on the restraint she felt was necessary to fit in:

> I stay around a lot of white folks. Rich white folks. You know, and I mean there's a certain way we gotta act, and we can't have a lot of noise, can't have a lot of people hanging around our house. We very rarely sit on the front. We don't sit unless we sitting outside watching our sister play or whatever. But I like living in the neighborhood that we live in 'cause it's quiet. There ain't all that confusion, it ain't everybody outside just acting a fool, you know what I'm saying. Trash ain't everywhere. I mean it's a clean environment. It's the kind of place I'd raise my children. . . . [But] it's a lot of prejudice, a lot of that.

Ramara had lived in her neighborhood for a couple of years and described it as "like a white populated area. Not a lot of kids. It's not loud or anything like that. There are gang people on our street but they don't, like, disrupt the peace or anything like that. It's mainly quiet and just like, it's not like a regular street, it's different." Comparing her neighborhood to surrounding neighborhoods, she explained: "Other neighborhoods, it's always like one house that's a ghetto house or something like that, and that play the loudest music. And my street or my neighborhood is not really like that. It's not ghetto. I guess 'cause it's whitely populated. Or, I don't think that should have nothin' to do with it, but that's what I think. That's why it's like that." While some youths attributed such differences to the racial composition of their neighborhoods, research has shown that it is the structural features of such neighborhoods that matter, including their greater access to resources that facilitate both social capital and neighborhood collective efficacy.[95]

In addition, even a number of the racially integrated neighborhoods were still situated within broader ecological contexts with high rates of crime. For instance, Michelle, Destiny, and Janelle described their immediate neighborhoods as quiet, but each noted that there was street action nearby. Each lived in racially heterogenous neighborhoods. Felicia described living in an area of south St. Louis that has been in the process of gentrification in recent years. She had lived there for about seven months and had previously lived on the north side. She described her current neighborhood as "pretty quiet" but said that at night she didn't feel safe "because I'm not too far from the [public housing projects] and I'm also not that far from [another high crime area]."

Frank also lived on a predominantly white block that was in close proximity to crime: "My neighborhood, it's in the cooler neighborhood. Ain't really that many Black people live in there. . . . On the street I stay on, [it's] mostly white. But like a [little way up the block, past the] corner . . . at the end of the alley, it's a house where all Black people stay at." In this nearby area, Frank said, "my cousin and them, they sell drugs over there. . . . Man, over there, you hear gun shots almost every day. Ambulances, police, almost every day." Likewise, Wayne explained:

> My street [is] right in the middle of a real nice neighborhood. . . . It's like real big houses [nearby], you know what I'm talking about. I live right there where all those nice houses are so it's pretty much quiet on my street. But like a few more blocks over it gets worse. Guys on the corner pretty much selling drugs. Police out there all the time and stuff like that. Pretty much like your little ghetto.

In interpreting these accounts, one important issue to keep in mind is that many of the youths in this study had experienced a great deal of residential mobility. More than two-thirds of the girls and one-half of the boys reported that they had moved in the past three years. Even more striking, one-half of the girls and nearly one-third of the boys described multiple moves during this period. In some cases, youths' moves led them to relatively safer neighborhoods. However, such residential instability also contributed to a broadening of the places in which they spent time. In this sense, while it is important to understand the neighborhood contexts where youths reside, it is also important to take into account their broader patterns of interactions within the larger community. As Sampson and his colleagues note, "many behaviors of interest . . . unfold in places (e.g., schools, parks, center-city areas) outside of [youths'] residential neighborhoods. . . . Adolescents occupy many different neighborhood contexts outside of home, especially in the company of peers."[96]

Particularly for youths who had moved to unfamiliar neighborhoods, or those who lived in neighborhoods that were absent other adolescents or even other African American families, spending time in their old neighborhood or the neighborhoods of family and friends was quite common. For example, Doug had lived in his current home in a predominantly white neighborhood for about a year and complained, "aw, there's nuttin' to say about my neighborhood. I live in south [city]. Nuttin' goes on there much. . . . I don't hang out there for real." He noted that "we're the only Black family that live on our street" and described spending most of his time on the north side, in the neighborhood of his extended family, friends, and girlfriend.

Likewise, Darryl had moved twice in the last year and had lived in his current home for about a month. He described his neighborhood as "boring. It's like, I live around a lot of white people." As a consequence, he explained, "after work I go down to my grandma house, 'cause my grandma be needin' help to take out her trash and stuff and I still have friends over there so I be doing stuff with my other friends over there." Gail described her aunt's home as "like my second home, that's like where I be at, you know. I just look at that like another home." Distinguishing the two neighborhoods, she explained:

> I live on a busy street, so it's always noisy on my street 'cause cars comin' over or whatever. But as far as kids, uh-uh [no], 'cause don't no kids live by me. But where my auntie live, it's like, parks and kids and everybody in the neighborhood just go and be playing together, you know. And then, that like when most of the stuff start, you know.

Asked to clarify what she meant by "stuff," Gail continued: "I mean, just like normal stuff. Kids fightin', grown people gettin' drunk and just fightin', you know, lil' crackheads trying to sell people stuff to get money to buy beer and drugs, you know." Thus, while Gail described her aunt's neighborhood as having more crime problems, spending time there provided her with greater opportunities to socialize with family and friends than her own neighborhood.

Most youths in our study lived in dangerous neighborhoods. For the small proportion who did not, the relative safety of their neighborhoods came at a cost: safer neighborhoods also tended to be isolating neighborhoods, where youths lacked the familial and social ties that adolescents crave. Given the broad structural distributions of race, poverty, and crime, such youths necessarily traversed into more dangerous terrains for social purposes. Consequently, a striking feature of youths' accounts, including their comparisons across neighborhoods, was the extent to which their points of reference were crime and violence. What this suggests is that youths' "cognitive maps of their neighborhoods and areas of social interaction" are centered around the expectation of crime.[97] Recall Ramara's comment that the quiet neighborhood she lived in was "not like a regular street. It's different." And Gail's description of "fights," "crackheads," and "drunks" as "normal stuff." Rather than safe streets being perceived as the norm, youths who lived in such places recognized them as atypical, just as youths in dangerous neighborhoods saw them as normal. These perceptual frameworks speak volumes about the spatial vulnerabilities and routine exposures to danger faced by the youths in this study.

Conclusion

Youths' general neighborhood descriptions provide an important backdrop for my analysis of the social contexts of violence against young women. This detailed overview reveals that while variations were present that placed some youths in more immediate risk than others, overall youths' accounts—and their understanding of the nature of neighborhoods—provides evidence of the importance of neighborhood contexts in structuring exposure to violence. Most of the young people in this study lived in communities that can best be characterized as extremely disadvantaged, and youths themselves reported that drug dealing, street gangs, and associated gun violence were commonplace. The minority of youths who reported that their immediate neighborhoods were relatively quiet focused on the age or racial composition of their neighbors but also emphasized their proximity to crime and danger and their need to hang out in other (often more dangerous) places in order to socialize with family and friends.

As described, urban disadvantage has important gendered dimensions. Of particular relevance for this study is growing evidence that the structural inequalities that create disadvantage also result in increases in both cultural support for the victimization of women and its visibility.[98] In chapter 2, I examine these issues in greater detail. I discuss how gender shapes neighborhood participation and neighborhood dangers, focusing specifically on gendered exposure to victimization and violence against women. I conclude the chapter by examining young women's strategies for managing neighborhood risks.

Chapter 3 shifts from the neighborhood setting to schools. Because youths spend a significant amount of time in school, it is an important arena for examining both gendered peer interactions and gender-based violence. Schools are embedded within broader communities, and thus the available resources and social interactions within schools are shaped by their location within communities of concentrated disadvantage.[99] The focus in chapter 3 is on school-based sexual harassment, its meanings and consequences. Chapter 4 builds from the findings in chapters 2 and 3 to focus on more severe forms of sexual violence, including sexual coercion, sexual assault, and gang rape. While most of these incidents occurred in peer settings within the community, youths' interactions within schools also provided an important foundation for creating social support for the sexual victimization of young women.

In chapter 5, I shift the attention from sexual violence to physical violence in dating relationships. I examine the extent and cultural support for dating violence against young women but also focus on how gender inequalities shape young women's use of dating violence and its meanings within dating relationships. I tie everything together in chapter 6, discussing the implications of the study for research on urban disadvantage and violence against women, and conclude with an overview of some of the policy implications that emerge from this research.

2

Gender 'n the 'Hood

*Neighborhood Violence against
Women and Girls*

For adolescents in disadvantaged urban communities, neighborhoods represent a major feature of social life. Youths congregate on the streets and in parks, and they cruise around in cars or on foot, socializing and playing music. In some cases, they also sell drugs, fight, and defend their neighborhood or gang territories. These activities, however, are deeply gendered. Young men are more often and more intensely involved in delinquent networks in their communities. And though adolescent girls and boys sometimes share their involvement in the social facets of neighborhoods, their participation often presents different kinds of risks for victimization and thus results in variations in the enactment of strategies to ensure their safety and well-being. In addition, because of the gendered meaning systems that guide interpretation and behavior, violence against women takes on distinctive features in disadvantaged neighborhoods, and these are ultimately detrimental to young women's well-being.

In chapter 1, I provided a general overview of youths' descriptions of their neighborhoods, including some notable variations across gender. Most striking is the extent to which youth described neighborhood dangers as both commonplace and ordinary. In addition, girls' and boys' descriptions suggest that these action spaces are male dominated, as evidenced by boys' greater participation in and awareness of the nuances of neighborhood conflicts. Here I consider some additional features of male domination in neighborhoods by examining the problem of gender-based violence.

Urban disadvantage has important gendered dimensions. This is certainly evident in research on the urban street world, where researchers have provided consistent and extensive evidence of the salience and institutionalization of gender inequality, including violence against women.[1] It is also evident from nationally representative research, such as the National Crime Victimization Survey. The work of criminologist Janet Lauritsen indicates that, compared with other racial groups—where gender disparities in rates of victimization are pronounced—African American young women have rates of nonlethal victimization that are similar to those of their male counterparts, and these young women are more likely to be victimized by the people they know, including those in their neighborhoods. Lauritsen's area-level analyses reveal that the relationship between race and victimization risk is largely accounted for by those facets of extreme disadvantage that I documented in chapter 1.[2] This is why, though there is evidence of greater cultural support for violence against women in distressed urban neighborhoods, it is important to always keep its structural basis at the forefront. Robert Sampson refers to this as the *cultural structure* of such communities, to highlight the fact that cultural adaptations emerge in response to the structural conditions in which people—in this case urban Black adolescents—find themselves.[3]

In this chapter, I turn the attention explicitly to the nature of violence against women in youths' neighborhoods, examining their experiences with sexual harassment and violence, as well as other public acts of violence against women.[4] I consider how gender structures neighborhood risks, the visibility of gender-based violence, and the strategies young women employ to maintain their safety and security while going about their daily lives. Throughout the chapter, I pay special attention to how youths interpret and make sense of violence against women in their communities.

Gendered Perceptions of Neighborhood Risk

As discussed in chapter 1, youths' neighborhood descriptions consistently included reports of various kinds of criminal activities, including drug sales, gang conflicts, and gun violence. Their accounts suggest that many have witnessed a great deal of community violence. As illustrated in table 2-1, this is confirmed by their responses to survey questions about exposure to violence.[5] For instance, nearly all of the youths had seen people being hit or physically assaulted. Though some of these incidents occurred in school (see chapter 3) or at home, fully two-thirds of the youths indicated that they had witnessed such events in

TABLE 2-1
Exposure to Violence

	Girls (N = 35)	Boys (N = 40)
Seen people hit	33 (94%)	40 (100%)
Seen physical assault	27 (77%)	39 (98%)
Seen guns shot	27 (77%)	38 (95%)
Seen someone shot	21 (60%)	28 (70%)
Seen robbery	16 (46%)	30 (75%)
Seen stabbing	15 (43%)	21 (53%)
Seen drive-by shooting	14 (40%)	17 (43%)
Seen someone killed	12 (34%)	19 (48%)

neighborhoods. In fact, the more serious the violence witnessed, the larger the proportion of youths who reported that it had occurred in neighborhoods. A total of 36 youths reported having witnessed a stabbing; 33 of these incidents occurred in neighborhood contexts. Likewise, all of youths' reports of witnessing gunfire occurred in neighborhoods. It is especially striking that many had witnessed serious gun violence. Fully 60 percent of the girls and 70 percent of the boys had witnessed someone being shot. Of these 49 incidents, only two occurred in sites other than neighborhoods.[6] Likewise, more than one-third of the girls and nearly one-half of the boys had witnessed someone being killed. All 31 of these homicides occurred in the community.[7]

A growing body of research has examined the impact for youths of witnessing such extraordinary violence. This work indicates that witnessing violence is related to increased aggressive behavior, increased emotional and psychological distress, a heightened sense of vigilance, and increased risk of personal victimization.[8] Notably, several studies suggest that "repeated exposure to high levels of violence may cause children and adolescents to become uncaring toward others, and desensitized toward future violent events."[9]

What is missing from these studies, however, is an examination of the impact of exposure to violence against women, particularly in the community. Research has examined the consequences for children of witnessing violence among adults in their families,[10] but studies of community violence nearly always measure incidents such as those listed in table 2-1 and have not made distinctions between violence witnessed against women and other violent events.[11] This is because until recently, when scholars thought about urban violence, it was conceptualized primarily in gender-neutral terms or was assumed to be male on male. The consequence is that we have little information about how young women are affected by repeated exposure to male violence against women, including its psychological impact and its effects on girls' gender identities and their relationships with both males and other females. This is a critical gap in our knowledge, made all the more significant by my findings here, which suggest that not only do young women face gender-specific risks in public spaces but also that violence against women often takes on features of public spectacle.

Before considering such incidents in detail, let me begin by examining how youths perceived neighborhood risks to be shaped by gender. During the interview, we asked a series of questions to tap into youths' beliefs about the gendered dimensions of neighborhood risks. One question that drew a varied response was whether they felt the neighborhood was safer for males or females. Regardless of whether youths believed males or females were safer, or, conversely, faced greater neighborhood dangers, the majority of their responses drew from gender-specific meanings about the nature of neighborhood risks.

Youths who believed that young men faced greater dangers focused on how young men's neighborhood activities structured risks against them. Specifically, they noted young men's participation in gangs and drug selling, along with the much greater likelihood for male violence to involve firearms. Young women, they believed, were insulated from such dangers because they were less involved in street action and rarely used guns; they believed that street conflicts over gangs and commodities from the drug trade tended to be the purview of young men.[12] For instance, Tisha explained, "it's probably safer for females, 'cause the males, they involved in them gangs and stuff. And I mean, you don't really hear too much about females shootin' each other the way you do males." Doug concurred: "A girl is cool, but the guys, it's just plain and simple. Like if we see you, and we don't know you in our neighborhood, we gonna jump you."

Alternatively, some youths believed that their neighborhoods were so dangerous that gender didn't insulate anyone. Curtis explained, "the neighborhood I'm living in now, it ain't safer for nobody." Likewise, Tommie said that "when all the drive-bys and stuff was goin' on" in his neighborhood, it was dangerous for "everybody. The kids, *everybody*." And Alicia explained, "I don't think it's safer for neither one, 'cause . . . a girl can get shot just like a boy can." Nonetheless, youths often alluded to gender-specific risks, even within a broader sense of generalized danger. LaSondra said her neighborhood was safe "for nobody. Nobody." Clarifying, she explained, "females get raped, males get killed." Likewise, Dwayne said, "I don't think [my neighborhood's] safer for neither one. Anybody can get hurt." He continued, "if [girls] look good, somebody might try to touch 'em or something. And they might not want them to touch them and they might say something to 'em. And the dudes in my neighborhood, they might try to beat them up 'cause the girl wouldn't let them touch 'em."

As these last comments suggest, youths who emphasized the dangers posed to girls in their neighborhoods often focused on gender-specific issues. While risks for males were tied to gangs and offending, youths emphasized the dangers to girls caused by predatory male behavior. The threat of sexual violence was a common theme, and young women often spoke specifically about the dangers posed by nighttime. Britney explained:

> We face . . . a lot of stuff. Males, if you don't want to give it up they'll probably try to take it. If you walking by yourself and in the dark they'll probably approach you and want to, you know what I'm saying, do something with you. That's why you don't never walk by yourself after dark. [I] always keep [protection] with me when I walk by myself.

Likewise, Gail noted: "I don't know if it's just me being paranoid. I'll be walkin' at night and people just be walkin' behind you. . . . I mean, I don't know, everybody get scared to walk at nighttime, so I guess it's just normal. . . . [I] just keep lookin' over my shoulder to make sure ain't nobody walkin' behind me." And LaSondra said:

> Over there, you have to watch. Especially when you walking or something, 'cause you never know who might be behind you. When I walk, I look around and sometimes when I'm walking I forget to look around. Next minute somebody's behind me. Like, where'd this person come from? I just start walking faster. That's scary. Especially if it's nighttime too.

Felicia's concerns stemmed more specifically from the physical layout of her neighborhood. Recall her comment in chapter 1 that she felt safe there "in the daytime, [but] not at night" because of her proximity to a public housing project and another high-crime area. She said, "in the daytime don't too many people try too much because there be too many people outside." However:

> When I'm coming home from work at night or be coming out from my friends' at night . . . you gotta enter through the back, which is a alley. And it's like, there's one parking lot and then there's another parking lot. . . . You know, by me being a girl I try . . . to keep the gate closed, and move up the steps as soon as I can. 'Cause there's no telling what's gonna happen coming through there.

While fear of being alone at night is a common reaction among women generally, in Felicia's case, this was explicitly tied to both her knowledge of crime in the neighborhood and the infrastructure she had to navigate in order to get home. Her focus was not a generalized fear of the dark but a reasonable perception of the risks young women faced in neighborhoods where criminally involved men congregated in public spaces.[13] In fact, though Britney earlier noted that girls "face a lot of stuff" in general, she felt particularly unsafe walking though the parking lot near her housing project, specifically because "it be all grown men standing out there . . . drinking and smoking weed, selling drugs and everything. . . . You know, and when you walk past trying to go to the |gas| station, you don't know what they can do, what could happen. They can grab you in the car and rape you and whatever."

Young men also emphasized sexual dangers in their discussions of girls' neighborhood risks. Antwoin said it was safer for males " 'cause like the females, all the dudes be wanting to try to freak, you know, have sex with 'em, all that kinda stuff." Darnell explained, "you don't catch no girl walking, you know what I'm saying, on the northside. Not in no nighttime. Like my girlfriend, she stay like up the street from me. . . . I walk her home 'cause I don't trust her walking by herself, unless she got somebody with her." Asked what he thought might happen, Darnell explained:

> I don't know, I just can't trust things like that, you know. 'Cause things happen, things happen. Like you don't know if somebody'll jump out the bushes. Or wherever you going you can have somebody following you. . . . Like she could've been on her way to my house, somebody could've followed her, and I could've let her walk back home by herself and something would've happened to her.

Thus, nighttime posed different kinds of dangers for young women and young men. For young women, it signaled the potential for sexual danger; for young men, it was when the streets came alive with gang and drug violence. In both cases, though, perceived dangers came primarily at the hands of males.

In addition to their focus on sexual dangers, youths' perceptions of girls' neighborhood risks were tied to their beliefs about men's greater ability to protect themselves and to the vulnerabilities for women that emerged from perceptions of them as "weak." Jamellah explained, "it's always safer for males. They could protect theyself better than a female can. That's in any neighborhood." She continued:

> A girl could walk down the street and she hafta fear about somebody stoppin' and rapin' her and makin' her get in the car. And a boy could walk down the street and wouldn't hafta worry about that. 'Cause what woman gonna wanna rape a man for? And then a man is more likely to try to do something to a female anyway, 'cause we not as strong as a male.

Similarly, Britney believed males were less likely to be "messed with" because they were more likely to "carry a gun." In contrast, she said "dudes" believe females are "weak—won't do nuttin', won't say nuttin'."

As a consequence, Britney, like Jamellah, felt women were at greater risk for predatory behavior, including sexual assault, because they were deemed easy targets. April believed her neighborhood was safer for males for similar reasons:

> Ain't no nigga gon' mess with no 'nother nigga. They'll mess with a female 'fore they mess with another dude. 'Cause they more powerful than us. They know they can do, we like sensitive and all that stuff. We ain't gon' act like what no nigga do. We might try to fight back but we all for that hollerin' and ain't no dude gon' do that. . . . A dude'll pull a gun out on you. [With females], they can do something, knock it outta our hands or something, even if we had a gun.

A number of young men concurred. Curtis explained that "males more, I guess, rugged. Males more harder." Likewise, Kevin said, "women seem more vulnerable. So most people, like dope fiends and stuff, they'll rob women and stuff. They ain't gon' rob no man that's walking down the street 'cause they know he—especially a young man —probably got a gun or something on 'im." James explained, "dudes, I mean they can pretty much handle theyself and they ain't gotta worry about nuttin', they're safe. Females, somebody [can] overpower them. . . . I mean strength wise . . . [it's] easy to take something from them 'cause there ain't too much they can do for theyself." Likewise, Maurice noted that "females can't protect theyself," explaining: "Who'll be the first person you rob, a male or female? It's like a big buff dude versus a feminine woman, you know what I'm saying, who the person gonna stick out to 'em? That woman."[14]

Thus, many youths culled from exaggerated notions of gender difference (males are buff, rugged, powerful; females are feminine, sensitive, vulnerable) in their explanations of young women's risks in dangerous neighborhoods. These widespread belief systems did not just affect youths' perceptions of gender and risk but contributed more broadly to a hierarchy on the streets in which females were situationally disadvantaged vis-à-vis males and therefore often viewed by males simply in terms of their sexual availability.[15] As Kenisha complained, "dudes get more respect than females. . . . It's just the way it is over there. The males, they have more authority than girls." Such gendered status hierarchies affected how young women were treated in public places and how others responded to incidents in which females were mistreated. Moreover, these inequalities limited the recourse available to young women for challenging gender-based violence.

In fact, gendered status hierarchies and the sexualization of young women meant that a number of youths looked to young women's behavior or dress in explaining their neighborhood risks. Kristy said that "dudes be safer than the gals . . . 'cause I mean, they don't be walking around in hoochie clothes and stuff. They don't give people the wrong idea about what they want." Likewise, when Tisha was asked whether young women faced any particular dangers, she replied, "oh yeah, like when they out there wearin' all them tight clothes and all that, you know. They get a bad rep, they can be raped, anything like that." Asked whether girls faced particular dangers, Eugene said, "yeah, like people comin' and rape them or something, 'cause girls wear short stuff and . . . fellas think, well, dawg, you know, I'm fina get up on [that], I'm fina touch on her or something. And they get mad if somebody touch 'em. They gotta look [at] what they wearing and when they sending signals like that."

LaSondra provided a more layered analysis of how girls' behavior shapes sexual risk, tied to her own experience of being raped in her neighborhood. She noted that young women faced sexual assault and stalking, then quickly shifted to an emphasis on girls' culpability: "But these girls, sometimes, you just should see what they wear. They look like they just want somebody to touch 'em." The dialogue continued:

> *Interviewer*: So you think those girls are partly to blame for what comes to them?
> *LaSondra*: They ain't to blame, 'cause it ain't they fault. It's the person who do it to them, it's they person's fault.
> *Interviewer*: But you think that if they dress that way, you run a higher risk?
> *LaSondra*: Yeah. But sometimes you don't have to dress that way. Take me for instance, I have on baggy pants and a long t-shirt. They'll still try. 'Cause that's how I was [dressed when I was raped]. I had on some baggy pants with a boy's shirt, everything. They still try to talk to you. But some girls, they just want attention. They just wear stuff like all the way up to here and shirts up. I just look at them girls, I be like, it's sad. They look like hookers. . . . You know, and when they wear that stuff, they make the boy think, "Aw yeah, we gonna get this." They take it if they want it. 'Cause the girl might let 'em or might not let 'em. She gotta know it's the way she act and the way she dress.

As LaSondra's dialogue illustrates, many youths believed that dressing in a provocative manner drew attention to girls from men or boys who could pose significant dangers to them. While not a necessary condition for being targeted for sexual assault, revealing clothing was believed to heighten girls' risks. At the same time, LaSondra herself vacillated between holding young women accountable and blaming the perpetrators of violence. Making reference to her own victimization, she recognized that her experience provided an ill fit with popular interpretations of girls' culpability, yet she was unwilling to discount this position entirely.

In sum, youths who believed their neighborhoods were less safe for females than males emphasized both the sexual dangers facing women and the perception that women were weaker and thus easy targets.[16] In fact, regardless of whether they believed males or females faced greater danger, youths' explanations rarely deviated from gender-based interpretations of neighborhood risk. Their accounts provide further evidence of the extent to which public spaces operated as male-dominated terrains, providing avenues for male engagement (and, thus, victimization risk) and sites in which the presence of young women could be read as opportunities for sexual conquest.

Disadvantaged Neighborhoods and Violence against Women

I noted earlier that studies of community violence rarely make distinctions between violence against women and other violent events. However, youths' discussions of neighborhood risks clearly emphasized its gendered dimensions. In fact, recent research has found that—in addition to other forms of violence—violence against women is also heightened in disadvantaged communities. Recall that Michael Benson and his colleagues suggest that the higher prevalence of violence against women in disadvantaged communities is linked to both the social isolation present in such communities and the difficulties these neighborhoods have in developing collective efficacy.[17] In addition, research on offender networks suggests that public violence against females is quite common and highly visible.[18]

In fact, three facets of violence against women were present in youths' accounts of their neighborhoods: exposure to public incidents of physical violence against women, including intimate partner abuse; young women's complaints of widespread sexual harassment in neighborhoods; and incidents of sexual assault and coercion.[19] Most youths, like scholars, initially thought of urban crime in their neighborhoods in terms of masculine endeavors—gangs, drugs, and guns. However, once they were asked directly about forms of violence that target women specifically, they had plenty of stories to recount.

Witnessing Physical Violence against Women

Though scholars typically assume that intimate partner violence occurs primarily behind closed doors, many of the youths here described witnessing such incidents in public view. Youths' accounts of such incidents may seem somewhat peripheral to their own lives, particularly since much of the public violence they described involved adults and rarely included individuals they were intimately familiar with. In actuality, such incidents are quite meaningful, because they impart essential messages about how violence against women is to be interpreted and responded to. Thus, it is important to pay attention here not just to the descriptions that youths provided but also to the tone and implications of many of their comments. These provide evidence of the interpretive lenses brought to bear on such events, illustrating how youths were taught to think about violence against women.

Asked whether she had ever seen a man hurt a woman in her neighborhood,[20] Tisha responded:

> Yeah, it's this girl next door. I don't know if she a crackhead or what, her boyfriend just always beatin' her up. She always comin' [over], like, "Call the police for me!" But then when the police get there she don't wanna press charges or nothin' like that. I don't know, I guess she stuck on stupid. She like getting beat up I guess.

Tisha said that the woman "done let him [back] in [her home] over and over, and she know what he gon' do to her. So that's on her. We don't call the police for her no mo'. Just let her get beat up." Because, in Tisha's eyes, the woman had not taken sufficient action to extricate herself from the abusive relationship, she was seen as culpable and thus unworthy of further assistance.

In addition, Tisha speculated about whether the woman was a "crackhead." Other youths also referenced substance abusers in their descriptions of violence. Christal said she had seen "crackheads fightin' they boyfriends," and Tawanna described seeing a "prostitute standing around" who got beat up. Such labels functioned to distance the victims from the young women who witnessed the events and to suggest that the violence was deserved and the victim blameworthy because of her status. Gail said it was "lil' drunk, alcoholics [that] be fightin' up the street . . . just lil' drunkies, drunk people just gettin' drunk. Crackheads, drunks, you know. . . . We'll be laughin' at 'em or whatever." Thus Gail's response was unsympathetic. She described a recent incident:

One time I seen a man hit a woman with a bottle. But again, they was drunk, you know. . . . Well we ain't really see it from the beginning. We just heard them arguin' [and went to look]. She was running down the street talkin' 'bout some, "He tryin' to kill me, he tryin' to kill me!" [*laughs*]. . . . He was like, "Come here, come here." She was drunk, going back and stuff. And she talkin' 'bout, "You don't hit me." And he —bang—just stole her [hit her with the bottle]. . . . [Then she] kept yellin, "Oh, he gon' kill me, he gon' kill me!" And knowin' us, we just laughin'.

Tami described a recent incident she witnessed involving the man across the street, who was routinely abusive toward his girlfriend:

I don't know what they was arguing about. When he came outside he was telling her to get her stuff, and she don't run it, he run it. He be hittin' her upside her head and she be, "Why you hittin' me? Stop hittin' me!" and stuff. But she don't be fightin' him back or nothin'. He be hittin' her . . . upside her head, she was just walkin' down the steps.

Asked how she reacted upon seeing the man hitting his girlfriend, Tami explained:

We was laughin'. Then we was like, that's a shame and they shouldn't put up with that stuff. They should go'on, leave, but I guess they ain't got nowhere else to go so they just put up with the stuff. . . . But we figured it wasn't none of our business. It came outside [so] we was just lookin' to see what was goin' on.

Tami's comments suggest that her reaction to the event was complex. On the one hand, she and her friends found it an amusing public spectacle. On the other hand, Tami expressed some empathy for the woman she felt was likely trapped in the situation. Finally, she noted that it "wasn't none of our business," indicating the important norm of staying out of others' affairs.

Kristy described a similarly complex—though delayed—set of reactions upon witnessing the brutal beating of a woman:

Kristy: It was like Friday, it was kind of dark out. The people next door, the girl like 17, the dude about 25. I guess she had said something to him, and the next thing we know everybody out on the front, watching him pull her up the street by her hair. It was [hair weave] tracks everywhere. We was laughing. But then when the girl ended up in the hospital we was like, man he shouldn't had did that. But then, we should've did something too, you know, we seen him beating on her, we could've stopped him. It was more than enough of us.

Interviewer: So how did you react to that when you saw it?

Kristy: I mean, it was shocking. Kind of funny. 'Cause she was getting whooped. But the result of it was, whew!

Interviewer: Did you do anything about it?

Kristy: No, I ain't feel like it was my place, you know, ain't have nuttin' to do with me.

Interviewer: How did other people react?

Kristy: Code of silence. They didn't say nuttin'. They just watched.

Despite her subsequent sense that she and others present could have done something to intervene, Kristy's reaction while the lengthy assault happened was surprised amusement, and those around her watched and laughed as well. Her description of the event offers evidence of both the neighborhood rule of staying out of other people's business and the level of desensitization and callousness that develops toward violence against women in such settings.

Terence said that there were "a couple of dudes in the neighborhood that be beatin' on they females." He continued:

Like they'll be arguing in the house, and then she tryin' to leave or whatever, he might come out the house, get to arguin' with her. And 'fore you know it, he puttin' his hands on her or whatever, slappin' her around, telling her to get back in the house, "You ain't goin' nowhere," or whatever. People around the 'hood just sit there watchin' like, "He wild, he wild," let him go on about his business.

He described a recent incident in which his next-door neighbor was hitting his girlfriend "all up in her face, in the back of her head or whatever, smacking her" as she tried to leave. Terence said the incident went on, in public, for "like fifteen minutes" until they "went back into the house." Even then, he heard the violence continue. Asked whether anyone thought to call the police or otherwise intervene, he said, "naw . . .

[everybody] was just sitting there looking, laughing, a couple of 'em. . . . I guess they get a kick out of that stuff or something."

Likewise, Dawanna saw "this man . . . grabbin' this lady by her face and pulling her down the street." She explained, "she was yelling, but I ain't hear, you know, if it was like, 'Help' or anything like that. But when I walk down the street I was finding all her jewelry, you know, in a line going up to her house. [He was] pullin' stuff off her face, pullin' her face, hittin' her in the side." Asked whether she called the police or did anything else to intervene, Dawanna said, "I mean I didn't do nuttin' 'cause I mean, in my eyes that's their problems, that's not mine."

Shaun described participating in an altercation with a woman in his neighborhood that combined physical violence with sexual degradation:

It was me and my homies, we was walking down the street, gonna get on the bus. . . . And my homie . . . was talking to some lady, and she was real drunk and she was saying something. She was calling him a nigger or something like that. And he was like, he asked me if I wanted to see her strip, and I was like "Yeah." [So] we ripped her dress off. She was like, "Damn, you wanna see something?" She took her bra and her panties and her shoes off and she threw her shoes at him. And she was swinging on him and stuff. And he kicked her in her stomach and she fell and she got up and she was still swinging. And then his brother stole [punched] her in the face and she was knocked out, she was laying in the street.

Shaun and his friends then got on a passing bus and left. Kevin was one of the "homies" present, and recounted the story in similar detail. He said, "the bus came, so we had to get in the bus. [But] a bunch of [people at] the bus stop was staring and stuff." Fearing someone may have called the police, he and his friends rode until "another bus came, and we jumped off and got on the other bus just in case."

In fact, three young women did recount incidents in which they or someone in their family called the police. In two cases, an adult member of the young woman's family was present and took the initiative. In the third, the incident involved a woman who had been beaten and robbed by a stranger. Jamellah witnessed the incident as it happened near her house, explaining, "the dude got her by her shirt, just grabbin' her, punchin' her in her face. And she was like, 'Help, help, I'm getting robbed! Call the police!' " After the man took off, Jamellah brought the woman to her house, called the police, and waited with her "for like thirty minutes." Since the police "ain't never show," Jamellah "waited on the bus stop with her . . . and she caught the bus home."

Rennesha said that recently a young girl who lived down the street ran to their house and told them that her stepfather was beating her mother. She explained, "the lil' girl was cryin', telling me what happened . . . [she] just looked so sorry." Though her family called the police, Rennesha said they "never did come." Finally, Kenisha saw a man brutally beating a woman across the street and "called my grandmother to the door. I was like, 'Look how he doin' her.' And my grandmother was like, 'Call the police,' so I called the police and [they] came." Following her grandmother's lead, Kenisha explained, "I felt like any man shouldn't hit a woman first of all. I don't care what the situation is. And the way he was doing her, I don't care how much money that she owed him or whatever the case was, he didn't have no business putting his hands on her." Kenisha said there were a number of people present when the incident happened, some of whom were "standing around." One young woman attempted to intervene, telling the man, " 'It don't make no sense how you doing her. [If] it was a man, you wouldn't beat on no man like that!' " Nonetheless, Kenisha noted, "it was a good six people out there, and it was only that one girl who was trying to break it up."

There were times, then, when neighborhood residents attempted to intervene on incidents of violence against women. It appears that this was most likely to occur either when a responsible adult was present and took initiative or when the incident involved someone perceived as an innocent victim, as with the woman robbed by a stranger. Intimate partner violence, in particular, was defined as a private affair. Cherise, for instance, described an incident at the bus stop in which a young man got angry with her and "smacked me in my face." She explained, "there were people standing around [but] they didn't help. They jus' thought that was maybe my boyfriend or something, they didn't want to get involved." In addition, when youths were in the company of peers, incidents of violence against women took on a carnivalesque flavor, with group dynamics that encouraged watching and taking pleasure from the spectacle rather than intervening. Even when youths felt a pang of responsibility to do something, strong norms toward nonintervention won out.

In fact, Britney was explicit about this normative expectation. Residents at her housing project witnessed a lengthy assault in which a neighbor choked and beat his girlfriend when she tried to leave, then held her at gunpoint and forced her into his car. However, they refused to cooperate when the police arrived. She explained:

> People in the neighborhood, they be like, "We not gonna tell you nuttin', 'cause you the police," stuff like that. They was like, "You the police, we ain't fina tell you nuttin' about this person and that person." So the police couldn't get no information. So they walked away. And I couldn't tell 'em, the kids couldn't tell 'em. 'Cause they would've got on us for being a snitch.

Thus, the consequence of neighborhood norms that required people to mind their own business, coupled with distrust of the police and slow or poor police response, meant that many incidents took place in the public eye, but few interventions followed. As Britney noted, even if she wanted to provide information to the police, she believed her hands were tied as a "kid" among adults who refused to cooperate.

I noted earlier that public incidents of violence against women were significant because of the messages they taught youths about how such violence is to be interpreted and responded to. Central among these—which even young women learned and often internalized—was that women were to blame for their victimization. Moreover, they saw for themselves that intervention on behalf of female victims was rarely forthcoming. Such responses taught young women the profound lesson that they are likely to be on their own when it comes to dealing with gender-based violence.

Of course, norms that discourage residents from getting involved in neighborhood crime are not reserved for female victims. Scholars have tied this pattern to the broader problem of limited collective efficacy and even the reasonable fear of retaliation in high-crime urban communities. However, two features of violence against women are distinctive. First is that norms toward nonintervention were deepened further by the definition of intimate partner violence as a *private* problem, even when it occurred in public. This makes such violence an even more isolating experience for its victims. Second is the fact that most youths' accounts of violence against women included reports of spontaneous laughter. What is especially striking about this is that youths' accounts of male-on-male violence did *not* include descriptions of laughter or other evidence that these events were looked on with such amusement. Perhaps this stemmed from greater concern that such conflicts could escalate to gun violence. Whatever the reason, it was violence against *women* that youths "got a kick out of" seeing, thus further demarcating such violence as unimportant.

Sexual Harassment in Neighborhoods

In addition to witnessing physical violence against women in their neighborhoods, a common problem described by young women and corroborated by young men was the routine sexual harassment of girls. While the issue of sexual harassment has received a great deal of scholarly attention in the institutions of school and the workplace, limited attention has been paid to harassment in public spaces such as neighborhoods.[21] In all, 89 percent of the girls we interviewed reported experiencing some form of sexual or gender harassment. While they were more likely to report having experienced harassment in school (77 percent; see chapter 3), more than one-half of the girls (54 percent) described incidents that occurred in their neighborhoods.[22] Two kinds of neighborhood sexual harassment emerged in youths' accounts: sexual come-ons or comments by young men in the neighborhood, and harassment by adult men, which girls often found much more ominous.

SEXUAL HARASSMENT BY ADOLESCENT PEERS

Young men's behavior was described as problematic in two situations: when they engaged in inappropriate sexual banter or touching with girls they were friends with, and when they approached young women they didn't know. Cherise complained about the behavior of some of the young men she hung out with in the neighborhood:

> When we be playing or something, they try to touch me on the fly. But we usually don't fight over it. We might, you know, I might just push him or something 'cause they might be cool. . . . I don't know what they might be thinking, but maybe they might try to take advantage of you or something. . . . I just know that they try to touch me and I don't like it.

Nicole exhibited a similar ambivalence when describing the behavior of her male friends in the neighborhood: "You gon' have to watch out for them boys though. . . . They just got problems, that's what I think. But they cool though, I hang out with 'em. But they'll say lil' [sexual comments], but they won't say nothin' nasty. . . . They be playin' with you." While Nicole appeared uncomfortable with the young men's sexual banter, she went along with some of it because she enjoyed their company. She continued, "they'll make you laugh with 'em, you know. They like to have fun or whatever, make you laugh." Thus, she vacillated between interpreting their behavior as "playful" and problematic.

In fact, Nicole's ambivalence was even more apparent when we consider the question that elicited her comments: "Do you think girls face any particular dangers in the neighborhood?" While she ultimately interpreted her friends' behavior as "playful," her discomfort was evidenced by the fact that her account was triggered by a question about the risks young women face in the neighborhood. Later in the interview, she was more explicit about her concerns. Asked how the neighborhood could be made safer for girls, she said:

> I think it could be made safer if the boys would think 'fore they talk. You know, you should always think. . . . Like you come up to a lady, you should approach her in a better way instead of being like, "Ah, yo' when we gon' do this? When we gon' fuck?" Naw, un-un. You ain't suppose to do that. You should just ask her, "Would you go with me? Would you be my lady?" You know, ask her in a appropriate way, you know, don't just come up to her like she a hooker or something.

When neighborhood friends were the ones engaging in this behavior, young women would typically negotiate the situation so as not to escalate to a conflict or damage the friendship, despite their discomfort with the young man's behavior. Young men used "play" claims to explain their behavior, which girls sometimes went along with, though seemingly uneasily. Jamal explained, "we don't try to take advantage of them. . . . We probably just have fun with them. Try to play with them." Jamal emphasized what he described as "joking" sexual banter, noting: "Taking advantage [is] like grabbing or touching them, we don't do that. You might catch one or two try to slap a girl on the butt, that's the most." Likewise, Raymond said, "the only time I see girls get hit on [is] when they playing around."

In addition to negotiating "play" banter with male friends, a number

of girls complained about how boys approached them in the neighborhood, including those they didn't know or know well. Nicole's earlier
comments are illustrative. Similarly, Alicia described what happened after a young man came up to her friend and "said, 'girl, you fine. Why
don't you back that ass up?'" Alicia's friend "told him don't come to
her like that, that's real disrespectful," but the young man replied,
"'How is that disrespectful?'" In fact, some young men seemed oblivi-
ous to (or at least feigned ignorance of) girls' interpretations of such
sexual comments. For instance, asked whether he knew of males in the
neighborhood who tried to take advantage of girls, Tony replied, "naw,
I don't know nobody that do that. . . . They [just] be tryin' to mack.
Probably be like, 'Hey baby, can I get your number?' or something, or 'I
want to get to know you.'" Reminded that during the survey he indicated that girls could be uncomfortable with such behaviors, Tony said,
"oh yeah, sometimes when they just be playin'. But I don't think they be
meanin' it though. . . . Probably be sayin, 'You ugly,' callin' em B's
[bitches] and stuff, then they'll laugh." Though he admitted that such
incidents may feel serious "to the girl," Tony insisted that young men
"don't be serious" when they behave in such ways.

While Tony downplayed the significance of such behavior, Dwayne
was highly critical:

> It was a girl walking down the street, she had some little shorts on and
> a little top. And at first [the guy] try to talk to her, and she didn't want
> to talk to him. So he touched her and she told him not to put his hands
> on her no more or she gonna go get her big brother. He done slapped
> this girl. So she went to go get her big brother and stuff. That's how
> stuff be getting started. That's how people be getting killed . . . putting
> they hands on people they don't even know.

In fact, Dwayne described intervening on behalf of his girlfriend to get
the young men in his neighborhood to leave her alone. He explained,
"like my girlfriend, she be like walking home and stuff and I be too
busy at the house and I can't walk her home. They be trying to put they
hands on [her] and stuff. So I be going around talking to them little cats
about putting they hands on my girlfriend, so they don't be doing that
stuff no more."

As Dwayne's earlier description illustrates, a number of youths reported that when a young woman rebuffed the advances of a young man she didn't know or know well, he often became angry or disrespectful toward her. Walking through her neighborhood, Anishika said, sometimes "one of them lil' thugs or something tryin' to talk to me. . . . They'll get mad or something if I don't say nothin' to them, they be like, 'Well fuck you then.' I don't say nothin' back 'cause . . . I'm not even trying to get involved with nobody like that." And Katie said, "some boys I know, like if they see some new girls walkin' down the street or something, they'll try to talk to 'em or whatever. And then if the girls don't give 'em no play, they'll call 'em out of they name. . . . He'll curse her out or something, talk about her." Jermaine said that "like if gang members try to talk to the girls, and the girls don't want to talk to 'em, they like, they start arguing, like, 'I don't want to talk to you anyway, you ugly,' or something like that."

Antwoin described similar incidents, though he appeared to implicate the young women: "The boys over there, they don't like the girls [who are] stuck up. They don't like stuck up girls over there." Asked what qualified as being stuck up, he explained, "like they don't like talking to boys or something. When a boy say hello or what's up, girls don't wanna talk to 'em." When girls didn't respond to young men's advances, Antwoin said, "they be like, 'F [fuck] you, B [bitch].'" Here incidents turned to gender harassment when young women ignored or responded negatively to young men's advances. Kevin explained: "We might be clownin' or something and say something stupid, make a little, make a comment to 'em, like we might try and talk to a girl and she look at you like you crazy or something, like we ain't good enough for her. Then [you] just start going off on her or something."

In addition, girls were sometimes seen as culpable when incidents of sexual harassment occurred, in this case penalized either for *not* acting sufficiently "stuck up" or for dressing in ways that were defined as provocative. Ronald's comments are illustrative:

Like if she come down the street wearing some real skinny shorts and a shirt that's real little she'll get some attention. I think that's mainly why they do it, to get attention. Some dudes, they be like, "Let me get your phone number," and then she be like, "Naw." This one dude say, "Why you gonna come outside wearing that if you gonna act all stuck up?"

While Ronald was critical of young women who dressed "to get attention" but didn't respond favorably to boys' advances, Janelle suggested that the problem boiled down to some girls' failure to stand up for themselves:

> The guys will normally do that to a female that they know. . . . They'll make the sexual comments or they'll hit on them because they know that that female is not going to do anything. . . . Like if a male comes to a female and says something or hits on her and the female stands up for herself, then it'll be a different story. He won't treat her like that anymore because she has more respect for herself than another female might have for herself.

What we see, however, is that girls faced a double bind: not standing up for themselves meant that sexual harassment was likely to continue and would be seen as deserved or even desired, while standing up for themselves often prompted an angry response. Given male domination of public spaces, young women were in a lose-lose situation. None of the strategies available guaranteed positive outcomes. Held accountable for young men's sexualization of them if they appeared too friendly or compliant, they risked escalating into a conflict—or at least insults and name-calling—if they challenged or ignored young men's sexual advances. I revisit these tensions in chapter 3, as there were many parallels between the dynamics of peer harassment in the neighborhood and at school.

SEXUAL HARASSMENT BY ADULT MEN

Young women expressed greater apprehension and less ambivalence about sexual harassment by adult men in the community. These incidents, more so than incidents involving peers, heightened girls' sense of vulnerability and made them fear for their safety. Nykeshia explained:

> The one person I feel uncomfortable around in my neighborhood [is a man that] always askin' me to do something [sexual] with him. And I told my momma about it and she told me, "Just stay away from him, as far as you can, and I hope he stay away from you." She called the police about it 'cause he had asked me in front of my momma. . . . He just denied everything and they was like, "We don't have proof that he asked you that . . . we [can't] do nothin' about that."

Nykeshia was fifteen when interviewed and said this man (who was four years her senior) had been harassing her "since I was about thirteen." She said he behaved this way toward other girls in the neighborhood as well. The police were less than helpful, and, to make matters worse, the officer who responded to the call was one that Nykeshia's friend said had sexually assaulted her. Nykeshia noticed that her friend, who "was over there" at the time, quickly "went back in the house" when the officer arrived. "I went in the house too, 'cause I was wondering what she was backing back for, she was just backing back." Thus, not only was the officer's response to the man's behavior ineffectual, but Nykeshia had evidence that the man called to protect her had sexually assaulted her friend. Since the police failed to intervene, she had little recourse but to try and avoid the man and hope he never hurt her.

Shauntell, who was just twelve, described a similar problem with a man in her neighborhood:

> He stay directly across the street from us. I'm real cool with his lil' brother. [But] he just got outta jail. And me [and] my best friend, we walked down the street after school and he comes across the street, stand there and he watched me go all the way up on my front until I get in the house. I . . . go in the living room and looked out the window, he starin' straight at the window. . . . I goes outside and he'll come from across the street and come sit on our steps and just sit up there and stare at me. I look at him, I be like, "Problem?" And he shook his head no. I go [sarcastically], "See something you like?" . . . I looked like a lil' tomboy and I sit like [a tomboy] and he'll look between my legs. I closed my legs. Stuff like that. I just don't feel comfortable around him and he just got out of jail.

Despite her discomfort, Shauntell said her auntie told her, "don't worry about it." She continued, "I got too many people over there for him to think he gon' do something to me."

While Shauntell took some comfort in her belief that having relatives in the neighborhood would keep the man from assaulting her, Britney specifically called on her uncle to sanction a man who was menacing her:

> Older [women], they'll walk past, [and neighborhood men will] be like, "How you doing?" But like me, if I walk past, grown man say like,

"Hey baby what's your name?" and I'm 14 years old, they can be 25. I be like, "I'm only 14 years old sir." And they'll be like, "Ain't no problem," you know what I'm saying. And that's not right. So one man approached me and he said, "Hey baby what's your name?" I say, "I'm 14 years old," and he said, "I ain't ask you [your age], I said what's your name." I keep on saying I'm 14. He said "I'm 25 and I don't care." I said, "Well I'm 14." Then he kept on saying it. So then my uncle had rolled up, [and] he didn't know that was my uncle. So my uncle got out the car and was like "What you saying to my niece?" He like, "I was asking her do she know where somebody stay at." I said, "No you didn't, you asked me what's my name and I kept telling you I'm 14, you a grown man." My uncle had said, "If you ever talk to my niece like that again [you will deal with me. So] he walked off.

As Britney's account suggests, girls felt that they were a particular target for adult men in the neighborhood because they were teenagers and thus seen as easy to take advantage of. Young women expressed great discomfort about being sexualized by adults and, consequently, tended to be especially leery of groups of men.

Young men also described the widespread nature of adult male harassment of adolescent girls. Andrew said in his neighborhood, "females get harassed so much." He believed it posed a real danger for young women:

Like an older person come through and they'll see a young girl walking through. She can have a pretty shape, pretty face or whatever, and they'll see her and they'll try to dog [her].[23] They try to talk to her or whatever, and the female will tell them no, or that they're too young or they too old for them, or they not interested. They get mad and get to calling them bitches and ho's, disrespecting them. [Then the girls] get mad, they get to cussing them back out. Sometimes the dudes get mad and threaten 'em, saying, "I'll do this to you," or "I'll do that." . . . And a woman know they can't whoop a dude, so.

Andrew surmised that "older guys" targeted teenage girls because "I guess they feel like with a younger girl they can take advantage of them." He described being upset when his younger sister was targeted: "See like I got a little sister, and I feel bad when she come home and say a man came and did this to her and tried to do that or whatever. . . . It makes me mad to the point where if I see the dude that did it, it feel good to fight him. But it ain't gonna prove nothing, so ain't no point. . . . I mean, a man gonna be a man regardless."

Likewise, asked whether there were men in the neighborhood girls felt uncomfortable around, Ricky said yes, explaining:

> I don't mean to say it like this, but they act like typical niggas, you know what I'm sayin'. I mean you got them—the girls fear the guys that be out there constantly using the B-word [bitch] and constantly talkin' about sex and always wanting to sell drugs and smoke weed and drink. It's mainly those guys they fear. I mean, [the girls] know we not a threat 'cause we pretty much universal. We like to kick it, chill with females and stuff. . . . [But] it's some of the guys we hang around. We don't necessarily associate with 'em or nothin' but it's the particular older guys that's say from like 19 to 25.

He said a few of these men "go look for females to talk about and cuss out, and they look for females to give 'em a reason to hit 'em or say something very disrespectful, or try to find a reason to touch 'em or something." Ricky said such incidents occurred "on a everyday basis with the particular guys I'm talking about. I mean, they just love disrespecting women." While nonintervention was the norm, Ricky explained that "I would say something. Like, 'Man, you wouldn't want nobody to talk to your mother like that.'" In response, though, he would be told, " 'Ole' punk ass nigga get out of here,' or something. I mean it's just they attitudes man."

Several young women described a final, related form of harassment that resulted from living in areas with active drug markets: the threat they believed drug addicts could pose to them, and the dangers of being mistaken for a drug-addicted woman themselves. LaSondra described a recent incident:

> It was nighttime. See, my mistake. I was walking by myself from my friend's house, at first she was watching. This man was a crackhead, he ran up behind me and say, "You know [where I can get] drugs?" And I said "No." So he ran across the street, bought some crack, and ran back down her block. I turned and I was walking, I was at the corner of my block, and as I was going in the house, before I got in the house, this man pulled up and said, "You need a ride girl?" I say "No." But I

made sure he like left, and then I went on my porch and went in my house. I told my momma too. I don't like that.

Lisa complained of a similar incident: "I'm sittin' in a car, my boyfriend was in the back of the car seat and I was fina drop him off at home. This boy gon' tell me, 'What's up with you? Come here let me talk to you." [I replied,] 'Do you think I'm a crackhead?' 'Cause I don't like that."

And Dawanna emphasized how the drug trade contributed to the visible sexual abuse of women around her neighborhood. She said that girls had to "watch out for some of the males that be around the neighborhood, 'cause it's a couple of them that force females to, you know, do this and do this, and do certain things. . . . Basically sexual things, or like drugs and stuff like that." She explained why she was uncomfortable around some of the men in neighborhood:

> It's many of them that sell drugs around here, do drugs, and do certain things to other people. Be renting cars out from people that they sell the drugs to, and sometimes they bring 'em around my house and they be doin' certain things. They have 'em doing sexual active stuff right there, and there be a group of kids right there. . . . Right there on the street where everybody can see.

Seeing men take advantage of drug-addicted women in full view of neighborhood youth made Dawanna "feel uncomfortable." She explained, "I have nieces and nephews that's over there and I don't want them seein' no bad influence and then they grow up and they been through all that, and I don't want them comin' out as anything like that." While not a direct form of harassment, the public sexual mistreatment of female drug users further accentuated the sexualization of women in the neighborhood.

The neighborhood-based harassment of young women, then, was particularly widespread and amplified by the fact that groups of men—young and old—often congregated in these spaces. Whether older men, perhaps unemployed and with time on their hands, sometimes drug-addicted, or young men actively involved in drug sales and gangs, these groups often looked on young women primarily as potential sexual conquests. Young women were routinely frustrated by the disrespectful sexual come-ons they received by young men, but they were often downright threatened by the behavior of adults. While not all men or boys in their neighborhoods behaved in this way, it was a common enough problem to be a regular cause for concern and was tied directly to the structural inequalities that shaped their communities.

Sexual Assault and Coercion in Neighborhoods

Sexual assault was also an ongoing neighborhood danger for young women. In fact, the girls in this study reported very high rates of sexual victimization. More than one-half (54 percent) reported some form of sexual victimization, including rape (29 percent) or attempted rape (14 percent), or being pressured or coerced into unwanted sex (43 percent). Nearly one-third (31 percent) reported multiple sexual victimizations. These are staggering figures, especially considering that the average age of the young women we interviewed was just sixteen.[24]

In chapter 4, I provide a detailed analysis of the problems of sexual assault, coercion, and gang rape. Nonetheless, it is worth a preliminary discussion here because most of the incidents of sexual assault that youths described took place in and around the neighborhoods where they lived or spent time. While such assaults rarely occurred in public settings within the neighborhood, young women were often targeted through their neighborhood and other peer connections and were made vulnerable by the abundance of men present in public spaces. Here I focus brief attention on some of the neighborhood dimensions of sexual assault, then return to a more detailed analysis after examining school-based sexual harassment in chapter 3. As with sexual harassment in neighborhoods, peer harassment in schools provided an additional overlay of sexualized interaction that facilitated the sexual abuse of young women across settings.

Sexual assaults and sexually coercive behaviors in youths' neighborhoods were often an extension of the broader sexualized treatment young women experienced. This is largely why young women were so leery of groups of men. As with sexual harassment, young women's risks for sexual assault and coercion were varied. Among peers, alcohol and drugs were often used to lower a young woman's level of awareness or incapacitate her. Rapes involving physical force more frequently involved adult men, though they happened with peers as well.

Recall Antwoin's earlier comment that the neighborhood was less safe for girls than boys because "like the females, all the dudes be want-

ing to try to freak, you know, have sex with 'em, all that kinda stuff."
He continued, "females, they be having trouble [in the neighborhood],
like boys be wanting to run a train on 'em[25] or something, like two boys
on one girl in a sandwich or something. One boy be hittin' her from
the front, one boy be hittin' her from behind." Antwoin described such
activities taking place fairly often around the neighborhood, and it
appeared that young men preyed on particularly vulnerable young
women. In fact, it is worth noting that Antwoin's earlier complaint
about "stuck-up girls" followed directly after this commentary about
running trains on girls. Stuck-up girls, apparently, were those who refused to engage when young men made sexual advances, yet it was
these same advances that were used to lure girls to precisely the kinds of
coercive situations he said made the neighborhood unsafe for them.

Shauntell described similar events in her neighborhood involving her
male relatives and their friends: "I done known girls that done just
walked down the block, and I ain't gon' even lie, my cousins, my brothers, snatch 'em up, take 'em around the corner and watch 'em and do
some of I don't know what to 'em." She recounted a recent incident:

> The other day, two girls over there that just ran away from home, they
> came over here 'cause one of 'em use to go with my cousin. And they
> was all just over here doggin' 'em. All them boys took 'em around . . .
> the corner [to one of the boy's houses], he got his own house. . . . My
> cousin not givin' a care about the one girl [he used to go with]. He not
> carin'. They take her, take her sister, and do some of, I don't even
> wanna name it all. Then [the girls] come out cryin', sayin' "I'm fina go
> home." [They were doing] some of everything. Get 'em drunk, high,
> beat 'em, raped 'em, tortured 'em, everything.

Shauntell said that because one of the young men lived on his own, thus
providing the boys with an unsupervised locale for their activities, "they
do it all the time." Though she appeared to implicate her cousin for
not caring about the girl he had previously been involved with, Shauntell also blamed the young women and was unsympathetic when they
tried to talk to her about what had happened: "I come home from
school and go over, [those girls] still there. Then they come to me,
'Shauntell—.' [I said], 'I don't care, 'cause you shoulda went home."

Sexually coercive behavior often appeared targeted toward young
women who seemed easy to take advantage of. A common strategy, as

Curtis described, was to "like get them drunk." Likewise, Kristy said some of the gang members she knew would "give 'em some GH, you know, B [GHB, gamma hydroxy butyrate, a common "date" rape drug], you know, like at a party." Ricky said young women in the neighborhood were particularly at risk in the context of parties: "They have to be extra careful about leaving. And they have to watch what they do. [Watch their drinking] and getting high. I mean, you got some smooth talkers in our neighborhood, so." Asked why he thought the guys in his neighborhood did that to girls, he explained:

> I think it's just to get a image, a name. To make theyselves look big. . . . I can't really explain it. A lot of guys do it just so other guys can be like, "Aw, man, he'll do this" or "He'll do that." Like for example, "We did this and we did that, and it was [so-and-so's] gal." Most of 'em just do it for a name, man, just for a image. Try to look like something they not.

Thus an important feature of girls' sexual abuse was the status rewards such behavior provided within male peer groups. In addition to Ricky's emphasis on young men's attempts to build a name for themselves through their coercive sexual conquests, Lamont suggested that disadvantaged neighborhoods gave rise to young women he defined as "freaks": "In the ghetto, every ghetto I can tell you . . . you see all these . . . freaks. It's babies, little bitty babies walking around with coochie cutters [tight-fitting shorts] on. You know that they gonna grow up to be freaks. Just 'cause you know what they been influenced by." In some cases, the early sexualization of girls likely made them vulnerable to sexual abuses in adolescence.[26]

However, many youths defined the girls themselves as sexual agents in these encounters and blamed them for their victimization. For instance, though Kristy described her friends using GHB to sexually abuse young women at parties, recall her earlier comments that she believed "the dudes be safer than the gals . . . 'cause I mean, they don't be walking around in hoochie clothes and stuff. They don't give people the wrong idea about what they want." Kristy said the neighborhood would be safer for girls if they "wear respectable clothes and don't go around sleeping with everybody."

Girls were also blamed when they were perceived as not having taken proper precautions in other ways. For instance, April described a recent incident in which a young woman was raped in the park near her home. She said, "my momma best friend stay across the street and she called the police. She heard it, that girl screaming or whatever. She was lookin' out . . . the window and they threw the girl in the trash can and stuff like that. . . . They was throwing her in the trash can after they did what they did." April blamed the young woman, because she had been walking through the park "at nighttime . . . and it was dark. It was about twelve, one o'clock nighttime. Ain't nobody gon' be out, woke, walking. . . . I walk through the park every day. I just ain't no fool to walk in no park at no nighttime. That's just how it is, it's common sense."

LaSondra described being raped by a man as she walked home from her friend's house one night. She said "it was dark, nobody was outside." As a precaution, her friend "walk[ed] me half the way, and I crossed over to go home and she walked back the other way." LaSondra was passing through a gas station on her way home when the man approached her. "He was just looking at me, and he said, 'I seen you and your friend earlier.'" The man then got LaSondra into his car and raped her: "He was heavy-set, he be holding me down, like I can't run, I can't get away." Afterward:

> He just dropped me off in this one spot and then he just pulled off. It was so scary, I was shaking, I was crying, I was running, you know, trying to find somewhere to go. I seen some people that went to my school and they let me use they phone and I called my momma. I tell my momma everything that happened and so she took me to the hospital and she called the police. The detective peoples came over and stuff and she talk to them and they didn't find him. . . . I was crying, shaking like all night in the hospital bed having flashbacks.

While LaSondra's mother was very supportive of her, she was disappointed with the police. She explained, "police don't do nothing. Some of 'em just give up, they could care less. . . . That's how they are, they could just care less."

Janelle also described being raped by a young man in her neighborhood:

> I was over at a friend's house, this girl, and he came over there. And you know, he was sitting down and he was talking to me and conversa-

ting with me at first, you know. And then he got to trying to touch me and stuff, and I was like, "No, go away," pushing him and trying to avoid the whole situation. But me being a female, males have more strength. So he holds me down and there's not much I can do about it because, you know, I'm not as strong as him.

Janelle said the rape happened when "my friend had went to the store." Afterward, she said, "I was scared to tell somebody so I didn't tell anybody. . . . I guess I thought if he found out that I told somebody he would somehow try to do something else to me." She was also fearful of reporting the incident to the police: "I mean, after he got out [of jail] or whatever and they did charge him with it, if he would've got out he would have been mad about the fact that I got him locked up, so he might have did something more."

As this brief discussion illustrates, sexual assault was an ongoing neighborhood danger for young women. Girls faced this danger both at the hands of their male peers (the focus of chapter 4) and from adult men who congregated in their communities. As with sexual harassment, youths tended to hold victim-blaming attitudes toward young women who placed themselves in situations that made them vulnerable to sexual mistreatment, while taking as a given the "rewards of rape" for males in their communities.[27] Young women who described sexual victimization reported few resources for addressing these problems. The perceptual schemas youths brought to bear on incidents of sexual assault, coupled with norms of nonintervention, meant that young women's personal networks were not a promising avenue for support; moreover, police response was experienced as ineffectual or as an option that could not offer sustained protection.

Gendered Risk-Avoidance in Neighborhoods

How, then, did young women adopt strategies to safeguard their safety and well-being in their neighborhoods? Given the gendered patterns I document in this chapter, it is not surprising that there were variations across gender in youths' descriptions of the kinds of precautions they took to stay safe. Two themes ran through young women's accounts: avoiding public neighborhood spaces, altogether and especially at night; and relying on the company of others (especially males) for protection, including drawing security from the belief that having neighborhood networks of family and friends would ensure their safety. Young men, in contrast, focused more attention on staying within the boundaries of their own neighborhoods, not engaging in activities that might lead to retaliatory violence, and traveling in groups or with weapons.[28]

Time and again, we were struck by young women's proclamations that they simply avoided being outside in their neighborhoods. Alicia said she felt safe in her neighborhood, because "I don't be outside over there, I sit on the porch. I don't go nowhere." Likewise, Jackie explained, "I stay in the house. . . . I don't go outside at all when I'm at home. When I'm around my grandma's house I go outside sometimes. I know mostly everybody over there. But when I'm at home, I don't go outside unless I'm going to the store, but I don't talk to nobody." Likewise, Anishika said that while "I been staying [in the same neighborhood] all my life . . . I don't be on the block. I don't be outside like that." She clarified, "I might sit outside for a minute or something . . . [but] I just don't be outside." And Nykeshia said she "rarely" went outside when she was at home, noting that she only went "on the front and back of the house. You know, I just don't trust my neighborhood." Finally, Tisha gave a lengthy response to the question of whether she felt safe in her neighborhood:

> Well, I don't be outside for real. So yeah, [I feel safe] 'cause I'm inside my house. 'Cause I don't wanna be involved in nothin' that goes on around there. I mean, I got my friends already, don't none of 'em live around there. I don't mess with nobody around there, I don't got no reason to go outside and conversate with them or nothin'. I know what they about and that's not what I'm about.

Though the most prevalent theme in girls' descriptions of risk-avoidance was to limit the time they spent on the streets, girls did spend some time in public spaces in their neighborhoods, including, in some cases, in social situations. At these times, they described either explicitly relying on others for protection or believing that their personal connections would protect them. LaSondra said, "I just don't walk at night by myself. If I'm gonna walk somewhere at night, I'm gonna call one of my friends on the phone or get my next door neighbor that's there so he'll walk with me." Likewise, April said, "if you walk somewhere at nighttime, you just gon' be with some dudes or walk and have something [a knife or mace] on you. . . . I do both—walk with dudes and have something. 'Cause [the dudes] might run, you never know." Gail touched on multiple themes:

> I'm not really outside all the time. I might stay in the house and watch TV or whatever. . . . I don't really go nowhere by myself. I mean, I live down the street from a donut shop where it be a lot of grown men just sitting around and stuff. But I don't think they'll harm me, 'cause they like know my uncles and my daddy, and like, they know everybody we live around.

Though she expressed apprehension about groups of adult men in public spaces and described her tendency to avoid them, she also believed that her (male) family and community ties would help insulate her from becoming a target of men looking to take advantage of girls. Similarly, Shauntell said, "I got a lot of family [in the neighborhood] and I know they ain't gon' let nothin' happen to me."

In general, having extensive ties in the neighborhood provided young women with a sense of security, and these ties developed particularly through residential stability. Katie said she had been in the same home her whole life, and she believed that her relationships with others in her neighborhood would protect her: "I feel safe when there's a lot of people outside 'cause they know me and they wouldn't let nuttin' happen to me." Cherise said, "I get along with pretty much everybody, I know everybody. I've been staying in my neighborhood for about ten years." Jamellah articulated a similar set of beliefs, though with a bit less confidence than Cherise:

> I usually do feel safe in my [immediate] neighborhood. Because I been there, my mother grew up there, that's my grandfather's house, she grew up there. And we been staying there for like six years, so I know basically everybody. And it's all old people in this neighborhood, where I'm walkin' down the street and I'm saying, "Hi, how you doin'" to every house on the street.

However, Jamellah was more concerned in the broader neighborhood, where she had to travel daily, because "that's where all heroin

users be at, and you know how they be over that drug—going crazy."
There, she was concerned primarily about being robbed, but she hoped
her long ties to the neighborhood would insulate her:

> I be lookin' nice, you know, I have on a nice jacket . . . I don't never
> take off my necklace or my earrings, and I be like, I hope they don't do
> nothin' to me. I know 'em though, 'cause I grew up over there. But still,
> when a person on heroin, they mind go crazy. They don't care. You
> could be they momma, if ya got something they want, they gon' take it.
> . . . I usually keep a job and they know that. I'm just, I got respect over
> there, so. That what put me in the mind like, ain't nobody gon' mess
> with me over there 'cause they all been knowin' me since forever.

Finally, Cherise added that she insulated herself from neighborhood
dangers through her lack of participation in criminal neighborhood activities: "I don't get affected by all these problems. Crack dealers get affected a lot . . . the boys that sell drugs get affected. People get killed
over gangs do, they get affected."

Thus, to the extent that girls felt themselves to have strong and long-
standing ties in their neighborhoods, they believed they would be offered protection against more serious forms of community dangers.
Having male relatives in the neighborhood could help place them "out
of bounds" among adult males who targeted young women for sexual
manipulation and violence. Likewise, the presence of an individual they
could call on to walk with them in traversing the neighborhood—particularly at nighttime—gave young women confidence in their relative
safety.

Unfortunately, there remain several limitations to these strategies.
First, the vast majority of young women reported a great deal of residential instability: two-thirds described having moved in the last three
years, and fully one-half reported multiple moves. These patterns are
strongly tied to the kinds of economic deprivations youths and their
families faced, but nonetheless they placed limits on the young women's
ability to rely on collective community ties for protection. Second,
young women's faith in the adult men and adolescent boys they knew
was sometimes misplaced, and compelling evidence of this is shown in
the next several chapters. Research consistently finds that women are
significantly more likely than men to be victimized by intimates and
other individuals they know, and this is reflected as well by the dispro-

portionate rates of sexual assault perpetrated by dates and acquaintances (and even family members), as compared with strangers.[29]

Third and finally, young women's primary strategy for staying safe in their neighborhoods—staying indoors and at home—also had its limitations. Much violence against young women occurs in unavoidable public spaces (such as schools), as well as in private or semiprivate locales, like their own or friends' homes and parties. While insulating them from some neighborhood risks, staying at home was ultimately not effective in protecting young women from violence and also came at a considerable cost, because it limited their ability to fully participate in public life.[30] Of course, public life in disadvantaged neighborhoods is severely hindered by the structural dislocations and lack of resources available in these communities. As discussed in chapter 6, socioeconomic improvements in such neighborhoods could provide dramatic benefits for young women—not just in terms of generally improved life conditions but also in better ensuring their safety and security and their ability to claim a right and stake in neighborhood life.

Conclusion

Three overarching themes emerge in youths' discussions of the gendered dimensions of neighborhood dangers. First, youths' accounts indicate that young men were much more likely to be active participants in neighborhood-based street networks. Their neighborhood descriptions (where boys spoke of "I" and we," while girls spoke of "they"), their depictions of young men's (but not young women's) neighborhood risks being explicitly associated with gangs and drugs, and their accounts of girls' treatment on the streets all reveal that public community space was, in many ways, *male* space. Though this was particularly the case at night—when young women suggested that dangers lurked largest— male domination of public spaces was nonetheless ubiquitous.

Second, many facets of neighborhood risk were structured by gender, and youths brought gendered perceptual frameworks to their understandings of neighborhood violence. Like other forms of violence, violence against women was both widespread and highly visible. Youths recounted witnessing public violence against women around their neighborhoods, and young women expressed concern about the pervasive sexualization they faced, including sexual harassment by adolescent and adult men and their fears and experiences with sexual assault in their neighborhoods.

Third, neighborhood residents' (including adolescents') responses to violence against women were decidedly unhelpful to the victims, as were their experiences with the police. Victim-blaming attitudes were widespread, among both young women and young men, and norms favoring nonintervention often won out, frequently leaving female victims to fend for themselves. In some cases, such violence even became a source of entertainment, particularly when youths were in the company of their peers.

For adolescent young women, the public nature of violence against women likely had a meaningful impact. Its visibility created a heightened vigilance and awareness among girls of their own vulnerability, but it also resulted in coping strategies that included victim-blaming as a means of psychologically distancing themselves from such events. To the extent that violence could be seen as something that happened to *other* women and girls—those who could be understood as "deserving" of it—young women could construct a sense of self that they believed shielded them from such risks.[31] Moreover, in a setting where norms were not favorable for intervention into violent events, the result was that youths became desensitized to such violence. Because the ability to stand up for oneself is a key avenue for respect in disadvantaged communities,[32] girls who failed to do so—particularly when their actions could render them culpable in some way in the eyes of others—faced sanction, at the very least in the form of lack of empathy.

3

Playin' Too Much
Sexual Harassment in Schools

Urban neighborhoods characterized by entrenched poverty, segregation, physical decay, and crime problems are dangerous places for young women. Leaving aside homicide, they face rates of victimization that are comparable with those of their male peers, and they have gender-specific risks associated with the congregation of men and boys in public spaces and their tendency to view young women through a sexualized lens. However, adolescents don't spend all of their time within their neighborhood and community action spaces: much of their time is spent at school. Thus, in this chapter I turn the attention to girls' experiences with gender-based conflicts in schools, focusing specifically on the problem of sexual harassment.

Youths' interactions within schools, of course, cannot be understood in isolation. As criminologist Denise Gottfredson explains, "Schools are community institutions."[1] They are strongly affected by the larger social processes, resources, and characteristics of the communities in which they are embedded. Schools in impoverished urban communities have limited resources and difficulties in attracting and retaining the most talented educators. In addition, they face unique challenges as a result of competing or inconsistent community norms, limited collective efficacy, and the distinctive needs of many students from disadvantaged contexts.[2]

These problems are exemplified in the St. Louis Public School District, where the youths in our study were enrolled. For nearly a decade, the district has been under threat of a state takeover as a result of consistently poor student test performance, low attendance and graduation rates, high dropout rates, serious fiscal problems, and accusations of political patronage. It has been characterized as "crumbling," "failing," "in crisis," "in decline and decay," "perpetually unstable," and "underperforming [and] violence-plagued."[3] In fact, since the time we began our research, the St. Louis Public School District has been unable to perform successfully enough to receive full accreditation from the state. In 1999, the district's total accreditation score was just 23 points out of 100, far shy of the 66 needed for an accreditation rating.[4]

In addition, the city school district has suffered from decades of falling enrollments.[5] It continues to face chronic problems with teacher hiring and retention and must rely on a large population of substitutes. During the period of our study, nearly 8 percent of the district's teaching positions remained vacant, and a similar proportion of "teachers, guidance counselors and librarians [did] not have proper state certification."[6] Teachers cited low pay, lack of parental and administrative support, and discipline problems as primary among their concerns. In fact, at the time of our research, "St. Louis teacher salaries ranked 73rd out of 76 school districts" in the region.[7]

In chapter 1, I note that the majority of the youths we interviewed (87 percent) attended one of the St. Louis Public School District's then alternative high schools. These schools, which served youths expelled from mainstream public schools, had the highest dropout rates in the region (82 percent), with a graduation rate of just 6.5 percent.[8] From 1998 to 2002, not a single student at these schools finished at or above the state standard in test performances. The student body was more than 90 percent African American and around 70 percent low income. One of these schools, described by state evaluators as having "cracked walls and ceilings, broken windows, asbestos problems and dim lighting," was slated for renovation prior to its closure.[9] And just prior to our investigation, this school's principal was one of four district principals terminated after a *St. Louis Post-Dispatch* inquiry revealed their lack of certification.[10]

The ten youths in our sample interviewed at a local community center also attended schools with poor outcome measures, though not quite as severe as those at the alternative schools.[11] One of these schools was in such infrastructural disrepair at the time of our research that it was later rebuilt on a new site in the early 2000s. However, it "continues to be plagued by gang-related problems and has failed to overcome its reputation as an academic abyss."[12]

As a consequence of these myriad problems, school offered little respite from the many problems the youths in our study faced in their neighborhoods. This includes violence. Though serious incidents remain

TABLE 3-1
Reported Crime in St. Louis Public Schools

	1998/1999	1999/2000
Assault/battery	179	161
Drug offenses	78	87
Rape/sexual acts	0	5
Weapons possession	96	105
Weapons used	17	12
Total disciplinary infractions	6,342	5,211

Source: Pierce, 2000 (St. Louis Public Schools data).

rare, "youths are at elevated risks for victimization when they are in school."[13] In fact, recent analyses of the National Crime Victimization Survey reveal that over one-half of youths' experiences with victimization occur at or on the way to and from school. This includes one-half of all violent victimizations.[14] Moreover, as with other school indicators, school violence is geographically patterned: "Schools in urban, poor, disorganized communities experience much more violence and other forms of disorder than do schools in rural or suburban, affluent, organized communities."[15]

The St. Louis Public Schools are no exception. Discipline problems rank as one of the "top concerns" of the teacher's union, and the School Board has convened multiple task forces in an attempt to address violence and other disciplinary concerns.[16] Each of the district's middle and high schools have metal detectors and uniformed security officers, in addition to the district's mobile security unit.[17] Table 3-1 provides a count of officially reported incidents of school crime in the St. Louis school district during the time of our research. Weapons offenses and violence were even more common than drug offenses. And, as with official statistics generally, it is likely that these figures are just the tip of the iceberg since they represent only offenses that received formal response.

So what does all of this have to do with gender-based violence and sexual harassment? There has been a great deal of scholarly and popular attention to the issue of school violence in the last decades. Unfortunately, the school violence literature exhibits a limitation parallel to that I raised in chapter 2 concerning urban violence: it is frequently conceptualized and studied in gender-neutral terms or assumed to be a primarily male phenomenon. Thus, young women's gender-specific risks for violence and abuse are often not fully considered.[18]

In contrast, there has been a great deal of research outside of criminology on the problem of sexual harassment in schools. In fact, scholars in psychology and education often lament the fact that our conceptualizations of school violence often overlook the gendered dimensions of these challenges. As Nan Stein and her colleagues explain:

> School reform efforts which address school safety have focused on the prevention of physical violence, particularly related to the presence and use of weapons in schools. . . . This construction of school safety as zero tolerance, first for guns and now also for drugs, eclipses other more pervasive aspects of school safety, including daily threats to psychological and social safety, especially sexual harassment. . . . The omission of gender from the dominant construction of school safety and violence contributes to the disproportionate focus on the most extreme forms of violence while the more insidious threats to safety are largely ignored.[19]

In fact, there is a burgeoning literature on sexual harassment in schools, despite the fact that it is rarely conceptualized within the broader framework of youth violence. This research has examined the extent and consequences of sexual harassment for young women, and some scholars have paid particular attention to how the organizational and ideological contexts of schools shape sexual harassment. A significant finding of this research is that sexual harassment in school has tangible negative consequences for its female victims, including harmful effects on school performance, the curtailment of social networks, peer rejection, and negative emotional outcomes.[20] Thus, it does pose, as Stein and her colleagues contend, an "insidious threat" to girls' well-being.

Unfortunately, though, much of what we know about sexual harassment in the educational setting has not specifically examined how disadvantaged community and school contexts shape young women's experiences. There is strong evidence that schools in impoverished urban communities are faced with more severe violence and disorder, as well as institutional difficulties addressing these problems. Combined with the evidence I presented in chapter 2 that the visibility and cultural support for violence against women is heightened in disadvantaged community contexts, there is good reason to suspect that sexual harassment and its consequences may be especially acute in this school setting.[21]

Gendered Conflicts at School: Sexual and Gender Harassment

During the survey portion of our interviews, we asked youths a series of questions to gauge the prevalence of behaviors researchers classify as harassment.[22] Tables 3-2 and 3-3 indicate their responses to these questions. The vast majority of young women (89 percent) reported experiencing incidents of gender or sexual harassment, with most (77 percent) reporting that such events occurred in school.[23] The most common incidents girls reported were those involving inappropriate sexual comments (71 percent), while just under 50 percent reported being grabbed or touched in ways that made them feel uncomfortable. Young men were most likely to admit to calling girls names or putting them down (70 percent), while just over one-half (53 percent) reported that they had either made sexual comments (48 percent) or grabbed or touched girls inappropriately (38 percent).

Two factors likely account for the small differences in young women's and young men's reported prevalence of experiencing versus perpetrating such incidents. There were young men in our sample who expressed disapproval of sexual harassment and defined these incidents as such. Thus, it is likely that some boys are disproportionately responsible for

TABLE 3-2
Girls' Prevalence of Sexual Harassment Experiences (N = 35)

Have boys ever called you names or said things to make you feel bad about yourself?	18 (51%)
Have boys ever made sexual comments to you that made you feel uncomfortable?	25 (71%)
Have boys ever grabbed or touched you in ways that made you feel uncomfortable?	17 (49%)
Girls who answered "Yes" to one or more of these questions	31 (89%)
Girls who reported such incidents happened to them at school	27 (77%)

TABLE 3-3
Boys' Prevalence of Sexual Harassment Perpetration (N = 40)

Have you and your friends ever called girls names or said things to put them down?	28 (70%)
Have you and your friends ever made sexual comments to girls that might have made them feel uncomfortable?	19 (48%)
Have you and your friends ever grabbed or touched girls in ways that might have made them feel uncomfortable?	15 (38%)
Boys who answered "Yes" to one or more of these questions	32 (80%)

sexually harassing multiple girls. In addition, as discussed in more detail later in the chapter, young women and young men also brought different interpretive lenses to sexually suggestive or explicit encounters. Girls routinely described such incidents as offensive and troublesome, while boys were more likely to characterize them as harmless "play."[24]

Youths' survey responses provide baseline information about the prevalence of sexual and gender harassment. Even more telling, however, is that many youths told us such events were a frequent occurrence around school. Michelle explained, "way I see it, it happen often." Ramara concurred: "Every day . . . all through the day." And Raymond said, "all the time." In fact, the following dialogue with Alicia was typical:

> *Interviewer*: How often would you say that girls and guys argue at school?
> *Alicia*: I guess every day. . . . If a boy touching a girl where she don't wanna be touched or something. [Or] it's something the boy say to the girl or something. . . .
> *Interviewer*: How often would you say stuff like that happens at school, where a guy touches a girl inappropriately?
> *Alicia*: Every day.
> *Interviewer*: What about saying inappropriate stuff to a girl?
> *Alicia*: Every day.

Young women also noted that such incidents occurred in a variety of locations around the school, including, as Tisha summed up, "classroom, hallway, cafeteria, gym, it could happen anywhere." Likewise, Jackie explained, "like in class and in hallways. It could happen any place. They [boys] don't care." And Jamellah noted, "Like when you walking down the hall, that's where it normally happen at. . . . Basically, or when you out in the yard out here . . . going home from school, or coming to school."

Youths also described a range of incident types, including forms of gender harassment, as well as verbal and physical sexual harassment. Several girls suggested that these behaviors were systematic and indicative of young men's devaluation of young women. Anishika said, "most of the boys is disrespectful. That's all. Like call the girls B's [bitches] and stuff. And then like, if you don't, if the girl don't want them to touch 'em, they get mad and all that stuff. They basically always want to mess with the girls, touch on 'em and all that stuff." Asked to clarify what she meant when classifying young men's actions as "disrespectful," Jamellah explained, "call her out her name, grab on her butt, you know what I'm saying, something like that. That is disrespectful. Pull her hair. *Anything*. They think of anything to do to irk a girl." Raymond concurred:

> Dudes period have attitudes, all of 'em, no matter what. All dudes got a attitude. . . . Some guys need to know how to treat women with respect and don't put they hands on them. [But you] can't [change them. They] look at 'em like she looks like she like that, so I can start an attitude with her. That's how it be going.

Youths' comments demonstrate that sexual and gender harassment were not rare events but, instead, were an everyday feature of the cultural milieu at school. In addition, these events were highly public in nature, occurring in nearly every location within the building and grounds. They typically occurred in the presence of other students, and sometimes in front of school staff as well. These were important contextual features of school-based sexual harassment that shaped youths' interpretations of the events, their likelihood of escalating, and the range of informal and formal responses available to young women.

Basically, these problems appeared to be systemic, not just at the alternative schools where we interviewed (which could be expected, given that the youths were expelled from mainstream schools for behavioral problems) but also at the other schools youths attended. The youths we interviewed who attended other schools in the district told us parallel stories, and the alternative school students reflected back on their experiences before transfer.

Gender Harassment

Scholars use the term "gender harassment" to refer to comments and behaviors that are not explicitly sexual in nature but nonetheless convey disrespect toward women. Psychologists J. Nicole Shelton and Tabbye M. Chavous define it as "generalized sexist remarks and behaviors that convey negative and degrading attitudes about women."[25] Boys and girls described such incidents as routine and said that particular derogatory terms were guaranteed to lead to anger. Walter explained, "a girl get mad if a dude call her a bitch and all that stuff. That's the main word the girls get mad on." Likewise, Terence noted that such conflicts were typically "like lil' petty stuff . . . you know, they call a female a B [bitch] or whatever. You know, ain't no girl gon' stand for it, so they get amped. 'Fore you know it, they trying to fight 'em."

Conflicts between young women and young men were triggered in a number of circumstances, some of which were instigated by the boy, some by the girl, and some by other peers. Youths typically classified these broadly as "he say/she say." Tisha explained: "It works both ways. . . . Some of the girls, they be playin' with boys too much. Then they'll start playing rough with 'em, then they wanna get mad, stuff like that. Or either [the boys]'ll be saying something to upset the girl, stuff like that." Arthur concurred, "I mean, it's just bickering. . . . I mean, anybody can get in an argument right, you know, quickly." And Raymond explained, "he say/she say stuff [can happen] when dudes or girls be in each other's business." And Larry noted, "She'll call him a scrub, he'll call her a pigeon.[26] . . . Somebody playing too much. Anything for real [can lead to conflicts between girls and dudes]."

Despite the focus in this chapter, it is important to acknowledge that disputes between girls and boys could emanate from multiple sources and situations, and they were not always and clearly unidirectional. Age, popularity, physical attractiveness, friendship networks, economic and social resources—all of these, in addition to gender, come into play in determining who will have conflicts with whom, and to what consequence. Put another way, gendered power does not exist in a vacuum but overlaps with other sources of status and power.[27] Nonetheless, gender inequality, and the powerful social ideologies that support it, provided young men the social advantage of "masculine power" in these circumstances. This is why feminist theorists conceptualize gender harassment as a powerful "form of social control that reifies women's lower rank . . . [and] reinforces dominance over women."[28]

The young men in our sample described having and using an expansive repertoire of gendered terms with which to assail young women when conflicts emerged. As Raymond explained, "I call girls names . . . everything . . . B's [bitches], ho's, rats, triflin' tramps. . . . [Those names] be the first thing that come out my mouth to a girl who make me mad." Likewise, Walter said:

> If a girl say something about me and then I don't like her, I call 'em like bitches and ho's and stuff like that. . . . I don't got a problem with girls,

it's just when girls come to me . . . and they say something to me I don't like, that's when I get mad. . . . [For instance,] the first couple of days [of the school year] here, this girl, she just kept staring at me. And then she say, "What the hell you staring at?" Then I be like, "Your dirty ass" and stuff like that. Like a girl say something to me I don't like, I turn around and say something back. Then I put it in a more feeling hurting way. . . . I be calling 'em all, like all that I can think of.

Thus, young men had an arsenal of derogatory gendered terms at their disposal when in verbal altercations with young women, with the weight of gender inequality in their favor. In addition, this language system was particularly pernicious because it went hand in hand with other forms of gendered mistreatment, including sexual harassment. Though scholars distinguish gender harassment as conceptually distinct from various forms of sexual harassment, in practice the two are often intertwined.

Verbal Sexual Harassment

In broad strokes, sexual harassment refers to unwelcome sexual conduct. It can take on a range of forms, which researchers classify roughly into categories such as verbal, physical, and visual, and can be more or less threatening or coercive in its execution.[29] The youths in our study described a variety of forms of verbal sexual harassment, ranging from sexual comments or propositions, comments intended to ridicule a girl's appearance or sexual attractiveness, and sexual threats, as well as bragging, spreading rumors, or taunting a girl about her alleged or actual sexual activities.

Kenisha explained, "boys sayin' stuff out the way, like saying stuff like about sex or something, and the girls'll react." Rennesha said it's "mostly about sexual acts. Like he'll make like a nasty comment and she'll get mad." And Destiny complained that "the boys get to talkin' about your butt, talkin' about this, talkin' about that. They get on your nerves." Alicia described a young man telling her, " 'yo' booty big.' " She explained, "ain't nobody wanna hear that, saying it all loud in front of other people."

Sometimes such comments were intended to ridicule the girl. Rennesha described a recent incident she witnessed: "This one boy told this girl [that] she's got a fat butt but she can't have sex good. And she got mad . . . they was arguing back and forth." Bobby said when he was with his friends, they would see a girl they found unattractive, "and it be like, 'Dang, you ugly girl!' or something like that. And you get to talkin' about her." Alicia told of an incident she witnessed in class on the day she was interviewed:

> This girl, she kinda big or whatever, and he was talking about her weight and she got mad and they started arguing and cursing and stuff. . . . People be laughing, encouraging the boy on, and making him keep doing it and doing it. So my teacher had sent them down to the office. . . . She sent the girl [too] because the girl was cursing.

There are notable themes in Alicia's account, including the role of peers in escalating harassment and problems with how teachers sometimes responded to such incidents. I revisit these issues later in the chapter.

In addition to comments and ridicule, several young women reported experiencing or witnessing verbal harassment that was threatening in its intent. Destiny told us, "just yesterday this boy was talkin' about [my friend], tell me his friends were gonna haul her down and freak all over her. And she like, 'No you all not!' And she got mad and she went to tell the principal." Similarly, Katie was in class when a classmate came over and "was like, 'Yeah, I'm gonna get you over to my house' or whatever." His insinuation, she noted, was that he would get her to his house for sex. Katie said her classmates heard the exchange and simply laughed at the boy's comments. When she threatened to tell the teacher, the boy "left it alone," but she also believed the teacher overheard the interaction yet said nothing: "He just sat there. He act like he ain't listening to us talk but I know he do. . . . He probably just waitin' for one of us to come and tell him."

As the following conversation reveals, Nicole was directly threatened by two boys at school, and she did not believe her experience was unique:

> *Nicole*: [Boys will] go tell a girl, "I'ma rape you." That's what they'll tell a girl, for real, up here, they will. I'm like, "Naw, we takin' that to the court. That's gon' get you locked up." I know two boys up here said that to me, and I went straight to the principal. I was like, "You said you was gon' do what to me?"

Interviewer: Two boys said that to you? Like what happened?

Nicole: 'Cause one of 'em wanted my number and the other one, he was going around lyin' sayin' I go with him and we had sex or whatever. I was like, "I don't like you, I never did like you and I can't trust nan one [none] of y'all." . . . When I got to the office, I said, "You said you was gon' rape me." And they was like, "We ain't say that." I said, "I got witnesses," and I told [the principal]. I said, "Hold on, I'll be right back with witnesses." So all the girls was like, "They did say that, they did."

Interviewer: Did you think the boys would actually carry that through? Did you think they meant it?

Nicole: [Nod]. And I brought my brother up here, my 23-year-old brother, and he said, "You put yo' hands on my baby sister, we gon' have some problems, and I mean I'm killin' both of y'all." . . .

Interviewer: How often would you say boys threaten girls like that?

Nicole: . . . They don't hardly threaten us but they'll say they lil' words just to try and get us scared. But I ain't scared of them. Not me. 'Cause I'm goin' to tell.

Nicole's dialogue illustrates another important theme: Often conflicts between young women and young men were ongoing, with individual incidents situated within a longer pattern of interactions.

A final form of verbal sexual harassment youths described as common involved young men bragging or spreading rumors about sexual encounters with young women. Nicole explained: "The boys, they just play too much. . . . They talk about 'em, they dog 'em: 'I did this to her and she gave me head behind the building.' I'm like, 'What is you tellin' us for?'" Lisa told us that the semester before we interviewed her, her friend was repeatedly taunted "every day at 5th period. . . . This boy was like tellin' everybody [that my friend] had sex in the alley, she do this, she had sex with all these boys." Lisa said such incidents were commonplace, explaining that usually:

The boy, he'll say something about the girl or they'll start a rumor about the girl. A boy'll be talking to [dating] one of the girls that go here and then he'll come back and bring it back to the school, whatever they did outside of school and then it'll just be a big ole' argument and turn into fights.

Asked to describe such an incident, she continued: "This boy did something to this girl, he said that she did this and that to him or whatever. He brought it back to school, and she was feeling real bad about it or whatever. . . . He was sayin' he had sex with her and that she sucked his stuff."

Young men also said it was commonplace for boys to tell stories about sexual encounters with girls at school. Tyrell explained, "dudes, they always talk about when they have sex with a girl or whatever. . . . That's all dudes talk about when they talk about girls." Ronald said one of his friends routinely tormented a girl in his class. Ronald described the girl as "like a freak," because "she went over to his house [and had sex] with him one day . . . and half the people in that school she been with." He continued the story in the following exchange:

> *Ronald*: He call her all kinds of names. . . . It be funny sometimes. It's jokes he be making about her, it be funny. . . . He just say something, then she get an attitude and say, "That's not true." Then all the boys in the classroom who been with her look at her like, "You ain't gotta lie."
>
> *Interviewer*: Like what might he say and she says that's not true?
>
> *Ronald*: She faced 'em up [had oral sex with them]. . . .
>
> *Interviewer*: And he does this in front of the whole class?
>
> *Ronald*: Yep. . . . Nobody like her in that class. . . . He just walk up next to her and I start laughin'.
>
> *Interviewer*: Does the teacher . . . know that he's saying stuff like that about her?
>
> *Ronald*: Teacher don't care. All he do is just give us our work. He just sit there and do nuttin'.
>
> *Interviewer*: And the other students around don't normally say anything?
>
> *Ronald*: Nope. Girls be laughin' at her [too]. . . . It be funny.

At its most insidious, the escalation of such stories had devastating consequences. They tended to be targeted, as Anishika explained, at "the girls that got like bad names . . . the girls that's disrespectful to theyself." She described the most serious incident of this nature that we came across:

This one girl that use to go here, she dropped out or whatever. She was
. . . going here, doing fine and stuff. She a real pretty girl, she had a
whole lot of talent, rap and everything, I mean, wasn't nothin' wrong
with her. It's just the simple fact [she had sex with] like almost all the
boys. . . . She'll like 'em, and then they'll make her think that they like
her, but they got a girlfriend and stuff like that. . . . They'll do it to her
then she'll just suck they stuff. And she'll admit that she do that stuff,
but I don't know what for. . . . I think she just do it for attention and
she has low self-esteem or something and she just don't love herself
'cause she just doin' it like that. . . . [Then] she just dropped out 'cause
everybody be like, "You a dick suckin' girl," callin' her all [kinds of]
stuff. . . . They [even] took pictures of her doing it in a van. . . . They
took pictures, they brought [them] to school.

Anishika felt sorry for the girl, and chastised the boys who abused her:

They was like, "I'll bring [the pictures] and show you." And I'll be like,
"Why y'all gon' do that?" you know what I'm saying. . . . I mean,
"Why would you do it? Because y'all know her self-esteem is so low."
She just doin' it so people could like her. . . . [The boys] should just
make that girl feel confident and build up her self, not lower her self-
esteem more. But I mean, it just some boys that don't care and don't
think. . . . I use to be tryin' to encourage her and stuff, and then she just
dropped out of school. . . . That's why I think she stopped comin'.

Sexual rumors were particularly troubling because they caused damage to girls' reputations. Girls who had sex with boys outside the context of a well-delineated relationship, or were known to have had past
sexual encounters with boys at school—especially oral sex—were defined and talked about by others as "nasty." Sexually based rumors, regardless of their validity, facilitated the continuation of the sexual harassment of the particular girl about whom the rumors were based and
often were perpetrated by more boys than the original source of the rumor, and even by some girls. In fact, as Anishika's account illustrates,
spreading sexual stories about particular girls could lead to even more
exploitative sexual behaviors, such as taking and circulating photographs.

Such incidents also illustrate the extent that school interactions were intertwined with youths' activities in the community. In Lisa's language, boys "bring" their neighborhood exploits "back to the school." Thus, girls' neighborhood reputations—or presumed reputations—followed them to school. The following exchange with Ronald is illustrative:

> *Ronald*: Like let's say a new girl come to the school and like one of my friends know her, they be like, "She a freak man," and then they like, somebody talk to her and they just tell 'em that she a freak. Put it on front like that.
>
> *Interviewer*: And how do your friends usually know?
>
> *Ronald*: Nine times outta ten, they used to be with that person.
>
> *Interviewer*: They used to be with her? Do you ever think your friends are lying about the girl?
>
> *Ronald*: Sometimes I do. 'Cause I hang with a whole bunch of liars, lie about everything. . . . Like little petty stuff, like them going to a concert, they'll lie about that. Or they'll lie about them playin' on a basketball team, lie about stuff that don't even matter.

Sometimes, it seemed it took only one young man to pass on a story. True or not, it had the potential to take hold. For the girl, social ostracism and ridicule followed.

Physical Sexual Harassment

Aside from the sometimes devastating consequences of sexual rumors, most young women believed that physical forms of sexual harassment were more egregious than verbal harassment. Destiny explained, "when they be talkin' about my butt, I don't like it, but I don't trip off of it 'cause it's stupid to me. Lookin' and feeling are two different things, and they can look and they say what they wanna say, long as they ain't touchin' me I don't care." Likewise, of comments, Tawanna said, "I don't pay them no attention. . . . I don't pay it no mind." But she distinguished this from touching: "I don't like that. I hate when they do that. . . . They know better not to." And Marcus explained, "you can talk all you want, but as long as you don't touch 'em." In fact, physical forms of sexual harassment often led to escalating conflicts between boys and girls.

Nonetheless, such incidents occurred with some frequency. Cherise complained of young men "trying to touch on you or your breast or something, trying to play it off." And Yvonne explained that she was especially bothered by young men's

> touching and stuff. Trying to touch on your boobie or your breasts or whatever. And how they come at you, you know what I'm saying, it ain't cool. . . . It seem like we always gotta be on their head because, you know what I'm saying, you wouldn't want nobody treating your daughter like that. If you had a daughter, you know what I'm saying. Show me respect.

Some young men were open about engaging in such behavior, as the following exchange illustrates:

> *Interviewer*: Have you ever like touched girls when they're like, you're standing in the hallway and girls come by, you touched her?
> *Lamont*: All the time. All the time. In gym I do. . . . 'Cause I mean, that's fun.
> *Interviewer*: What do the girls say about that when you do that?
> *Lamont*: Most of the time they keep walking. . . . I mean, sometimes I get in trouble for it, but I really don't be trippin' off it.

Likewise, Frank said, "it happen a lot. I do it myself." Asked why, he explained: "Oh man, I don't know. Hey 'cause, these girls, they got big butts. Just, I'm like, damn, you just out there, guess they want somebody to touch ['em.]. . . . Pow, be smackin' them booties and all that [*laughs*]." Frank also emphasized how being in the company of other young men facilitated such behaviors:

> We be up in the hallway, we be like, we see a good looking girl walk past, we be like "Damn!" Be like, "Man, I'm goin over there." So we like go over there, I'm gonna hit it and quit it. Hit it and quit it, that's all we be doing for real. I be like, "I dare you to touch her butt." Like, "Man you go, you go touch her butt."

Bobby gave a similar account: "Say you walkin' with one of yo' friends or whatever and uh, they was like, 'I bet you can't go over there and touch her butt' or something like that . . . and then [you] go over there [and do it]."

Despite their recognition that some girls found touching quite troubling, young men often excused the behavior so long as it wasn't explicitly coercive. Walter said, "I've seen some boys try to grab or touch 'em,
but they ain't never really force them or nothing like that." And Travis
explained, "I see it happen, but man, I ain't ever seen it happen to
where it's the point to where, boy touch a girl and the girl says 'stop'
and he keep on doing it." However, he clarified that this was also due to
the school context: "Boys, some boys know what backing off means. If
a girl say 'No,' that means no. You need to leave 'em alone. Especially
in school anyways. School will get you in trouble."

Gender and Interpretations of Sexual Harassment

As Walter's and Travis' comments suggest, young men rarely took sexually harassing behaviors as seriously as young women did. In fact, numerous studies have found that girls believe sexual harassment is more
harmful than boys do, and this gap is especially pronounced among adolescents.[30] Comparing young women's and young men's accounts, there
were both important disparities and notable overlaps across gender.

Contested Play Claims: Humor or Disrespect?

Young men often downplayed the seriousness of sexual harassment
by couching it in terms of "play." Antwoin said, "yeah, I grabbed a girl
bootie a couple of times . . . we was playing." Such touching, he said,
was best understood as "like playing around. Sometimes the boys'll be
messing with the girls and they'll just grab they bootie or something."
And Carlos explained, "oh yeah, I touch they booty, touch they titty . . .
shit, they like it. Gotta talk to 'em, play with 'em. . . . I love it, it's
cool." Similarly, asked why he and his friends touched on girls, Curtis
said, "I don't know, just to have fun. Just playing."

"Just playing," however, was a characterization young women
roundly rejected. Instead, to quote Nicole, girls found boys' sexually harassing behaviors to be "too much playing." Sharmi's biggest complaint
about boys was that they were always "playin' too much." She continued, "when dudes hug up on me a lot, I don't like it . . . I get annoyed.
[They] play too much." And Katie complained, "most of the time boys

and girls get into it because boys, they play too much. . . . Like they try to touch you and stuff, or try to talk about you, or put you down in front of they friends to make them feel better. . . . Just talk about you or something like in front of they friends so they can laugh."

Katie's comments tapped into an important feature of boys' play claims: the primary audience for this "play" was other young men. As Anishika argued, young men's "humor" was for the benefit of their friends, and at the expense of the young woman:

They just tryin' to be like this person and that person. They already know, they know what's right. They know right from wrong. But when it's a lot of 'em, they think that stuff is cute, calling girls B's [bitches] and rats and all that stuff. They think that stuff cute, and some of these girls think that stuff cute. But it's not cute.

In fact, Frank's and Bobby's accounts, described earlier, are indicative of the role male peers played in facilitating young men's behaviors. Thus, Frank continued, "some people, when they see [you touch on a girl], they'll laugh or they give you some props. They give you like a little five or something like that. That's what the dudes do." Other boys were equally explicit in attributing boys' behavior to their attempts to show off for and gain status among their male friends. Asked why boys talked to girls in sexually explicit or derogatory ways, Tony surmised, "probably to impress they friends." Likewise, Travis said, it's "for attention from their friends. Like it's an ego thing . . . you know, just to show off in front of their boys."

A number of girls said boys simply used play claims as an excuse for their behavior and described explicitly rejecting these claims. For example, angry after a young man made sexual comments about her, Destiny said he responded to her anger by saying, " 'You ain't even gotta get that serious. I was just playin' wit' you.' " She replied, " 'I don't care. I don't want you playin' with me like that, stop playin' with me like that.' " And Nicole explained, "sometimes boys make it like, act like it's funny. But it's not. 'Cause you touchin' a girl and she don't wanna be touched. So don't touch me, period. Don't even think about touchin' me." Alicia described an incident that happened the day she was interviewed and was especially angered by the boy's failure to view the incident as anything but humorous:

This happened today as a matter of fact. I was walking down the hall and [this boy] hit me on my butt real hard. He made me mad so I punched him. I know him, but he just play too much. He getting on my nerves, it's so irritating. So I punched him and he started laughing and running. He thought it was funny, but I was just mad, I ain't find it funny.

Instead of finding young men's behavior "playful," young women believed it was a reflection of boys' disrespectful attitudes and treatment of girls generally. For example, asked why she thought young men engaged in harassing behaviors, Jamellah explained, " 'cause they ain't got no respect for themselves or the female . . . just don't got no respect for women or theyselves, for real." Cleshay concurred: "I think they not raised right or something, I don't know. That's how they know to be towards females. . . . I don't know what it is, but they got this superior [attitude]." Kristy said there was "a lot of animosity" between girls and boys, tied to young men's beliefs that girls were inferior: "They quick to disrespect you, and don't expect you to stand up to 'em 'cause you a female and they male."

In fact, a great deal of research has examined the functions and meanings of sexualized and gender-based humor. Sociologist Meika Loe, for example, argues that sexual joking and harassment "are used as social distancing techniques that reinforce [the woman's] vulnerable position and maintain her inferiority."[31] Returning to Anishika's position that while young men knew right from wrong but behaved this way to amuse their friends, it is not surprising that researchers have routinely found that humor at the expense of women functions to shore up the masculine identities of individual young men specifically and their male peers generally. To put Anishika's point in academic language, the problem "lies not so much in [male] ignorance but in acts of ignoring" young women's points of view.[32]

Indeed, despite young men's routine use of play claims, their own accounts belied the notion that their behaviors were simply intended as harmless fun. For example, several young men said part of the fun in taunting girls was getting an angry response. Robert explained:

When you smoke weed you get, you feel like you wanna laugh. You know, and so they'll start jonin' and you know what I'm saying, start talkin' about somebody and we'll just be sitting there playin'. And then they'll see a girl, they'll start messin' with the girl. That's how that start. . . . They'll just call her ugly or something or laugh. Just to get a laugh. And then, you know, she'll get mad.

Moreover, several young men described treating girls in a derogatory way specifically to demarcate their (male) space and make it clear to the girl that she wasn't welcome. Asked why his friends mistreated girls, Marvin remarked, "most of my friends, they can't stand most of them girls." He continued, "we call her out her name, tell her to get away from us . . . call her a bitch or ho. . . . She'll laugh, she think we be playin' with her. We tell her, we ain't playin'." And Shaun explained:

> Well, most of the time we be talking or something and the girl get in your conversation when she ain't got no reason to be in your conversation. And girls be nosey and stuff, always talking about something. Then we say something to 'em, "Excuse me" or something, they get smart and then gotta get smart with them. . . . I don't really talk to girls. . . . [We] tell 'em "Go on somewhere," you know what I'm saying, calling 'em names and stuff. . . . Call her a bitch or something. . . . [Then] most of the time [the girl] say something like, "Don't play with me," or something like that. Then it's like, "Leave me alone." That's how most of my homies is, "Hey, get out my face, ain't [got] no time to be arguing with no girl."

At the same time, several young men were openly critical of other young men's behavior. Despite suggesting that boys treat girls badly "to impress their friends," Tony continued, "but I don't be likin' that stuff, 'cause tellin' a girl, callin' a girl a B [bitch], it's like sayin' you'll call your mamma a B [bitch] or something." And Jamal explained:

> I feel if the dude touch [the girl], they deserve what they get. If the girl hit them, you got to accept that she hit you. 'Cause you, you know what I'm saying, you made her feel nasty. Made her feel nasty by touching her in the wrong way. If she want you to touch her, she'll holler at you and you can touch her then. But just touching her to get your good thing going, I don't see it. Ain't no purpose in it.

Very few boys shared Jamal's strong opinion. When pressed, however, many young men admitted that not all girls found their behaviors "fun." For example, Cooper said boys grabbed and touched girls "every day" but did not define such incidents as problematic because he said "they like it." Asked why he thought so, he explained: "They smile. I mean, they don't show no sign of they don't like it. Like, they like being touched." When the interviewer persisted, however, Cooper conceded, "I mean, some of 'em don't like to be touched, some of 'em do."

Likewise, Dwayne said that when girls were grabbed or touched, "they don't say nothing. They be laughing or smiling or something." Asked to clarify whether all girls responded that way, he clarified, "not all of 'em, some of 'em be yelling and screaming and stuff. [But] most of 'em be laughing and smiling." And Travis noted, "you got some girls that when a boy call 'em a name, they just figure, 'Aw, well, he always playing like that, talking stuff,' but you got some girls that, if you call 'em a name and they ain't used to being told something like that, they'll just jump up in an outrage, you know, and start something, and it'll turn into a big issue." Note the implication of Travis's words: it wasn't boys' behavior that made the situation "a big issue" but girls' "outrage." Such incidents were indeed a big issue for girls: by not responding with sufficient outrage, they risked being labeled a "hood rat."

Finally, one additional factor belies young men's characterizations of their behavior as "just play." Asked when harassing behaviors took place or whether they were directed at particular girls, a number of young men described targeting young women they deemed to be "stuck up," unwilling to show sexual or romantic interest, or otherwise unimpressed with the boy. Such responses were a challenge to young men's perceptions of gendered superiority. Darnell complained:

> The girls, they cool, but they just think they too much. They think they too much. Like if you say something to 'em, they think they like, all that. But at the same time, guys are like really thinking they['re] like nothing, you know. I know I think they ain't nothing to me, you know. They ain't really nothing to me. They just girls I see every day.

Kevin described an incident in which his cousin "just started jonin' on [this girl], talking about her shoes and stuff and made her mad." He explained, "for real, it's just saying bad things to 'em and making 'em feel bad about theyselves." Asked why they behaved that way, he continued, "because some girls be trippin'. They be thinking they too good or like they really worth something." And James described being with his friends:

> When they try to talk to the female and [the girl'll] be like "Naw," or the female like, you know what I'm saying, [the boy'll] ask her a question, try to talk to her, make conversation, [but] she have an attitude, talk crazy to him. . . . She might say, you know what I'm saying, "Get out of my face" or something or . . . talk down on 'em or something. [The boys] might just click on 'em and cuss 'em out, call 'em out they name.

Likewise, Curtis said, "we'll see a girl in like a short skirt or short shorts, and we be kind of talking to her, and she don't, she ain't giving nobody no play. So we just get to playing with her, touching on her butt and all that."

Boys' attention toward girls—especially in the presence of their peers—was often an expression of sexual rather than romantic interest. Young men received status among their peers for sexual conquests, while girls faced the risk of stigma and derision for their sexual activities, particularly when they did not occur in the context of an ongoing relationship. Anishika interpreted boys' behaviors with this in mind: "[The boys] do it [touch on girls] so much. It could be somebody, tell you the truth, they don't be liking for real. They just be wantin' to just, you know, just do one thing [e.g., have sex] then leave it alone and stuff." This placed young women in a classic double bind. Responding negatively to boys' advances could result in the kinds of escalating harassment that Curtis, James, and the other young men described. But failure to fend off boys' advances led to escalations of a different sort. Once a girl was perceived as sexually available, she faced ongoing derision and mistreatment.

Selective Targeting: "Wild" Girls and "Hood Rats"

Along with the important disparities in girls' and boys' interpretations of sexually harassing behaviors, with many girls rejecting boys' "play" characterizations, there was a notable overlap across gender. Despite their criticisms of boys' actions, many young women suggested that "some girls" brought such behavior on themselves—by being sexually "fast," dressing provocatively, or craving male attention. No young woman described *her own* experiences with sexual harassment in these terms, but many projected this interpretation onto other girls' experiences.

Anishika's earlier description of the young woman called "the dick-sucking girl" by her peers was at the kind end of this continuum. She remained sympathetic toward the young woman, who she believed was talented but lacked self-esteem, and chastised young men for abusing the girl's self-image further. Other young women were less compassionate. Cleshay, despite being critical of young men's perceptions of "superiority," nonetheless believed that some girls precipitated their mistreatment:

> Well, women could start [by] learn[ing] they seasons. They be coming up in here in mini-skirts up to they butt and it's cold, 50 degrees outside. Then they bending over in front of these boys. Sometimes women do bring it on theyselves, you know what I'm saying. They throwing messages, and then once a boy got a message already in his mind, she wanna act like that ain't the message that she gave him.

Likewise, Cherise critiqued young women she said don't "got respect" for themselves, which she measured both in terms of their clothing choices (for instance, shorts that left their "butt hanging out") and their behavior. She explained, "they treat women that act that way like they need to be treated—stupid. They stupid, you get treated stupid. . . . I mean, if you carry yourself like you ain't got no respect for yourself, that's how they gonna treat you." Comparing her own response to boys' behaviors to those of "stupid" girls, she explained:

> I mean, you try to touch on me, I'm gonna check you. If you try to touch on me, you being disrespectful. I'm saying, you [engaged in] sexual harassment. Some girls just play that [*imitates giggling*]. Laughing at it. That's how you know if a girl is a freak or not. That she want to be touched for real.

LaSondra's interpretation of young men's behavior was based on the advice she received from her male cousin, who, she said, "tell me how boys treat girls, talk with girls, and why they do it and stuff like that." It combined what she believed was the reality that young men would mistreat young women when they could and the perceived responsibility that fell on young women to police their own behaviors:

> See, my cousin say you don't go out and find a man, no one should ever look nasty and go out and find a man. . . . He tell me how you gotta act and dress and he say don't be dressing all trashy and trampy and stuff. He say 'cause that's gonna make a dude think everybody have sex with her and stuff like that. I listen to my cousin and he may think I don't listen to him, but I listen to him. He say all dudes gonna be like, "She's a rat, everybody have sex with her, I bet I could get her too," and he say they won't think nothing of it.

In some ways, LaSondra's cousin's interpretation of boys' behavior appeared to be on the mark. A number of young men in our study said one function of sexually harassing behaviors was to test young women's responses. Girls who appeared receptive to boys' actions stood a good chance of being labeled "rats." Frank explained, "I just look at the girl, I see how they act. 'Cause when I first came [to this school], I was just sitting by myself, see how people act, see how they are. Like, 'Oh, she wild, I can [mess with her],' or 'She quiet, I ain't messin' with her.' . . . I just seein' what I could do." Dwayne described a friend who was suspended after touching a girl. Asked why he thought his friend touched her, Dwayne explained, "probably want to see how it feel, see what up [with her]." He described his own process for detecting whether a girl would allow him to touch her: "You gotta like just talk to 'em, be like, man, just tell them the things she likes to hear [and see how she responds] . . . if she be smiling."

Cherise was explicit in describing how young men tested the boundaries of what girls would allow them to do:

> I don't give hugs. Boys in this school ask me, "Can I get a hug?" "No!" 'Cause once I give them that hug, next thing you know they gonna want to ease their hands down to holding your butt when they get a hug. Next thing you know they gonna try to feel on your chest. I don't play that. No. You and mine, we give handshakes. The only person I give a hug is my boyfriend. And then, I mean, the girls that treated like they're ho's is the girls that let them. Hug the boys. And then they let them touch on their butts, squeeze on them, push 'em, hit 'em. That's how it comes, just by a little simple hug.

Once a girl was seen as sexually available, many boys described classifying them as deserving continued mistreatment. Dwayne continued, "I don't think nobody gonna change [guys'] attitudes about no girl. I don't treat my girl[friend] like no hood rat, but I treat a rat like a rat though." Likewise, Andrew explained, "if I'm disrespecting a female, [it's] because they nasty. . . . It's some girls that are just wild and don't care who they sleep with or who they have oral sex with, stuff like that. . . . [Wear] bootie shorts, they be like all up above they hips and stuff." Marcus said such girls "ain't got no respect for theyself." Of one girl he and his friends targeted, Marvin explained, "they call her a rat . . . she was like a little freak. Let anybody touch on her. . . . She wouldn't say nuttin'. She'll start laughin'." Though he and his friends "touched on" the girl, socially they distanced themselves from her. Marvin said a boy he associated with "ask[ed] everybody, 'Do you all go with her?' I'll be like, 'Man, no. She just a little freak we be around.'" Likewise, Dwayne described "a little group" of girls who "let people touch on 'em," which he and his friends nicknamed "the Rat Pack." In fact, Bobby acknowledged that "that's why girls be actin' so stuck up and be tryin' to play hard to get. 'Cause they think that person said, 'Aw, you a rat,' stuff like that [*laughs*]."

Like Anishika, though, there were a few young men who remained puzzled by some young women's seeming willingness to put up with abusive behavior. Doug used the following analogy to explain:

> The ones that like it, you know, they'll always come around, and you'll always see 'em. They like . . . like say for instance you go down the street, you know a dog right there that's trying to bite you. You gonna try your best to avoid that dog. But you know, some people mess with the dog and try to go straight to it and let the dog try and bite 'em or something, and chase 'em up and down the street like that.

Here Doug clearly acknowledged that young men's behavior was dangerous for girls, rather than simply playful. Picking up on this, the interviewer asked, "So you're a dog?" Doug replied, "No, I didn't say that. Then again, I would in a way." Except when pressed, his primary emphasis remained on the young women who were targeted, not on the problematic actions of young men.

Likewise, asked what could be done to change young men's negative attitudes toward girls, Tyrell explained, "the girl . . . gotta respect theyself. Don't let no dude do whatever they wanna do with 'em or talk to 'em how they wanna be talked to." The conversation continued:

> *Interviewer*: Why do you think girls let guys treat them like that?
>
> *Tyrell*: I still don't know, man. I be wondering about that too. Some dudes be tripping, they be like, 'Suck my dick!' or something. And then the next day the girl'll be all in the dude's face. I don't understand that, I don't know why girls do that. I still don't know, I just think it's something in girls' brains that just erase stuff, just act like they forgot. Like they don't know how to hold a grudge with no dude.

Tyrell does raise an important question: Why did some young women seem to "put up with" abusive behaviors by young men? There are a number of issues to consider in addressing this question. To begin, research consistently reveals that some youths disproportionately experience repeated victimization by their peers. While the exact causal mechanisms are not fully understood, there is evidence that some combination of individual psychological traits, the effects of previous victimization experiences, and the labeling effects that result from previous victimization do make some individuals more vulnerable for continued mistreatment.[33] Scholars Sandra Houston and Naomi Hwang suggest:

> Victims of unwanted childhood sexual contact may learn age-inappropriate sexual behavior and also learn to use sexual behavior as a tool for gaining affection. The stigmatization associated with unwanted sexual contact can lead to lowered self-esteem, which could then lead to an increased vulnerability to further victimization.[34]

Their research revealed that young women who had experienced sexual victimization during childhood were more likely than nonabused girls to experience sexual harassment in high school. However, such young women were *not* less likely than other girls to perceive these experiences as harassment. Thus, a victim-labeling process is likely at play. In the study reported here, for example, as the label "hood rat" proliferated among youths' peer networks, two factors contributed to further victimization. First, as more young men became aware of the label, larger numbers of boys began targeting the girl. Second, the label itself led to greater peer isolation and thus decreased the likelihood that girls would have social support in addressing the problem.[35] Both of these processes were apparent in youths' accounts.

In addition, we must consider the fact that girls' and boys' interactions with one another took place in the context of gender inequality and held particular weight because youths, unlike adults, "tend to be in continuous contact with one another in school and recreational settings."[36] Some young women's apparent unwillingness to "hold grudges" against young men reflected the status hierarchies that existed between them. These girls may have believed they could enhance their own popularity through affiliation with high-status boys, despite the fact that these same boys were likely to be the very ones who gained status, in part, through their adherence to facets of masculinity that include the denigration of women.[37]

To be sure, many young women did employ strategies to resist young men's harassing behaviors. Some girls talked or fought back, and some went to third parties for intervention. Nevertheless, as young men's discussions of "stuck-up" girls revealed, most strategies of resistance resulted in negative consequences. Girls who stood up to boys were often not perceived as entitled to do so. Their actions were read as a challenge to male definitions of the situation, as well as to young men's social dominance over young women. This left young women little wiggle room to successfully negotiate boys' harassing behaviors.

Responding to Sexual Harassment: Girls' Strategies, Escalations, and Double Binds

Young women described four basic strategies for addressing young men's sexual harassment: engaging in avoidance techniques to decrease the likelihood of being targeted; going to a third party for intervention, including school personnel, older family members, or boyfriends; ignoring young men's behaviors, particularly in their less-serious forms; and finally—most commonly—"standing up for themselves" through verbal and/or physical rebuke. The latter strategic choices were the most frequently discussed forms and were especially fraught with risks for escalation.[38]

As the previous discussion revealed, young women who were perceived as taking no action against sexual banter or harassing behaviors faced stigmatization[39]: they were often seen as deserving abuse and were met with powerful and lasting derogatory sexual labels. Thus, the decision to ignore young men's behaviors had to be counterbalanced with the perceived seriousness of the affront. As Tawanna's earlier remarks suggest, girls might choose to "pay them no attention" when boys made comments, but girls drew the line when these were especially crude or vicious or when boys touched or grabbed them. Janelle cautioned: "I feel if you don't respond, they're gonna keep on doing it, and they're gonna keep on doing it. But if you say something to them, you know, more than likely they won't say anything else, not of that sort. . . . He won't treat her like that anymore because she has more respect for herself than another female might have for herself."

Janelle's belief that "saying something" to young men would lead to a positive outcome was rarely borne out in youths' accounts. But her comments are nonetheless in keeping with young women's uniform assessment that girls needed to stand up for themselves. In fact, as Jackie described, the onus of responsibility sat squarely with the female victim: "You might be walking down the hallway and they just come up behind you and touch your butt. And everybody be standing right there and you just look around feeling embarrassed. [Everyone says,] 'You let that boy do that and you ain't goin' do nothing about it?'" Shortly thereafter, the conversation continued:

Interviewer: You said that when a guy comes up and touches a girl inappropriately, the other kids will say something. To who? To him or her?

Jackie: Probably the girl. If she didn't do nothing about it, they probably will. [They would expect her to] I guess hit him. [If she doesn't], they just be saying lil' stuff: "You ain't gon' hit him back?" Lil' stuff like that.

Thus, girls were expected to be more proactive than simply ignoring young men's behaviors, particularly when the incident included physical contact. From the young women's point of view, the appropriate response for a girl was to register her disapproval—and thus mark her respectability—through either a verbal or physical admonishment.

Occasionally, such strategies worked.[40] A few girls described incidents in which they challenged a young man's behavior and he backed down. Destiny said once when a boy "touched my butt . . . I just turned around and hit him, sayin,' 'Stop playin'!' And he walked away." And

Alicia described witnessing an incident in which the young woman verbally bested the young man: "One time I seen this boy grab this girl['s] butt. He didn't know her. She got mad, then she started cursing him out. This was in the hallway, she was real loud or whatever, and he was feeling stupid. . . . He said a little something back, but he didn't make any sense, so he feel stupid."

More typically when young men backed down, they did so while framing young women's concerns as illegitimate. One means of doing so was to laugh at the girls' reactions. Ronald recounted an incident in which "the dude touched this girl['s] butt." The girl "said, 'I don't like you, I hate you!' and all this stuff, and she started smackin' and swingin' on him. . . . He just laughin', thought it was funny." And Robert explained, "my partner got into it [yesterday] with a girl 'cause he called her a bitch. . . . She tried to throw a [cafeteria] tray at him, but it missed and he ain't jump at her or nuttin'. He wasn't fina beat her up, he just laughed at her." Such strategies, when adopted by young men, undercut young women's concerns about the problematic nature of sexual and gender harassment, as well as their ability to effectively address the issue.

Moreover, it was much more common for youths to describe that girls' efforts at standing up for themselves resulted in an escalating conflict. Jackie surmised this was because "boys want to have the last word, they want to be right." Girls and boys both said that when young women rejected boys' verbal advances, these incidents often shifted from their original sexual content to derogatory gender-based name calling. Ramara explained:

> A boy will like come up to me and be like, "What's up with me and you?" and stuff . . . and I'll say, "I don't wanna talk to you" or something like that. And they'll be like, "Well forget you then. I don't like you anyway . . . with yo' stanking" blah, blah, blah, you know. And they'll just say a whole . . . string of stuff 'cause they mad they got rejected and stuff.

Young men reported similar interactions. Recall their earlier discussions of targeting "stuck-up" girls, and James's description that his friends "just click on 'em and cuss 'em out" when girls "have an attitude" in response to his friends' attempts to "talk to" them. Kevin noted, "if it's a bunch of us and the girl walk past, somebody try to talk to 'em and she look all stupid [at him, we'll sing this] rap song. It's called *Bitches Ain't Shit,* and the chorus is 'Bitches ain't shit, but ho's a trip.' We just be going off on 'em."

Thus, girls' primary method for standing up for themselves in the face of verbal harassment—sometimes necessary to avoid victim-blaming labels—often led to ugly reproaches, which shifted from come-ons to put-downs. William explained, "dudes just expect 'em to come over when they call 'em." When, instead, girls refused to see boys' advances as complimentary or flattering, their rebuffs were read as disrespect and dealt with harshly. Moreover, as Kevin's and James's stories reveal, the public nature of these exchanges and the presence of male peers both heightened young men's need to save face when met with girls' "disrespect" and provided them with powerful allies who both facilitated and participated in the retaliation.

Violent Escalations

Young men's physically harassing behavior, including sexual touching, grabbing, and groping, were met with even stronger reactions by many young women. Yvonne situated her own reactions to her previous experiences with sexual violence:[41]

> I don't like to be touched on by guys that I don't know them. I don't like it and I click, you know what I'm saying. And that's a lot of [the] reason why I stay in trouble at school. Because I talk loud and I have a big mouth and I get loud. And when I [get] like that, that's just from past experiences and I can't explain it to them because they don't know [what happened to me] and I don't want them to know. So I got to protect myself from them. I be trying to let them know, "Look nigga, don't touch me like that," you know what I'm saying.

Conflicts emerging from disputes over sexual harassment sometimes escalated beyond verbal confrontations and culminated in physical violence. Occasionally, young men initiated this violence as a response to girls' verbal reproach. Anishika noted, "sometimes when you don't want them to touch you and stuff, they'll get mad, hit the girl and all that stuff." And Cleshay explained, "I seen a dude smack a girl. First he was messin' with her a lot, then she asked him to stop it. He kept messin' with her, and when she got up to move, he grabbed her and smacked her real hard."

More often, youths described young women initiating physical violence, typically as a response to harassment that itself was physical (and arguably violent) in nature, such as when young men grabbed their breasts, buttocks, or vaginas or when their sexual reputations were challenged. LaSondra explained, "I don't fight girls, but boys, yes . . . 'cause they try to touch me." Ricky believed that girls who were more street-oriented were more likely to use violence as a strategy, as the following conversation reveals:

> *Ricky*: A gal might walk past, [and one of the guys] be like, "What's up baby?" And if she don't say nothin,' then, "Aw, bitch go'on."
> *Interviewer*: What's the girl's response to that?
> *Ricky*: I mean, if you run into somebody that care about school, you know, I mean she'll say something like, "Naw, yo' mamma laid down, the bitch is the one that had you!" You know. But if you run across somebody that's half into it and they don't really care, I mean, it'll be a fight or something. A few punches might get throwed. She might end up hittin' him.

Alicia, for instance, when asked whether she reported a young man's behavior to school authorities, said, "no, what happened, I was too mad. I ain't trip off going to tell nobody. I wanted to punch him myself 'cause he play too much."

Young men often claimed that girls' physical violence was not met with violent sanction. Raymond explained: "Ain't no real straight up fighting with the girls and the boys. . . . The girl get in the dude face, but people pull her off, pull her back. . . . [The guy] just be like, 'Get out my face,' or something. . . . 'Somebody get this girl out my face before I hurt her' or something." And Travis noted, "half the time when a boy call a girl [out] they name and the girl try to fight them, half of the time you see the boy just running, you know, 'cause the boy don't really wanna fight the girl."

Darnell likewise argued that "they don't really have no conflicts up here where like guys'll try to fight girls. You know, they don't do things like that. I had a conflict up here once with a girl. She tried to get me to fight her, but I don't see myself as fighting no girl, 'cause it's, it just, it ain't my style." Asked to describe the incident, he explained:

[She was] going off at the mouth, [and] she came up to me and pushed me, so I was like, "Don't push me." So I got, you know what I'm saying, [to] using foul language, cussing her out, like you know, "You don't have to put your stinking hands on me," or whatever. And then, so she ran up on me, hit me three times, and I pushed her and she fell into the wall. I picked her up and I asked her if she was alright and I apologized. But she should've been apologizing to me, 'cause she hit me three times.

Darnell seemed genuinely distraught over his physical encounter with this young woman, which began when he inadvertently bumped her rather than being initiated over sexual harassment. He explained, "I won't put my hands on her 'cause I don't fight girls. You know what I'm saying, make me feel bad if I hit a girl."

But as I examine in further detail in chapter 5, norms against using physical violence against girls were contingent. Young men often defined violence narrowly (for instance, punching is violence, but pushing is not), and there were many exceptions to the general rule. These made violence against girls both acceptable and amusing in certain circumstances. Even young women described themselves and other students laughing when girls were caught off guard by young men's violent responses. The following conversation with Sharmi is illustrative:

> *Sharmi:* The girl hit the dude and the dude choked her. . . . She punched him in the chest. They got into it for something, I don't know [what. Then] he just grabbed her by the neck and started choking her [until] the security guards came and he let her go.
> *Interviewer:* . . . What were the other students around doing?
> *Sharmi:* Laughin' at her. . . . 'Cause she thought he wasn't gon' do nothin' back to her.

In fact, several young women provided accounts of being met with retaliatory violence once they challenged a young man's right to touch them. Yvonne described two such incidents:

I got put out of my regular school because I had a fight with this dude or whatever. 'Cause I was on the cheerleading squad and um, he was a football player, you know, and he had rank up at the school. He was real popular, you know what I'm saying, and we was cool because we used to get high together . . . and we like stay in the neighborhood around each other or we used to. But [when] we started going to school together he just started acting real funny towards me. And I'm a large breasted girl. So we [the cheerleaders] was doing our little pyramid and he kept on coming over there and he kept on hitting me like that [touching her breasts] and I tell him to "quit playing with me, quit playing with me!" He was like, "I don't have to quit playing with you." He was trying to show off in front of his friends or whatever. So I went over there and I kicked him in, you know what I'm saying, his thing or whatever. And um, that's when he got . . . he start choking me or whatever.

She had a similar encounter at her current school:

In the classroom with this dude, he sitting in a chair, I was at a desk [and] I had on a blue-jean skirt. And he kept on rubbing my thigh or whatever, and I was like "Why don't you move?" and I pushed him. And then he pushed me in my head and I got up in it, because nigga you touching me, you know what I'm saying. So, I stood up or whatever and I pushed his chair to the side. And he hopped up like he was gonna hit me or whatever, but the teacher came over there, which was a dude or whatever. He took my side and I like I told him, we don't talk no more. We used to be real cool, but we don't talk no more after that.

In both instances, young men Yvonne thought she was "cool with" violated their friendships by sexualizing their behavior toward her. When her verbal requests to stop failed to elicit compliance, she reacted with violence and they responded in kind.

Sheron described witnessing an incident in which a young man "said that the girl had oral sex, and I guess hurt her feelings or whatever. . . . So she got mad, just started hitting him. . . . Smacked him . . . in his face. . . . He hit her back [and] they just got into a big ole' fight." And Alicia described being "shocked" by the amount of force a young man used in a classroom altercation: "She got up and pushed him . . . to tell him, don't touch her. He got angry and pushed her real hard." Terence described a similar incident in gym class: "She hit him first . . . slapped him . . . after that they was arguin' for a minute. . . . She was just, you know how girls talk—'You ain't this, you ain't that' or whatever. He got tired of her. She hit him, so he hit her back, pushed her in her face.

. . . He pushed her a couple of times, it was pretty hard too." Likewise, Tami told of an incident in the cafeteria: "They was fightin' [and] he pushed the girl and she slid under the lunchroom table. And then she got back up and pushed him back, and he just spit in her face." Tami reported that the other students were "laughing," and the incident ended only when the security guard came and broke it up.

In fact, because young women knew that some boys would respond with violence, some reported making strategic decisions to avoid physical confrontations. For instance, Alicia described a "nasty" fight she had with a boy that began when he "was trying to jon' on" her. The incident devolved into ugly name-calling on both sides. She explained, "I got up in his face, talking stuff. I knew I couldn't beat him up or nothing, so I was just loud and in his face, going off on him, cursing him out." Likewise, of a fight she witnessed, Anishika said the girl "was mad and stuff, but she already know she was just frontin' [acting], 'cause she wasn't gon' hit him and stuff. 'Cause he the type, he'll hit her back."

Other incidents appeared headed toward violence when they were broken up.[42] Jamellah described an event that happened the week prior to her interview:

> This girl was in the lunchroom. And the boy, he had put a [cafeteria] tray between her legs and had said, "I'ma treat you like I treat the rest of these ho's up here." And she turned around, walked to the back, picked up the tray [*laughs*] . . . and she said, "You got me fucked up!" And then he said, "Ugly ass bitch!" She charged at him with the tray [*laughs*] and the assistant principal grabbed her. . . . [The boy] standing there, talkin' 'bout some, "Come on, I'ma whoop your ass!"

All of these incidents further demonstrate the double bind young women were faced with as they attempted to challenge and negotiate young men's sexual harassment. Young women's attempts to defend themselves elicited the threat of violence or a violent reprisal, while their actual concerns—not wanting to be treated in a sexualized or otherwise demeaning manner—were discounted.

Role of Peers: Amping It Up and Intervening

Evidence throughout this chapter illustrates the role of peers in both facilitating sexual harassment and escalating the conflicts that often ensued. As with their descriptions of gender-based violence in neighbor-hoods, the vast majority of youths described nonintervention in school as the norm and emphasized the entertainment value of male-on-female conflicts.

On the whole, youths were discouraged from intervening by norms that encouraged individuals to stay out of others' business. Cleshay explained, "sometimes we say something about it, but what can we do? They gonna just say shut up or mind your own business and stuff like that." And Leon said, "they feel like they gon' do what they want to anyway. So if I tell 'em, they won't listen."

More than simply failing to intervene, however, youths said their peers routinely worked to "amp up" the conflict. Recall Alicia's description of a boy "jonin' on" an overweight girl: "people be laughing, encouraging the boy on, and making him keep doing it and doing it." Likewise, of the "nasty" fight she had with a male peer, she said the other kids were "laughing and making us go more and more and just . . . they wasn't even trying to stop it or nothing. They was just encouraging me and him going on and on." And Rennesha said students typically reacted by "looking, instigating. . . . Most of the time, [they] just instigating. 'Aw, he said yo' momma—' or something like that." Kenisha said the other students "run up to it, influence it, laugh, join in on it."

Leon described a recent fight in which "[the girl] said something to [the boy], and he said something to her, and he ran towards her and got to grabbin' her, chokin' her and all type of stuff. . . . We was suppose to be in class, but by them fightin,' half the third floor was out there in the hallway to watch." And Jamal said, if "there's a crowd around, like they'll try to soup the girl or boy up to hit them . . . try to see the action going on." Eugene concurred: "They amp it up, they get excited. . . . Excited like, 'Ah, it's gonna be a fight!' and stuff."

Michelle's description of a recent incident illustrates how peers helped escalate sexual harassment against young women:

> We was down in the gym and we had to change our clothes or whatever and the teacher didn't say nuttin' 'bout my shorts bein' too short so I had on some shorts and a boy was like "Yeah this my butt, this my butt" and . . . then somebody told him "Well if it's your butt go over there and touch it" and he came over there and touched me and I told him "Don't touch me! If I didn't tell you to touch me don't touch me"

or whatever. He got to talkin' "Don't be frontin'[43] now" like that or whatever.

Michelle said the other boys continued to encourage the young man, not just to touch her but to use physical violence in response to her rebuttal: "[The other boys were] instigating, 'Oh, that's your gal, that's your butt? Smack her down then, tell her to shut up!'" Thus, rather than just "minding your own business," other students often joined in to escalate the conflict for their own entertainment.

Nonetheless, there were both circumstances and relational ties that sometimes encouraged intervention. The popularity, friendship groups, and age of both parties had some impact on how youths responded. Dawanna explained, "it depends on who's fighting for real or who it is or whatever. 'Cause if it's they friend, then you know, they stop it or whatever, and then if it somebody they don't know or something, they just standing there watchin' or whatever."

Young women in particular said that their friends would stick up for them. Ramara noted, "if it's the boy's friends, he'll go off on the girl with him and stuff, and if it's the girl['s] friend and stuff, they'll be like, 'Leave her alone! Anyway, you just mad 'cause you got played' or something like that." Britney said:

> The other day I got into it with a boy because he said something to me. . . . I said, "Shut up talking to me!" and he got mad. So we just started arguing and stuff. . . . He said, "Bitch you better shut the fuck up 'fore I slap you in your mouth!" . . . Then my friends had came over like, "If you touch her we gonna jump you," so he didn't do nuttin'. He walked away.

Nicole also described intervening in an incident:

> This boy, he had went with her a long time ago, about two years ago. And he was touching her and she kept tellin' him, "Leave me alone!" So I came down the steps and she asked me would I help her, so I just pulled him off of her. . . . He was touching her, trying to make her give him a kiss. And so I was like, that was too much playing. I just grabbed him by his arm and walked this way with him and started talkin' to him. So I was just like, "You shouldn't do that if that girl don't wanna

be touched." He was like, "Man, I went with her for a long time." . . . [In the meantime] she ran up the stairs, she was just trying to get away.

Nicole's two brothers also witnessed the incident, but they "was just laughing. I was like, 'Y'all ignorant.'" Though she did not elaborate, it is likely Nicole felt safe in intervening precisely because her brothers were present, thus deterring the young man from turning on Nicole.[44]

Destiny described accompanying her friend to the principal's office to corroborate the girl's complaint against two boys who had sexually threatened her. Her friend asked her to come along, "'cause she ain't know if everybody was gonna tell [what they had witnessed]. I was like, 'Yes, I will,' 'cause I hope if somebody was doing me like that, somebody'll go with me to tell." And Jamellah's encounter indicates how gender inequality could be tempered by age:

> We was in lunch line and [this little boy] kept on pulling my hair, playing with me, just playing with me. Talking to me, talking to me, and I was ignoring him. And he got mad and started talking back, you know what I'm saying, talkin' all type of crazy stuff. And I am like the oldest female up here. So I am like, "You a little boy to me. Stop talkin' to me, you not on my level. I don't got nothing to say to you. Stay in a child's place." And then he got up in my face—that wasn't the end of it—he got up in my face [saying] "You think you all that? You walk in this line . . . and don't say nothin' to nobody. You ain't better than nobody! . . . Look girl, I'll hurt you." [And I said,] "Naw, little boy, you'll get hurt!" And one of the boys that actually is my age . . . was like, "Man, you need to calm down. . . . Hold that down man, leave her alone, you see she don't wanna play with you, leave her alone." And he grab me and was like, "Calm down don't trip off of him, you be steady, he a little boy."

Here the age difference between Jamellah and the boy gave her the upper hand, and a young man her own age intervened on her behalf.

On the whole, what we have seen in this section is the difficulties young women faced in their attempts to challenge sexual and gender harassment. On the one hand, failing to "stand up for yourself" came with the likelihood of victim-blaming labeling and sometimes led to escalating abuse. On the other hand, young women's attempts to stand up to young men—verbally or physically—also placed them in a precarious position. Rather than recognizing the legitimacy of girls' concerns, young men often read girls' responses as "disrespect," and they retaliated with harsh, gendered putdowns, threats, or violence. And while peers would occasionally stand up for the young woman, they were much more likely to "amp up" the conflict, watch, and laugh. Thus girls were often alone in their attempts to address harassment, with few viable options at their disposal.

Limits of School Responsiveness

But what of school policies and personnel? Unlike the neighborhood violence examined in chapter 2, the incidents analyzed here all took place on school grounds, where teachers, administrators, and security personnel were both present and legally obligated to ensure the well-being of their students.

I began this chapter by outlining the difficulties faced by St. Louis city schools for addressing the educational and safety needs of their students. The school district has faced chronic performance and fiscal crises, and it continues to grapple with the recurring problem of school violence. As such, it epitomizes the struggles of schools in impoverished urban communities. In addition, as I demonstrate throughout this chapter, the sexual and gender harassment of young women in these schools is an entrenched problem.

Given the pervasiveness of school-based harassment, it may be surprising that only a minority of girls described relying on school personnel in seeking remedy for sexual harassment. Recall when two young men threatened to rape Nicole, she not only went to the principal but also brought witnesses to corroborate. She explained, "the girls I hang with, they tell. I be like, 'Sexual harassment! He just touched me!'" Likewise, Tawanna said when young men grabbed her, "I tell the teacher or something." Katie said when guys touched them inappropriately, girls would "curse 'em out or tell a teacher or tell [the] principal or something." Asked what happened when they told, she explained, "[teachers] bring 'em down to the office and talk to 'em and be like, see if everything's cool or whatever, then they just leave and they don't say anything to each other." And Rennesha said teachers would "tell us, 'That's sexual harassment' or whatever."

Recall that Katie also described threatening to tell the teacher after a young man in her class made what she considered sexual threats. Though she said the threat succeeded in diffusing the boy's behavior, she was frustrated that the teacher "just sat there . . . probably just waitin' for one of us to come and tell him" rather than taking the initiative to intervene on his own. In fact, a primary reason girls described not going to teachers was because they felt many of them failed to take such incidents seriously. Katie said it was up to young women to take action for themselves, as the following dialogue suggests:

> *Interviewer*: Are there teachers usually around [when sexual harassment occurs]?
> *Katie*: Sometimes. But they don't pay no attention. [Security guards] don't pay no attention [and students] don't pay no attention either.
> *Interviewer*: So it's usually the girl that has to speak up for herself?
> *Katie*: Yeah.

In fact, the majority of young women described most teachers as ineffectual or unconcerned.[45] Britney explained that teachers were often present when incidents occurred, but "sometimes they don't even really say nothing. They just sit back and watch us." And Cleshay noted, "I mean, teachers gonna see what they wanna see, that's how I see it." Likewise, Yvonne said teachers "really don't too much say nothing. They just go about they business just like we do." She clarified:

> Some of the teachers get concerned. But most of them are like, "Go on about your business" or whatever. . . . I think the teachers aren't concerned enough. They don't take time out enough. But of course you have your dedicated teachers that are here to work with the students, that want to help. But the majority of them, I just think they here for a paycheck and a fashion show. Just like the students.

Like Yvonne, Kenisha said, "it depends who the teacher is. . . . Sometimes they'll send 'em down to the office . . . stop it, talk to them."

Alicia blamed her teacher's inadequate response on lack of ability: "My teacher kinda old, so he was trying to break up [a conflict], trying to do something. But he old, so he couldn't really do nothing." Ricky attributed teachers' responses to both fear and what he considered the understandable indifference that came with experience working in chaotic, urban schools:

I mean, a lot of teachers, I wouldn't say they necessarily scared, I mean, [but] a lot of kids just take those teachers for granted. I mean, will talk to 'em bad, I mean, don't show 'em any respect, and I mean, if they try to break up a fight, you might have a student that'll be bold enough to just swing on a teacher. So for a teacher, it's basically just for the safety of they job.

Later, he elaborated further on his perceptions of why teachers did not intervene more:

'Cause man, you got them kids [*laughs*] you know how, if you was teaching a class, right. I mean, and a student is callin' you out your name. . . . You got a 15 or a 16 year old callin' you all type of "black muthafuckas" and all type of, you know what I'm sayin', everything but your name, you know. You ain't gonna keep takin' that. . . . So they feel they can only do so much.

Thus, though Ricky offered an insightful explanation of the myriad motives for teachers' actions or lack thereof, the upshot was that many girls felt that sexual harassment was not taken particularly seriously by school personnel, even when they did take minimal action.[46]

Recall Destiny's description of going to the principal's office with her friend after boys in her class threatened to "haul her [friend] down and freak all over her." Nonetheless, she was dissatisfied with what she felt was both the teacher's and principal's lackadaisical response. "They was like, 'They ain't do nothing too bad to her.' It just like they was givin' them another chance. Like [if they had touched her, that] would be a different story, but they wasn't doing nothing but talkin' so they was gonna give 'em a chance." Likewise, Lisa's account of her friend who was tormented "every day at 5th period" by a young man who claimed "she had sex with all these boys" included a description of insufficient action by the teacher:

One day we in 5th period and it just so happen that my friend's teacher wasn't there. And so [a whole group of boys] had come in our classroom. So they in our room or whatever, and he gets to talkin' about us just to make everybody laugh at her. So they started goin' off and then he got loud, then she got loud and [the teacher] sent them out of the classroom.

Lisa said none of the young men were further sanctioned for their behavior. They were merely asked to leave.

Nicole's description was perhaps the most dramatic example of teacher nonintervention. She explained:

> My sister and this boy [got into it in the gym]. He had touched my sister in her privacy part, so she picked up a weight and threw it at his head. And it hit the wall instead of hittin' him, so she [grabbed] some more and just chased him down the hallway. . . . And she came up and just hit him and that's when I ran up and then I hit him. So we was just out there fightin' with him. . . . [The teacher was there,] he'll let you fight though. . . . He knew about the weight, and he saw when my sister ran out of the classroom. . . . So they was out there tusslin' and wrestlin', so I came up. I'm hittin' him a couple times, so we just jumped on him. [The teacher didn't come out] until we got to the end of it. . . . [Then] he was like, "Stop that, stop that." And I was like, "Naw, too late for all that."

Three key problems are apparent in young women's discussions of the nature of teacher interventions. First, such a seemingly cavalier approach sent a message to students that sexual and gender harassment are not sufficiently troubling to warrant serious intervention. Youths' accounts clearly demonstrated otherwise. Harassment contributed to long-term stigma for those girls who acquiesced or consented to sexualized interactions (and, as discussed in chapter 4, set the stage for more serious forms of sexual abuses). For those girls who challenged it, harassment led to escalating conflicts with young men and sometimes to violence. These were in addition to the detrimental consequences other researchers have documented, including harmful effects on school performance and negative emotional outcomes.[47]

Second, because teachers did not appear to take a strong hand in addressing sexual harassment, young women were left to remedy the problem themselves. One result was that conflicts often escalated to the point of requiring the intervention of school personnel. Once conflicts reached this stage, young women often got into trouble themselves for doing what they believed was necessary to defend themselves. Recall Alicia's earlier description of a "kinda big girl" in her class that a male classmate was "jonin' on" about her weight. She said the other students were "laughing, encouraging the boy on, and making him keep doing it and doing it." By the time the teacher intervened, the young woman was "arguing and cursing" with the young man, and she was sent to the principal's office for cursing. Likewise, Britney said she was removed from her class "because I defended myself. And they ain't send him. They let him stay in the classroom so I had to get out and go to another classroom." In the most severe case, recall Yvonne's earlier description of being expelled from her "regular school" when a young man refused to quit grabbing her breasts and she ultimately responded with violence.

Third, and relatedly, because school personnel seemed to take a reactive rather than proactive approach to addressing sexual harassment, the onus of responsibility for challenging boys' behavior fell to young women. One problematic facet of this was placing young women in the position of having to decide—and thus be accountable for—whether to request that young men be written up for their behavior. For instance, Ronald said when teachers witnessed sexual harassment, "they'll ask the girl if they want them to write him up." The result was that, in addition to the types of immediate escalations I described earlier, young women sometimes faced negative repercussions for reporting young men's behaviors. When Nicole went to the principal to report the two young men who threatened to rape her, she said other students were "like, 'She snitch too much.'"

Likewise, recall Michelle's description of the incident in her gym class when a young man was encouraged by his friends to grab her buttocks and "smack her down" when she responded angrily. When the teacher finally intervened, he put Michelle in charge of the decision to report the young man and appeared to have ignored the young man's threat to her in response:

Interviewer: What did the teacher say?
Michelle: Nuttin'. He pulled him to the side and I don't know what he saying, but all I know is he was telling him, "Don't put your hands on her 'cause if she wanna write you up for sexual harassment that's what she gonna write you up for." And [the boy] like, "She better not write me up for that!" And I [was] tellin' the teacher, "Just for that I wanna write him up."

Michelle said, ultimately, "the gym teacher talked to both of us and told us don't even worry about it as long as he don't put his hands on me no more." With the teacher unwilling to penalize the young man himself, and given the boy's implied retaliation threat, she said, "I never did get around to writing him up."

Nykeshia described a young man who "had got in trouble in class, and I guess he took it out on the class. By me sitting by the door, I don't know if he was trying to spit in the trash can or not, but he directed his spit towards me and spit in my face." When she told the principal what happened, "he was like, he'll take care of it. But [after] I told, [the boy] was like, 'Yeah, I'll get you after school.'" Since that time, the young man had continued to harass her: "He call me out my name, walk up and bump into me. Like I could be on one side of the hallway and he'll be on the other, and he'll see me coming, walk towards me and bump into me." Nykeshia said the principal told her not to respond to his behavior and, instead, said, "Every time you have a problem, keep coming down and telling 'em." Despite doing so repeatedly, she said school personnel had yet to take action, because "they said it was my word against his."[48] She said he continued to bother her "like every week."

Lisa described an incident similar to Nicole's, in that she was also labeled a "snitch" by her peers.[49] In addition, the young man retaliated for her reporting his behavior, and she struck back and was suspended for the semester. Continuing her earlier description of the incident in which "this boy . . . was sayin' he had sex with [this girl] and that she sucked his stuff," Lisa said because the girl was "feeling real bad about it or whatever . . . I brought it to [the assistant principal's] attention." She explained, "I told him, and when I came outta [his office], they like, 'You a snitch! You tellin'' this and that. And the boy spit in my face. And that's when I tried to cut him." Asked to elaborate, she continued:

> [The girl was] cryin' and this and that, and [the assistant principal] wanted to know what's the big thing—you know, what the big deal was. And I told. . . . He called me and the rest of the girls, he called us in the office. And we was tellin' and I told him who [the boy] was and everything. [When we came out of the office, the boys] was like, "You a snitch, you a snitch!" . . . Just, "You a snitch!" and cursin' me out. So I just started going back off on him and he spit in my face. . . . He started talkin' stuff and he started callin' hisself jonin' on me and so I started jonin' on him back and everybody was laughin'. So [that's when] he spit on me. . . . I pulled out a knife . . . [but the teachers] got my arm [and] grabbed the knife. Then when they took the knife, I took my shoe off

and I started hittin' him with my shoe. . . . [Then] the guard grabbed me. He was walkin' me, tryin' to calm me down.

Lisa said the school "put me out for a semester, but they let me come back." However, she reported that "nothin'" happened to the young man; he was suspended for just "three days."

Indeed, a few youths did report knowing of boys who were suspended for their behaviors, particularly when the incidents involved sexual touching or grabbing. Alicia said she knew of "one boy [who] got suspended. I seen this, it happened to this boy and this girl. He touched on her breast and she told. He got suspended for like three days."

And of the incident in which the boy put a cafeteria tray between a girl's legs and made sexual comments, Jamellah said the girl "called her mother up and stuff and got him suspended for three days for sexual harassment." Doug said he had gotten suspended for groping a girl, explaining, "it ain't work out like I had hoped it would, but I learned my lesson: not to *touch 'em*, touch 'em." Frank knew of a young man suspended for sexual harassment but, despite describing his frequent participation in such behaviors, noted, "oh, I ain't ever got caught." Katie said she "never knew anybody that got suspended for" touching girls, though she believed it was an appropriate response to a first offense.

Other girls, however, believed that suspension was an insufficient punishment and futile exercise. Asked what she thought the school could do to reduce sexual harassment, Tawanna said, "all they can do is suspend them [but they] come back and do the same thing." And Yvonne explained, "they need to give 'em a harsher punishment. Suspending, I think suspending us from school don't mean jack. Nothing to us. We wanna be at home. We wanna be able to sleep 'til 12 o'clock, watch TV all afternoon, eat, then go outside and have fun." Kenisha concurred:

Instead of them trying to get us involved—order detention, something —the first thing that come to the principal['s] mind is "Send 'em home." . . . [Nothing's] gonna get solved by sending 'em home or suspension. I think they need a better, something better than suspension. 'Cause it's not doing nuttin' but giving [them] what they want. . . . Sending 'em home, they ain't doing nuttin' but hanging out on the street.

Other youths were even more pessimistic about the limitations of school interventions and believed there was nothing—short of Nicole's suggestion to "take all the bad kids from this school"—that could be done to solve the problems of sexual harassment specifically and student conflicts generally. She explained, "the boys gon' do what they wanna do, they not gon' listen. They don't even listen to their parents." Likewise, Vanessa said, "ain't nothing gon' stop them kids from doin' what they're going to do anyway." And Sheron noted, "really it would stop for a little minute if [the school] were to do something. But it'll start right back up, so I don't think that would [solve the problem]."

Conclusion

This chapter has revealed four important dimensions of school-based sexual and gender harassment. First, such behaviors are a multifaceted and systematic facet of girls' experiences in school. Youths described a variety of forms of harassment, ranging from name-calling, sexual comments, sexual rumors, and sexualized touching, groping, and grabbing. Sexual harassment was an everyday phenomenon that girls routinely had to guard against and contend with. And while young men often characterized such behavior as "play," their own accounts and girls' experiences of harassment belied this interpretative framework. Instead, the characterization of sexual harassment as "play" functioned to both consolidate young men's masculine identities and conceal the threat such behaviors posed to young women.[50]

Second, such behaviors caused a multitude of harms to young women. Those girls unable or unwilling to challenge some young men's sexualization of them faced ongoing mistreatment and often were faced with sexually derogatory labels with lasting impact. These led to social isolation, taunting, and peer rejection. And, as I show in chapter 4, they also set the stage for more serious forms of sexual abuses. School-based sexual harassment was sometimes a testing ground used by young men to identify girls who were susceptible to sexual mistreatment outside of school, just as sexual interactions in youths' neighborhoods were carried into the school as part of the labeling process.

Third, the harms of sexual harassment were not reserved for those girls who endured the labels of "freak" or "hood rat." Young women employed a range of tactics to negotiate school-based sexual harassment but at every turn were disadvantaged in the strategies available to them. Ignoring young men's behaviors could lead to victim-blaming. Likewise, young women's avoidance strategies meant limiting their interactions with peers. Just as in girls' neighborhoods, such strategies could provide some insulation from problematic encounters with young men, but they came at the cost of limiting young women's ability to fully participate in public life. In addition, in the school context, the ability to successfully avoid threatening or troubling behaviors by young men was made more difficult by the social organization of schools. Harassment occurred in all areas of the school—in hallways, classrooms, the cafeteria, gym, and school grounds. Unlike in their neighborhoods, when girls could simply stay to themselves in their homes, avoidance was not an effective strategy in schools because youths were in continuous contact with one another.

It is striking that most young women described addressing harassment by using strategies researchers have classified as assertive or aggressive: demanding the behavior stop or expressing anger, hostility, or threats. Much research, based primarily on white and middle-class samples, has found that women and girls are more likely to use internal or indirect responses in addressing harassing behaviors.[51] Alternatively, sociologists Janice D. Yoder and Patricia Aniakudo's research on African American women firefighters found that all of the women in their sample used strategies similar to those discussed here, and, like the young women in our sample, these women were critical of women who were passive, indirect, or went along with the harassment.[52] Yoder and Aniakudo argue that situational factors play an important role in shaping women's response choices. Likewise, our research suggests that girls' externalized responses to harassment were grounded in the significant role that standing up for oneself plays in disadvantaged urban milieus.

As with the other strategies available to young women, however, standing up for themselves came at considerable cost. Girls' responses to harassment, when assertive or aggressive, often resulted in more vicious mistreatment, especially in the forms of gender harassment and violent overtures. Their attempts to defend themselves were read by young men as disrespect, and the incidents quickly escalated into hostile confrontations when young women challenged young men's sexual and gender entitlements. Thus, young women were in a lose-lose situation. Every available avenue for responding to sexual harassment reproduced their disempowered position vis-à-vis young men.[53]

Finally, perhaps most troubling, youths described school personnel as either indifferent to sexual and gender harassment or taking a primarily reactive approach to the problem. Young women very much felt they were on their own in handling harassing behaviors, unsupported by most of their peers and teachers. The result was that girls were often as likely as boys to get into trouble over harassment when they employed verbal and especially physical strategies to defend themselves. In addition, they faced peer sanctions when the burden of reporting the behavior fell to them.[54] The strong community norms against both intervention and reporting offenses to authorities, shown in chapter 2, translated to the school context as well, further narrowing young women's options for addressing this systematic problem.

To be sure, schools do have a responsibility to address sexual harassment: such behaviors create a hostile environment for young women, causing the school "to become hostile, intimidating, or offensive and unreasonably interfer[ing] with" young women's schoolwork.[55] In 1999, the U.S. Supreme Court ruled that educational institutions are legally obligated to take action against school-based sexual harassment, and failure to do so is a violation of Title IX. While this ruling was important, it remains an insufficient remedy for such harassment, both because of the strict criteria employed[56] and because legal liabilities applied through the use or threat of lawsuits are "largely reactive, piecemeal, individualized responses. . . . They take place after the fact and only provide a remedy for an individual victim after the harm has been done."[57]

Young women like those in our sample—from distressed urban communities, attending chronically troubled schools—are further disadvantaged. School resources are limited, staffing problems are acute, and the primary security concerns involve gang violence and weapons violations. Moreover, parental involvement, financial resources, cultural capital, and knowledge are necessary prerequisites for the threat of litigation to be an effective measure against sexual harassment. On these counts, urban poor young women face nearly insurmountable hurdles.[58]

For school-based sexual harassment to be effectively minimized, "interventions should be proactive and comprehensive and should focus on the elimination of factors that contribute to a hostile school environment."[59] This is all the more daunting for schools embedded in urban poor communities. As discussed in chapters 1 and 2, the deep structural disadvantages found in youths' communities limited the development of the social capital and collective efficacy necessary to maintain strong pro-social community norms and led to legitimate distrust of broader community institutions. The result was the development of strong oppositional cultural norms that favored individual autonomy, discouraged "snitching," and supported negative gender stereotypes that encouraged and validated the mistreatment of young women.[60]

As I discussed earlier, the former of these have been linked to the extent of school violence and disorder. And though sexual harassment is a widespread problem facing schools throughout America,[61] my research suggests it is especially acute and fraught with risks for violent escalation in chronically distressed schools. As troubling is the reciprocity of interactions between school and neighborhood contexts. The sexualized and gendered mistreatment of young women in schools was embedded within parallel neighborhood-based processes. Even with the kinds of limitations documented here, school-based sexual harassment was constrained by the presence of adult institutional supervision. In neighborhood settings, the often unsupervised community milieu posed much greater risks for young women. Through its emphasis on male sexual entitlement, "the denial and denigration of female sexual pleasure or agency, and the objectification of [young] women," school-based sexual harassment often functioned "as a kind of dress rehearsal" for gendered interactions in the community, including widespread sexual coercion and violence.[62]

4

Respect Yourself,
Protect Yourself
Sexual Coercion and Violence

In chapter 3, I argue that there was a relationship between school-based sexual harassment and violence against girls in their neighborhoods. This was evident in youths' descriptions of how girls' neighborhood sexual reputations carried over into schools but also in young men's accounts of using sexual harassment as a testing ground to identify those young women most likely to acquiesce to sexual behaviors in neighborhood contexts.[1] I expand on this theme here, focusing on the nature and situational contexts of sexual violence, including the role of unsupervised parties, drugs, and alcohol on sexual aggression, as well as the widespread problem of "running trains."[2] I conclude the discussion in this chapter by examining young women's strategies for addressing sexual victimization risks.

Extent of Sexual Violence against Young Women

A striking finding in our research was the high rate of sexual violence experienced by the young women in our sample. As mentioned in chapter 2 and as table 4-1 details, more than one-half (54 percent) of the girls we interviewed reported experiencing some form of sexual coercion or assault. In fact, nearly one in three young women reported multiple experiences with sexual victimization.[3] This is an alarming amount of sexual violence, particularly given that the mean age of our sample was just 16.

The extent of girls' repeat sexual victimization was especially troubling. In all, 11 girls (31 percent) reported multiple victimization incidents. Take Alicia, for example: 18 when we interviewed her, Alicia was first pressured at age 14 into unwanted sex by her boyfriend. Later, this

TABLE 4-1
Girls' Prevalence of Sexual Assault and Coercion (N = 35)

Have you ever been sexually assaulted, molested, or raped?	9 (26%)
Has anyone ever tried to sexually assault, molest, or rape you?	6 (17%)
Has anyone ever pressured you to have sex when you didn't want to?	13 (37%)
Has anyone ever had sex with you when you didn't want to, but you were unable to stop them because you were high or drunk?	3 (9%)
Has a group of men or boys made you have sex with them when you didn't want to but felt like you didn't have a choice or couldn't say no?	3 (9%)
Has your current/former boyfriend[a] ever pressured you to have sex with him when you didn't want to?	9 (26%)
Has your current/former boyfriend[a] ever made you have sex with him when you didn't want to?	2 (6%)
Has your current/former boyfriend[a] ever used physical force to make you have sex with him?	4 (12%)
Have you ever been sexually abused by someone in your family?	5 (14%)
Girls who answered "Yes" to one or more of these questions	19 (54%)
Girls who answered "Yes" to more than one of these questions[b] or reported multiple incidents in a single category	11 (31%)

[a] These questions were posed separately for current, last, and any former boyfriend. Responses are combined here.

[b] Follow-up questions asked for each question allowed for the removal of duplicate answers here. See note 3 in the text for further information.

same young man raped her and also arranged for his friends to "run a train" on her at his house. Then, when she was 16, a young man in the neighborhood had sex with her when she was drunk and high and unable to fend off his advances. Felicia was sexually abused by a family friend when she was 6 years old. She described being pressured into unwanted sex by young men in her neighborhood "a lot" and described two incidents, at ages 14 and 16, when she was drunk and high and thus unable to consent. Felicia also described witnessing several rapes, including in her neighborhood and at a hotel party. Nine additional girls described similar life experiences.

A great deal of research has examined young women's risks for sexual victimization and repeat victimization. Though my primary focus here is on the situational contexts of such events, our research can be used to illustrate how the young women in our sample correspond to previously identified risk factors. First, it is not race but racial inequality that increases young women's risks.[4] Specifically, it is youths' embeddedness in high-risk, high-crime communities.[5] Age also has an effect. The National Crime Victimization Survey (NCVS) consistently shows that adolescent girls and young women have the highest rates of rape victimization.[6] For adolescents, two constellations of factors have been identified as increasing risk for sexual victimization: participation in delinquency and previous experiences with abuse or other family problems.[7] These factors have also been identified as posing particular risks for revictimization.[8] Delinquency, for example, may expose young women to deviant peers who may be potential perpetrators, while traumatic or troubling family experiences can expose young women to high-risk men and also affect both coping abilities and social support.

So how did the young women's experiences in our study fit with previous research? Our sample already overrepresents the likelihood of these risk factors. As described in chapter 1, we selected youths for inclusion when they were at risk for or involved in delinquency. In all, 66 percent of the girls we interviewed reported having engaged in serious delinquency, including drug sales. Table 4-2 reveals that these young women were disproportionately represented among those who had experienced sexual victimization: 61 percent of girls who had engaged in serious delinquency reported sexual victimization, compared with 42 percent of girls without a history of serious delinquency. This was also the case for multiple victimization experiences: 39 percent of delinquent girls reported revictimization, compared with 17 percent of nondelinquent girls. Put another way, while 66 percent of young women reported involvement in serious delinquency, serious delinquents were 74 percent of those who experienced sexual victimization and 82 percent of those who experienced multiple victimizations.

Turning to problems within the family, the vast majority of young women (86 percent) reported at least one of the following: witnessing physical violence among adults in the household (54 percent), being physically abused by a family member (31 percent), a lot of alcohol use in the home (43 percent), a lot of drug use in the home (37 percent), and having a family member who had spent time in prison or jail (66 percent). Table 4-3 shows how the presence of such family problems correlated with experiences of sexual victimization. Only five girls reported none of these family problems. Among these girls, just one— Nykeshia—described having been the victim of a sexual assault. She had been raped several years earlier by her mother's then boyfriend, and neither she nor any young women in this category reported other experiences with sexual assault or coercion.[10]

While 86 percent of girls experienced family risks, a larger propor-

TABLE 4-2
Correlates of Girls' Sexual Victimization and
Revictimization with Delinquency

	Participation in Serious Delinquency (N = 23)	No History of Serious Delinquency (N = 12)
Sexual victimization	14 (61%)	5 (42%)
Multiple victimization incidents	9 (39%)	2 (17%)

TABLE 4-3
Correlates of Girls' Sexual Victimization and
Revictimization with Reported Family Problems

	No Family Problems (N = 5)	One or More Family Problems (N = 30)	Multiple (3+) Family Problems (N = 16)
Sexual victimization	1 (20%)	18 (60%)	9 (56%)
Multiple victimization incidents	0 (0%)	11 (37%)	7 (44%)

tion of girls who had experienced sexual violence (95 percent) came from families with at least one of the identified family risk factors. Interestingly, the number of family problems did not appear to have a cumulative impact on girls' initial risks for sexual victimization. In all, 60 percent of girls with one or more family problems, compared with 56 percent of girls with more than three family problems, reported a sexual victimization. In contrast, having multiple family problems was more strongly correlated with multiple experiences with sexual violence. In all, 44 percent of the girls in families with multiple problems had been repeat victims of sexual violence. In fact, of the 11 girls who experienced more than one incident of sexual violence, seven (64 percent) came from families with three or more family problems. Two came from families with two of these family risk factors, and just two came from families in which the only reported problem was having a family member who had spent time in prison or jail.

Because our sample is relatively small and nonrepresentative, I can't draw conclusive patterns from these findings. Nevertheless, these results suggest that some contextual factors are likely to increase girls' risks for victimization. In fact, not surprisingly, having multiple family problems was also correlated with participation in serious delinquency. Of the 16 girls who reported three or more family problems, 14 (88 percent) also had engaged in serious delinquency. Researchers have documented a number of ways in which these problems are interlinked. Family environments can themselves be criminogenic, but they can also push girls away from home and onto the streets with their peers, where exposure to delinquency and associated risks are more likely.[11] Moreover, a problematic family environment may decrease the extent of social support and hinder girls' coping abilities when sexually victimized, which can also contribute to the likelihood of repeat victimization.[12]

The research evidence is quite strong that previous experiences with victimization, including sexual abuse, heighten individuals' risk for future victimization.[13] Many studies have focused on how the effects of early sexual victimization can change the victim's behavior in ways that might increase later victimization risk. This includes a lowered sense of personal efficacy, feelings of powerlessness, low self-esteem, isolation, more insecure attachments, increased risk for drug and alcohol use, and learned expectancy (i.e., viewing coercion as a normal part of sexual interactions), as well as what researchers call "traumatic sexualization," resulting in increased sexual precociousness and risk taking.[14] However, sociologist Liz Grauerholz proposes an ecological model for understanding the problem of sexual revictimization. She argues that an exclusive focus on individual-level changes in victims can result in victim-blaming and also overlooks mediating contextual and ecological factors.[15]

In the case of young women in our sample, repeat victimization was particularly likely because they were living in high-crime neighborhoods where groups of adolescent boys and adult men often congregated unsupervised in public spaces. Thus, part of the risk for repeat victimization resulted from heightened exposure to potential victimizers. Some researchers argue that a victim-labeling process is also at play, such that potential offenders can identify young women who may be particularly vulnerable to mistreatment, either from specific knowledge of past interactions or from cues such as social isolation, marginalization, and limited personal efficacy.[16]

In chapter 3, I discuss how the various facets of sexual harassment contributed to this process. These included the proliferation of sexual rumors about girls' previous sexual behaviors and some young men's use of sexual harassment as a staging ground to test young women's ability and willingness to stand up for themselves. Next, I expand this analysis by examining the social contexts in which peer sexual coercion and sexual assault took place within youths' neighborhoods and the broader community.[17]

Contextual Features of Sexual Aggression against Girls

As shown in table 4-1, sexual violence took on a range of forms: from young women being pressured into unwanted sex, to more explicitly coercive forms, up to and including the threat or use of physical violence. For this reason, feminist scholars conceptualize sexual violence as existing on a continuum, with normative heterosexual sexual acts at one end and rape at the other. This is a useful conceptual tool, because it allows us to interrogate how normative constructions of sexuality are implicated in sexual violence.[18] For instance, the sexual double standard has shown little sign of abating in the last decades. While virginity is no longer expected for young women, they continue to be judged more harshly than males for having sex outside of a committed relationship, for having multiple sexual partners, and for early initiation into sex. Thus, young women are expected to be the "gatekeepers" of their sexuality, which limits their sexual autonomy in exchange for peer acceptance.[19] Young men, in contrast, are rewarded by their peers for sexual conquests and are encouraged to engage in sexual activities without emotional attachment. In fact, research has shown that the greater young men's attachment to these facets of masculinity construction, the greater their likelihood of engaging in sexual aggression.[20]

As I describe in earlier chapters, researchers have found that such masculinity constructions are heightened in urban disadvantaged communities. While the reasons for this are complex, researchers have linked the development and maintenance of heightened masculinity both to blocked opportunities for the achievement of other types of masculine rewards and to the dominance of male peer groups in such settings.[21] Importantly, adherence to such ideologies also means discounting young women's interpretations of sexual violence.[22] Sociologist Neil King argues that men's "certainty" about women's consent is based on patriarchal definitions of gender and sexuality built on the belief in male entitlement and constructed in concert with male peers.[23]

Thus, it is not surprising that none of the young men in our sample explicitly admitted to engaging in sexual violence. Just three boys (8 percent) said they had sex with a girl when she was too drunk or high to resist, and four (10 percent) admitted to pressuring their girlfriends into unwanted sex. Although 18 young men (45 percent) said they had "run trains" on girls, they defined such incidents as consensual. Altogether, nearly half of the young men we interviewed (48 percent) described involvement in sexual behaviors that researchers would classify as coercive or violent. Yet none of them saw their behaviors as sexual violence.[24]

"Persuasion," Coercion, and Sexual Compliance

Not surprisingly, then, a number of young men framed their own and other boys' actions as "persuasion." Tyrell explained, "I think it's easier to persuade girls than it is like for people to persuade dudes into doing stuff . . . like as far as sex or anything like that, you know." Of young men's behavior toward girls, he explained:

> They don't be like forcing 'em or like, "I'm gonna beat you up," you know what I'm saying, "[I'll] choke you or kill you if you don't do this." But you can easily talk to girls and have 'em thinking [that you care about them]. . . . You know how they heads [are. It's] that easy. . . . You just talk to 'em. You tell 'em what they wanna hear, they gonna give you what you want, thinking that you really care about them for real, but you really don't. You'll have 'em loving you, but you ain't even care about 'em.

Likewise, Shaun said, "I wouldn't say [we] make 'em have sex. [But we] run a game on 'em or something . . . convince her . . . just be talking." In these instances, young men were not engaged in sexual coercion per se, but they used manipulation techniques in adherence with the normative conceptions of masculine heterosexuality described earlier.

Bobby described a recent incident that was more coercive and clearly tied to male peer competition:

> We had went to a telly [hotel]. It was me, my brother, his girlfriend, and her lil' sister. We was all sharin' the same room with 'em. So I consider her as like a rat, which, I don't know, 'cause it just happened [because of] how I talked to her, you know what I'm saying. And she just up and gave it to me, you know what I'm saying, just that fast, so I don't know.[25]

In fact, Bobby described planning to pressure the young woman into sex in advance:

> Before we even got there, [my brother and I had a competition], "I bet I hit [have sex with] my gal before you do," you know what I'm saying. While he up there hittin' [his girlfriend] I'm like, "Aw, man, I can't let this go down like this." I be like, [to the girl], "Okay, what you wanna do while we up in here?" You know, the girl be actin' all scared to say something, be like, "I don't know." . . . I asked her, "Okay, what you wanna do, you wanna have sex?" She say, "I don't know." I say, "Do you? I just asked you." I say, "Do you?" She say, "I don't care."

Some researchers distinguish sexual coercion from sexual assault based on the techniques used to gain compliance. Maria Testa and Kurt H. Dermen, for example, define coercion as intercourse obtained through verbal or emotional pressure, while sexual assault is achieved by force or its threat. They argue that there are important conceptual distinctions between the two, in part because low self-esteem and low assertiveness are risk factors that predict women's risk for sexual coercion but not rape. Young women with these psychological or behavioral characteristics are then targeted by young men, who believe they will have an increased likelihood of success.[26] In fact, some research has found that verbal coercion, such as that described by Bobby, is the most common form of sexual aggression.[27] While there is evidence of a complex range of gendered reasons for compliance with unwanted sex, psychologist Nicola Gavey suggests that some women may choose to comply to avoid the threat of sexual assault.[28]

Ricky, who was critical of other young men's behaviors, explained that they often targeted girls they believed would be vulnerable, either because of their naiveté or because of their social circumstances: "A lot of times they try to find girls that ain't up to the level that they should be. I mean, they might be a little slow on how things go and how the streets work. And then they just prey on innocent people, really, you know what I'm sayin'. It's usually the ones that they know [are] vulnerable." Of social vulnerabilities, he explained:

> Say for instance [the girl's] mother might put 'em out [of the house], right? Put 'em out for like a week straight 'fore she'll let 'em back in. And they might need somewhere to sleep, 'cause it's cold or something.

And they feel like if somebody let 'em in, it's [sex] just something they suppose to do, you know. Or, [the guy decides], "Well, I'ma smoke this weed with her and I'ma drink this with her, and eventually we gonna do this [have sex]," you know. She ain't got nowhere to go. I mean, that's usually how it goes.

It is clear from Ricky's description that ecological and social contexts were thus critical for understanding the nature and risk of sexual violence.

Few of the young women we interviewed provided detailed narrative accounts of incidents in which they felt pressured into unwanted sex.[29] Sheron, however, described numerous instances of both sexual coercion and sexual violence. Just 15 years old when we interviewed her, Sheron had been sexually abused by her uncle when she was 13, and she reported having had 20 sexual partners in the short time since. Many of these were the result of coercion. She described having been pressured into unwanted sex by young men at her school a half a dozen times in the previous six months, and she had been gang raped twice in the last six months. Here she described her ambivalence about being pressured into sex by a former boyfriend:

This was my ex-boyfriend. And we were in the basement [at my auntie's house]. And I wanted to, but I didn't. But at the same time, you know, I felt that I ain't have no choice. 'Cause, you know, it's something I wanted. It's something I did, and I didn't want to have sex at that particular time. 'Cause I was in a relationship with somebody, but at the same time I still cared about him. And I just felt like, I was like, you know, what I got to lose? I ain't got no choice, you know, so I just did it.[30]

She also described being pressured by her current boyfriend, who used techniques identified by researchers as common in cases of sexual coercion in relationships:[31]

[My boyfriend] was just like, um, "Do you wanna have sex?" And I was like "No." And he was like "Why?" I said " 'Cause I don't want to." And he was like . . . "Then if I go home, I'm gonna do it to someone else." And just peer pressure, and I was just thinking about it, you know. I'm supposed to be his girlfriend and why, you know, why won't I have sex with him? He going home having sex with somebody else [if I don't]. So I felt that was a lot of pressure on me, him saying that [and so] I had sex with him.

Asked how all of her experiences with sexual coercion had affected her, Sheron explained, "I don't trust myself around so many males and having sex with them, so I've stopped it. I don't, I don't have sex with [anyone now] 'cause I can't trust myself around no male. . . . I don't trust their intentions."

Given the extent of her sexual victimization, Sheron's case was atypical. Nonetheless, her experiences and history distinctly illuminate the patterns I raised earlier about sexual revictimization. She came from a home with many traumatic aspects. In addition to the sexual abuse by her uncle, who was staying with her family at the time, she said she was physically abused as a child and witnessed adult violence in her household. She also described extensive drug use in the home and having family who had spent time in prison. Perhaps because of her family experiences, Sheron described ongoing participation in serious delinquency. Her repeated victimization resulted, in part, from her exposure to delinquent young men in the neighborhood.

In addition, it is clear that a victim-labeling process was present, given that she was repeatedly targeted by young men at her school. And by her own account, Sheron felt herself to have limited efficacy in her interactions with young men and felt she was too easily influenced by them. As discussed in chapter 5, her current boyfriend was also physically abusive. In addition, she told us that all of her friends had experienced sexual violence. Thus, Sheron seemed to view coercion and violence as an expected part of her interactions with young men—her reason for now trying to avoid them.

The number of sexual partners Sheron had in a matter of less than two years is also significant. In part, this number was high because of the sexual coercion she faced. Researchers have found a connection for adolescent girls between having multiple sexual partners and viewing young men as having control over the nature and terms of sexual interactions.[32] In fact, of the four girls who reported having had more than ten sexual partners (Alicia, LaSondra, and Cherise, in addition to Sheron), all reported multiple incidents of sexual aggression.[33]

Sexual Assault

Though much of the sexual violence perpetrated against young women fit the legal definition of rape, I focus here on those incidents young women themselves classified as rape or attempted rape.[34] Many young women reported deep concerns over adult men in their communities and were shaken up by their acts of sexual harassment, but LaSondra's report (described in chapter 2) was the only stranger rape we came across in our research. Instead, young women were more likely to describe sexual violence perpetrated by young adults who they came into contact with socially. This is not surprising, since most sexual assaults are perpetrated by acquaintances.[35] Janelle's experience, also described in chapter 2, was typical. Recall that she was hanging out at her friend's house, as was a young adult male. When her friend went to the store and Janelle was left alone with the man, he held her down and raped her.

Other incidents had similarly innocuous beginnings. Cherise described regularly hanging out with a young adult in his mid 20s who lived in her neighborhood. She said, "all of my friends come out and used to play Nintendo games, come over [to his house], watch TV, you know." She described herself as somewhat naïve at the time, "I mean, at that age, I was 14, and I . . . you know, I didn't really know nothing for real." She said because the man was "short" and hung out with adolescents, "I really didn't think about [how old he was]." Looking back, she explained, "well I supposedly went with [dated] this man . . . [but] all I really [did was ask], 'Can I get a dollar?' here, 'Can I get a dollar?' there." Then, when she was hanging out at his house by herself, he raped her:

> I was over at his house watching *Xena*, I remember exactly what was on, *Xena*. And this guy forced himself on me. He forced, or whatever you want to call it, he forced himself on me. And I felt so scared, so I just let him do it. . . . I [tried to resist] at first, but I felt, it was like, when he made like a facial expression I was too scared. I mean, I felt like if I was to tell him, "No, stop!" maybe he would've hit me or beat me up or did something to me . . . so I just went along with him. And that was when I lost my virginity.

Cherise's ambivalent allusion to the perception that "I supposedly went with this man" provides evidence of the predatory nature of many adult male/adolescent female relationships. She was young and trusting, and the man—11 years her senior—capitalized on her naiveté in order to sexually assault her.

Lisa, who was 17 when we interviewed her, described an attempted rape when she was 13. As with Janelle and Cherise, she described the perpetrator as a young adult, in this case around age 19:

> It was Fourth of July and we was with these boys [who were] my cousin's friends. . . . It was me and my cousin and him and [my cousin's] friend. And so we was just ridin' with them all day, ridin' with them. We was kickin' it or whatever. And then his car broke, so he had to go get his car fixed. I'm like, "Well I'm fina catch the bus home," 'cause . . . my cousin was fina walk down to my auntie house but I wanted to go home. . . . I said, "Do you have a dollar so I can get on the bus?" He like, "Yeah, I got a dollar. You gotta come get it." His house like right across the street.

Lisa said she waited for a few minutes on the stoop of the young man's house, but "he up there for a long time" so she finally went inside. She explained, "I didn't think the boy would be something like that, because I just, I know him. So I ain't even trip off of him like that. . . . I didn't think he would come at me like that." She continued:

> I'm sittin' on the couch, I'm lookin' in his house, I'm lookin' at his stuff [while I'm waiting]. So he come in, he like, "I ain't got it, I ain't got it." Well, so I'm fina go, so I'm walkin' downstairs, [and] he gon' pull out a gun. And I started crying. And he started—I had on this lil' shirt, I had on some real lil' biddy shorts and the shirt to match it, you zip it up and it was like a blue jean—and he was tryin' to unzip my shirt. And I'm just screamin'. . . . [He's telling me], "Bitch, shut up! Shut the F [fuck] up!" Just kept [stutters as she recounts], steady, steady cursing me, [pause] unzipping my shirt. . . . I was screaming and cryin'. . . . And then the people outside . . . it was a four family flat . . . they was like, "Open the door! Open that door! Open the door!" And the lady finally got the door open and I just ran out of there.

Lisa later told her cousin what had happened, and together they called the police. She explained that when the police arrived, they discovered the man "was already wanted. . . . He got a warrant out for his arrest . . . [so] he got locked up anyway."

Yvonne's experience was similar, but with the added complication that she was "high as a kite" when it happened. As with Lisa, it was only through the fortuitous intervention of others that her sexual assault was prevented:

> I was with my cousin and her best friend [at her best friend's house]. Her best friend's daddy a crackhead, and I don't like being in those types of environments because when I was younger I had to deal with that, and that's a part of my life I'd rather not even go back to. . . . We was over there or whatever, and we was all in the room. And her daddy wouldn't give her no money, so she all upset, crying or whatever. And of course, being the friend that [my cousin] is, you're going to go and comfort your friend. So they left out the room and started talking. Um, a dude, he was like about 19 or whatever, cocky, he came into the room or whatever, and I was high as a kite. I was high, I was drunk . . . and it was like, I really couldn't defend myself. But if my cousin wouldn't have walked in the room, it would've happened. And I know it would've, because I was out like that.

Yvonne continued, describing what happened:

> He was like, "What's up baby girl?" talking all, trying to talk all sweet to me. And I was looking at him . . . and I was like, "Nigga, what do you want?" And he was rubbing on my leg, and I was like, "No!" I couldn't really like take him, I was so drunk. I was so drunk and um, he was . . . he got to rubbing all on me, and finally I was like, I can't keep on fighting him. . . . He was pulling at my shirt or whatever and I'm like, "What you doing?" and I was just like dazing and dozing off. And my cousin walked in the room while he trying to take my clothes off or whatever, and he had me all up on the bed. And she was like, "What you doing?" You know what I'm saying, jumped on him or whatever. She was slapping me, "Wake up, wake up! It's time to go home, wake up, wake up." Trying to get me conscious or whatever, bring water in there for me. I was throwing up.

The contextual similarities in each of these young women's accounts are striking. Most alluded to or described themselves as young and naïve at the time, and—as Ricky described—young adult men preyed on these vulnerabilities. As early teens at the time, the young women were attempting to socialize in their communities and were as yet un-aware of the dangers these older men could hold for them. An additional similarity was that the perpetrators either explicitly attempted (as in Lisa's case) or seized on the opportunity to get the young women alone. Such isolation strategies are common with acquaintance rape.[36] Given the norms of nonintervention documented in chapter 2, Lisa was particularly fortunate that a neighbor took considerable effort to intercede on her behalf. And Yvonne benefited from the timing of her cousin's return. Although drugs and alcohol played a heavy role in many young women's experiences with sexual violence, in hotel and other party settings, such interventions were far less forthcoming.

Role of Parties, Alcohol, and Drugs in Sexual Aggression

Numerous studies have identified the linkages between alcohol use and sexual violence. Much of this research has focused on college populations, and especially fraternities, as these are often unsupervised social contexts in which elevated substance use takes place and risks for sexual violence can be especially high.[37] Importantly, sociologists A. Ayres Boswell and Joan Z. Spade argue that it is not alcohol consumption per se that elevates risk for sexual violence; instead, the characteristics of the settings play a prominent role in promoting behaviors that foster a climate conducive to sexual aggression.[38] In their comparative study of college fraternities, for example, they found that parties in those fraternities with high risk for sexual violence often had skewed gender ratios and limited social interaction between the males and females present, and they were dominated by heavy drinking. In addition, men tended to treat women "less respectfully, engaging in jokes, conversations, and behaviors that degraded women."[39]

Likewise, researchers Patricia Yancey Martin and Robert A. Hummer identified key features of high-risk masculinity in such settings, including the valorization of violence, competition among men (as with Bobby's earlier account), and the use of alcohol as a weapon to reduce women's resistance to unwanted sex.[40] H. Harrington Cleveland and his colleagues argue that alcohol provides multiple functions for men's enactment of coercive sexual acts. In particular, alcohol use by women "allows men to label them as easy or loose . . . providing [these men] with the ability to rationalize their behavior. . . . Moreover, alcohol may reduce a woman's ability to detect risk cues . . . and may lessen the effectiveness of female resistance to male aggression."[41]

As discussed, some young men in disadvantaged neighborhoods demonstrate a heightened concern with masculinity constructions that include rewards for demonstrations of physical prowess and sexual conquest. In addition, particularly given the few social alternatives available in their communities, partying held a prominent place in these adolescent and young adults' social lives. This was particularly the case for those involved in delinquency. In all, 95 percent of the boys and 74 percent of the girls we interviewed described having used alcohol or drugs. More than two-thirds of the boys (68 percent) and one-half of the girls (51 percent) described consuming alcohol or drugs in the past six months. Not surprisingly, all of the boys who described engaging in sexual incidents that researchers classify as aggressive, as well as all of the girls who had experienced multiple victimizations, described using alcohol or drugs. Much of this substance use took place at parties or get-togethers, held unsupervised in the homes of adolescents or young adults or in hotel rooms rented for this purpose.

I am certainly not arguing here that all sexual activities taking place in these contexts are coercive or violent. It is likely that some girls engaged in consensual sexual activities when they were at parties. One problem, however, is that it is difficult to establish genuine consent in such circumstances. In addition, youths reported that some young men purposely strategized to get young women high or drunk in order to have sex with them. Such efforts are undeniably coercive in nature. Other times, like Yvonne's earlier account, young women were unconscious or nearly unconscious. In such situations, they were clearly unable to consent, making these incidents sexual assaults.

Not surprisingly, young men were most likely to view sexual interactions in these settings as consensual. Young women were more likely to interpret incidents as consensual when they were witnesses and the girl in question was either a stranger or a casual acquaintance. This facilitated viewing the girls' behaviors as victim-precipitated. Janelle explained:

> We don't go too much to house parties, but we go to a couple depending on whose party it is. . . . The guys, they respect me, uh, but there's

always a certain female that's, you know, easy—however you want to say it—and they'll react to them a whole different way than they would me because of how they carry theyselves and how I carry myself.[42]

Asked whether the young men took advantage of such girls, Janelle elaborated, "they don't have to. They don't have to take advantage of those girls, they just tell them what they want and that female's gonna give them what they want." She said such young women got high or drunk on their own, without prodding from young men. Asked why they behaved that way, Janelle surmised, "really, I think a lot of girls are like that because their parents don't teach them no better, you know . . . or just because they want to be well known and they think . . . that's how they're gonna get well known."

Likewise, Ricky—who earlier described that young men often preyed on vulnerable girls—also clarified:

Then you got some girls, though, that's just mainly what they do it for. That mainly why they get high. Some of 'em just fiendin' for sex. It's just something they do. That's what you would call something like a hoodrat, or a project chick, or something like that. You know, a chicken-head or something. Girls that just like gettin' dogged out.

With the introduction of crack cocaine, ethnographers identified the term "chickenhead" as one of many used in drug economies to refer to women who exchange drugs for sexual acts, most notably oral sex.[43] It is not clear if this was Ricky's specific referent, though if so, it is notable that he defined their behavior not as desperation for drugs but desperation for sex.

Other young men did not make the distinctions Ricky did between vulnerable girls and hoodrats and simply focused on young women they classified in the latter category. For instance, Walter said that young men weren't taking advantage of girls at parties, " 'cause girls, they'll sit there and dance on you. They'll come to you and dance. But then when a girl get drunk, then they act a whole lot of crazy. But then the dudes be drunk at the same time, so you really can't say." And Cooper surmised, "she set herself out like that."

Destiny described a recent incident she witnessed, and she firmly believed the girl had been a willing participant:

> *Destiny*: It's like, it was a group of us, and they brought some friends, and people brought some friends. And we was just sittin' there chilling, and the girl drunk too much and stuff and was lettin' them feel all over her and stuff.
>
> *Interviewer*: Did anybody say anything to them?
>
> *Destiny*: Man, I mean they was drunk. I mean, they wasn't drunk, but they was high too. But they know what they was doin'. And to me, she know what they was doin' to her. I don't care what nobody say, she knew how to stop that. . . . I don't care what nobody say, "She was too drunk"—she wasn't too drunk to know that that boy was feelin' on her. We drunk the same [amount] and smoked, and nobody—I was like myself.

Later in the conversation, she continued, "she wants it. I mean, it ain't like she was just [passed] out and they done did that. She's up, talkin' like me and you talkin'. So she want them to do it to her." When Destiny next saw the young women, she was skeptical of the girl's claim that she didn't know what had happened: "She was like, 'I ain't know, I ain't know!' I was like, 'How you ain't know when you were talkin' like everybody else?' Man, I don't care, I still think she want them to do that to her."

In other cases, youths believed that alcohol and drug consumption impaired young women's judgment, either by getting them to do things they otherwise would not, or because they were not clearly aware of what was happening. Shaun explained, "you [both] get drunk or whatever, she be feeling like doing the same thing. Just probably, she probably wouldn't feel that same way if she wasn't drunk or whatever." And Tyrell surmised, "like a girl . . . get too drunk or whatever, and then don't realize what she doing or whatever. And they got on a little skirt or whatever, dudes feeling all on 'em. Whatever. Shit, they don't be saying nothing."

Research has shown that those women most at risk for sexual coercion are also likely to have sex-related expectancies associated with alcohol use. For instance, they are more likely to report that, when drinking, they engage in riskier sexual practices and sexual behaviors that they would not engage in when sober. Such externalizing beliefs are consistent with other correlates of sexual coercion risk, including lower self-esteem and less assertiveness or efficacy.[44] Thus, there is evidence that some girls are at heightened risk for engaging in the types of sexually provocative behaviors youths described. Nonetheless, their behaviors should not be viewed out of the contexts in which they took place, including the presence of young men eager to capitalize on their reduced sense of self-control.

Moreover, there was strong evidence in our data that some young men did not simply capitalize on girls' drunkenness but purposefully cultivated it. They did so not just to get girls to "loosen up" and be more willing to have sex but, in some cases, to incapacitate them. Dawanna explained, "there's been a time that some females drink and then smoke, and [get] mixed up, and sometimes they don't know what they doin'. . . . Some of the males would try to, you know, take advantage of 'em 'cause they drunk." Lisa was nearby when a young man she knew worked to get a girl too intoxicated to resist his sexual advances:

He had a blunt [marijuana cigarette] . . . [and] he steady [telling the girl] "Smoke this, smoke this! Drink this, drink this!" and my sister say, "He tryin' to get her drunk, he tryin' to get her high so they could do something." He just kept on doing [that]. He had some Cisco[45]— "Drink this, drink this!" You don't give her no Cisco like that [unless it's to take advantage of her]. And then he smokin' the blunt with her, [but] he let her smoke most of it.

And Terence explained:

I've known [some of my friends] to put they hands on a female before. I wouldn't, I'm not saying that they have exactly done it [raped a girl], but I wouldn't put it past 'em. . . . I wouldn't put it past a couple of 'em . . . just by they attitude. . . . I've seen them drinkin', smokin' with females before they had sex with 'em.

Like Ricky, Terence was adamant in his disapproval. He said when his friends bragged about such incidents, "I tell 'em, you know, 'Go on.' 'Cause they know how I am. I don't condone none of it for real. If you gon' talk about it, don't talk about it with me." This was why Ricky insisted that "participatin' in those parties and stuff" posed the greatest risk to young women: "Dances, hotel parties and stuff like that, [girls] have to be extra careful in stuff like that."

Even a few young women described having male friends or relatives who bragged about such behaviors. Ramara said one of her friends "will say, uh, 'I'ma have a party and I'ma get so-and-so drunk and I'ma see if I can hit [have sex with] her,' and you know, stuff like that. I be like, 'Ok, that's all on you.'" She thought he engaged in such behavior because "he conceited . . . he think it's all about him." She explained, "he know he doing wrong. He say, 'I know that, I know that. But it's fun!'"

Likewise, Tisha often witnessed or heard about her brother and his friends' sexual coercion of girls:

> I mean, I done seen them. You know, they'll go over, like they'll be over my house or whatever, they'll pick up my little brother then they'll pick up some girls over there where they at. Get them messed up or whatever so they can try to do it to 'em. Then they talk about it all day long.

Asked to describe a recent incident, Tisha laughed and said, "they probably doin' something like that right now." Then she explained:

> We was all sittin' over in front of my daddy house or whatever, some lil' girls came down the street, they started talkin' to 'em or whatever. They had hooked up with 'em or whatever. They came back over there that night and they was sitting on the front, then like—the back of my daddy house, it's just like, it's a apartment building, six lil' apartments. On the back of it, it's like six little porches or whatever. They tried to [*laughs*] take the girls over on the porch . . . tried to do her [have sex with her] on the porch.

Shauntell, who was just 12 when we interviewed her, witnessed her cousin rape a young woman at a party:

> [We were] at a get together . . . [and] the girl, she got high and drunk. And she was just sittin' there on the couch just chillin' listen to music and my cousin told her to come here. She got up and went to him. He was like, "Come sit here with me for a minute." She was like, "For what?" He said, "Come here." . . . She said, "Well, why she can't come in here with me?" . . . He said, "Well, come here Shauntell." So I went with him [too]. And uh, we went down there . . . in the basement. . . . And my cousin said, "[Shauntell] can sit right there." I sat there. At first [the girl] likin' it, but when he started takin' off his clothes and taking off her clothes, she start tellin' him to stop. And I'll look, I be like,

"Man, don't do that man." He was like, "Shauntell, go upstairs." She was like, "Naw, Shauntell, don't leave me." . . . So I just sat there, closed my eyes and covered my ears. And he did [it] with her. . . . All I know is I just kept hearing her say stop.

Shauntell's cousin later told her that he had purposely gotten the girl drunk to coerce her into sex in retaliation for her earlier rejection of his advances: "He said that she wanted it and she deserved it. . . . He was like, 'Because she was comin' on to me before we got to the party, and [then] she tried to front me out in front of my boys, and that's what she get.'" Shauntell described the experience as "scary. 'Cause I was imaginin', I was just thinking, what if that was me in that position?"

Kristy described barely escaping being raped at a party when she was passed out: "There was a lot of drinking and we were using some drugs. I had passed out. So like I'm coming to, I seen myself somewhere I know I shouldn't be and [with a guy I] hardly even know. So I began fighting my way up, you know, put up a little fight." Kristy said she left the party and went "to a relative's house [to] sober off a little bit." Then she "told a true friend, and we went and retaliated." She and her friends "jumped him," but "jumping the dude got us into a little bit more trouble than we imagined. 'Cause he called the police and, well, two of my friends got assault charges."

Finally, I noted earlier that researchers have found that in party settings where masculinity constructions are heightened, young men also engage in conversations and behaviors further degrading to women. In addition to the types of sexual coercion and violence examined in this section, two additional incidents we learned about are noteworthy in this regard. Dawanna said that she "hang[s] around mostly dudes." She described leaving a party with them, along with a girl who "was so intoxicated that, you know, she didn't care what she was doin'." While Dawanna rode with her friends "to take her home," one of her friends had sex with the girl: "She just yellin' out his name and then all of a sudden she just took off her clothes and junk, and he just, they was just at it." Rather than simply having sex with the drunken girl, Dawanna's friend "threw her clothes outside . . . of the car and drove her home and laid her down in the front [yard naked]. . . . He threw her clothes out and took her home like that." Dawanna felt bad for the girl and covered her with "the extra shirt that I had on." Of her friend, however, her reaction was just to tell him, "You trippin'!"

Lisa also witnessed the degradation of a young woman by a friend of her boyfriend's: "[He'll be like], 'Let's go to the liquor store, let's do this,' he'll take [the girls and] they'll get drunk. So the other night, they got drunk, they got real drunk. He peed on this girl, made her go to his house, take a shower, then he had sex with her." She elaborated:

> We was all sittin' around my boyfriend car or whatever, they drinkin' or whatever. I'm in the car, 'cause I'm ready to go. So they drinkin' or whatever. I don't know, I hear them laughin' or whatever and [makes mocking noises]. I turn, he done peed on the girl. I'm like, "Come here, he done peed on her! He pissed on her!" I'm like, "No, he did not just pee on that girl!" They like, "Yes he did!" She like, "Uh uh." . . . She didn't know he was fina pee on her, she didn't know. But he peed on her, everybody laughed, it wasn't nothing she could do. . . . Then he like, "Come on baby, you want me to take you, you can go take a shower at my house. Come on, come on baby." She was just like, "Uh uh," but she went anyway.

Lisa appeared to take the incident in stride, explaining, "see, that's just how they do girls. That's just how his friends are with girls." Ironically, she believed she was insulated from such behaviors because of her boyfriend: "They figure, well hey, this Ronnie's girl and we gon' respect her." Of the young woman, she argued, "all of them girls out there, down there where they stay, that's the way they like to be treated, 'cause that's where they head at."

"Running Trains" on Girls

A final form of sexual aggression all too common in our research was the phenomenon of "running trains" on girls. Youths used this phrase to refer to incidents that involved two or more young men engaging in penetrative sexual acts with a single young woman. Researchers typically classify such incidents as gang rape, because it is difficult to establish consent when an individual girl is outnumbered by multiple male participants. However, as mentioned earlier, young men viewed these events as consensual. Nearly one-half (45 percent) of the boys we interviewed described having engaged in trains. In fact, five boys—Bobby,

Kevin, Lamont, Shaun, and Wayne—described multiple incidents in the past six months.

"Running trains" was correlated with participation in serious delinquency in our sample. Of the 18 young men who described running trains on girls, 14 (78 percent) also reported participation in serious delinquency.[46] In fact, the five boys who described perpetrating multiple incidents were actively involved in serious delinquency at the time, and all five were involved in gangs. The three young women in our sample who were victims of gang rape were also involved in serious delinquency, and all three said there was a lot of gang activity in their neighborhoods. Thus, their immediate community context and participation in neighborhood activities with delinquent peers exposed them to potential perpetrators.[47]

Numerous studies "locate group rape in the contexts of broader structural violence, including profound marginalization and diverse forms of deprivation" such as those found in our respondents' communities.[48] As sociologist Karen Franklin argues:

> Although young men may experience temporary powerlessness due to their age, [and] more long-term powerlessness due to their economic class and/or race, they still maintain relative superiority due to their sex. Group rape . . . [is a method] of demonstrating this male power over individuals with less social power.[49]

In addition, however, such events are also disproportionately found in more privileged settings, such as fraternities, athletic teams, and the military.[50] What these disparate sites have in common is that they are male-dominated contexts, each with preoccupations with exaggerated masculinity, including a strong sense of male superiority and sexual entitlement. Anthropologist Peggy Reeves Sanday argues that what makes such settings ripe for group sexual misconduct is the emphasis on "exaggerated male bonding, dominance behaviors, rejection of dependency, devaluation of things feminine, and repression of female input."[51]

Group processes also play a central role in gang rape. The enactment of such violence increases solidarity and cohesion among groups of young men, and there is also a behavioral contagion effect. Participants' actions escalate in the process of enacting the event with their male peers, and responsibility for their joint actions is diffused. The victim has symbolic status and is treated as an object. And performance plays a central role, "as group rapists ritualistically take turns, converse about taking turns, watch each other, and engage in simultaneous sex[ual acts] with victims."[52] Lamont's account of his experiences running trains on girls exemplifies both the use of the girl as an object and the mutual performance among male peers:

> I mean, one be in front, one be in back. You know sometimes, you know like, say, you getting in her ass and she might be sucking the other dude dick. Then you probably get her, you probably get her to suck your dick while he get her in the ass. Or he probably, either I'll watch, and so she sucking your dick, or while you fuck her in the ass. It, I mean, it's a lot of ways you can do it.

Not surprisingly, research has found that gang rape incidents are more likely than individual rape incidents to target victims who are strangers or casual acquaintances (which facilitates the use of the girl as an object) and involve younger victims and perpetrators. In addition, these events tend to have more severe sexual assault outcomes, including multiple penetrative acts (i.e., oral and anal, as well as vaginal penetration). Because of the threat inherent in the presence of multiple offenders, there tends to be less victim resistance (which young men may choose to interpret as consent), and gang rape incidents are more likely to be successfully completed than individual rape attempts.[53]

As noted earlier, young men defined girls' participation in trains as consensual.[54] For instance, Wayne was adamant that girls agreed to have trains run on them: "It don't be like we just intoxicated or intoxicate her and then do it. Don't nobody really want to have sex with a drunk girl anyway. It's like um, they be cool with it, you know." He suggested that young women did so because they wanted the young men to like them: "They [hang out] with us, they like us. It's like, they want friends, you know, and it's like, it's just something we do. . . . I don't feel that I be takin' advantage of them."

In fact, a few young men described the young women as willing and even eager participants. Frank recounted a recent incident:

> There's this one girl, she a real, real freak. . . . She wanted me and my friend to run a train on her. I was like, it's, whatever. I went to go get him, we went back to her house. . . . [Beforehand], we was at the park,

hopping and talking about it and everything. I was like, "Man, dawg, I ain't hitting her from the back." Like, "She gonna mess up my dick." . . . He like, "Oh, I got her from the back dude." So we went up there . . . [and] she like, "Which one you all hitting me from the back?" [I'm] like, "There he go, right there. I got the front." She's like, "Okay." And then he took off her clothes, pulled his pants down. I didn't, just unzipped mine 'cause I was getting head. She got to slurping me. I'm like, my partner back there 'cause we was in the dark so I ain't see nuttin'. He was back, I just heard her [making noises]. I'm like, "Damn girl, what's wrong with you?" [More noises] [I'm like], "You hitting her from the back?" He's like, "Yeah, I'm hitting it."[55]

Likewise, Robert described a girl encouraging him and his friends to run a train on her for his birthday:

She came over and I was throwing a birthday party, you know. And she just told me, she asked me, did I want my birthday present? You know, I said yes. So she said, "Come on," then she told me to bring them two [friends] and I bring two of my other partners. And we went upstairs and we ran a train on her.

However, some of young men's accounts—even when they argued "running trains" was consensual—revealed evidence to suggest the incidents were experienced by the girls as coercive or threatening.[56] The following conversation with Terence is illustrative:

Terence: It was some girl that my friend had knew for a minute, and he, I guess he just came to her and asked her, "Is you gon' do everybody?" or whatever and she said "Yeah." So he went first and then, I think my other partna went, then I went, then it was like two other dudes behind me. . . . It was at [my friend's] crib.
Interviewer: Were you all like there for a get together or party or something?
Terence: It was specifically for that for real, 'cause he had already let us know that she was gon' do that, so.
Interviewer: So it was five boys and just her?
Terence: Yeah. . . .
Interviewer: And so he asked her first, and then he told you all to come over that day?

Terence: We had already came over. 'Cause I guess he knew she was already gon' say yeah or whatever. We was already there when she got there.

Interviewer: Did you know the girl?

Terence: Naw, I ain't know her, know her like for real know her. But I knew her name or whatever. I had seen her before. That was it though. . . .

Interviewer: So when you all got there, she was in the room already?

Terence: Naw, when we got there, she hadn't even got there yet. And when she came, she went in the room with my friend, the one she had already knew. And then after they was in there for a minute, he came out and let us know that she was gon', you know, run a train or whatever. So after that, we just went one by one.

By Terence's own account, the young woman arrived at a boy's house that she knew and may have been interested in. Waiting for her on her arrival were four additional young men whom she did not know or know well. And they had come in advance specifically for the purpose of running a train on her. Terence did not consider the possibility that the young woman may have felt threatened or that she hadn't freely consented. Instead, because his friend said "she was down" for it, Terence took his turn and left.

There were similar inconsistencies in Tyrell's account:

This girl was just like, I ain't even know her, but like I knew her 'cause I had went to work [where she did] last year. . . . Then my boy, when he started working there, he already had knew her, 'cause he said he had went to a party with her last year. And he was gonna have sex with her then, but . . . [her] grandmamma came home or something, so they ain't get to do it. So one day he was just like, we was all sitting watching this movie [at work[57]] and it was real dark or whatever. And she had come in there or whatever, and he was just talking to her, and he was like, "Let's all go 'head and run a train on you." She was like, "What?" And she started like, 'You better go on." Then, like, [he said], "For real, let's go over to my house." And then, you know what I'm saying, she was like, "Naw."

Later that day, Tyrell and his friend were leaving work and saw the girl "walking over there to the bus stop." His friend invited the girl over to his house, and she agreed to go. Tyrell admitted, "I think she liked him," and this was the reason she came over. However, because they had previously introduced the idea of running a train on her, Tyrell and his friend decided that her consent to go to his house was consent to have a train run on her. The discussion continued:

> *Interviewer*: Do you think she really wanted to do it?
> *Tyrell*: I can't really say. 'Cause at first she was like laughing and stuff, like, "Don't!" But we didn't pressure her. I didn't say nothing to her for the rest of the [work] day. I probably talked to her, but I say nothing about like that. And then she just came with us, so I mean, she had to want to.

According to Tyrell, the fact that he and his friend did not mention running a train on the girl again during the day they spent at work together meant they had not "pressured" her. Apparently it didn't occur to him that their silence on the issue allowed the girl to interpret the earlier comments as innocuous. Instead, he insisted that "she knew."[58] Of what happened once they got to his friend's house, Tyrell's account became a bit more murky: "I just remember—'cause I was high—I remember we had went in there . . . and I [put a] CD on. Then he was like, "So, what's up?" Said, "You better get on." Tyrell described the girl's clothes being removed but was vague about whether she or his friend removed them. Of the incident itself, he continued:

> I just can't even remember, I remember next thing I know we was having sex with her. I ain't kiss her or nothing though, I ain't kiss her though. . . . She was doing oral sex on me while he'll be having sex with her from the back. Then I had sex with her from the back while she giving him oral sex.

His account of the young woman's behavior afterward also belies his insistence that she had engaged willingly. According to Tyrell, "she missed like a week of work after that." And while he believed the girl liked his friend before the incident, he said, "I know she didn't like him after that. . . . She don't even talk to him at all. Every time they see each other they'll argue." This was exacerbated because when Tyrell and his friend returned "to work the next day, he telling everybody. I'm like, 'Damn, you shouldn't do the girl like that.' He telling everybody." In addition, Tyrell said "she go to my cousin's school now, and she be talking all stuff like, 'I hate your cousin!' But I don't care, I mean I don't even care. She shouldn't have did that." Asked whether he thought she felt bad about it, the conversation continued:

> *Tyrell*: I can't even say. I don't even know her like that. I really can't say. She do that kinda stuff all the time.
> *Interviewer*: She does?
> *Tyrell*: No. I'm just saying. I don't know. If she don't she probably did feel bad, but if she do she probably wouldn't feel bad. . . . But if she didn't really wanna do it, she shouldn't have did it.

Notice Tyrell's inability to take the point of view of the young woman, even with strong evidence that she was both traumatized and angry about what happened. He slipped easily into noting that "she do that kinda stuff all the time," but when pressed, he conceded that he had no basis on which to draw such a conclusion. Nonetheless, he placed the onus of responsibility for avoiding having a train run on her squarely on the girl, once again overlooking the fact that being isolated and outnumbered likely affected her perceived ability to do so.

Sheron's experience was similar to the incident Terence described participating in. In this case, however, her ex-boyfriend brought his friends to her house. She explained:

> He called . . . and be like, "Is somebody there . . . can I come over?" So one night I was like, "Yeah." So um, he comes and brings all his friends with him, and I'm like, you know. We went together, but we had broke up, and he came in the room and we did whatever [had sex] and then it was dark in there. So somebody else, I saw the door and somebody else came in there. And they are just like, "Well, if you gonna do it to him, then you have to have sex with me too." And I was like, "Why?" And he was like, "Well, if you don't have sex with me, then you gonna have to give me oral sex." So I knew that I wasn't gonna do that and that. And [my ex-boyfriend] said, "We not gonna leave until you have sex with him." So I feel that, you know, I ain't have no other choice. . . . I guess they planned it or whatever.

To Sheron, the incident was definitely sexual coercion. While she willingly had sex with her ex-boyfriend, whom she still cared about, she did not consent to sex with his friend but acquiesced because she was out-numbered and pressured. This is in keeping with research that finds women are less likely to physically resist gang rape because they fear an escalation of violence if they refuse. Her ex-boyfriend and his friends planned the assault. He first made sure she was alone in the house, then took her by surprise by bringing along several male friends. She said the incident "made me feel bad. 'Cause just . . . he'll let his friend, you know, have sex with me, his ex-girlfriend, [who] he say he care about."

Cherise's experience of gang rape occurred at a party, after she "got drunk," perhaps had GHB slipped into her drink, and passed out. She explained:

> They raped me. Came home, don't know how I got home. I know I was in a car though. And [when I] woke up, [my] privacy was swolled. I knew they had did something. They put something in my drink, maybe to make me forget. And the only [way] that I did know was because my privacy was swolled. . . . I don't remember nothing about it. That's the bad thing about it. I don't remember nothing. All I remember is my privacy was swoll.

Like Kristy, Cherise responded to the incident by getting a group of young men—in this case, her cousins—to retaliate. Once they got to her house, she called the young men she believed responsible and invited them over. She explained:

> I believe the reason they came over there was because they know they put something in my drink and they thought I didn't remember about it. Maybe they was planning on doing it again. So, we called them over there and they got beat down. Beat down! That's the good thing.

The party context heightened young women's risks for individual sexual assaults, and it also heightened their risk for gang rape. Accord-ing to Ricky, "that happens all the time, *all* the time." He continued:

> I mean, it was an incident when we went to a party like two weeks ago. I mean, this guy brought his girlfriend. And she told him before they even came, "I'm goin' home after the party." Don't expect something [e.g., sex] you not gettin', in other words. . . . And [so] he got her drunk and high and told her he was carrying her home. And [instead he] took

her to the hotel and let three or four of his other friends be with her too. And, I mean, when she came to him about it, he smack[ed] her. [*long pause, disapproving laugh*] That's the type of stuff that go on, man.

Alicia also described an incident that occurred when she and two of her friends went to a hotel to party with three young adult men. She explained, "we didn't think they would try to do nothing like that . . . they tried to talk to us, but we looked at them like big brothers and stuff. . . . We 16, they like 21." All three of the girls were drinking and smoking marijuana. When one of Alicia's friends got sick and began throwing up, one of the young men offered to take her and Alicia home. "So we left out the room, me and my friend. My other friend was still in there [with two of the men]. And they close the door, he was all messing with her and she say, 'Why don't you all quit playing!' And they was still messing with her, she was like, 'Why don't you all quit, why ain't y'all quit! . . . Stop, stop!' "

Alicia heard enough commotion to be concerned. However, the young man who had offered to drive her and her friend home tried to get her to leave her friend behind:

> [He] was like, "Come on." We got in the car . . . [but] we didn't wanna leave our friend. We was like, "Wait a minute, we gotta wait on her." . . . He kept saying, "Whatever happens tonight just happens." So they weren't tripping off it. I'm the only one tripping off it. They like, "Whatever happens happens."

Fortunately for her friend, Alicia refused to leave without her. Though she was concerned about going back "up in that room and let them try and do nothing to me," she went back, knocked on the door and "asked them to stop messing with her." The young men then opened the door and "they took us home." Alicia was surprised when a little later that night, these same young men "came back and had blow[ed the horn] . . . and wanted us to come back down 'cause they was gonna go back to the hotel. . . . We was like, no. We ain't going with them."

One final gang rape incident merits discussion. This case was unique, in that it was instigated by a young woman seeking revenge on a girl with whom she had a long-standing conflict and also because of the extreme and public nature of the event. Felicia was a witness to the incident and said it began because a friend of hers had a fight with a girl at school some months earlier and was expelled as a consequence. Felicia's friend "told me that if she ever seen her again, she was gonna make sure that she regret it." She continued:

> It was on prom night . . . [and] somebody invited the girl up to our hotel [party]. . . . My homegirl . . . realized that it was the girl that . . . got her put out of school. She um, [threatened the girl] . . . and told her that if she didn't give all the dudes in the room a blow job she was gonna drop her [off the balcony]. So she got down, she gave all the dudes in the room blow jobs. And um, one of the boys stuck his finger up in her and was like, "Well, she's a virgin, who wants to sleep with her?" She was like, she wasn't no virgin and he was like, he don't care, she was tight and [he] want to sleep with her. She said "No" and he smacked her and tossed her up [had sex with/raped her].

Felicia said though there was a large crowd present, no one attempted to intervene on the girl's behalf. Afterward, "most of the girls was like, 'You didn't have to do her like that, it wasn't necessary.' I mean, that's how we was, and a lot of the boys said the same thing. I mean, it was like three boys out of the whole crew that said she deserved it." Nonetheless, at the time, none of the youths present took action, and a number of young men participated even though they didn't believe the girl "deserved" it. Those who disapproved simply left. Felicia explained, "everybody was trying to go. They wouldn't have no part of it." And despite saying she believed "it wasn't necessary," Felicia also noted, "that's on her. 'Cause I feel she put herself in that position. I mean, you put yourself in a position for this. She put herself in that position." Ironically, recall that Felicia herself had been the victim of sexual violence on multiple occasions.

Girls' Strategies for Addressing Sexual Aggression

It is not sufficient to focus exclusively on girls' experiences with victimization. Despite the extensive violence faced by many young women in our sample, they developed strategies to manage the risk for sexual coercion and assault and to prevent repeated victimization. In fact, the girls' approach to addressing sexual danger was encapsulated in the advice Yvonne described giving her younger sister: "Protect yourself, respect yourself. 'Cause if you won't, guys won't."

Yvonne's advice illustrates the widespread pessimism many girls had about some young men's behavior in their communities. As Sheron argued, "a boy gonna do what he wanna do, regardless." Asked what could be done to curtail young men's mistreatment of girls, Ramara concurred: "[*laughs*] I don't know for real cause you can't stop somebody from doing what they feel like doing and stuff." And Jamellah surmised, "I mean, it's no way for it to stop. 'Cause a male always gon' come around a female. It's like a life cycle. It is always gonna happen." Nicole's response was almost identical to Sheron's: "Man, I don't think I could say nothing about that. The boys gon' do what they wanna do, they not gon' listen." In fact, many of her friends had been victims of sexual aggression. She lamented:

> I feel sad for 'em. . . . We'll sit there and have our lil', you know, we'll cry with each other, you know. 'Cause we gon' be there through thick and thin. It's hard for me to just sit there, just watch them talkin' and then tears start comin' down they face. And then it hurts me to see that half of my Black people are getting raped because boys are so, you know, doing petty stuff to us 'cause they want to get in yo' panties. You should come to them in a better way instead of trying to rape them 'cause you wanna get in they pants or whatever. . . . So that's why I call some of these boys up here stupid.

Similarly, Tawanna complained, "some of them [boys] think they the world. . . . They think they so cool to do that. They not so cool." Nonetheless, she surmised, "it ain't gonna change."

In principle, all of the young women we spoke with were adamant that sexual violence was wrong. Asked whether she thought it was ever okay for a guy to force a girl to have sex with him, Jamellah said, "none whatsoever. . . . I mean, a girl got they right to choose. If she ain't want to give none, she ain't got to give you none. It's her body. God made that body for her. Even if, you know, [you want it], that body still hers. Not yours." Likewise, Yvonne replied, "no, it's never okay. Not even if she misled you to where she was kissing on you or whatever, and then when it came down to the nitty gritty, she was like, 'No.' It's never okay. Never, ever." And LaSondra noted, "no, because man, that make the woman feel worthless."

However, given their strong sense that young men's behavior was often intractable, along with their recognition of the prevalence of nonintervention norms, young women accepted that they bore the responsibility for keeping themselves safe. They felt, realistically, that the only way to avoid sexual abuse was through their own actions. This is a theme we have seen again and again, with regard to neighborhood dangers, sexual harassment, and now, as well, sexual aggression. Young women felt very much on their own in managing their risks for sexual assault.

As discussed in chapter 2, some young women did so by restricting their social lives, particularly in their neighborhoods. These girls avoided spending time on the streets and also avoided going to "parties and clubs and stuff like that." Limiting their exposure to delinquent young men and high-risk settings, they believed, could insulate them from sexual violence. Such an approach, while strategically sensible, came at the cost of limiting their participation in public life. Moreover, girls occasionally were victims of acquaintance rape in sites they believed themselves to be safe in, including in their homes and those of their friends.

For young women who wished to participate in neighborhood and adolescent social activities, the first part of Yvonne's adage came to bear. Fundamental to these girls' beliefs about how to insulate themselves from sexual violence was the notion that girls should "respect" themselves. Janelle explained, "a guy's not gonna respect a female that don't have respect for herself." As discussed in chapter 3, young women's conceptualization of "respect" was multifaceted, focusing both on having sexual integrity and on being assertive enough to stand up for yourself. Tisha explained:

I mean, [girls] gotta make it safe for theyself. They, I mean, they attract what they want. I mean, it got a lot to do with they attitudes. If they can, you know, correct they attitude, you know, find a presentable way to dress. Not all that lil' skirts and shirts, showing they chest and all that kinda stuff. And then, they make theyself, they gotta *demand* respect. That's what it is—they don't demand respect. So they get what's dished out to 'em. What they don't want for real.

Not surprisingly, some girls emphasized the issue of sexual respect. Gail surmised, "it's some girls that really do, you know, stuff like, do

stuff to boys to make them, you know, wanna do stuff to them."
Sharmi said, "rape, well, if they wouldn't dress the way they dress.
Some of the girls, they dress so triflin' they ought to be ashamed." And
Rennesha noted:

> I really think we, I mean, it's us [females] who have to do it. I mean,
> carry yo'self like a woman. Don't dress this way if you know it is going
> to catch his eye too much. I don't think nothin' could be done [to
> change young men], it take you to do what [you] need. And if you
> know he gon' do this if you do that, don't do that.

Ironically, Cherise—who had been both raped and gang raped—was
one of the harshest critics of other girls, going so far as to explicitly
blame them for their sexual mistreatment. Recall Cherise's comment in
chapter 3 that if a girl acts "stupid, you get treated stupid. . . . I mean, if
you carry yourself like you ain't got no respect for yourself, that's how
they gonna treat you." Later in the interview, the conversation returned
to Cherise's characterization:

> *Interviewer*: So you think that women are partly to blame for the way
> they get treated?
> *Cherise*: I actually, I mean, I hate stupid girls. Actually yes. Truthfully
> yes [they are to blame]. Because if they act a certain way they would-
> n't get treated [that way]. But they act that way so they [get] treated
> that way. Not saying they deserve to get treated that way, but if you
> act that way, you can't help but get treated that way. So in other
> words, you probably do deserve it. I mean, nobody deserves to get
> [raped]. . . . I guess they feel that they are nothing, so they get
> treated like nothing.
> *Interviewer*: So you think that girls have to be like, show that they are
> just as tough as the boys?
> *Cherise*: No, not tough. But they have to carry themselves in a respect-
> ful way. In other words, if you have respect for yourself, you get re-
> spect. If you don't have respect for yourself, people will see it, and
> that's how they'll treat you. Like dirt.

Cherise's dialogue, like that of Tisha's, illustrates girls' multifaceted understanding of respect. A young woman doesn't have to be mannish or
"tough," but she must "carry [herself] in a respectful way"—one that

rejects sexual objectification and announces the willingness to stand up for herself.

Having been the victim of multiple rapes, however, Cherise knew as well as anyone that self-respect was insufficient to avoid sexual violence. Her description of how she coped with her own victimization experiences brings us to the final part of Yvonne's adage: "Protect yourself." Of her first experience, raped at a man's house while watching TV with him, Cherise said, "actually, maybe you could say [the experience] helped me. That's why I won't put myself in that situation no more. . . . I'm very wiser." Likewise, of her gang rape, she explained:

> It just has made me wiser. More aware of what's going on. . . . Made me think about what I do before [I do it]. I think about what I do, the consequences of that. And it also made me think about the different, how crazy people are, and how I gotta be careful with dudes, men.

She continued, describing more specific strategies she now employed to protect herself:

> It ain't gonna happen no more. 'Cause I'm not gonna drink no more. If I drink I'm gonna get my own drink. That way can't nobody put nothing in my drink. If I go to a party and I leave my drink, my drink's just gonna be left there 'cause I ain't coming back to it. It ain't gonna happen no more.

Thus, while "respect yourself" referred to a young woman's sexual integrity and assertiveness, "protect yourself" referred more specifically to strategies young woman could employ as they became more streetwise and knowledgeable about the variety of sexual risks they faced at the hands of young men. Asked how her experience with attempted rape affected her, Lisa described making behavioral changes: "I don't know that it affected me in any way like that [e.g., emotional trauma]. [But] I'm not gonna go up in a boy house by myself that I really, really don't know like that." And of her experience, Kristy surmised, "well, I don't trust people and I don't drink."

Finally, there was evidence in our data that some young women made the effort to protect their female loved ones when they were in a position to do so. This theme emerged specifically among young women who themselves had been victims of sexual violence. For instance, it was in the context of describing how her attempted rape affected her that Yvonne described the admonishment she gave her younger sister (which opened this section). She routinely talked to her sister to educate her about what she needed to watch out for:

> I'm just real protective of myself and my sisters. 'Cause I have, you know what I'm saying, my sisters are my world. If anything was to happen to them, I don't know what I would do. . . . [My experience] just make me look at them in a different light. You know what I'm saying, I be just constantly on my younger sister. . . . 'Cause she pretty, got a body out of this world, and guys, they be on her, you know what I'm saying. [So I] be on *her*. And I be telling her to protect yourself, respect yourself. 'Cause if you won't, guys won't. And drinking and smoking, that ain't nothing, it ain't worth it. All the emotions that you go through when you get high all the time and you drink, and your body, it ain't ready for that. You know what I'm saying 'cause I'm 17, my body ain't ready for it and I know it. You 15 and your body ain't ready for it neither. You know so, [what happened to me], it just make me look at things in a different way.

Alicia's earlier description of refusing to leave her friend behind at a hotel with three men is also a case in point. Perhaps because of her own experiences with sexual violence, she put herself in her friend's shoes and surmised, "I wouldn't want them to leave me." Likewise, Cherise described protecting an intoxicated friend from young men at a party: "[She] got drunk, but she was with me. See, I wasn't with a friend [when I was gang raped]. And the dudes was trying to get her to go [with them], and I was like, 'No!' . . . I stayed sober just because . . . she was drunk."

Unfortunately, such protections rarely extended beyond a young woman's immediate circles. Girls who were strangers or mere acquaintances were more likely to be viewed, as Felicia earlier surmised, as "putting [themselves] in that situation." In addition, such strategies—though ostensibly realistic, given the social contexts examined here—placed a heavy burden on young women. And, given the magnitude of sexual aggression in these young women's lives, it is clear that girls' individual efforts alone were woefully inadequate for keeping them safe. Without broader social supports available to address the problem in any systematic way, the ultimate responsibility for avoiding sexual violence remained in the hands of girls themselves, leaving them, once again, in a precarious position as they negotiated their daily lives.

Conclusion

In this chapter, I examine the nature and situational contexts of sexual aggression against young women in urban disadvantaged communities. More than one-half of the girls we interviewed had experienced some form of sexual violence or coercion, and nearly one-third had experienced repeated sexual victimization. Youths described a continuum of sexual aggression, from pressuring and coercing girls into unwanted sex to brutal gang rapes. While the former were much more common experiences for young women, nearly one-half of the young men ran trains on girls, and it appeared part and parcel of the "coming of age" experiences of many urban young men.[59]

Chapters 2, 3, and 4 have progressively demonstrated how broader patterns of girls' neighborhood mistreatment, visible violence against women, crime and delinquent peer networks, and the prevalence of sexual harassment in schools all coalesced to create social contexts that heightened young women's risks for sexual victimization. These risks were exacerbated for young women with extensive family problems and those who participated in serious delinquency. Much of the violence girls faced took place at unsupervised parties, where alcohol and drug use was widespread. Such social contexts not only made young women more vulnerable to sexual mistreatment but also enhanced the likelihood that girls would be viewed as either willing participants or deserving victims.

Moreover, there is little evidence that young women had social support for addressing their risks for sexual violence. Girls' most common strategies involved problem-solving, which focused on making behavioral changes to better protect themselves from future risk. There is evidence that such coping strategies can be psychologically beneficial to victims of sexual violence, to the extent that these increase their perceived efficacy.[60] However, it is simply insufficient and unacceptable for young women to face such systematic violence without broader institutional support and intervention.

As I discuss in chapter 6, girls were either unfamiliar with or wary of formal community agencies that provide assistance for crime victims, including female victims of male violence. In fact, only Nykeshia, who had been raped by her mother's then-boyfriend, described receiving counseling and other social service support. And this occurred specifically because Children's Services became involved once her rape was reported. More commonly, girls described relying on a trusted friend or family member to cope with their victimization experience, or they simply kept it to themselves. Several girls called on male friends or relatives to seek revenge for sexual violence, but few called the police or sought remedies through the legal system. This is not surprising, given the general and gender-specific distrust of the police found in urban African American communities.[61] Moreover, research has shown that institutionalized racism often blocks African American women's use of community agencies that have the resources for addressing violence against women.[62]

However, even efforts to improve young women's access to formal institutional support when they are victimized are inadequate for addressing the risks they face in their communities. Like the school-based sexual harassment policies discussed in chapter 3, such resources offer assistance to victims only after they have been harmed. They offer little remedy for improving the broader patterns of gender inequality, violence, and disorder present in young women's communities. As my analyses here have demonstrated, this is where the problem of violence against young women lies. Thus, much more comprehensive solutions are needed to protect young women from the entrenched risks present in their daily lives.

5

The Playa' and the Cool Pose
Gender and Relationship Violence

The public nature of physical violence against women in youths' neighborhoods, and its sometimes carnivalesque treatment, had a meaningful impact for girls. It taught them, among other things, that women often deserved their mistreatment and, consequently, that they were unlikely to receive broad social support or even immediate intervention when they were the victims of such violence. A great deal of research has found linkages between witnessing intimate partner violence as children and being at greater jeopardy for perpetration or victimization later in life.[1] For adolescents, such systematic exposure to violence in their neighborhoods and homes risked normalizing these interactions within the contexts of intimate relationships.

What is perhaps unique about relationship violence, particularly when compared with the kinds of sexual mistreatment and violence examined thus far, is that some studies find similar rates of relationship violence perpetration across gender, particularly in its less-serious forms.[2] This is especially the case among adolescents, where there is also evidence that relationship violence may have features distinguishing it from partner violence in adulthood. For instance, dating violence among adolescents is more likely to be mutual rather than one-sided and is also more likely to take place in the presence of others, most notably at school.[3]

Not surprisingly, in response to survey questions about dating violence, the youths in our study reported prevalence rates of victimization in dating relationships comparable to those found in other studies on adolescent dating violence. As table 5-1 shows, youths reported a sizeable amount of dating conflict and violence.[4] In all, 33 percent of the girls and 44 percent of the boys reported that a dating partner had threatened to hit them; more than one-half of the girls and just over one-quarter of the boys described a partner throwing, smashing, or

TABLE 5-1
Prevalence of Reported Relationship Victimization (N = 72)[a]

	Girls (N = 33)	Boys (N = 39)
Called names/verbally abusive	16 (48%)	9 (23%)
Put down in front of others	9 (27%)	5 (13%)
Accused of cheating or flirting	25 (76%)	26 (67%)
Cheated on	24 (73%)	6 (15%)
Threatened to hit	11 (33%)	17 (44%)
Thrown, smashed, or kicked something	17 (52%)	11 (28%)
Pushed, grabbed, or shoved	19 (57%)	22 (56%)
Slapped	7 (21%)	15 (38%)
Kicked, bit, or hit with fist	7 (21%)	11 (28%)
Hit with something	6 (18%)	6 (15%)

[a] Three youths report not having had a boyfriend/girlfriend and are not included in the table.

kicking something when they were angry; over one-half of both groups (57 percent and 56 percent, respectively) described being pushed, grabbed, or shoved by a boyfriend or girlfriend; and 21 percent of girls and 28 percent of boys described being kicked, bit, or struck with a partner's fist. There was a great deal of gender parity in youths' survey reports, though young men were more likely to report being slapped by a girlfriend, while young women were more likely to report behaviors categorized as verbally abusive (called names, put down in front of others) and were significantly more likely to report having had a dating partner cheat on them (73 percent versus 15 percent for boys).[5]

Though youths' reported prevalence of relationship victimization revealed gender parity on some items, and for some acts young men reported higher rates of victimization, it is important to put these numbers in context. Despite similar base rates of relationship violence, research consistently shows that young women are significantly more likely than young men to experience more negative consequences from partner violence, including being significantly more likely to sustain injuries, require medical attention, and fear for their safety.[6] In addition, if we base our understanding of partner violence only on youths' responses to survey items that ask whether a partner has ever pushed, slapped, or hit them, we overlook youths' gendered "interpretations, motivations and intentions" concerning partner violence, and fail to understand "the contexts of violence, the events precipitating it . . . the sequence of events by which it progresses," as well as its consequences.[7] In addition, it is impossible to determine the severity of a given incident based only, for example, on an affirmative survey response that a youths' partner "hit" them.[8]

Focusing specifically on girls' victimization, 61 percent described having experienced some physical violence in a dating relationship,[9] and 13 girls (39 percent) described having been kicked, bit, hit with a fist or object, beaten up, or choked by a boyfriend. In all, 24 of the girls we interviewed reported currently having a boyfriend. Of these, 11 (46 percent) described being physically victimized in this relationship. Moreover, of the 28 girls who reported having had two or more boyfriends, 16 (57 percent) described experiencing violence across multiple relationships. In addition, as discussed in chapter 4, more than one-quarter of girls reported being pressured into unwanted sex by a boyfriend, and 12 percent described being raped by a dating partner.[10]

In this chapter, I provide a contextual examination of the nature, circumstances, and meanings of partner violence in young women's and young men's dating relationships. To better contextualize this examination, I begin by situating youth's experiences with relationship violence first in the context of gendered power dynamics in their peer culture. Here I specifically examine how dominant definitions of masculinity influenced same-sex and cross-gender relations in ways that set the stage for conflicts in dating relationships. Next, I move to a discussion of the primary facets of relationship conflict described by young women and young men, focusing on jealousy, distrust, and control issues and examining how these were shaped by gender. These were often the proximate triggers for violence in youths' relationships.

Table 5-1 showed gender parity with regard to violence but also suggested that broader gendered patterns were present in youths' relationships, including high rates of infidelity among boys and a greater likelihood for girls to report verbal mistreatment. These emerged as themes in youths' narrative accounts and were indicative of important contextual features of dating relationships that affected gendered power dynamics, relationship conflicts, and beliefs about and experiences with dating violence. Having situated the analysis in these contexts, I conclude by examining how gender shaped youths' use of and responses to violence in dating relationships. Comparing female-perpetrated, male-perpetrated, and reciprocal relationship violence, I pay special attention to how gender shaped youths' interpretations of dating violence, the normative aspects of dating violence, and the contexts, progression, and consequences of these events.

Hegemonic Masculinity and the Social Organization of Gender Relations

As noted in chapter 1, a characteristic feature of adolescence is the "shift from the relatively asexual gender systems of childhood to the overtly sexualized gender systems of adolescence and adulthood."[11] This shift has different meanings and consequences for girls and boys. As discussed in the preceding chapters, young women face a sexual double standard in which they receive status from their peers for their association with and attractiveness to males, but they are denigrated for sexual activities deemed "promiscuous." In contrast, young men are rewarded and receive status for their sexual activities with young women. Among the youths we spoke with, being a "playa'" (player)—using girls for sex and having multiple sexual conquests without emotional attachment—was described as a prominent model for male behavior that offered the potential for status and prestige within male peer groups. These hegemonic facets of masculinity heightened girls' risks for sexual coercion and assault.[12] And while not all of the young men in our study strove for such an identity—and some were openly critical of its more extreme forms—they each described ways in which it affected their dating relationships and the messages and support they received about girlfriends from their male peers.[13]

One problem I made note of in chapter 4 is boys' descriptions of feigning interest in a relationship in order to convince girls to have sex with them. Recall Tyrell's belief that it was easy to persuade girls into sex by getting them to think "that you really care about them for real, but you really don't." Ricky, who was in a steady relationship and critical of this behavior, described such young men as "smooth talkers" and said they behaved this way "just to get an image, a name. To make themselves look big" with their peers. Dwayne described his technique as follows:

> *Dwayne*: You gotta spend some time with 'em first. You can't just go buy her something and expect just to take her home the same day. You gotta chill out with her for a little minute. Like talk to her and stuff.
>
> *Interviewer*: Do you do that because you want to spend time with her or just because you want to have sex with her?

Dwayne: Yeah, that's why I do it sometimes. I do it just because I wanna have sex.

As discussed in earlier chapters, some young men described becoming mad when their efforts failed, and young women also told of instances when their rebuffs were met with young men's anger. In some cases, this led to the kinds of gender harassment examined in chapters 2 and 3. At its extreme, recall Shauntell's account in chapter 4 of her cousin raping a girl because he believed she " 'was comin' on to me . . . and [then] she tried to front me out.' " Continuing his discussion, Dwayne said that he "get[s] mad and stuff" when a girl is unwilling to have sex with him: "I be like, 'Man I bought you this, I done bought you that, and you ain't gonna do that?' I be like, 'I see you some other time' or something. I ain't gonna stay over there if she ain't gonna give me none. I go home or I go to my girlfriend's house or something."

Dwayne's comments suggest that the playa' ethos also included the belief that if a young man spent cash on a girl, he was entitled to sex. Ronald explained, "alright, let's say you took her to McDonalds, you know, alright I can't understand [expecting sex for] that. But if you took her to a real expensive restaurant and you spend a lot of money I think that you should [expect sex]. . . . If you spend all this money on her then you gotta get something." In fact, 18 young men (45 percent) reported that their friends had conveyed such messages to them, and another 11 (28 percent) said their friends believed their girlfriends should have sex with them when they want to.

Alternatively, girls who succumbed too readily to boys' sexual advances—even under false pretenses—not only faced derogatory labels and were liable to be targeted by additional boys (as discussed in chapters 3 and 4) but also were disempowered in their dating relationships. Kristy said of several of her friends, "like they knew this boy a week or something, but then they still let him do what he wanna do to 'em, but then they get mad when he don't wanna call 'em back. It's funny to me but they get mad, but they keep letting it happen so it's they fault." Many young women, though generally critical of the playa' mentality, nonetheless blamed girls for being too gullible. Recall Tisha's description in chapter 4 of her brother and his friends picking girls up and "get[ting] 'em messed up or whatever so they can try to do it to 'em." She continued: "I mean, it's wrong of them to try to take advantage of people like that, but I don't really care. 'Cause if the girl stupid enough to do it, then she must want it done."

Thus, to qualify as a real girlfriend, girls were expected to police their own sexual desires and also resist young men's advances. For example, asked to describe his relationship with his girlfriend, the first thing Travis emphasized was that he knew his girlfriend was not sexually "loose":

> I've been going with my girlfriend for six months. You could say we taking everything pretty slow you know. She the type that it took me awhile before we had sex. She ain't the type that like after the first week or something I could've had sex with her, it ain't like that 'cause anybody that's like that I mean, I wouldn't want to be with nobody that's like that. To where it's that easy for me to have sex with 'em.

In contrast, Bobby was in a fairly new relationship with a young woman but didn't respect her and was ambivalent about the relationship because he felt she had sex with him too readily. In fact, this was the incident he described in chapter 4, when he and his brother had a competition to see who could first have sex with the girls they were out with, and Bobby told of pressuring the girl until she acquiesced.

His ambivalence about having her as a girlfriend came through in his interview: "This girl I got now . . . well, I don't consider her as my girlfriend *for real,* 'cause, you know . . . [she had sex with me] the first day we met." Bobby then asked the male interviewer, "okay, if you had met a girl on yo' first date, you had sex with her on yo' first date, what would you think? What would *you* call her?" While he acknowledged that the sex "just happened [because of] how I talked to her," he was nonetheless reticent to fully acknowledge her as his girlfriend. This disempowered her in their relationship and negatively affected the way he treated her.

The sexual double standard and the cultural ethos of the playa' was also associated with a clear message boys received from their peers: love equals softness. For some, this encouraged the avoidance of committed relationships, as Ronald's description exemplifies: "I'm a one-month person. I like movin' on." But even among young men in committed relationships, the message had an impact. The following conversation with Tyrell, who was in a long-term relationship, illustrates a number of key consequences:

Interviewer: Do any of your friends talk to you about their relationships with their girlfriends?

Tyrell: Sometimes. . . . [But if] they be like, "Well yesterday I [went out
with] this girl, I took her out to eat and to the show then dropped
her off at home," we be like, "So?" Nobody care about that. We talk
about like, they'll say stuff like, "Man I hit [had sex with] this girl
yesterday" talking about how good it was, that's all dudes talk about
for real.

Interviewer: They talk about their girlfriends?

Tyrell: Ain't just be their girlfriends for real, any girl, anybody. They
don't be like, "I love her so much" or stuff like that. Ain't nobody
wanna hear that man. It don't get talked about. It was like last week,
it was me and my friend and he was like, "I'm gonna get my baby's
momma name tattooed on my neck and get my baby's name tattooed on the other side my neck." They was talking about him and
stuff, talking about he so soft and in love and all that kind of stuff.
. . . He was just being quiet after that. I mean don't nobody wanna
hear that. I mean I'm sure everybody got somebody they probably
love, [but] they don't be broadcasting it like that to everybody. Don't
nobody care about how you in love with this person.

Interviewer: So you all just talk about sex?

Tyrell: Yep, that's all I talk about for real. My cousin, I talk to my
cousin like that, but nobody else. [When they see me with my girl-
friend] they be like, "Who's that?" and I be like, "My friend." I
don't even say "My girl" 'cause one time I got mad at her. She was
like, some dude was like, "Where you gonna go?" and she was like,
"Over to my friend house, [she] stay right there." And then he came
and told me what she said. I was mad. So every time we go somewhere and they be like, "That's your girl?" and I be like "No it's just
my friend man." She be looking at me like I'm crazy but just like
yesterday I did the same thing, [Someone] was like, "That your girlfriend?" and I be like "No, we just friends."

In fact, many of the young men we interviewed described not being
open about their relationships with their friends and, instead, talking
with one another primarily about the sexual facets of their relationships
or about other girls.[14] Like Tyrell, several other young men who were in
long-term or serious relationships described having one trusted confi-
dant that they could talk to openly about their relationship. On the

whole, however, this talk was discouraged or sanctioned through ridicule. In contrast, most of the girls we talked to described openly talking with their friends about their own and their friends' relationships, including what Rennesha called "normal stuff, like we went here and there last night," and their fights and conflicts. Michelle said her friends would "come and talk to me about they relationship, like if they just got into it with they boyfriend. Or should she do this, should she do that." As Lisa summed up, "everything that go on with our boyfriend we tell."

Both girls and boys described positive facets of their relationships—as evidenced by the fact that nearly one-half of the youths were in relationships of a six-month duration or longer. In fact, boys were more likely to highlight positive features of their relationships—most notably the intimacy and emotional support they received from their girlfriends. For instance, Travis explained that there was "a special bond between" him and his girlfriend because "I could talk to her about anything." Girls spoke especially positively about boyfriends who did not pressure them into having sex but generally seemed to be more ambivalent about their relationships. Yvonne noted, "we real close, we talk a lot to each other. He more like a friend. He's real dependable and I enjoy being with him sometimes when he don't get ignorant." Likewise, Cleshay described her relationship as "good. It only have rocky spots but twice, but that's because he cheated on me. . . . But other than that he's a decent guy. I like him, he cool."

Boys in particular, then, valued intimacy in their relationships, as this was less available in their friendships with other boys where status depended on not revealing these qualities. Boys found competing expectations in their romantic relationships and their friendship groups, which were a source of potential conflict with their girlfriends. In fact, young men's concern with their appearance in front of friends led many to adopt what sociologists Richard Majors and Janet Mancini Billson describe as a "cool pose"—a mask to conceal vulnerabilities that is characterized by detachment, control of emotions, aloofness, and toughness.[15] These authors describe the cool pose as an adaptation strategy often embraced by urban African American young men. For instance, as Tyrell suggested, part of the reason he sometimes refused to acknowledge his girlfriend in front of others was because he felt she was inappropriately friendly to another young man—a circumstance that could make him look weak in front of his peers. Among the young men we spoke with, the cool pose was a core feature of normative masculinity, particularly in public presentations of self.

Given its emphasis on sex without emotion (and often with elements of manipulation), playa' behavior fit well with the cool pose. Likewise, boys' minimization of their commitment in relationships, further facilitated through sexual talk about both their girlfriends and other girls, helped project a detached persona. Some youths described boys treating their girlfriends badly in front of friends in an attempt to uphold this image. Dwayne explained, "like say if me and my friend Lester around or something, I got this friend named Pete, he be like talking to his girl first, and if we ain't there he be talking to her all cool and stuff. But when we come around he try to play like he pimping her or something. Like, 'Girl shut up. Ain't nobody tell you to say nothing.'" Dwayne attributed Pete's behavior to "trying to show off." Likewise, Walter said he had friends that "like if you around 'em and their girl[friend] come around they'll be like, 'Get away from me, leave me the fuck alone,' and that they don't wanna be bothered." But like Dwayne, Walter suggested this was primarily a public image: "Something telling me they probably just act that way when they around us. When they go home with her it'll probably be a whole different story, they acting nice and sweet. So we never know."

To be sure, not all young men adhered to these features of localized hegemonic masculinity, and some were openly critical of its more extreme forms. Young men who strove for such an identity were more likely to participate in delinquency and associate with delinquent peers. In addition, gang involvement and participation in drug sales provided access to money and status-enhancing possessions. Wayne complained that young women tended to be attracted to such young men, because of their popularity and material assets. He explained, "I try to tell girls . . . 'You're pretty enough to have any man you want to, and don't just accept whatever comes to you,' you know what I'm saying. . . . But then again, they still attracted to . . . all that gold and all this other stuff . . . [if] he got a car, you know what I'm saying." Asked why he thought girls were attracted to such young men, he continued:

'Cause they feel that they gonna get some of that, you know what I'm saying. Some girls feel that once they have sex with a man, they expecting something like, you know what I'm saying, "What you gonna give me now? Now that I've had sex with [you]." Some girls, girls think like that nowadays, you know, which is really not right. . . . They like to be seen with boys that got something. You know, they want the best man, who dressed the best and all this. . . . For girls, it's like, that's what they look for first, to see if this dude's got money, you know what I'm saying. And by the time they find out his personality ain't no good, it's too late, you know what I'm saying.

More harshly, Marcus complained, "most [girls are] all the same—they money hungry. . . . They say, 'Naw, he broke, I ain't messin' with him.'" Ironically, then, to the extent that young women were drawn to boys with greater peer status, they were also more likely to become involved with boys more at risk for mistreating them. Both these public features of normative masculinity—the playa' and the cool pose—came with consequences for relationships.

Jealousy, Distrust, and Control: Gendered Relationship Conflict

The playa' climate and the cool pose were significant facets of hegemonic masculinity that structured gender relations to the disadvantage of girls. This masculinity also created a pervasive cultural ethos that led to widespread jealousy, suspicion, distrust, and conflict in relationships. Even youths who were genuinely trying to maintain committed relationships described the negative consequences of this ethos for building and sustaining trust. Combined with the sexual double standard, these facets of masculinity served to disempower many girls in their relationships with young men, with consequences for the nature and outcomes of relationship conflicts.

It also meant that girls tended to have a greater emotional investment in their relationships, particularly early on, when it was unclear whether the boy was truly interested in them or "running game." In addition, young men sometimes intentionally fostered girls' insecurity. Tyrell, for example, said that "when I started going with [my girlfriend] I was just running games, just talking to her like, 'I care about you' and all this stuff, but I really didn't care about her." Now though, he said, "I do love her or whatever, be in love with her," even though he still sometimes refused to acknowledge this in front of his peers.

Some boys also fostered this greater emotional stake from their girlfriends by purposely doing things to make them jealous and uncertain about their commitment to the relationship. Bobby, for example, described "playing" with his girlfriend by pretending to be on the phone with another girl. Once when she called, he "be like, 'What's up?' and then be like, 'Hold on, let me go tell this girl I'll call her right back.' You playin' with her, [put the mute button on the phone], then you take it off and be like, 'Yeah, alright what's up?' [She] be like, 'How you gon' have me on hold while you sittin' up there talkin' to [another girl]?'" Cooper described purposely angering his girlfriend by saying "I was with another girl even though I wasn't." Tyrell and Travis both said they made comments about how attractive other girls were in the presence of their girlfriends. And Ricky said he would sometimes ignore his girlfriend or do things to make her mad because "it's easy to frustrate her and I know I can so I be doin' it to see how she gon' react that day. I just mess with her."

Girls also described these types of situations. For instance, Shauntell got angry because her boyfriend purposely walked past her arm-in-arm with another girl and ignored her. In the most extreme form of emotional manipulation, several girls reported that their boyfriends would pressure them for sex with the threat that if she did not provide it, he would seek it elsewhere. For instance, recall Sheron's description of her boyfriend's use of these tactics in chapter 4. Such behavioral techniques assisted young men in maintaining a cool pose and allowed them to maintain greater emotional control in their relationships by undermining their girlfriends' confidence and security. Youths did not describe this range of behavioral strategies being adopted by girls in relationships. In part, this was because to do so would function to put the girl's sexual reputation in jeopardy.

Gendering of Jealousy in Relationships

Both young women and young men described jealousy as a key problem in dating relationships. Many described it as universal rather than gender-specific: recall from table 5-1 that more than three-quarters of girls and two-thirds of boys reported having been accused of cheating or flirting by a partner. Jamal, for example, explained that jealousy was a mutual issue between couples, "either one see another one in the hall with a different gender and you know how you talk and just stir things up, that type of thing. . . . That's the main reason for any couple [to argue], just cheating. Somebody thinks things going on in the house."

Moreover, youths' peers often instigated conflicts over jealousy by informally policing the behavior of members of dating couples and reporting back to one member of a couple when the other was seen engaged in potential relationship "misconduct" (i.e., talking to, flirting with or calling a member of the opposite sex, or actually infidelity). Dwayne explained:

> Like if your girlfriend don't come to school or something and you'll be sitting there just bullshitting or something, a girl just come and sit by you. And then I be talking and somebody else be like see us talk and they spread a rumor. They be like, "They was talking, they went home together," and stuff like that.

Jermaine described difficulties in maintaining trust in his relationship because he and his girlfriend lived in separate areas of town. He said his relationship was "good" because "like she love me, I love her," but nonetheless explained:

> I stay a long way from my girlfriend and I can't tell what's going on over there, and she can't tell what's going on on my side, so we just get that, that little feeling, you know what I'm saying. We trust each other, it's just like to a certain extent we don't trust each other. 'Cause like, say for instance, she don't trust me, but she trust me, but she don't trust me that much when I'm around a bunch of girls. She think I'll probably try to do something. And I don't trust her when she around a lot of dudes 'cause I think she may try to do something.

In his case, the lack of informal peer networks to report on a partner's behavior was what undermined trust in his relationship. However, as Dwayne explained, their presence often functioned in the same way.

Though youths described these issues affecting both males and females, their discussions also revealed gender-specific elements to both jealousy and the conflicts that ensued. Because of the playa' environment, it was more likely for girls' jealousy to be based on valid concerns. Continuing his earlier conversation, Jamal explained, "women have the tendency to always think that men are dogs and we gonna do what we want to do anyway [and] for most guys it's true." Recall again from table 5-1 that 73 percent of the girls reported that they had been cheated on, compared with only 15 percent of the boys. In fact, 25 of the boys we spoke with (64 percent of the 39 who were currently or had been in a relationship) said that they had cheated on their girl-friends.[16]

A number of young women described these events in the course of talking about their relationships. Jamellah, for example, had recently ended a three-year relationship with a young man five years her senior after she found out he had been cheating on her. Her description of what happened also illustrates the nature of informal policing and her application of the sexual double standard in her evaluation of her boy-friend's infidelity:

> *Jamellah*: I was in his neighborhood and that's the same neighborhood I used to hang out in and my god sister, she always over there. And the girl was bragging about having sex with him, and [my god sister] came and told me. And it was just like—she not the only one who came and told me, like three other girls came and told me [at] the same time she did. I'm like, oh my god. . . . And this girl, she was his age too, she like 24, 23. But she was pregnant, she got like five kids. She ain't have no high school diploma. She ain't doing nothing with herself but smokin' weed and drinkin', smoking' weed and drinkin'. Ain't got no job, on welfare. Just looked like she wore out and then she was having sex with everybody too. Everybody out [in] the neighborhood she done gave some to. So I was like, "You gon' cheat on me with *that?*"
>
> *Interviewer*: So when you found out about it, did you confront him or what happened?
>
> *Jamellah*: I confronted him, and he denied it and denied it. He still deny it to this day but she didn't even, the girl, I could tell because every time when she would see me she would look at me all crazy, and this a grown woman! And like my sister, she hang with the girl, so like, I'll be around and I wouldn't say nothing to her but she'll be like, "If y'all want y'all men then y'all betta keep 'em away from me, cause I'ma drop down on it." Saying lil' stuff, tryin' to get to me. So I just knew. And a dude even came here to school and told me, [this was my boyfriend's] friend, so I know [that he did it]. . . . Then it got to the point when I'll be around him and I just be like upset. Like I did-n't break up with him that soon. 'Cause I couldn't after being with him for so long, it's hard to break up with somebody. But it got to the point where I be around and everything . . . [and] the hurt really

make me mad, and that insulted me. I'm up here trying to do something with myself, I ain't got no kids, and you are going cheat on me with that? A hood rat at that. So, I was like, it had got to the point where I didn't want to be around.

Even when conflicts did not involve outright cheating, boys' associations with other girls fueled suspicion. Alicia had recently begun dating a boy but complained that he "got too many girl friends. He have too many friends that's girls. I don't like that. It makes me jealous sometimes. He be talking on the phone to 'em and when I'm over at his house they call him. There be too many of 'em, too many girls paging him and stuff. I don't like that." Likewise, Eugene said, "I have a girlfriend, then I have girl friends. She my main girl then I have different other girlfriends, 'cause I'm too young to be tied down so I talk to other people and stuff." He said he and his girlfriend argued sometimes over what he called "stupid stuff. Like, 'Who is that girl? How she know your number? Who is that calling?' or something."

Terence explained that such conflicts emerged because girls did not know where the relationship stood: "Somebody might page my boy and his girlfriend'll go off 'cause she think it's another female or something, she just don't know what kind of relationship they got together or whatever and they get to arguin' over it." In some cases, girls' jealousy was not founded, and boys reported being frustrated by their accusations. Ricky said he thought it stemmed from "insecurity. They don't fully trust you but at the same time they care about you." Of conflicts with his long-term girlfriend, he explained, "I be around a lot of females, man, to be honest. I mean, I don't mess with 'em, it's just a lot of females live on my street and we grew up [together]. . . . I be tryin' to explain to my girlfriend, she just don't get it."

While girls' concerns were more likely to be founded, in most cases boys' jealousy did not appear to result from actual infidelity. Instead, it came from their knowledge that the playa' climate meant it was likely other young men would try to talk to their girlfriends, and sometimes from suspicions generated by the young man's own behaviors. Tyrell was distrustful of his girlfriend in part because she confided to him that after they began going out, a boy she had previously had sex with tried to get her to have sex again. She told Tyrell that she had said no, but he remained suspicious: "He stop, far as I know. She say she ain't do nothing else but I don't believe her 'cause I don't really trust nobody." Tyrell admitted that part of the reason he did not trust her was because of his own behavior: "I think if you'll do it one time, you'll do it again. I know I have. I had did it [cheated on her] again [after getting caught]. Stuff like probably hugging and kissing people, going to see 'em. So I think she do the same thing but I really don't know."

Tami said she and her boyfriend argued occasionally when "he actin' stupid" by accusing her of cheating or flirting with other guys. She said once this occurred after she was seen talking to another boy in the cafeteria at school:

> Like we was in the lunchroom and this dude was up in my face and he was asking me why my boyfriend wasn't over here talking to me. So I was like, "I don't know, I guess he down there with his homies" or whatever. And he was like, "He should be up here with you cause somebody else could try to get you." I was like, "I don't know what's wrong with him." And then [my boyfriend's] partna, my play-brother, he came and was like, "Tami, who was that you was talkin' to in the lunchroom?"

Tami and her boyfriend later fought because "he was hearing things" about the incident, but she said, "I ain't trip off of it for real because I know I ain't doing nothing like that." Likewise, Destiny described her long-term boyfriend as extremely jealous despite his suspicions being unfounded. He had been locked up for a period during their relationship and routinely accused her of having been unfaithful while he was confined. She explained, "I don't even like havin' sex for real, even with him. [I told him,] 'If I ain't doin' it with you, I ain't doin' it with nobody else!'"

Tisha described being extremely upset when her boyfriend repeatedly accused her of cheating. She said their arguments generally occurred when "he was talkin' 'bout I was cheatin' on him. . . . He listenin' to what other people say. And that really affected our trust or whatever, just for even mentionin' that he think I'm cheatin' on him 'cause I know I'm not." Finally, Tisha said, "the last time [he accused me], I told him, I was like, 'If you gon' keep accusin' me and stuff then it ain't no reason for us to be together.'" After she gave him this ultimatum, "he don't really come to me with it no more. I know he hear stuff 'cause people talk

a lot or whatever. He'll ask me about it, he'll be like, 'I ain't tryin' to ac-
cuse you,' blah, blah, like that, 'Did you do this?' and stuff like that. He
really doin' the same thing, he just tryin' to be nice about it."

In sum, while jealousy was a salient issue for both genders, girls were
much more likely to have experienced infidelity and other relationship
conflicts that exacerbated insecurity and distrust. While adolescent relationships do not have the permanence of most adult relationships, and
some amount of relationship concurrency is to be expected,[17] it remained the case that infidelity and jealousy showed gendered patterns.
In addition, young men sometimes exploited girls' jealousy and insecuri-
ties by threatening infidelity or showing interest in other girls as a manipulation strategy. Boys' distrust appeared less grounded in the realities
of their girlfriends' behaviors, while girls' concerns were heightened by
the playa' climate and exacerbated by many of their boyfriends' behaviors. Moreover, because of the sexual double standard, accusations of
girls' infidelity were also implicit challenges to their reputations—a
meaning that was lacking when boys were accused of being unfaithful.
As a result, jealousy was qualitatively different across gender and contributed to girls' relative power disadvantage in dating relationships.

Management of Relationship Conflict and Control

The other area where significant gender differences emerged with regard to jealousy and distrust was in the relative efficacy of partners' responses. Both girls and boys described attempting to intervene or exert
control over their partner's behavior, particularly when they were sus-
pected of flirting or cheating. However, girls were less successful in their
attempts than were boys. Specifically, both girls and boys described a
pattern of male unresponsiveness during conflicts stemming from girls'
jealousy that often functioned to escalate girls' angry reactions. Recall
Eugene's description of having a "main" girlfriend and other girls on
the side who routinely called him in his girlfriend's presence. His account of a typical conflict and his reaction to his girlfriend's attempt to
intervene in the situation illustrates the linkages between playa' behavior, jealousy, the cool pose, and girls' (failed) attempts at control:

> Like, if we sitting down just chilling, me and her and then somebody
> just call and sometime I would play like, "Ah, yeah, that's my boy," you

know, this and that. But she like, "Who is that?" I'm like, "The girl
next door," and then she like, "What she want?" and I'll say, "See what
I'm doing," and she like, "Why she askin' what you doing?" I'm like, "I
don't know." Then she get mad. I'm like, dawg. She like, "Do she call
here a lot?" I'm like, "Naw, she just called here then." I'm just chillin'.
She like, "I don't like her callin' here." I'm like, "Yeah, okay whatever,"
and then she get mad and stuff. She'll ask me a question like, "You
messed with that girl or something?" I'm like, "Naw I ain't messing
with her. Why you tripping off her?" She get mad. And I'm like, "Well
so?" And then she'll get mad and leave or I'll leave. I'm like, "Well I'll
leave, bye." I'll just leave, walk away. . . . She'll like cuss me out when
she get mad and stuff, she want me to say something back to her. I'm
like, whatever, just burn out [leave], go somewhere, disappear with my
friends.

Ideally, walking away from a conflict until cooler heads prevail is an
effective and healthy approach. For example, Doug was in what he described as a "strong, steady relationship" and said both he and his girlfriend "keep ourselves distance, away from like fighting, like we feel
mad at each other we just won't talk to each other for a minute. Cool
down then come back." But, instead, boys most often described using
disengagement as a strategy to maintain control or send the girl a message. Darnell said when he had conflicts with his girlfriend, "what really
make her mad is when I walk away from her. She get upset when I do
that." And Leon explained, "I'll just walk away and I might ignore her.
That'll make her think 'Well he ain't talking to me so I must of did
something to make him mad.' Just stay away from her. I won't say
nothing to her."

Describing conflicts with her ex-boyfriend, Ramara confirmed, "if we
had a argument he'll just walk away, he wouldn't yell at me or nothin'.
That's what made me mad 'cause I would want him to yell at me and
stuff but he never did it, he'll just walk away." Walter offered the most
exacting description of this strategy: "If we like get into an argument
and it's like a real bad argument and I don't like what she said or something like that I won't say nothing to her for like a week. And if she call
I just tell my stepmother and father to keep telling her that I ain't here. I
wait for like a week and then I'll probably call her."

This type of "cool" strategy was rarely adopted by girls. While a large number of youths described boys refusing emotional engagement during conflicts, just two instances of girls adopting this strategy emerged, and both involved girls in lengthy relationships. Destiny explained:

> If he see me talkin' [to another guy] he's real jealous, and when he talk to a girl I just sit there and look. He get really mad then. I be all, "You play too much, bye. I'm not stoppin' you 'cause I don't care." Well, I do care. But that's what I tell him. And that makes him real mad [for me to] act like I don't care because he think I love him. Well, I do love him but I'm like "So long, whatever, I don't care, I don't need you" and all this. That makes him mad.

This counterexample suggests it is not the case that girls and boys were so different but, instead, that youths' relative power within relationships had a strong impact on the strategies they were most likely to adopt and their consequences. This power was heavily influenced by gender, but not determined by it. Destiny appeared able to maintain an emotional upper hand by employing a strategy similar to what many boys found effective, and the result was a similar psychological reaction by her boyfriend as was found for many girlfriends.

In contrast to young men's descriptions of their own emotional disengagement strategies, a number of them complained that girls were emotionally out of control, and they viewed girls' concerns and their attempts to exert control in the relationship through this framework. For example, Kevin explained:

> She get mad when she page me or something and I don't call her or she don't know where I'm at or she call my house and I don't answer the phone or something and I don't want to tell her where I'm at. Sometimes she just talk too much. I want her to leave me alone. She be trippin'. Make me feel like I'm gonna bust her head. Most of the time when she get to talking and stuff I'll leave then I come back and she be mad, talking shit, where I've been at and all that. And it really ain't called for. Women crazy.

Likewise, Ricky said, "females have the tendency to go overboard sometimes." He explained that men are "stronger mentally and physically, so you can't really blame them." Only one young man reported appreciating this sort of behavior from his girlfriend. Jamal said his girl-friend "say she's the jealous type. She like to know where I am and what I'm doing at all times. But I don't care, she can know. Some men say they don't like it. I like it 'cause that shows that she's concerned." Nonetheless, boys' typical way of framing girls' behaviors allowed them to dismiss the gender inequalities that fostered girls' insecurity and emotional reactions and, instead, to frame girls' behavior as rooted in naturalized gender difference.

In contrast, conflicts emerging from male possessiveness or jealousy were more likely to result in the male getting his way. Recall that Tyrell was concerned about a boy that his girlfriend Kadesha had a previous sexual relationship with. The young man in question was the half-brother of Kadesha's cousin, but was not related to Kadesha. After she told Tyrell of the incident, he forbade her to spend time at her cousin's house without his permission:

> She had told me but I was mad or whatever so I was like, "You ain't going back over there." I told her, "You ain't going back over there," and like I said, "We can break up, but you ain't going over there while you going with me." So she hadn't went over there since. So she went over there this Memorial Day so I was like, "It gonna be daytime anyway so go ahead and go over there" so I let her go over there then. And then she tried to go over there yesterday and I'm like, "Now you ain't going over there today" or whatever, but she ain't get mad 'cause she understand. I like, "I break up with you right now, you ain't gonna go over there." Have me thinking she cheating on me or whatever.

In fact, though few boys admitted to such direct controlling behaviors themselves, many of the girls described their boyfriends exerting control in their relationships. This was particularly the case when they were in long-term relationships. For example, Britney described a recent conflict with her boyfriend of five months:

> His cousin like me so if I go like to the store with his cousin he'll be like, "Why you go to the store with him? You know he like you," and I'll be like, "'Cause he asked me and I want to go anyway and you was-n't around so I couldn't ask you and I didn't want to go by myself." And he be like, "It don't matter, you ain't supposed to go 'cause he like

you." And I be like, "You can't tell me what I can and I cannot do." He
be like, "I'm your boyfriend, I can do what I want."

Young men's attempts at exerting control often manifested themselves not just in keeping their girlfriends from talking with other boys
but also in controlling their physical appearances. This again reflects the
influence of both the playa' ethos and the sexual double standard: girls
were specifically discouraged from wearing clothing that, as Katie described, "draw too much attention from other people." She said her
boyfriend "always tryin' to tell me what I can wear, what I can't wear,
like [he says I can't wear] short shorts and tight shorts and stuff like
that. [He wants me to wear] church girl clothes, long skirts, he just like
for me to be covered up." And she admitted that she would sometimes
change her clothes simply to avoid conflicts.

Recall that Jamellah had been in a lengthy relationship with a young
man five years her senior. She said they would typically argue over "lil'
petty things [like] something I got on is too short. . . . He always, by
him being older than me, always trying to, you know, sometimes treat
me like a child, telling me how to dress sometimes." Michelle said what
she liked least in her relationship was "when he up in my face, 'How
many other boys you be talkin' to today?' And just stupid stuff like
that." He often initiated these fights when "I go get my hair done [or]
when I'll buy me an outfit or something. He be like, 'Who you wanna
impress now?' or something like that." Lisa complained that her boyfriend "talk like he my daddy, like he be tryin' to tell me what to wear,
what not to wear, sayin' I look like a hoochie . . . I look like a rat when
I put that on, I look sleazy. He just say stupid stuff." She said though
she regularly told him "that he hurt my feelings," his reply was, " 'I'm
tellin' you the truth . . . I'm sorry, you can't wear that.' "

Despite male efforts at control generally being more effective, girls
did not always stay in controlling relationships, and they also sometimes resisted their boyfriends' control. Kenisha, for example, had recently ended a two-year relationship because she eventually found her
boyfriend's controlling behaviors to be too much:

He was the type of person, he'll want me in at a certain time and all
type of stuff. Didn't want me to go to my friend's house spending the
night, didn't want me around my own brother. He was type of person

that wanted me over his house all the time. And I felt like he needed help so I just left him alone.

It is striking that young men's controlling behaviors appeared to manifest themselves primarily in long-term relationships, while girls' attempts to exert control were more likely to begin early in the relationship when they were especially unsure of where the relationship stood. Young men clearly had the upper hand in new relationships, when the possibility remained that they were just "playing" the girl. Consequently, they could draw from a repertoire of behavioral strategies that functioned to sustain power imbalances in their relationships, including using the playa' ethos and detachment strategies to undermine girls' security.

While these remained salient issues even in long-term relationships, it was nonetheless the case that as relationships progressed, the potential existed for such power imbalances to lessen as boys themselves became emotionally invested in the relationship. This was when young men were more likely to outwardly attempt to exert control over their girlfriends' actions. These issues—gender and jealousy, emotional detachment, and control—remain salient contextual factors that shaped the nature of relationship violence and youths' interpretations of the meanings of these events.

Real Men and Emotional Women: The Gendering of Dating Violence

Dating violence did not occur in all of youths' dating relationships. Nonetheless, as shown in table 5-1, the majority of young women and young men described at least some experience with minor forms of violence in relationships. In addition, because dating violence among adolescents was often public in nature, most of the youths we talked to had witnessed dating violence among their peers, regardless of whether they had experienced it themselves.[18] Notably, the meanings youths brought to bear in their interpretations of dating violence were widely shared, regardless of whether they described personal experiences with dating violence.[19] Consequently, in this section I draw both from youths' accounts of their own experiences and from their interpretations of incidents they witnessed and heard about involving their peers. I situate their accounts in the contexts of youths' shared (and where present, discordant) understandings of such events and highlight their linkages to the salient gender dynamics examined in the previous sections.

Four types of dating violence were routinely described by the youths we spoke with: female-initiated violence against a male dating partner, male violence in response to female-initiated violence, nonreciprocal male violence, and mutual "play" violence.[20] Girls were as likely to describe initiating violence as to describe nonreciprocal male violence (and some described both types occurring in their relationship). However, none described reciprocating when males initiated violence. Boys were twice as likely to describe female violence as to report that they had engaged in violence, and they primarily described their own violence as a response to female-initiated violence. We found two notable differences in girls' and boys' reports: first, of those girls who initiated violence, nearly three-quarters said their boyfriends responded with violence. In contrast, nearly two-thirds of boys described female-initiated violence in their relationships as nonreciprocal. Second, despite the extent of girls' reports of nonreciprocal male violence, only two boys admitted to having engaged in such violence themselves.

These differences may partially result from our sampling—specifically, that ours was not a sample of dating couples. However, they likely also stemmed from two phenomena related to the definition of and meanings attached to male violence. Young men's accounts of female-initiated violence as nonreciprocal were in some measure the result of gender differences in the labeling of an act as violent—specifically, young men's greater differentiation between striking a girlfriend (violence) versus pushing or grabbing her (nonviolence).[21] In addition, youths of both genders described a much stronger set of normative constraints governing male-perpetrated, as compared with female-perpetrated, dating violence. Youths described particularly strong norms against nonreciprocal male violence, making it likely that some young men would be reticent to admit involvement in such incidents.[22] This gender difference in the reported prevalence of boys' violence was one of several notable gender differences in youths' accounts. Except where specific gender differences are highlighted below, girls' and boys' accounts were strikingly similar with regard to the gendered meanings they applied when interpreting the causes, consequences, and normative place of violence in dating relationships.

Young Women's Dating Violence

Girls' use of violence in dating relationships was interpreted within the framework of their perceived emotionality. Jermaine explained that "girls get mad real easy so [they] can't hold it back." Likewise, Lisa said that, while "a boy ain't gon' trip, a girl will trip faster than a boy will." Since girls did not face the constraints of the "cool pose," they had more latitude to express their emotions, including through the use of minor forms of violence. Still, the consequence was that they were often viewed as emotionally out of control. This meant that in some instances —depending on the severity of their violence and their boyfriend's own willingness to use violence—girls' actions were seen as excusable (i.e., "they can't help it"), whereas in other instances, their "out-of-control" emotions were viewed as in need of (male) control.

Young men did not define girls' violence as threatening. Describing what happened when a girl called him when his girlfriend was at his house, Andrew explained, "she got mad or whatever and she got to going off and she slapped me or whatever. It wasn't really nothing, really." Marvin reported that his girlfriend once got mad and threw a baseball at him, but "it missed [and] I laughed at her. It made her madder but you know she just got frustrated and just sat there." Likewise, Ricky said, "if we have an argument or something, she'll just like hit me, punch me in my chest or something or like slap me on my back or push me in my head or something. It ain't, I mean . . . it's not too much." Again, minimizing his girlfriend's use of violence, Walter described: "She was thinking I was cheating on her. I brung up another girl, but it was my cousin and she didn't believe me so she hit me in the face. I didn't really take it like it was a deep, deep thing. I got mad and looked at her like I wanted to hit her, but I wouldn't and I balled up my fist but I never did."

Because girls' violence was not viewed as physically threatening, the majority of youths espoused the belief that under most circumstances boys should not hit girls back (but see below). Many felt girls often used violence because of this tacit understanding. Ramara explained that "if [he] think he a man, he should be man enough to take what a woman give to him. If she cussin' him out, he supposed to be able to take it. If she hit, he just supposed to walk away, you know." As a consequence, Bobby noted, "you know how girls are, they'll hit you, you know what I'm saying, 'cause they know, hit a dude and a dude ain't gon' hit 'em back. So that's how they get carried away by hittin' boys." Darnell said his girlfriend "know I ain't gonna fight her, that's why she'll try to fight." However, this was a contingent belief, and there were situations in which male violence was an approved response to girls' actions.[23] As Jamal explained, "some females put themselves in that position [to get hit], that's how I see it. 'Cause some women think they know that their man won't hit them back, that's why they hit them. Some men get fed up."

As Andrew's and Walter's accounts suggest, girls' violence was often precipitated by anger resulting from jealousy or the belief that a boyfriend had been unfaithful. In keeping with the playa' ethos, Robert said that in addition to being in a long-term relationship, he "got other girlfriends on the side." Once after cheating on his girlfriend, he said she "got mad 'cause when she came [over] I had a passion mark on my neck and she smacked me." Unlike Robert, Wayne did not adopt a playa' mentality and was in what he described as a "good relationship, probably going to last for a nice while." Once his girlfriend had used violence:

> She had called and I had called her a different girl when she called. I'm like, uh, "Who is this, Monica?" but that wasn't [my girlfriend's] name. She was like "Naw this ain't," well she hung up on me. I'm like that had to be my girl so, she called back and was like, "Who'd you just call me?" and "Who's that?" We had an argument. I'm like, "I don't want to talk about it over the phone, I'm gonna come over there." So, I go over there and she was all mad and stuff, you know stomping around and whatever, yelling. Tried to slap me and all that kind of stuff.

Girls' accounts of such violence were similar to that of boys. Kristy said she had been violent in her relationship only once, and the result was a two-month breakup: "I had confronted him because I heard that he had been unfaithful. So I confronted him and he got loud about it and he called me a B [bitch]. So I pushed him, then he pushed me back and he was like, 'Just leave, get out my face 'fore I hit you.' I was like, 'It's like that?' He's like, 'It's like that.'" Lisa was one of two young women who described having engaged in a serious assault on her boyfriend. At the time of her interview, she had a swollen black eye that was the result of this recent fight:

I got this [black eye] 'cause [*pause*] I didn't come to school Wednesday so Thursday when I came to school, this girl tellin' me that my boyfriend be comin' over to they house, this, this, this and that. So me bein' stupid, knowing the girl didn't like me anyway I shouldn't have listened to her. Me bein' stupid, went home tryin' to fight him. He blockin' the punches or whatever like, "Go'n, get off of me, go'n, stop, stop." He kept on tellin' me to stop, stop, go'n, go'n. So I'm steady hittin' him, steady hittin' him. I had on some sandals, I'm hittin' him with the sandals. I run outside, I'm hittin' him, I'm hittin' his car or whatever and so he said something to me as he was closin' his door and I punched him in his eye and he pushed the car up in park, he got out the car and smacked me and got back in the car and left.

Lisa said her mother "was upset with me" about the conflict. "'Cause her boyfriend was there, her boyfriend had said that he heard [about the fight] and he told her that I kept on hittin' [my boyfriend] and that he kept on tellin' me to go'n and I didn't stop. . . . My momma talkin' 'bout I'm not suppose to listen to what other girls tell me about my boyfriend."

Young women also described initiating violence as a result of anger or frustration resulting from what they perceived as their boyfriend's emotional detachment or uncaring response.[24] Kenisha's boyfriend was a friend of her brother's, and one night they came in at three in the morning. "I was like, 'Where y'all been, what y'all been doing?' He was just ignoring me so I had pushed him in his head and we had got to arguing or whatever." Alicia described a conflict that emerged "'cause I want him to walk me to the bus stop and he ain't feel like it so we got to arguing. I was like, 'It's all late outside and you won't walk me to the bus stop?' He like, 'It ain't that far' so I just got real mad and I hit him." Alicia said that "he ended up walking [me], he was playing but I ain't find it funny. I wasn't playing." Nighttime in a dangerous neighborhood made Alicia unappreciative of what she interpreted as his callousness. Asked whether she thought she was wrong for hitting him, Alicia gave a firm "no." Instead, "I was like, 'You better had came [to the bus stop].' He like, 'I'll go back home.'"

Finally, girls' violence sometimes resulted from a combination of perceived infidelity and a boyfriend's cool pose. Christal, the second of the two girls who described engaging in serious violence, said her ex-boyfriend "used to treat me alright, he just a ho', go with everybody and they momma." A jealous conflict emerged, and Christal "was like, 'Well I don't wanna go with you no more.'" Expecting him to fight for her, she was angered when instead:

> He was like, "Oh well." That's when I got mad and threw a brick. And the first time it missed and then I got it again and threw it and it hit him right between his legs. And then when he came in my face I slapped him and then he grabbed me, pulled my hair, and then he had threw me on the ground.

Ironically, though most girls believed their boyfriends should not hit them back when they initiated violence, in some instances—particularly when their anger resulted from their boyfriend's emotional detachment —girls seemed to be trying to push their boyfriends into an emotional reaction, even if that reaction was a violent one. Describing a fight she witnessed between her friend and the friend's boyfriend, Tami said:

> I don't know what they was arguin' about but she was all up in his face talkin' about "do it" and "do it." I guess she was tellin' [daring] him to hit her or whatever. And he was like, "Man I ain't gon' hit you," and he was tryin' to go to class and she grabbed him back and was all up in his face. I'm like, "You crazy."

Bobby described that his girlfriend would:

> Be like, "Aw you ain't gon' put yo' hands on me." So [she'll] come up all in yo' face like you know. A real man, you know, he'll let a girl talk, come up all in yo' face and you know how to walk away from her, 'cause you walk away. [Then she'll say,] "Don't walk away from me!" and push you or hit you or something. You turn around and grab 'em like, "You betta chill out."

There was a clear tension between definitions of "real men" as being able to respond with detachment and walk away, but also a desire among girls to break through that detachment and elicit an engaged response.

Girls' violence, then, was typically minor though occasionally more serious; young men did not see it as posing a threat. It emerged in the context of young women's responses to gender-based power inequalities that were sustained within adolescent peer groups and functioned to create specific types of relationship conflict. For girls, these were jealousy, distrust and anger over potential infidelities, and reactions against the emotional detachment strategies adopted by young men.[25] Importantly, the minimization of girls' violence and the attribution of it to their greater emotionality meant that their use of violence, as with their other attempts at control documented earlier, rarely resulted in greater efficacy in their relationships.[26] Because youths routinely framed girls' violence as expressive, girls' more instrumental goals and desires —to increase boyfriends' faithfulness and emotional engagement—were more easily dismissed. This is in keeping with research on the gendered meanings of partner violence, which consistently finds that men minimize the significance of female-perpetrated partner violence, thus limiting young women's ability to use violence in order to control their partners' behaviors.[27]

Young Men's Dating Violence

While girls' dating violence was attributed to their being emotionally out of control, youths' attitudes toward boys' dating violence revealed a more complex set of interpretations. Youths' discussions centered to a large extent on explicating the general inappropriateness but situational acceptability of male violence.[28] An overarching theme in nearly all of the interviews was that young men should not hit young women. This was a powerful normative constraint that was not matched with a counterpart regarding girls' violence. For example, recall that Alicia insisted when she hit her boyfriend there was nothing wrong with it. She later described an instance in which her boyfriend "slapped me in my face" after another boy made comments about her. Her boyfriend "was just like, 'Who is so-and-so?' We got to arguing and I was like, 'There ain't nobody else.'" After he hit her, Alicia "was crying and I was mad so I [called] his momma. I don't know what his momma did but he ain't hit me no more. . . . He say, 'I didn't mean to smack you that hard,' he say, 'but you deserve to get smacked.'" Though Alicia held different rules for herself and her boyfriend, her account also illustrates one of the circumstantial exceptions that allowed young men to use violence.

TABLE 5-2
TABLE 5-2
Youths' Attitudes about the Appropriateness of Male Dating Violence (N = 74)

	Girls (N = 34)[a]	Boys (N = 40)
Do you think it's all right for a man to slap or hit his girlfriend if:		
She won't do what he tells her	0 (0%)	3 (8%)
She insults him when they are alone	1 (3%)	5 (13%)
She insults him in front of other people	4 (12%)	7 (18%)
She gets drunk or high	7 (21%)	5 (13%)
She won't have sex with him	0 (0%)	2 (5%)
He finds out she is going out with someone else	9 (26%)	10 (25%)
She hits him first when they are arguing	10 (29%)	16 (40%)

[a] One young woman did not respond to these questions.

To examine these contingencies a bit further, table 5-2 summarizes youths' responses to survey items about the appropriateness of boys' violence in relationships. None of the young women and just three young men believed it was okay for a man to use violence if his girlfriend would not listen to him, and only two boys (Darnell and Tommie) believed it was appropriate if she refused sex. However, a larger minority of youths believed it was appropriate if she insulted him, especially in front of other people, and slightly more boys than girls believed this to be true. In addition, more than one in five girls believed boys' violence was a legitimate response to girls' substance use, a slightly larger percentage than for boys. This was tied to the dangers posed by alcohol and drug use documented in chapter 4.

The largest proportion of affirmative responses were for two items. The first concerned girls' cheating on their boyfriends, which approximately one-quarter of youths believed warranted boys' violence. There was greatest approval for male responses to female-initiated violence. Although the majority of youths did not approve of such violence, a substantial minority (29 percent of girls and 40 percent of boys) believed it was appropriate. In all, 44 percent of young women and 60 percent of young men identified situational contingencies that they believed warranted male violence against a dating partner. These are important to keep in mind as I examine the overarching normative constraints against young men's dating violence.

Moreover, youths were much more likely to report that their friends had more permissive attitudes toward male partner violence than they held themselves. Table 5-3 reports youths' responses to the same questions posed in table 5-2, asking them to speculate on their friends' attitudes. What is shown is a great deal more perceived normative support among youths' peer networks for male violence. For example, nearly one-half of girls and boys believed their friends condoned male violence when girlfriends "insult" their boyfriends, and more than one-half thought their friends would approve when a girl cheated on her boyfriend or hit him first. Moreover, more than one-third of the boys said their friends would condone violence against a girlfriend if she wouldn't do what he told her. As discussed in earlier chapters regarding sexual mistreatment, youths' peer culture played an important role in shaping the contexts of violence, and perhaps even solidified youths' beliefs that their expressions of disapproval or attempts at intervention would be met with derision.[29]

Returning to the overarching norm against male violence, the imperative that boys not hit girls was primarily framed in one of two ways: first was the belief, grounded most clearly in hegemonic masculinity, that to do so was unmanly—men should fight individuals who pose a physical challenge, not individuals they know they can beat. Antwoin noted, "you a punk if you fight a girl," and Christal echoed his sentiment: "if a boy hit a girl, they a punk." Likewise, Rennesha said, "I feel a man has too much strength to hit a female, it is just not a man to hit a female. No matter what. Some girls think they tough, want to keep walking up. But still, you walk away. You a man." Cooper explained, "we have more strength than them. Why hit a female, when they hit

TABLE 5-3

Friends' Attitudes about the Appropriateness of Male Dating Violence (N = 74)

	Girls (N = 33)[a]	Boys (N = 40)
Do you think your friends would approve of a man slapping or hitting his girlfriend if:		
She won't do what he tells her	7 (21%)	14 (35%)
She insults him when they are alone	9 (27%)	12 (30%)
She insults him in front of other people	14 (42%)	19 (48%)
She gets drunk or high	13 (39%)	8 (20%)
She won't have sex with him	6 (18%)	5 (13%)
He finds out she is going out with someone else	19 (58%)	20 (50%)
She hits him first when they are arguing	17 (52%)	25 (63%)

[a] One young woman did not respond to these questions, and another reported that she had no friends.

you back it won't hurt for real. No competition in that." In addition to being viewed as physically unmanly, several young men also linked hitting girls with evidence of too great of an emotional investment in the relationship—a contrast to the valued cool pose.

The second framework for explaining why men shouldn't hit women was a more chivalrous variation of the first. Here the emphasis was specifically on girls' vulnerability and also linked with young men's respect for their mothers. Dwayne noted, "you don't hit no woman. You got more strength than them, you can hurt her good." Bobby said, "we stronger than girls. Can hit them and it hurt one of they bones for real." Kenisha took this angle as well: "I feel like a man don't never supposed to put his hands on a woman, because a man is above a woman always and a woman is a woman. That's just like a man wouldn't want no one to hit his mother so why you gonna go out and hit somebody else's daughter?" In fact, a number of young men said they were taught by their mothers and grandmothers not to hit girls. Ricky's explanation clearly links this norm back to the family:

> When you think about it, we already got the advantage 'cause we men.
> . . . All of us live with women, I mean, and I think about it like I wouldn't want my momma to be in a relationship and they have an argument then he feel like he can just punch on her, black her eye, choke on her or something like that. Then I think about it too, I got a sister. I wouldn't want my sister getting in no relationship with nobody and they feel like they can beat on her because they together and they call theyself a couple or whatever.

But the conversation with Ricky also alluded to one of the key contradictions in how youths viewed male-on-female violence: punching or beating up a woman was viewed as distinct from other forms of physical violence. He continued, "my friends don't too much hit they girlfriends. If anything, they'll just push 'em and yank 'em and grab 'em but it ain't really like a balled up fist or smack type of thing." Young women adopted this view as well, as Anishika noted, "I don't think a man should hit a female, period. I don't see nothing wrong with grabbing her or whatever, but hitting and grabbing is two different things to me." Thus, norms against young men's use of violence referred specifically to its most serious forms. But there were contingencies in the appropriateness of using serious violence, as well.

MALE VIOLENCE AS A RESPONSE TO
FEMALE-INITIATED VIOLENCE

Despite the belief that young men should be able to "take it like men," both girls and boys posited several ideologies that justified a violent response when a girl initiated violence. As Ricky's and Anishika's comments suggest, a tempered or controlled physical response received widespread approval. Terence explained, "you don't put your hands on females no matter what. And if it really come to it, you don't never hit 'em as hard as you could hit a dude or something." Of himself, Ricky said, "I can't hit no woman. I'm already weighin' 220, you know what I'm sayin'. . . . I already know I'm overpowering and for me to just fight her would just be worthless." Describing a recent conflict, he continued:

> We was standing outside here [at school] and she said why didn't I speak to her, and I said, "Man go'n, don't nobody wanna hear that." I guess she felt like, who you talking to? Like she was my momma or something and she slapped me in the back of my head. . . . I'm like, ugh, that's pathetic. I sorta like pushed her off me like, man ain't nobody tryin' to hear that. She hit me again and I came in the building and then she left.

Likewise, recall Wayne's description of the fight that occurred after his girlfriend telephoned him and he called her the wrong name. He said she "tried to slap me and all that kind of stuff," but that "I ain't ever put my hands back on her. I just kinda grab her, settle her down and you know just hold her, like, 'Why you tripping?' Pretty much restrain her from hitting me, that's all." And Marvin said "once I grabbed her [his girlfriend] 'cause she kept smacking me. I just grabbed her 'cause I didn't wanna hit her, I just grabbed her and told her to chill out."

Some youths believed more serious male violence was called for when the girl appeared to have forgotten her place. Asked to speculate as to why his friends sometimes hit their girlfriends, Larry responded: "Well most of the time I've been there, I know why. Gal be trippin'. Like one gal, she crazy, she be swinging on him. He be like, he be trying not to hit her but I be like, 'Don't keep lettin' her hit you like that dog, go'n, swing back or do something.'" Nicole said, "if you big enough to hit a man, you big enough to take that lick back." Walter concurred: "Certain times I feel that if a girl is man enough to hit you she man enough to get hit back." And Lamont said, "you punch me, I'm gonna punch you back. That's lettin' me know you think you big and bad, but if you hit me that let me know you big enough to take licks." Cleshay put this ideology in perhaps the starkest terms:

> When the woman step up to her husband like she a man and try to go head up with him, I think he should let her know, "You can't whoop me." Because some girls be needin' it. Like I know it's been times I done just stepped up to a dude like "What's up," like I'm just tough, bad, and all this other stuff and just swung on him. Now he should've knocked me on my butt, 'cause I'm feeling all big, bad, and bold, like I can beat everybody up. And all he did, he didn't want to hurt me. But sometimes you need to put people in their place.

In part, these contradictions about whether males should use violence were a reflection of different youths' attitudes. But such contradictions also coexisted within individual youths' accounts. For instance, Cleshay herself noted that "a man shouldn't hit no woman." Alicia said that "boys just don't supposed to hit girls. But I tell my little brother if she hit you, just hit her back." Christal best illustrated the layers of contradictions that sometimes emerged in a single narrative. While she was adamant that boys are "some punks" if they hit their girlfriends, she also said that "if a girl hit a dude, they deserve to be hit back." Reflecting on the fight with her boyfriend described above, she said "if you hit 'em, they'll probably like push you but they ain't gon' actually steal you [punch you in the face], smack you or do nothin' like that. If you keep on hittin' him, you stupid. 'Cause I know, can't no girl whoop no boy. I tried it, I thought I could, but [girls] can't for real."

Recall as well that Christal's fight with her boyfriend ended in their breakup. Nonetheless, she later said that if a boy hits his girlfriend out of jealousy, "that must mean that they really like you if they wanna hit you or whatever." In the same breath, she was complimentary of the young man she was currently interested in because "when I hit [him] he ain't hit me back. I smacked him and it left a hand print but he ain't hit me back, he just got mad." Thus, depending on the circumstance under which it arose, boys' violence had multiple and contradictory meanings attached to it—particularly for girls. None of the young men suggested that hitting a girl was an indication that they "really liked" her. That some girls suggested this interpretation was again related to the cool pose: an emotional response, even a violent one, was sometimes seen as evidence of emotional engagement.

NONRECIPROCAL MALE VIOLENCE

Two young women in our study—LaSondra and Sheron—were in relationships that fit the profile of chronic battering, in which there was "a systematic use of violence, the threat of violence, and other coercive behaviors to exert power, induce fear, and control" over one's partner.[30] Such relationships are intensely psychologically abusive as well. LaSondra had been in a long-term abusive relationship with a man 11 years her senior. Her boyfriend threatened her life, anally raped her, stalked her, and repeatedly physically assaulted and verbally abused her. She said the relationship "was good at first. He was real nice at first. Then after that [first] incident, then he start, I don't know. I still stay[ed] with him 'cause, you know, I was scared and stuff. . . . I thought he might kill me." The conversation continued:

> *Interviewer*: Did he make a threat to really kill you?
> *LaSondra*: Yeah. When he, that time when we walked to that alley to the short cut, when he choked me and said he'll kill me. And [he said] he'll kill me if I talk to somebody else, 'cause he don't want nobody talking to me, nobody looking at me but him. Or me looking at anybody else. And you know, I got male friends, and they just my friends. They not my sexual partners and stuff. He get jealous if he sees me and one of my male friends walking, or if I'm at work talking to another male friend he'll get jealous.

She also described him threatening her friend, when he perceived that the girl was critical of his treatment of LaSondra. She said that "my momma . . . left and went out of town, so I asked my friend to spend the night with me and she did." Her boyfriend took "me and my friend out" but then "threatened to hit my friend. He told me, he say, 'If she don't stay out of my business, I'm gonna slap her face.' He say, 'You need to talk to her,' but he said it like real mean." Such controlling and isolating strategies are common tactics of chronic batterers.

Of her rape, she explained:

> It was sad for real 'cause it's anal sex you know. He, um, wanted to have anal sex with me and I was like "Naw 'cause it's gonna hurt."

'Cause it look like it would hurt. So then he just pushed me down, I was flat on my stomach and he just pushed it in. It was hurting too. He just pushed it in. He just all on top of me and just pushed it in. . . . He knew I didn't [want to but] he didn't care.

LaSondra said that she "didn't talk to him for six months" after the rape, " 'cause it made me mad. . . . I don't want to be there with him when he did stuff like that." However, his apologies—also a common tactic with chronic batterers—eventually won her back over, and the abuse continued.

She also described closely monitoring her own behaviors because "he got a way of finding stuff out. . . . [He] used to stalk me, he used to watch me, like, he used to tell me too sometimes. He'll say, like, I'll watch your house at nighttime. To, you know, see who coming in my house so he could pick a fight or something." In addition, she continued:

He be talking to a lot guys and be finding out [anything I do]. And then, every time I see him I get this scary feeling, this like little feeling in my stomach. Or even if he look at me like in a mean way I get scared. I just ask him, I just say "Don't look at me that way." 'Cause that's scary. And he knew it scary so he keep looking at me that way. . . . He knew how it made me feel. . . . I was always crying every time he did something wrong to me or called me out my name and stuff. Call me a ho', a lot of names. Made me sad. . . . [Even] when we was having sex sometimes he be like asking me all these stupid questions. I don't even respond. He used to say to me sometimes, "When you gonna start doing what I tell you to do?"

LaSondra said they finally broke up after her mother "just come between us, because she ain't like the things [he was doing]. . . . And then he said like, 'She all in our business' and stuff, and he get mad at me, take it out on me 'cause my momma . . . said things to him." Her mother finally succeeded in leveraging their age difference—LaSondra was 16, and he was 27—to break up her daughter's abusive relationship.[31] However, they never called the police or otherwise sought assistance because LaSondra believed, "they can't help me. It wouldn't be worth it. . . . They just can't [help] at all. . . . Like the police, they [would] just take him and he be out of jail right back again. And he know where I live, and he know where I work, so." Nonetheless, she remained ambivalent about the breakup. Asked if she was glad the relationship was over, she explained, "not glad, happy-happy glad. I was okay. But, you know, I still got feelings for him, stuff like that."

LaSondra's case was exceptional, both because she was in a relationship with an adult and because of the chronic nature of the abuse she faced. Her experiences draw a vivid distinction between chronic battering and the more typical adolescent dating violence our research uncovered. Nonetheless, a number of young women described having friends in battering relationships, and youths reported that witnessing severe male violence among their peers was not uncommon. In all, 10 girls (29 percent) reported they had friends whose boyfriends had used violence against them, while 13 girls (37 percent) and 14 boys (35 percent) described having male friends who used violence against their girlfriends.

Despite the normative constraint against nonreciprocal male violence, youths did not uniformly condemn it. Instead, it was typically explained as either brought on by girls' behaviors (as evidenced in tables 5-2 and 5-3), the result of some boys having "bad tempers," or some combination of these. Girls and boys both espoused these beliefs, though with the notable caveat that girls were more disturbed by such events than were boys, particularly when the victim was a friend. Nearly all of the boys described taking a noninterventionist approach when they witnessed male violence. In contrast, girls routinely described attempts at intervention specifically when it was a friend being abused.[32] One of the intervention strategy girls employed was to talk to their friends and encourage them to leave violent relationships. These young women were frustrated when their friends "think he do it because he love her" or responded, "but I love him, it don't matter if he slapped me." Jamellah lamented, "you can't tell them nothin' cause they think they grown, they don't wanna listen to nobody." The second strategy, discussed below, involved direct intervention at the time of the assault.

Youths most often defined girls as deserving of male violence because they "runnin' they mouth." Of his girlfriend, Frank said, "man she just getting on my nerves. I tell her to shut up, I'm like, 'Shut up, just shut up.' Get all up in my face. Pow—shut up!" Likewise, Kevin described his use of violence:

> Like sometimes we'll be talking or something or arguing and she get loud and she start putting her hand in my face and stuff and I'll, she'll put her hand in my face and I slap her hand. One time I had just got, I

ain't try to, I just got mad and I, I smacked her, then she started looking at me crazy then she walked off or whatever. Sometimes she just, it be her fault for real. She don't know when to shut up. That's her main problem, she do not know when to shut up.

Girls sometimes espoused these beliefs as well. Dawanna said, "there's been situations where I been like, 'You need to smack her,' and then there's situations where I be like, 'Take her on!'" Asked why, she replied, "'cause how she's actin', how she's talkin', how she movin', how she carrying herself."

Sheron described nonreciprocal male violence in her relationship. Of a recent event, she explained, "he had my jacket and I was like, 'Hey can you give me my jacket?' and he was like, 'You know my name, my name not hey.' And he got mad and he choked me and then he threw my coat at me and walked off." Sheron said she was mad and "felt embarrassed . . . because he did it in front of everybody, all my associates at school." As described in chapter 4, he had also pressured her into sex. In fact, the day before her interview, they were on the phone and "he was talking about oral sex and I was like, 'No, you already know I don't do that' or whatever. And he was like, 'F [fuck] you then,' you know he hung up the phone or whatever." She speculated that boys were violent in relationships "just to show that they are the male in the relationship and they got control." However, in spite of her own experiences, she also condoned such violence in a wide range of situations—if the girl was disrespectful to her boyfriend, if she drank or got high, or if she cheated. And despite her misgivings about her boyfriend's use of violence, she said, "I think that a female knows what she's dealing with before she does get into a relationship . . . and I don't think that you should enter a relationship with anybody and you're not comfortable with them."

In fact, recall from tables 5-2 and 5-3 that girls were more likely than boys to believe that violence was an appropriate response if the girl was drinking. Sheron explained this was because "when you get drunk or high you can do anything." Likewise, Kristy said, "if she drinking and acting a fool, yeah put her in her place." In chapter 4, I discussed some of the dangers young women faced when they used substances, and this was likely the reason some of them approved of young men's relationship violence in such circumstances.

Sometimes, though girls did not condone the violence, they nonetheless explained it in terms of the young woman's behaviors. Yvonne described a recent incident she witnessed:

> My partner, his girlfriend be like having card games. . . . She can't hold her liquor, she can't get high and he don't allow her to do none of that which I think is good, but on occasion she be like "Get me a beer," you know what I'm saying. . . . And when she drink one, she gotta keep drinking, keep drinking, or smoking, smoking, smoking, so she got drunk or whatever, she was leaning all over him. She got hot and went to change and of course if your man there and you come out your bedroom with some shorts halfway up the crack of your butt and a little halter top, he gonna say something to you. He gonna get mad. He was already high and drunk and on top of that he was losing his money, so you knew he was gonna flip. So she come out there or whatever and she wrapped her arm around him and had one arm leaning on his friend and he said "Bitch, what's wrong with you?" and just threw her up against the wall. He was beating her up real bad and she don't never hit him back, never.

Despite suggesting the young woman brought it on by dressing inappropriately and drinking, Yvonne was disturbed by the assault and attempted to intervene: "I jump[ed] all up in his face and whatever, and my boyfriend be telling me, he say 'You ain't got nothing to do with this,' or whatever. Which she not my friend, but she a female and I don't want to see her getting beat up on." Asked how the young men present responded, she said, "they be laughing. Hee hee, ha ha and all that. And it's not funny and it's not cute to see no man beat up on a girl and she can't do nothing about it because she ain't as big as a man and she already petrified of you, you know what I'm saying. They think it's cute."

Destiny described a similar event among a couple she hung out with: "It's like he be talkin' to all these girls and stuff and she be tellin' him he can't do it so he get real mad at her and start beatin' on her, I mean straight beatin' her. . . . I'm the only one would sit there, 'Get your hands off her,' pull his hands up off her." Destiny said that "everybody used to call her so stupid and stuff, I used to call her stupid [too], but she loved him. I was like, 'Love's not that strong to be getting black eyes, he bustin' your head.' " Despite her willingness to intervene, Destiny's description of the young woman as "stupid" illustrates the pervasive victim-blaming attitudes common among the youths we spoke to.

As Destiny and Yvonne's accounts suggest, however, girls were more likely than boys to empathize with victims. Describing a violent friend, Larry said, "it's a gene, his daddy did it so I guess he gon' do it. He very angry and he can't control his temper." Of the friend's girlfriend, he surmised, "she with the nigga so she must like it." When witnessing his friend's violence, Larry said most often he "laugh[ed]": "That nigga crazy, he be trying to whoop his girl with stinsion [extension] cords, irons, and all that type of stuff. Sometimes it be funny to me, sometimes I feel sorry." Boys who were troubled when they witnessed violence most often described leaving rather than intervening. For example, Terence was at a friend's when the boy began beating his girlfriend: "I could hear him smackin' her or whatever. . . . I don't condone it or nothin' but I ain't tryin' to be around when it happen so I just left." Thus despite norms against nonreciprocal male violence, young men rarely faced negative sanction among their peers when they engaged in such behaviors. In fact, it was often attributed to an extreme version of the playa' mentality. Wayne explained, "they feel they got something to prove for domination or whatever . . . that they can run their girl or whatever." Kevin surmised, "some people think they pimps or something, they'll smack a girl and not think twice about it."

Conclusion

In this chapter, I document a series of gender inequalities in youths' peer groups with important implications for the nature of dating conflict and violence. These include features of localized hegemonic masculinity—the playa' and the cool pose—and a sexual double standard that rewarded male sexual exploits but sanctioned unconstrained female sexuality. In previous chapters, I discuss how these contributed to sexual aggression. The analyses here show that they functioned, as well, to structure the nature of relationship conflict and to diminish young women's efficacy within relationships.

This also was mirrored within relationship violence: young women's use of violence against their boyfriends was often rooted in their responses to the playa' (concerns about infidelity) and the cool pose (frustration at emotional detachment strategies); however, girls' violence was interpreted as ineffectual and perceived to be rooted in their greater emotionality. Young men's relationship violence, though condemned in the abstract, was situationally explained and justified as a reaction to their girlfriends' behaviors. It was seen as potentially dangerous, in need of temperance, but occasionally called for in order to reestablish the "natural" gender order.

The consequences were twofold. First, youths' construction of girls' violence as expressive—as a result of their greater emotionality—functioned to undermine their goals of challenging the inequities in their relationships. Second, young men's relationship violence was too often framed as a rational or acceptable response to young women's actions, was viewed with humor, or was silently disapproved of. Victim-blaming, callousness, and nonintervention were the norm.

Nonetheless, as with sexual assault, there were a few young women who described their efforts to intervene on young men's dating violence, both by encouraging their female friends to terminate violent relationships, and, occasionally, by attempting to intervene on violence when it happened. However, they were often discouraged from doing the latter, both because the incidents were defined as private and because intervention was perceived as placing them at risk for retaliatory violence. Yvonne, one of the few young women who described systematically attempting to protect other girls, told us, "my sister told me, one day it's gonna catch up with me, 'cause I always be trying to jump in other people's business, they gonna end up hurting me."

Thus, this chapter demonstrates that the meanings and consequences of young men's violence were strikingly different from those of young women. Girls faced much more serious harm from partner violence, particularly when it was nonreciprocal. This is particularly evident when we compare youths' descriptions of the female versus male partner violence they experienced and witnessed. While there may have been gender parity in youth's survey reports of dating victimization, these were not paralleled in youths' narrative accounts. Moreover, young men maintained greater situational control over violence itself—including whether girls' violence was permitted to occur or was met with violent sanction.[33] Compare this with the striking finding that none of the young women in our study described responding to male-initiated dating violence with violence. Relationship violence, like the other forms of gendered violence examined in previous chapters, was deeply grounded in gender inequalities.[34]

Once again, we return to the broader structural contexts in which youths' dating violence took place. Race-based and class-based inequalities strongly shaped the distinctive adaptation strategies of youths, including young men's heightened attention to the particular features of masculinity examined here. There is compelling evidence that these structural inequalities have great import for explaining both the nature of gender inequalities and the widespread use and acceptance of violence.[35] Nonetheless, the gender ideologies youths culled from, and the inequities they described, certainly are embedded within the fabric of gendered power and inequality within our society more broadly. Both of these facts pose an exacting challenge as we seek to improve the safety and security of urban African American young women.

6

Conclusions and Recommendations

In chapter 1, I argue that there has been a dearth of scholarly attention to the problem of violence against African American young women in distressed urban communities. For decades now, researchers have examined the criminogenic effects of disadvantaged community contexts and have documented the vast and overwhelming harms to young people that result from growing up in such settings.[1] For the most part, however, criminological research on neighborhoods has been gender blind or has focused specific attention on young men or adult offender networks. Research on young women, likewise, has focused primarily on their participation in delinquency, even when the emphasis has been on the blurred boundaries of victimization and offending.[2]

In addition, given the goals of feminist researchers—to problematize violence against women as a societal-wide phenomenon rooted in gender inequality—specific investigations of violence against urban African American girls have also been limited. As I suggest, part of the reticence to address this problem is grounded in legitimate concerns about further demonizing young Black men, who already face an abundance of harmful stereotypes that affect their treatment across any number of social institutions in America.[3] Ultimately, though, our inattention to such violence causes its greatest harm to young Black women, who are left to fend for themselves in addressing this systematic danger.

Because violence against women is an endemic problem in American society, of course we should expect that such violence would be particularly acute in impoverished community contexts where other forms of violence are widespread, community and personal resources are limited, collective efficacy is difficult to achieve, and young men are faced with a masculine street code that emphasizes respect, interpersonal violence, and heterosexual prowess demonstrated via sexual conquest.[4] Several recent studies bear this out,[5] and we have certainly seen it to be the case in the study reported here. Urban African American young women face widespread gendered violence that is a systematic and overlapping feature of their neighborhoods, communities, and schools. In addition, while young women employ a variety of strategies to insulate themselves from such violence, they do so in a context in which ideologies about gender work against them at every turn. They have limited support and few avenues—institutional or otherwise—for remedying the systemic nature of the gendered dangers present in their daily lives.

In chapter 2, I examine the nature of young women's neighborhood risks, showing that public spaces in disadvantaged communities are male dominated and, consequently, many facets of neighborhood risks are structured by gender.[6] Public acts of violence against women were widespread, with many youths recounting incidents they had witnessed. In addition, girls expressed serious concerns about their sexualization in community contexts. While they complained about sexual harassment by their male peers, they were especially leery of adult men and male offenders who congregated in public spaces in their neighborhoods and also believed that women's risks were heightened due to the presence of the drug trade.

Young women described numerous strategies for staying safe. Strikingly, many girls said they often avoided public spaces in their neighborhoods, opting to stay at or close to home when possible. When present in public spaces, girls often relied on the company of others for protection and sometimes called on male neighbors or relatives to walk with them, particularly at night. In addition, they drew security from the belief that their networks of neighborhood friends and family could insulate them from danger. Girls occasionally took comfort from the visible presence of police in their neighborhoods, but they rarely viewed the police as providing protection to neighborhood residents and were often disappointed in those instances in which the police were called to intercede.[7]

In addition to disappointment and distrust of criminal justice interventions, there were other limitations to girls' protective strategies. For example, their primary strategy for staying safe in their neighborhoods —staying indoors and at home—while insulating them from neighborhood risks, came at a considerable cost, because it limited their ability to fully participate in public life.[8] In addition, reliance on community ties were hindered by the great deal of residential instability reported by the youths in our sample, as well as by the dominance of nonintervention norms in their neighborhoods. Both of these patterns are strongly tied to the kinds of economic deprivations they and their families faced, but nonetheless placed limits on young women's ability to rely on collective community ties for protection. Gender had an impact as well, since violence against women in particular is often conceptualized as a "private" matter.

Moreover, young women's faith in the young men they knew was sometimes misplaced. There is clear evidence of this, not only in their discussions of boys' neighborhood harassing behaviors but also as discussed in chapters 3, 4, and 5. Young women faced the greatest risk for victimization at the hands of young men they knew, a pattern consistent with what we know about African American girls' risks in general, as well as with broader patterns of violence against women.[9] Finally, prevalent gender ideologies often resulted in the development of victim-blaming attitudes. When coupled with norms favoring nonintervention, violence against women often took on features of public spectacle, with girls and boys describing such incidents as a source of entertainment. Consequently, there was little empathy for young women when they were harassed or faced more serious forms of violence. Institutional and community supports were simply not widely available.

This was also the case when girls faced sexual mistreatment in school. In chapter 3, I discuss that girls actually reported more sexual harassment in schools than they did in their neighborhoods. Partly, this was because, unlike in their neighborhoods—where they could avoid interactions with young men by staying off the streets—in school they were unavoidably in continuous contact with one another. Thus, girls reported experiencing harassment in all corners of the school—hallways, classrooms, the cafeteria and gym, and the grounds in and around school. Young women described a variety of forms of harassment, including gendered name-calling, sexual comments and rumors, and touching, groping, and grabbing. Young men often characterized this behavior as "play," which functioned to conceal the actual harms to young women resulting from this behavior and undermined girls' attempts to remedy the situation.

Although girls employed a range of strategies in their attempts to prevent and challenge sexual harassment, each tactic came with constraining double binds. Ignoring boys' behavior was read as acceptance or acquiescence to it, and doing so led to perceptions that girls lacked respect for themselves—either because they "wanted it" or were too weak to stand up for themselves. More often, girls described asserting themselves by demanding the behavior stop and sometimes using defensive aggression to get their points across. Such externalizing responses were grounded in the important normative place of standing up for oneself in disadvantaged contexts, but these tactics also came at considerable cost. In many cases, the result was an escalating conflict, often egged on by peers and sometimes resulting in violent rebuke. In other cases, girls found their own behaviors penalized by school personnel rather than recognized as self-defense.

And in school, as in neighborhoods, young women described little institutional support for addressing sexual harassment. This is all the more troubling because school personnel have a clearly defined responsibility to protect the youths in their charge and create environments conducive to learning. To be sure, since youths' schools were embedded in distressed urban communities, their schools were chronically troubled as well. Understaffed, underfunded, and primarily concerned with weapons and gang violence, school personnel rarely saw sexual harassment for the serious problem that it was. Lack of concern for the harmful effects of sexual harassment is a serious problem in schools across America. Teachers and administrators often define it as a natural part of youths' shifts from childhood to more adult relations rather than as a "dress rehearsal" for the reproduction of gender inequality.[10] However, this was exacerbated further for the youths in our sample, given the systemic problems in their schools. Thus, yet again, girls often found themselves on their own as they negotiated this routine feature of their school lives.

Importantly, the analyses in chapter 3 also reveal that school-based sexual harassment often functioned in tandem with neighborhood dynamics. For instance, many of the sexual rumors at school were grounded in actual or perceived sexual interactions within youths' neighborhoods, and young men sometimes used school-based sexual harassment as a testing ground to gauge girls' receptivity or their ability to stand up for themselves. Such information was translated back to neighborhood settings, where serious sexual misconduct could more readily take place. In chapter 4, the focus shifts back to youths' community action spaces, where the sexualized treatment first identified in chapter 2 and examined in chapter 3 coalesced in the stark reality of widespread sexual violence against young women.

In chapter 4, I detail the nature and situational contexts of sexual coercion and assault against young women. Just as sexual violence is a continuation of the more routinized sexualization documented in chapters 2 and 3, such aggression exists on a continuum grounded in narrow constructions of heterosexuality that emphasize masculine concerns. Young women reported being pressured or coerced into unwanted sex, and they described actual or attempted sexual assaults, as well as gang rapes. In addition, recall the troubling finding that nearly one in three young women had experienced multiple sexual victimizations.

Research has consistently shown that women's risk for sexual victimization is at its highest in adolescence and young adulthood.[11] This risk is heightened further for young women in distressed urban communities. Just as scholars have documented the organizational characteristics, gender ideologies, and situational contexts associated with sexual violence in high-risk groups such as college fraternities, sports teams, and the military, I show some comparable facets of disadvantaged settings that encouraged sexual aggression against young women. As Elijah Anderson documents in *Code of the Streets,* behavioral expectations for young men in disadvantaged communities encourage cultural support for such violence, in part, through their emphasis on sexual conquest.[12]

Like fraternities and other high-risk groups, neighborhood networks in disadvantaged communities are male-dominated, with the congregation of adult men a visible presence. Youths described how some of these men targeted girls deemed particularly vulnerable or naïve and staged opportunities to sexually abuse or exploit them. In addition, as researchers have found with other groups, lack of oversight, supervision, and accountability further fostered a climate in which young women were mistreated with seeming impunity. As I noted, a great deal of research has documented the difficulties that residents in poor urban neighborhoods have in developing collective efficacy. Coupled with distrust of law enforcement—and the lack of social, political, and economic resources—the result is that norms favoring nonintervention often win out.

In fact, much of the sexual violence young women faced took place at unsupervised gatherings of young people, where alcohol and drug use was widespread. These contexts not only made young women more vulnerable to sexual mistreatment but also increased the likelihood that they would be viewed as either willing participants or deserving victims.

In addition, some young men purposely used alcohol and drugs as a weapon to weaken girls' resistance or incapacitate them. Yet again, girls described having few mechanisms available to them for support or intervention against such violence. They relied on themselves, on developing street smarts (though often only after an initial victimization), and on trusted friends or family members to cope with their experiences or, occasionally, enact retribution.

In chapter 5, I examine the problem of dating violence. Once again, this phenomenon was widespread but with the seeming twist that some young women also engaged in violence in their relationships. The meanings and consequences of girls' dating violence were vastly different from young men's, however, and both were grounded in gender inequalities associated with the masculine reward structures available to young men in disadvantaged communities. In previous chapters, I discuss how the sexual double standard that encouraged young men to view girls as potential sexual conquests led to sexual harassment and aggression. Here, I show how it contributed to dating conflicts and partner violence as well, serving to diminish young women's efficacy in romantic relationships.

While girls' violence was conceptualized as ineffectual and framed as stemming from their "out-of-control" emotions, young men's violence was recognized as a serious threat. Consequently, youths espoused norms against male-on-female dating violence, though with multiple caveats that justified young men's violence and blamed the female victim in a range of situations. Male-initiated partner violence was a serious problem in some youths' relationships, and many more young women described having friends in violent relationships. Young women often described their attempts to intervene, particularly by encouraging their female friends to exit violent relationships. However, as with the other forms of gendered violence examined here, victim-blaming and nonintervention were often the norm.

Recommendations: A Gendered, Ecological Approach

So where do we go from here? Violence against women is a ubiquitous social problem in American society, and such violence is intensified in the social contexts that shape youths' day-to-day lives in disadvantaged communities. It is heightened by the cultural adaptations that youths and other community members use to survive life in such distressed urban settings. In particular, when young men's constructions of masculine identity rely on keen attention to respect, violence, independence, and heterosexual prowess, young women are at greater risk for victimization. There is strong evidence that such masculinity constructions take hold in disadvantaged settings because young men's access to alternative avenues for garnering status and prestige are limited or absent.[13] Thus, any hope we have of ameliorating this endemic social problem must address the structural inequalities at the root of urban disadvantage. Such inequalities are not simply based on the race and class inequalities that pattern ecological disadvantage; they are deeply gendered as well.

The research I present here points to the clear need to address violence against girls in disadvantaged communities in a systematic fashion. Exactly how we go about doing so is perhaps best left to policy experts, who I hope will take up the challenge. But I can certainly point to the types of transformations that need to be made, as can the youths we interviewed. Unfortunately, there are no simple answers or easy solutions. Following Lori L. Hiese and Liz Grauerholz, I suggest that systematic, ecologically embedded approaches are necessary if we hope to ameliorate the problem. This means offering remedies that attend to the root causes of urban disadvantage, addressing the resultant costs and consequences, and improving institutional support for challenging gender inequalities and strengthening young women's efficacy. Certainly, the youths, themselves, had much to say about the changes they believed would make a difference in their lives.

Improving Neighborhoods

To begin, urban disadvantage has not simply "just happened." The concentration of poor African Americans in such community contexts is the result of deliberate policy decisions. As sociologists Robert Sampson and Janet Lauritsen sum up:

Many community characteristics implicated in violence, such as residential instability, concentration of poor female-headed families with children, multiunit housing projects, and disrupted social networks, appear to stem rather directly from planned governmental policies at local, state, and federal levels.[14]

Disinvestments in impoverished urban communities, decisions that concentrate public housing in these settings, the curtailment of municipal services, and negligence in the enforcement of city housing codes all contribute to crime—including violence against women—through urban decay, neighborhood destabilization, residential instability, and the resulting deterioration of the community-based resources and social networks necessary for generating collective efficacy.[15]

As Sampson and Lauritsen review, just as public policies have created concentrated disadvantage, there are also policies available that show promise in improving the situation by stabilizing communities. For example, improved municipal services and strict enforcement of housing codes would counteract physical decay in poor urban communities. Such environmental improvements offer promise for making neighborhoods more livable. Likewise, investments made to rehabilitate existing housing and provide new housing could also help preserve and stabilize urban communities, particularly when efforts are made to increase residents' ability to become homeowners.

Not surprisingly, when we asked youths their opinions about ways to make their neighborhoods safer, these were common themes. Marvin explained, "like most of these abandoned buildings that's over there, they could either fix 'em up or tear 'em down. . . . [That] would stop all the, you know, drug trafficking and all that stuff from goin' on over there." And Shaun said, "clean it up. . . . Take some of them vacant buildings out of there and put some real houses in." Likewise, he emphasized the need for businesses to reinvest in the community, explaining, "there's a big ol' Schnucks [grocery store] that used to be down there. Then they just closed [it]—the only store that was down there. So now I don't know what people supposed to do [to] go shopping and stuff." Of the public housing apartments she lived in, Sheron said, "the walkways are dark . . . they need more lights." And Katie summed up, "they should . . . clean up the neighborhood, then make it look nice so people'll wanna come around and whatever."

When neighborhoods are made more livable, residents are more likely to remain. The resulting stability can improve the collective efficacy of community members through the generation of social ties, which, in turn, increase protective mechanisms like the willingness to intervene on behalf of neighbors and monitor the behavior of young people.[16] Although these are not sufficient changes to protect young women from gendered violence, they are a necessary part of any efforts to enhance the likelihood of countering the dominance of nonintervention norms that leave young women to address such violence on their own.

Youths had much to say about the need for and benefits of improved collective efficacy. Eugene explained, "you should keep an eye on each other, you know, watch your community, help your community and stuff." Jamal proposed that it would help to "get people more involved, into a community. Getting people to get out and clean [it] up, getting to know more people in the community." In fact, Jamellah felt safe in her immediate neighborhood precisely because she felt such mechanisms were present: "It's like, you know how old people is, they always looking out of the window. All night, all day." April believed that getting "people [to] watch around the neighborhood" would be an improvement, and Kenisha proposed, "they need to get some events. It's a community center by my house, but to me it does no good because some kids, as they get older, they feel like they too old to participate in the activities."

Thus, in addition, youths—and young men in particular—desired community programs designed to better provide structured activities tailored to the interests of young people. These, they believed, could offer opportunities that would serve as alternatives to the streets. Wayne said, "I would say more programs to get into, like more Boy's Clubs and stuff like that. . . . [Activities] that'll keep people more busy rather than being out there." And James explained:

> People need stuff, need something to do, to motivate they time. They ain't got no type of recreation centers in they neighborhood. They ain't got nuttin' to buy they time, no basketball, you know what I'm saying. [If] they got a recreation center . . . they can be out there playing basketball and doing something. So they just, so they not out on the streets. If they ain't got nuttin' else better to do, they sit around with each other, they bored . . . [and] start trouble.

Young men also focused on the need for jobs and job training. Kevin explained, "if a lot of us could find a job or something, or something to do, instead of being outside on the street, if we wasn't out there, then we couldn't do what we doing. To find a job or a recreational center or something, somewhere to go after school instead of being outside, out on the streets." In particular, he believed that such opportunities could "instill inside young people's mind that it's more to life than having fun and drinking and smoking and doing stupid stuff. 'Cause a lot of stuff we do we know is dumb, and we know it ain't too much to get out of it, but that's just what we taught. . . . We regular people, just like everybody else, we just end up in wrong situations." Likewise, Terence said:

> The main problem like with drugs is 'cause it ain't no jobs out here for people, you know, in the 'hood, that they could be comfortable with. Or to really go to work and actually keep it up. So I mean, basically, you gotta find jobs for people in the 'hood, something they know about, something they can do, before you can even think to, you know, make a 'hood a better place for anybody.

It is somewhat striking that comparatively few young women focused on recreational centers and jobs, while these were central themes in young men's descriptions of the neighborhood changes they desired. In fact, it was several boys, rather than girls, who specifically suggested the need for activities inclusive of or designated for young women. Ricky explained:

> The young ladies in our neighborhood need more activities, 'cause a lot of them, they don't really have jobs or anything. I mean, and they just sit in the house and watch TV, and they tired of doin' that. [Then] they come outside and talk to us, and then, before you know it, they done picked up a habit of smokin' weed or something or picked up a habit like drinkin' or smokin' cigarettes. Before you know it, they like shootin' dice or they like being out all night with us. I mean, they just need more activities.

Travis articulated a similar position, though he focused specifically on the need for alternatives to early motherhood:

> I think that where I stay at, we need like a recreation center for women. Not for women, for the teenage girls. You know, because a lot of girls see . . . like their friends could come up pregnant and some girls think that's the way to be, but in a way it's not. You still gotta go to school. Half of the teenage girls that having kids, they don't even got a job. So they can barely take care of themselves, but they want to take care of a baby too. I think we just need a recreation center to where kids, teen-

agers, could just go sit down and talk to somebody about something that's on their mind.

This issue—having community agencies where there is somebody to talk to—was of critical importance to many youths we interviewed and is an issue I return to below.

So far, I have suggested the need for policies that could bring resources, stability, and environmental improvements to disadvantaged neighborhoods, as well as organizations to provide structured—and engaging—activities for young people. It is clear, in general, that such community changes would be beneficial to the young people in these settings. But how might they help ameliorate violence against young women? Alone they are not sufficient. Nonetheless, there is reason to believe they are part of the answer. For example, recall in chapter 2 that young women felt more secure in their neighborhoods when they believed they had networks of individuals willing to intervene on their behalf. As I note, because such neighborhood renewal efforts offer the opportunity to stabilize communities and make them more livable, we can expect that strengthened social ties will increase the likelihood that neighbors will look out for one another, and this also means looking out for girls.

In addition, recall from chapter 4 that sexual violence against young women most often emerged as a result of youths' involvement in unsupervised activities, including spontaneous get-togethers and organized parties. In addition, participation in delinquency heightened girls' risks for sexual violence and young men's likelihood of engaging in sexual violence. Youths believed that their participation in these high-risk activities were the direct result of not having alternative avenues available for having fun or earning money. Thus, perhaps in an indirect way, providing young people with structured activities to meet these needs would avert them from the social contexts that heighten the risk for violence against young women. Moreover, providing young men in particular with these alternatives could result in changing norms of masculinity that no longer rely on the "street code" for status and prestige. Such changes, as well, would be of benefit to young women.

Increasing Institutional Accountability

A common theme throughout this book is that young women are often on their own in protecting themselves from and addressing gendered violence. While efforts to stabilize communities and engage residents in one another's and the neighborhood's well-being are part of the answer, it is also of vital importance to increase the accountability of those social institutions charged with these responsibilities. As researchers Annie Woodley Brown and Ruby Gourdine argue, "violence is a multidimensional phenomenon and requires that efforts to address the issue not only focus on the aggressive behavior of individuals, but also assessment of and changes in the institutions that influence and allow certain conditions to exist."[17] Two most relevant to the current investigation are police and schools.

NEIGHBORHOOD POLICING

Youths had two overarching complaints about police practices in their communities: underresponsiveness, including slow responses to calls for service, and aggressive strategies that included disrespectful treatment, intrusiveness, and police misconduct, including violence.[18] These complaints are unsurprising, as research consistently demonstrates that residents in neighborhoods characterized by concentrated poverty and minority racial segregation are faced with disproportionate experiences with police surveillance and stops, disrespectful treatment, verbal abuse, the use of force, including excessive and deadly force, police deviance, along with fewer police protections and slower response times.[19] Sociologist David Klinger argues that part of the reason police are less responsive in poor urban communities is because officers come to believe certain crimes are normative in these contexts and thus not worth their effort, and they often view victims in such settings as deserving.[20] This has also been an explanation for the social ecology of police misconduct, disrespect, and the use of force, as both disadvantaged neighborhoods and their residents—particularly young Black males—are defined as suspicious and dangerous.[21]

The consequence of these patterns is twofold, both with direct bearing on the problem of violence against young women. First, aggressive policing strategies and misconduct create a deep sense of distrust and legal cynicism among residents of disadvantaged communities.[22] Consequently, community members are more likely to be uncooperative when police investigate crimes. Recall Britney's description in chapter 2 of residents in her housing project refusing to provide the police with information after they witnessed a lengthy assault in which a resident beat and choked his girlfriend and forced her at gunpoint into his car. Distrust of the police, then, heightened neighborhood norms of nonintervention, including for violence against women.

Second, young women's frustrations were heightened and they were dissatisfied when they or a family member called the police to report a woman's victimization. In several cases, they said the officers simply did not show up. In Nykeshia's case, not only was the officer unwilling to intervene against the man who routinely harassed and threatened her, but also she believed this same officer was the one who had raped her best friend. These complaints are representative of two arenas in which research demonstrates specifically gendered harms of common police practices. Feminist scholars have long argued that law enforcement is insufficiently attentive to violence against women, treating reports of sexual violence with skepticism and defining domestic violence as a private affair rather than the purview of "real" police work. And while important policy inroads have been made to improve police responsiveness to such violence, unsurprisingly, research suggests that differential response to African American versus white victims remains, with assaults against Black women less likely to result in arrest.[23] In addition, recent research suggests that police sexual misconduct is a serious concern, with some evidence that young women who are poor, racial minorities, and otherwise marginalized are most vulnerable to sexually abusive practices.[24]

Thus, few young women described going to the police when victimized. Recall that after LaSondra was raped by a stranger in her neighborhood, she felt the police were unresponsive and said they "don't do nothing. Some of 'em just give up, they could care less. . . . That's how they are, they could just care less." Felicia complained, "I mean, you even have the police out here raping people nowadays. So you can't count on them for protection." While young men's frustration with the police in their neighborhoods stemmed primarily from their negative encounters, for young women, this was coupled with what they believed was officers' lack of responsiveness toward crime victims, and women in particular. Janelle surmised, "I feel the police are there to protect and serve you, not to harass you for no reason."

It was not that youths desired less of a police presence in their communities. Far from it. Given the high rates of crime and associated dangers in their neighborhoods, what they sought was a different kind of policing—one that simultaneously engaged community residents, treating them with concern and respect, and selectively targeted and sanctioned those involved in serious crime, including crimes against women. Travis explained:

> First on my list, I think we need a whole different brand of cops. . . . I think if we had some nice cops, some cops that not just always in the act of trying to catch somebody doing something wrong, but that'll act more like, take a ride, see something going wrong, and try to get out the car, not just lock somebody up. Just talk to 'em, you know. Try to make them have a better day. Just like that. If we had that, then we would be much better.

Though young men complained vehemently about routine stops and searches, both boys and girls felt the police should take greater steps to disburse groups of offenders in their neighborhoods. Britney said she wanted

> the police [to] ride around a little bit more, make the dudes, make the men get off the lot. If they wanna hang out, hang out at a house or something, don't hang out on no lot. Crack selling on [the] Amoco [gas station] lot, quit. I mean, calm that down, make that stop. And just, if the security [guards are] scared, fire them. Hire someone that ain't scared to step up and tell them, "no, you can't sell no drugs. We gonna lock you up, you fina go to jail." . . . [If] police ride around more, make the dudes scared to sell drugs in that neighborhood, they'll clear out.

The key, for young men in particular, was selectively targeting the right individuals. For instance, while Marvin recognized that "it's hard to tell who dealin' drugs and who ain't," he still believed better police/community relations, and more careful attention to individuals' behaviors, would allow the police to "start doin' they job." Young men believed routine arbitrary stops of groups of young men were not indicative of genuine police concerns about neighborhood crime but, instead, as Darnell explained, provided evidence that the police "stop you just to mess with you for real."

In addition, both girls and boys believed officers' treatment of community residents contributed to hostilities. Carlos noted, "they need to change the way they talk to people." And Cherise explained, "I don't like police 'cause they mean. They don't know how to talk to people right, they disrespectful. They treat people like they ain't nothing, and especially Black people. They act like Black people are worthless." Research shows that the resulting distrust of police deters African American women from reporting incidents of violence against them.[25] Thus, current policing practices in many disadvantaged communities deny female victims their right to protection under the law.

Policing in and of itself cannot end violence against women. However, community policing strategies that treat community members with respect rather than suspicion, that engage residents and work to identify and meet their needs, and that are more sensitive to the dynamics and seriousness of violence against women would go far in making law enforcement more accountable. It is likely that such improvements would foster greater cooperation with the police and also increase the likelihood that young women could turn to them when they are victimized. Research demonstrates—and the youths we spoke to confirmed—that residents in disadvantaged communities are not more tolerant of crime than other citizens.[26] It is their cynicism about law enforcement specifically, and the criminal justice system generally, that hinders their willingness to fully engage with these institutions. Thus, finding ways to remedy systematic biases against disadvantaged community residents, including women, is an important step in ameliorating violence against young women in these settings.

SCHOOLS

Just as the police are charged with the responsibility of protecting and serving community residents, school personnel are mandated to provide a safe educational environment for students. And, as evidenced by the Supreme Court's 1999 ruling, this legal obligation extends to addressing school-based sexual harassment. As discussed in chapter 3, the St. Louis Public School District, including the schools our study participants attended, faced chronic problems that included serious fiscal troubles, poor student performance, staffing and resource limitations, and violence. Again, these problems are directly related to policy decisions about funding allocations, among other things, and the failures of local, regional, and federal decision-makers to invest in the education of poor urban youth. As criminologist Denise Gottfredson sums up, "schools serving the most disadvantaged populations lack the resources that make other schools effective."[27]

However, her research also shows that schools can adopt policies and practices that foster a climate conducive to students' educational and emotional well-being. Commitment and resources are necessary to achieve these goals. For example, without the ability to attract and retain

> the most talented educators, . . . [schools] contribute to poor educational practices—including the use of irrelevant, fragmented curriculum, rigid retention policies and disciplinary practices, and lower teacher expectations for student success. [These] adversely affect student performance in schools and increase the likelihood of delinquency.[28]

As Shauntell lamented of her own experiences in school:

> Most of the teachers can't control the class. It's mostly like a certain student in the class don't wanna work, so the teacher passes out worksheets and just tell us to do it. And most students . . . like myself, I know I get mad. How you just gon' put worksheets and books in front of our face and tell us to do it, and you not explainin', you not no teacher. If that's the case, we could teach ourself.

Alternatively, a commitment to providing a positive educational environment for youth—which includes well-trained and dedicated staff, responsiveness to student needs, a stimulating educational experience, infrastructural maintenance, and opportunities for youths to participate in school governance all have been found to improve school outcomes.[29] Moreover, it is of critical importance to find ways to ensure that educational personnel do not reinforce racial, class, and gender inequalities as part of the "hidden curriculum" of schools.[30] While such changes, in and of themselves, would not remedy the problem of school-based sexual harassment, they would likely have some bearing on the problem by improving the overall climate and culture in youths' schools.

More specifically, it is also the case that school violence initiatives primarily emphasize guns and gangs and often fail to conceptualize sexual harassment as an insidious form of violence that harms the educational opportunities and well-being of young women.[31] In chapter 3, I discuss that young women often chose not to go to school personnel when they were victims of sexual harassment. This had detrimental consequences when conflicts escalated, and girls themselves sometimes ended up in trouble. But much of the reason girls did not report incidents to teachers or other staff was because they believed doing so would be ineffectual. This was often borne out in their experiences. Numerous girls felt that school personnel should take a more proactive stance in addressing sexual harassment and other problem behaviors. Katie explained, "I think [they should] suspend them the first time and then the second time, they should report it to the Board of Education." Recall from chapter 3 that while Yvonne felt the school should "start being stricter," she believed suspensions "don't mean jack" since sending students home was often a short-term reward rather than a punishment.

In fact, educational scholar Valerie Lee and her colleagues argue that, given how widespread sexual harassment is in schools, "it is difficult to think that a policy of punishing the perpetrator and protecting the victim will be effective in eliminating" the problem.[32] Instead, they recommend policies aimed at prevention. For example, they suggest that the introduction of school curriculum on the topic would help "students understand, recognize, and address their own ambivalence about sexual harassment (indeed, about sexuality generally)."[33] Moreover, programs targeted specifically at girls could help them come together as a group, and recognize their common interest in "support[ing] each other . . . and creat[ing] strategies for change."[34]

Such practices, however, must be systematic and aimed not just at students but at school personnel and their practices. As researchers Jane Kenway and Lindsay Fitzclarence argue, "the dominant tendency . . . has been to individualize and pathologize . . . the violence which occurs within schools. . . . Such approaches have not encouraged schools to see themselves as amongst the many institutions which are complicit in the production of violent behavior."[35] Thus, legal scholars Sandra Kopels and David R. Dupper provide concrete policy recommendations, which include "proactive and comprehensive" interventions that also address "factors that contribute to a hostile school environment" for girls.[36] These include, for example, having school policies that clearly define harassment and delineate the procedures to be followed for promptly and effectively addressing incidents and providing avenues for victim assistance, as well as providing institutionalized programming for both school personnel and students that educates them on the seriousness of sexual harassment and informs them of the school's guidelines and enforcement measures. Moreover, teachers and other school personnel must be held accountable to these standards. This is a daunting challenge for schools in disadvantaged communities, but any hope to ameliorate the problem must involve the commitment of school resources, particularly since school-based sexual harassment not only disrupts girls' educational experiences but also carries over into community contexts that place girls at risk for more serious forms of sexual aggression.

Stabilizing Community Agencies and Facilitating Relationships with Caring Adults

Toward the end of our interviews with young women, we asked what they thought teenaged girls needed most to help them cope with the violence endemic in their daily lives. April provided a succinct answer that captured what many young women told us: "Somebody to talk to. That's all we really want." Youths in disadvantaged urban communities often lack stable relationships with caring adults they can turn to in times of need. In some cases, drug addiction or other family problems make parents unavailable in meaningful ways. In other cases, girls described not wanting to burden their loved ones with the painful knowledge of their victimization.

But many girls emphasized the importance for young women of having, as Cleshay put it, "a female role model in they life. . . . Somebody they can depend on, somebody they can talk to." Sheron explained, "some females out here, they don't have nowhere to turn. They feel that they're lost and don't have nowhere to turn. And some, they're not comfortable talking to their mothers, sisters, best friends, family members." Likewise, in a moving tribute to her grandmother, Yvonne contrasted her own caring adult with the absence of such a relationship in many of her friends' lives:

> The females I've been around and that I hang around with on a constant basis, what they want is to feel like they got their protection. 'Cause like my friends that I talk to, they have problems with they mother and they father or whatever, they don't have nobody to turn to. Me, on the other hand, I have a wonderful grandmother that's always been there for me, you know. . . . It's something about the touch of my grandmother that make everything seem okay. Makes me feel safe, makes me feel good, makes me feel like I'm on top of the world. . . . She

call me her shining star, her rose, and that's what I am. . . . I feel like if they had that, and they had that information, and they had that person, somebody to lift up they self-esteem, they would see things in a very different light.

Young women had limited knowledge of victim's service agencies. Only Nykeshia described receiving counseling services, after she was raped by her mother's boyfriend. She attributed receiving help to a caring adult who noticed that she was in need:

Some girls, you can look at 'em and tell something wrong with 'em. Like when that [the rape] first happened to me, I was at [a community] center, and I had . . . a computer class from Mrs. Jenkins. And she told me, she say, "Something going on in yo' family? 'Cause you don't act the same, yo' face . . . don't look the same and you don't look no males in the eye no more." I was like, I was asking her, "How you know something wrong?" She was like, "Just because of yo' attitude." She was like, "You can talk to me anytime that you need to."

Of the counseling she received, Nykeshia said, "it was helpful." As a consequence, she believed "if something really went wrong again, I'd contact 'em. 'Cause what they did do did something [to help]." However, none of the other girls we spoke to described such interventions.

In fact, a number of girls were suspicious of victim's services. In general, they experienced social service agencies as intrusive and questioned whether professionals were authentically concerned with their wellbeing. Asked whether she "ever talked to people, social workers or something" about her rape or gang rape, Cherise gave an adamant "no." She continued, "I don't want to. That's my business, it's private." April was also unwavering, though her account was also quite revealing. She insisted that she would not go to a stranger:

'Cause I got somebody to talk to. I got somebody that help me. . . . My Momma Bridges [at the group home]. Or I'll call you [the interviewer].[37] . . . 'Cause I feel comfortable around you. I don't just talk to people. . . . I don't be out here trying [to get] nobody to help me. I mean, I got all the help I need, don't need no more agencies and all that . . . don't trust 'em either.

As April's comments suggest, it was not the case that she felt she had no need for caring adults. The problem was a deep distrust of formal agencies. Likewise, Anishika explained, "if they just doing it and don't mean it [it's of no use]. But if it come from the heart, and they really, really do want to help this girl and stuff, then they should just tell her that 'I'm there for you,' or whatever. I mean, it's not even all about the money. It's just because you want to help this person." Thus, what young women sought were authentic relationships with caring adults. But they were especially torn between striking the right balance of closeness and distance.

For instance, some young women said it was hard to talk to their parents, because they feared disappointing or hurting them. Cleshay explained, "sometimes it's better to talk to somebody with no face, you know what I'm saying, than to look at your parent's face and see disappointment or anger or hear the words that's gonna come out they mouth." She continued, "I can't talk to my parents. But you do need somebody to talk to." Anishika described wanting to protect her mother, noting, "I know like some things, my momma, she just can't take." And Janelle explained:

> It seems like it's always easier to tell somebody you don't know . . . who won't say anything, like a doctor, counselor, whatever, than it is to tell your family. 'Cause you get scared of the fact that how they're gonna react towards something like that. . . . They might blame me, they just might get real hysterical about the whole situation. And it's like, even, you know, it's like with a mother and a daughter, if something happens to the daughter and she tells her mother, it's gonna hurt her too. And I really don't want to put my people through that.

At the same time, young women's distrust of formal agencies was tied to several types of concerns, which were revealed through their descriptions of who they could imagine themselves going to for help and why. First, young women sought someone they believed could understand them and their experiences and would not pass judgment. For instance, Katie said she would go to her aunt or cousin, " 'cause I think that they are like, more like understanding, like where I'm coming from. 'Cause they young, but they older than me." And Cleshay said she would go to "my boyfriend momma" because:

She somebody that you can talk to. And there's some people you can talk to, and they'll look at you and look down on you. And sometimes you don't need that either. So you can talk to her. She'll, she been through a lot, she wise, you know. She'll let you know, "Well, it's okay to make mistakes. But if you do this, that, and the other, I help you, I'll be there for you." You know. My momma, she'll be like, you got into [it] on your own, get out of it on your own.

In addition, young women emphasized the importance of having someone who would keep their conversations and experiences private. Sharmi, for instance, said she would go to her godmother, " 'cause she, if I didn't want her to tell nobody, she wouldn't tell nobody and I trust her." And Anishika said, "I trust my grandma. I mean, whatever I tell my grandma, it stays indoors, it don't go nowhere." Destiny explained, "I mean, it could be my auntie, my friend, or my boyfriend. 'Cause them three, they keep everything. I mean, it's just between us, you say it's just between us, it's just between us with them." Thus, of agencies, Jamellah noted, "I don't need nobody all up in my business."

What many youths wanted were stable relationships with caring adults whom they could talk to without the worry of disappointing or hurting them, but also without the concern that they would choose or be required to report the problem to others. Earlier, I described young men's desire for community centers where they could go for activities that would serve as an alternative to the streets. In addition, part of what they sought in such settings was the stability of relationships with adults they could rely on. In chapter 1, I note that some of the youths we interviewed were regular participants in a local community agency; however, shortly after we began our research, the agency lost its funding and closed its doors.

Youths lamented the loss of what had been a secure feature of their daily lives. In their comments, we can see the value of the programming and relationships they lost. Jackie explained: "We use to come over here after school, and stay from like 2:30 to 6:30. They use to help us with our homework, anything we needed help with. Or sometimes you could come up here, sit around, talk to Mrs. Quarles or anything. I've been up here for like three years until it closed down. . . . It was always somebody you could talk to." And Leon said, "it kept us out of trouble. We came up here every day. . . . [After it closed], everybody went back to doing what they did. Sellin' drugs or whatever." Ricky provided the most poignant account:

> I would say like, if we had community outreach workers . . . more of those people and people like Ms. Quarles, that basically focused on the young people and they concerns, I mean, it would be alright. For real. I mean, we need another community center, though. The one we have, I mean, to get there you got to go to a gang infested area. You know, I'm talkin' *totally* gang infested. I mean just walkin' up there anything could happen to you if they don't know you. . . . But we just need a lot of positive people to help the young people. . . . I mean, [the center that closed down] changed our focus about a lot of stuff. I mean, it helped build character with me. It helped me care about a lot more. It made me deal with people better, comin' up here. It changed my grades in school, it made my attendance right. . . . It opened my eyes on the other side of life. It's not that street, thugness type of life. It let me know it was a good side to life.

Unfortunately, as this example illustrates, providing stable programming and relationships is a particular challenge in disadvantaged urban neighborhoods. As community researcher Nicholas Freudenberg and his colleagues note, "limited resources, changing priorities on the part of public and private funders, and the resulting high staff turnover can make it difficult for youth agencies in low-income communities to respond to young people's needs effectively."[38] Many of the youths we interviewed, girls and boys, had a strong desire for stable adult role models and mentors who genuinely cared about their well-being, could be trusted to offer guidance and support without passing judgment, and truly understood the realities of their daily struggles in poor urban neighborhoods. Community centers like the one our interviewees lost offer much promise in this regard, but they cannot succeed without the commitment of ongoing funding to secure talented, dedicated staff. Unfortunately, both the public and funding agencies have too little interest in providing such services to adolescents deemed troubled or delinquent.

And again, we must ask the question: What does this have to do with curtailing violence against young women? I see the answer as twofold. Perhaps most obviously, as Ricky described, participation in programs with caring adults can provide alternative ways for youths to understand their place in the world. It can challenge fatalism and channel resilience. As Yvonne noted, caring adults can provide youths with a sense of their worth and potential. To the extent that such opportunities empower young people in disadvantaged communities, they can change their sources of status and prestige and limit their involvement in activities that place them at risk.

Second, ongoing involvement in such programs and with the caring adults at their heart can provide young women with necessary supports when they are victims of gender violence. Young women articulated a deep distrust of professional victim's service agencies, equating them with the impersonal social services they found intrusive, invasive, and inauthentic. They have some reason to be suspicious. Research has found that many service providers are not sufficiently committed to addressing violence against women and "consider that female victims but not male victims sometimes get what they deserve."[39] Moreover, there is evidence that victim's services are often inadequately prepared or unwilling to address the realities of African American female victims' lives in disadvantaged communities. Such biases have been found to hinder resource utilization among Black women when they are victimized.[40]

Thus, trusted community agencies—particularly if they find ways to partner with feminist organizations dedicated to assisting victims of sexual assault and partner violence—may be an important avenue for providing young women with the support and resources they need when they are victimized. Numerous studies have demonstrated the importance of social support for coping with experiences of sexual assault and partner violence.[41] Because young women are routinely blamed for their victimization, it is critical that they have strong individuals in their lives whose genuine concern can facilitate disclosure, challenge the insidious message that they are at fault, and guide them to available resources and programs for assistance.

Unfortunately, without additional remedies to ensure that caring adults themselves understand the nature and harms of violence against women, this is not guaranteed. For example, some research has found that African American women report greater community censure and less social support than white female victims when they disclose victimization experiences. As a result, they are less likely to seek out necessary assistance.[42] Thus, all of the recommendations I have made thus far must also integrate efforts to challenge gender inequality and change the community-based, peer, and internalized gender ideologies that harm young women and bolster support for violence against them.

Changing Gender Ideologies and Challenging Gender Inequality

Many of my preceding recommendations may appear somewhat tangential to the specific issue of violence against young women. But given that such violence is heightened by the particular social contexts and cultural adaptations that emerge in disadvantaged communities, I believe efforts to intervene on these institutional inequalities and social processes are critical to a comprehensive strategy. Nonetheless, gender inequality and the ideologies that uphold its various iterations are at the root of the pervasive violence uncovered here. No efforts can succeed without fundamental strategies to address these issues.

BUILDING SOLIDARITY AND ENHANCING EFFICACY AMONG YOUNG WOMEN

One of the most disheartening facets of my analyses here has been the extent to which young women adhered to ideologies that held female victims accountable for male violence. In neighborhood settings, while young women were sometimes ambivalent about the violence against women they witnessed, many also described viewing such incidents with amusement. In addition, in neighborhoods, schools, and other social settings, they often attributed boys' violence to girls' behaviors. Wearing revealing clothing, taking pleasure in boys' attention, drinking or using drugs, not being sufficiently assertive, and being emotionally "out of control" were all seen as provocations that contributed to sexual and physical violence at the hands of young men.

While problematic, young women's focus on the behavior of female victims made some sense, given the contexts they were faced with. Without broader social or institutional supports for addressing violence, they recognized that the ultimate responsibility for protecting themselves fell on their own shoulders. The result, as shown especially in chapter 4, was an often fatalistic attitude. Rennesha explained, "I mean, violence is a part of the world, and it's just gon' be like that." Sheron said, "a boy gonna do what he wanna do, regardless."

In addition, one of the reasons young women adhered to victim-blaming ideologies about violence against women was that such beliefs could function to psychologically distance them from perceived risks. As I describe in chapter 2, to the extent young women believed that *other* girls were at risk for victimization due to their behaviors, they could more readily believe that they, themselves, would be insulated from such violence. Unsurprisingly, then, when we asked young women their suggestions for how we might address violence against girls, many focused on changing how girls conduct themselves. "Wear respectable clothes," "mind they own business," "carry yo'self like a woman," "stay off the streets so late" "don't allow it," "stop doin' lil' stupid stuff," "make it safe for theyself . . . correct they attitude, and find a presentable way to dress" were all typical responses.[43] As discussed, however, strategies that blamed the victim failed to protect girls from gendered violence and were ultimately quite harmful.

The good news is that young women rarely applied such understandings to incidents involving their friends and loved ones. Instead, they often described taking steps to intervene, protect, and support them. An important goal, then, is to find ways to generalize young women's sympathetic recognition of their friends' experiences to women in general. This can be done in a number of ways. There is evidence, for example, that education and prevention programs that focus on sexual aggression and partner violence show promise in challenging young women's rape myth acceptance and improving their knowledge and attitudes about violence and control in dating relationships.[44] Thus, bringing such programming to schools and community agencies may help young women recognize the commonalities of girls' experiences that result from gender inequalities.

To be successful, however, such programs must engage young women in the process and incorporate an explicit understanding of the specific risks they face within the ecological settings of their daily lives.[45] A number of the girls we interviewed suggested that such an approach could be useful, both as an educational strategy and a means of strengthening young women's support of one another. For example, Nicole suggested "a teen program for all the girls." She believed it should focus on "sexual harassment, people who touchin' them when you don't want to be touched, boys forcing you to do things you don't want to do." In particular, she felt such programs would be successful if young women were encouraged "to step out there and say what they have to say. Don't be embarrassed 'bout it, 'cause it done happened to all of us before. So ain't no need to hide it." Likewise, Kristy said, "if that first victim stand up and tell somebody, I guess something could be done." Jamellah suggested:

> You could have like a class, like in a recreation facility, to show a woman like, how to protect herself for when she do decide that she needs to go outside when it get dark. Like, lil' classes where women talking about [what can happen]. . . . Have somebody that's been through [it] . . . going up there and talkin'. Lettin' 'em know how it is.

Bridget said it was important to "give them knowledge about how boys and men are." And Katie suggested, "they should . . . have open meetings so they just talk about it and stuff like that. Learn how to carry themselves more better so it won't happen again and stuff like that."

While it may be useful for young women to focus on identifying context-specific risks and risk-avoidance strategies,[46] there are numerous limitations to an exclusive focus on these issues. For instance, as discussed in chapter 2, young women's safety strategies often meant limiting their involvement in activities outside the home. Feminist scholars argue that the threat of sexual violence functions as a powerful mechanism of social control in women's lives precisely because it places systematic constraints on their behavior and participation in public life.[47] In addition, a primary focus on improving women's risk-management strategies reinforces, by implication, the conceptualization of violence against women as a *women's* problem.[48]

Thus, it is equally important to provide young women with the necessary resources to engage in "oppositional identity work"[49] that allows them to "identify and question cultural assumptions that uphold and reproduce gender inequality."[50] For example, a number of scholars have examined how both rape-prevention discourses and sex-education curriculum reinforce gendered definitions of sexuality and sexual violence that emphasize female vulnerability and young women's guardianship of their sexuality in opposition to male sexual needs or entitlements. Such approaches normalize coercive behavior on the part of young men and "hamper . . . girls' ability to develop a positive sense of themselves as sexual beings."[51] Instead, it is imperative that we assist young women to "think critically about the messages and images" they receive about gender and sexuality.[52] It is with such skills, individually and collectively, that young women can develop recognition of their rights and boundaries in relation to young men and "resist the dominant . . . stories through which their lives have been constructed."[53]

Feminist scholars often point to the strengths, resiliency, and independence of African American women.[54] Such qualities have emerged in response to legacies of oppression and can be drawn on to help young women create positive gender identities. Psychologist Gail Wyatt, for example, suggests using prominent African American female activists as role models in the empowerment of African American young women.[55] Other research likewise suggests the utility of "incorporating ideas related to cultural pride and ethnic identity" in violence-prevention programming.[56] However, we cannot just assume that young Black women have such strength and independence, particularly given the gender inequalities and other challenges they face in their daily lives in distressed urban communities. Instead, they must be provided the necessary resources to foster these qualities, particularly in their relations with young men.

Psychologist Niobe Way, for example, found that while urban adolescent girls are often outspoken in their relationships with parents, teachers, and female friends, they are less able to speak up with male peers.[57] Not surprisingly, then, several young women emphasized the importance of strengthening girls' independence and empowerment as a means of addressing the problem of gender violence. Felicia said programming should focus on "letting them know that even though they didn't have a male figure at home, that they don't have to want love from a man that beats them, or a boy just to have sex with them to feel loved. That they can feel love from anybody." And Britney explained:

> I know [some] teenage girls . . . wanna have kids 'cause they think don't nobody love them. But they don't know. . . . [They need to be shown that] you don't need no child, you too young. You don't need no boyfriend to support you, you can do it by yourself. Be independent, you know what I'm saying, and stuff like that.

Thus, empowering young women and providing them with safe spaces and opportunities to recognize their collective strengths and interests can help them support one another and challenge gender inequalities, including gendered violence. Nonetheless, "their own resolve and coping strategies should not be the only resources to support their growth and development."[58]

CHALLENGING STREET MASCULINITIES AND
BRIDGING THE GENDER DIVIDE

A number of institutional and community-based changes would offer young women greater assistance, but, in addition, any comprehensive recommendations would be remiss if they failed to focus on strategies that can address the attitudes and behaviors of young men. Violence against young women in disadvantaged communities is heightened as a result of dominant features of masculinity in these settings that promote male dominance, hierarchical gender separation, and high rates of interpersonal violence.[59] As anthropologist Peggy Reeves Sanday demonstrates, these social attributes are characteristic of "rape-prone" settings.[60] Likewise, researchers have found that norms favoring gender inequality heighten risks for partner violence against women as well.[61] So, it is necessary to develop strategies that offer promise for changing young men's narrow conceptualizations of masculinity and foster more egalitarian views of young women. As Terence and Darryl surmised, ending violence against women is "all up on the dude right there," "they gotta change theyself."

As discussed, structural dislocations associated with disadvantage play an important role in shaping dominant features of masculinity for young men in poor urban neighborhoods. Thus, a particular challenge lies in providing young men with alternative forms of status and prestige. This requires the dedication of resources to make the sorts of changes described earlier. But it also means educating young men, as well, about the harms of normative masculinity to themselves and the young women in their lives, and working to foster greater empathy and egalitarian connections with young women.

A great deal of research has shown that men who engage in violence against women report "a lower capacity for empathy" than nonaggressive men and that lack of empathy is associated with adversarial gender beliefs, avoidance of intimacy, and support for misogynistic ideas about women.[62] Scholars typically conceptualize empathy as having both cognitive and affective components. Thus, while educational programming may improve young men's "intellectual capacity to comprehend and identify another's perspective," as important is the need to develop their emotional capacity to identify with young women's feelings, desires, and interpretations of situations.[63] Some research suggests that programmatic efforts to enhance high-risk males' empathy offers promise for curtailing violence against women. However, in order for such strategies to be effective, young men must have "access to their own emotions" as well.[64]

In their evaluation of programs designed to educate young men about sexual violence, researchers Frans Willem Winkel and Esther de Kleuver found that victim-focused strategies—that is, those that emphasized the harms to women that result from sexual violence—were more effective than perpetrator-focused strategies. In fact, they suggest that the latter approaches, which emphasize deterrence through a focus on illegality and punishment, can have the unintended consequence of heightening support for rape myths.[65] Focusing on the harms of violence against women for its female victims thus shows some promise for cultivating young men's empathy.

Indeed, a number of youths' comments alluded to the utility of emphasizing boys' relationships with the women in their lives to help them generalize their concerns to women as a whole. Anishika explained:

> I mean, a lot of the males, I'm pretty sure they got female cousins, aunts, or sisters or something. They feel like if they sister or cousin or something is dating somebody, and that person did it to they sister, then they gon' wanna do something. But [then] they think it's okay for them to do it to a female and stuff. . . . When it all boils down, it's just because they wanna have friends, they want attention, they wanna be popular and stuff.

And Andrew noted, "Something should be done. I mean, I see like, I got a little sister, and I feel bad when she come home and say a man came and did this to her and tried to do that or whatever. I mean, it just bugs me, you know." Thus, capitalizing on young men's concerns for their female loved ones could offer a means of enhancing their empathy for young women in general. Tony suggested "put[ting] 'em in counseling or something . . . [to teach them] to treat a girl how you treat your momma or grandma." Terence explained, "the main reason I don't put my hands on females is 'cause I was raised that way, and you know, you don't put your hands on females no matter what."

However, a potential danger of this focus is the risk of reinforcing dominant definitions of femininity that emphasize female vulnerability in opposition to masculine strength.[66] In chapter 5, I discuss that the contingent norm against male use of violence was constructed, in part, on conceptualizations of women's physical and emotional weaknesses. This is perhaps a more benign version of gender inequality than blatantly misogynistic beliefs, but it is equally harmful to young women. Thus, it is important that efforts to intervene with young men also work to challenge young men's understandings of masculinity and male superiority.

For example, researchers Dana M. Truman and colleagues argue that "the positive association between traditional masculinity and date rape supportive ideology suggest that masculine gender roles be addressed in rape education and prevention programs."[67] They suggest that "a starting point for many men to personalize the ways in which gender socialization shapes their lives might be to discuss ways in which traditional gender roles may be harmful not only to women but also to men."[68] Likewise, psychologist Deborah Tolman and her colleagues argue for the need to challenge normative heterosexuality for young men, as a means of promoting their own as well as girls' sexual health. This "means being able to experience and acknowledge the emotional feelings associated with sexuality, being able to resist peer pressure to objectify girls and sex, and having access to images of male sexuality that do not extol sexual predation."[69]

However, just as I suggested for young women, it is important that such interventions incorporate an explicit recognition of the realities of young men's lives in disadvantaged communities, include an awareness and appreciation of young men's perspectives, and provide them with positive role models that foster "a strong sense of ethnic and racial identity."[70] For example, asked how we could change young men's attitudes toward girls, Ricky explained:

> You need somebody that's been through it for real. Somebody like us, I mean, later on in life. . . . I mean, we need more people that can come down and talk to people, and ain't really downin' 'em, tellin' 'em they ain't gon' be nothin'. I mean, they just need somebody that's gon' show 'em the way. I mean, just show 'em that it's better. You ain't gotta disrespect women all the time. Or she ain't gotta be a bitch every time you see her. Or she don't have to be this 'cause she ain't want to talk to you. Or you don't have to touch her 'cause she walk past or she look good and you couldn't help your[self]. I mean, we just need somebody to talk to, man. Won't nobody listen to us. Man, that's what it is. Won't nobody listen to us.

Finally, it is critically important that our efforts do not target young women and young men separately. "Boys and girls need more opportunities to relate to each other as equal, whole people."[71] Providing youths with opportunities for cross-gender friendships, activities, and engagement has been shown to decrease coercive sexual behaviors among African American young men and to foster more egalitarian relationships.[72] Such egalitarian values offer "positive alternatives to the traditional masculinities that . . . [are] detrimental to the lives and health of both [young] women and men."[73]

Conclusion

Violence against young Black women is an endemic feature of distressed urban communities. It is tied to the persistent nature of gender inequality in our society and is heightened by the racial and class inequalities perpetuated by our neglect of the urban poor. My goal in this book has been to illuminate how the structural inequalities that create urban disadvantage create social contexts and facilitate culture adaptations that heighten and shape the tremendous gender-based violence faced by urban African American girls. This is an acute social problem that harms young women, young men, and our society as a whole, and it requires comprehensive policy attention.

There are researchers and policy-makers dedicated to ameliorating the problems associated with urban disadvantage. As my research here has demonstrated, addressing gender inequality and its attendant harms must be part of that effort. In broad contours, I have made recommendations that offer productive strategies for attending to the multifaceted problems created by structural disadvantage, increasing institutional accountability, and simultaneously challenging the gender inequalities at the root of violence against young women. The young people we interviewed were often fatalistic about the violence so common to their daily lives. As Carlos lamented, "we gotta wait 'til the world end and then we gotta start all over again." It is up to all of us to prove him wrong.

Appendix
Study Participants (N = 75)

Name[a]	Age	Location of Interview	Interviewer
Girls			
Alicia	18	School	Toya
Anishika	16	School	Toya
April	16	School	Toya
Arsenia[b]	16	School	Norm
Bridget	15	School	Iris
Britney	14	School	Toya
Cherise	17	School	Dennis
Christal	14	School	Toya
Cleshay	17	School	Iris
Dawanna	15	School	Toya
Destiny	16	School	Toya
Felicia	17	School	Iris
Gail	14	Community center	Toya
Jackie	15	Community center	Norm
Jamellah	18	School	Toya
Janelle	17	School	Norm
Katie	16	School	Toya
Kendall[b]	19	School	
Kenisha	16	School	Iris
Kristy	16	School	Iris
LaSondra	17	School	Dennis
Lisa	17	School	Toya
Michelle	16	School	Toya
Nicole	14	School	Toya
Nykeshia	15	School	Toya
Ramara	14	School	Toya
Rennesha	14	School	Toya
Sharmi	16	School	Toya
Shauntell	12	School	Toya
Sheron	15	School	Toya
Tami	15	Community center	Toya
Tawanna	16	School	Dennis
Tisha	17	School	Toya
Vanessa	16	Community center	Toya
Yvonne	17	School	Iris

(continued)

Name[a]	Age	Location of Interview	Interviewer
Boys			
Andrew	17	School	Dennis
Antwoin	13	Community center	Norm
Arthur	16	School	Dennis
Bobby	17	School	Dennis
Carlos	13	School	Dennis
Cooper	18	Community center	Norm
Curtis	14	School	Dennis
Darnell	17	School	Norm
Darryl	15	School	Toya
Doug	17	School	Dennis
Dwayne	17	School	Dennis
Eddie[b]	18	School	
Eric	17	School	Dennis
Eugene	19	School	Iris
Frank	13	School	Dennis
Gary	18	School	Iris
Jamal	19	School	Dennis
James	17	School	Dennis
Jermaine	15	School	Dennis
Kenny	14	School	Dennis
Kevin	16	School	Dennis
Lamont	13	School	Dennis
Larry	18	Community center	Toya
Leon	18	Community center	Norm
Marcus	16	School	Dennis
Marvin	17	School	Toya
Maurice	14	School	Dennis
Raymond	17	School	Dennis
Ricky	17	Community center	Norm
Robert	16	School	Dennis
Ronald	15	School	Toya
Shaun	16	School	Dennis
Terence	18	School	Toya
Tommie	15	Community center	Norm
Tony	15	Community center	Norm
Travis	16	School	Dennis
Tyrell	17	School	Toya
Walter	15	School	Dennis
Wayne	16	School	Dennis
William	15	School	Dennis

[a] Pseudonyms.
[b] No in-depth interview.

Notes

NOTES TO CHAPTER I

1. McCall, 1994, p. 44
2. McCall, 1994, pp. 44, 50.
3. Rodriguez, 1993, p. 121.
4. For exceptions, see Benson et al., 2003; Bourgois, 1996; Dugan and Apel, 2003; Dugan and Castro, 2006; Lauritsen and Schaum, 2004.
5. Britton, 2000; Daly and Chesney-Lind, 1988; Smart, 1976.
6. Felson's (2002) research has been particularly controversial in this regard. For critiques, see Kruttschnitt, 2002; Simpson, 2002.
7. Of course, it's impossible to provide an adequate list of citations for this substantial body of scholarship. Susan Brownmiller's (1975) *Against Our Will* is certainly a classic early work (though not without its critics). There is now an interdisciplinary journal, *Violence against Women,* on the issue, and numerous other key works, many of which can be found in my discussions throughout this book.
8. For an overview, see Renzetti et al., 2001.
9. For a systematic treatment of this issue, see Davis, 1981.
10. Collins, 1990; Davis, 1981; hooks, 1981; Spelman, 1989.
11. In fact, several factors have hindered research on violence against young women in urban African American communities. The most obvious is the ease of access in interviewing college students and adults, compared with the difficulties inherent in interviewing underage youths about sensitive topics (Schwartz, 1997). Two additional factors are noteworthy. First is the tendency to study inner-city youths primarily in terms of their perceived deviance—as delinquents, teen mothers, school dropouts (for discussions, see Chesney-Lind, 1993; Gibbs, 1990; Leadbeater and Way, 1996). Second, this is combined with widespread stereotypes about violence against women that define some victims as "innocent" and deserving of attention, while others are seen as more culpable for their victimization. White middle-class women assaulted by strangers are at one end of the continuum, while urban African American young women—especially those involved (or perceived to be involved) in other risk behaviors—are at the other (Estrich, 1987; Walsh, 1987). As a consequence, our knowledge of

violence against African American adolescent girls is especially lacking (Burt et al., 1997).

12. For example, Gilfus, 1992; Maher, 1997; Miller, 2001; Richie, 1996.

13. Sanday, 1981.

14. For an excellent case study of a "rape-free" society, see Helliwell, 2000.

15. For example, Peterson and Bailey, 1992; Scully, 1990; Whaley, 2001.

16. Boswell and Spade, 1996, p. 133. See also Lefkowitz, 1997; Matoesian, 1993. The relationship of structural gender inequality to rape has been found to be complex. In perhaps the most sophisticated analysis to date, Whaley (2001) used longitudinal data to examine the relationship between changes in gender inequality and rates of rape. She found that, overall, rape rates are higher where gender inequality is more entrenched, and then, as women gain equality, there is a short-term backlash effect, leading to higher rates of rape in response to threats to men's collective power. She reports that, over time, however, gender equality has an ameliorative effect, leading to long-term declines in rape. Unfortunately, as yet, we do not have adequate data to fully examine these relationships. Whaley's study relied on the Uniform Crime Reports (UCR) to determine changes in rape rates, as this is the only longitudinal data available that can be linked to structural measures of gender inequality. However, there is strong evidence that police-reporting behaviors have changed dramatically over the period of her investigation as well, such that changes in UCR measures are a reflection of changing notification patterns and do not accurately capture changing rates of rape (Baumer et al., 2003).

17. For example, Boswell and Spade, 1996; Martin and Hummer, 1989; Sanday, 1990; Schwartz and DeKeseredy, 1997.

18. Martin and Hummer, 1989, p. 459.

19. Boswell and Spade, 1996.

20. Franklin, 2004; Lefkowitz, 1997.

21. Anderson, 1999.

22. Anderson, 1999; Bourgois, 1995, 1996; Majors and Billson, 1992; Messerschmidt, 1993; Mullins, 2006; Oliver, 1994.

23. Mullins, 2006, p. 25. Importantly, Anderson (1999) points out the presence of competing behavioral norms in urban disadvantaged communities, which he distinguishes as "street" versus "decent." While not all young men internalize the "street code," all must be competent in its behavioral rules in order to navigate the social terrains of their neighborhoods.

24. Though not specifically in reference to youths in disadvantaged community contexts, there is strong evidence that the types of masculinity construction described here are linked to the legitimization of violence against women, and that participation in delinquency and interpersonal violence are correlated with perpetration of such violence (Calhoun et al. 1997; Malamuth, 1981; Marcin-

iak, 1998; Truman et al., 1996; Vass and Gold, 1995; Willan and Pollard, 2003).

25. Bourgois, 1996; Bourgois and Dunlap, 1993; Fleisher, 1998; Hunt and Joe-Laidler, 2001; Maher, 1997; Miller, 2001; Raphael, 2004; Valdez, 2007; Wilson, 1996.

26. Oliver, 1994; Wilson, 1996.

27. Benson et al., 2003; Miles-Doan, 1998.

28. Boyle and Vivian, 1996; DeKeseredy and Schwartz, 1997.

29. Benson et al., 2003, p. 227.

30. Benson et al., 2003, p. 210.

31. Thorne, 1993, p. 135.

32. Eder, 1995; Lees, 1993.

33. Levy, 1991; Molidor and Tolman, 1998.

34. Foulis and McCabe, 1997; Marciniak, 1998.

35. Gibbs, 1990, p. 40.

36. Hunt and Joe-Laidler, 2001; Lauritsen et al., 1991; Miller, 2001.

37. Lauritsen, 2003.

38. All forms of violence are gendered, including when they are male-on-male (e.g., Mullins, 2006) and female-on-female (e.g., Miller and Mullins, 2006). However, I use the shorthand "gendered victimization" throughout the book specifically to refer to forms of violence against young women perpetrated by young men, including sexual harassment, sexual coercion and assault, and dating violence.

39. For an overview, see Alder and Worrall, 2004; Heimer and Kruttschnitt, 2005. In addition to scholarly accounts, there has been a surge in popular culture's attention to female violence specifically, along with the discovery of girls' "meanness" in general. For example, Simmons, 2003; Wiseman, 2002.

40. Chesney-Lind and Pasko, 2004; Gilfus, 1992.

41. Miller, 2001; see also Joe-Laidler and Hunt, 1997; Maher, 1997.

42. Hagan and McCarthy, 1997, p. 81; see also Short, 1998.

43. Because the data-collection process was a joint effort with my grant co-principal investigator and several graduate research assistants, I adopt plural rather than singular pronouns when discussing this facet of the project.

44. Snyder and Sickmund (1999) provide an overview of trends in youth delinquency, including the classification of youths as serious, violent, or chronic offenders.

45. I use "at risk" in part because it is a familiar term used by researchers and practitioners, but also because I believe it connotes concern for understanding the detrimental social conditions that affect youths' lives (see also Gibbs, 1990, p. 40). Other scholars have critiqued the term, however, suggesting that "the 'at risk' label . . . [has a] tendency to shift attention away from the social

conditions that place adolescents at risk and locate the risk within the adolescents themselves" (Taylor et al., 1995, p. 21).

46. Scully, 1990.

47. Lauritsen et al., 1991, 1992.

48. Lauritsen et al., 1992, p. 102.

49. Sampson and Lauritsen, 1990, p. 132.

50. In fact, the ideal situation for our study would have been to also include a third comparison group of "resilient" youths from the same neighborhoods. The study was originally designed to do so, and we spent nearly two years trying to gain access—through magnet and city schools, and church groups—to youths integrated into their communities in more pro-social ways. Ultimately we were unsuccessful, and so it is important to keep in mind that our sample only captures those youths with some involvement in risky behaviors.

51. Burt et al., 1997, p. 54.

52. Lauritsen, 2003; Lauritsen and Schaum, 2004. But see Dugan and Apel, 2003, who documented even higher rates of victimization among American Indian adult women.

53. In fact, criminologists are not alone in the tendency to focus on individual deviance rather than on broader harms resulting from disadvantage. For discussions, see Gibbs, 1990; Leadbeater and Way, 1996. For a critique of popular and scholarly treatment of race, crime, and victimization, see Mann and Zatz, 2002.

54. We did not attempt to target youth known to be victims or perpetrators of violence against women, however. Instead, drawing a broader (though not representative) sample allowed us some means of estimating the prevalence of such events in youths' lives and provided the opportunity to compare youths who reported such violence with those who had not, in terms of their experiences, beliefs, and the meanings they held about both gender and violence against women.

55. The majority of youths (87 percent) were drawn from the two alternative schools, while 13 percent (four girls, six boys) were interviewed at the community center. We did not find differences in youths' accounts across sites. The alternative schools are now defunct; they were closed as part of a restructuring of the St. Louis Public School District in the early 2000s.

56. The mean age for young women was 15.8, and for young men it was 16.1. More specific age breakdowns are as follows:

Age	Girls	Boys
12–13	1 (3%)	4 (10%)
14–15	12 (34%)	10 (25%)
16–17	19 (54%)	18 (45%)
18–19	3 (9%)	8 (20%)

57. In fact, we went beyond confidentiality by maintaining the anonymity of participating youth. We did not elicit or record their names except as needed to

schedule follow-up interviews, and we elicited no other direct identifying information. Completed interviews were kept in a locked file box or file cabinet, and youth were told not to make statements about intention to harm others in the future.

Parental consent is routinely required when interviewing individuals under the age of 18. This posed a problem for this study, as parental permission could jeopardize the anonymity of respondents and could present risks such as disclosure of child abuse, victimization, or participation in delinquency. To deal with this dilemma, we were granted a waiver of parental consent by the Institutional Review Board at the University of Missouri–St. Louis. The waiver was contingent on the appointment of a youth advocate to serve as a surrogate guardian for respondents. Olivia Quarles, then-director of SafeFutures, a program funded by the Office of Juvenile Justice and Delinquency Prevention to provide comprehensive services to at-risk youth, agreed to serve in this capacity. Potential research participants were provided with Ms. Quarles's name and phone number and were given the opportunity to contact her before making a decision to participate. Because parental consent was waived, great diligence was required to assess youths' voluntary participation and informed consent. Youth under age 12 were excluded from the study, and particular care was taken with those under age 14 to assess their competence to provide informed consent.

Finally, because the research focused on violent victimization, we took several steps to provide youth with information about available services. Linda Sharpe-Taylor, a psychologist and then-director of a gender-specific community-based program in St. Louis, served as a consultant for the project, and her contact information was provided to youth who participated. In addition, at the conclusion of each interview, we provided respondents with a detailed description of community agencies that provide intervention and assistance in abuse situations, sexual assault crisis centers, and other community services for adolescents. They also were offered assistance in making appropriate contacts with service providers (though none chose to take us up on the offer).

58. Occasionally, in-depth interviews had to be rescheduled—for instance, if the survey was completed toward the end of the school day and there was not sufficient time to complete it. The interview data are available for all but three youth (two girls, one boy). None of these youths refused to participate in the in-depth interview: in one case, the tape recorder malfunctioned; in the others, scheduling conflicts prohibited their completion. Interviews were conducted by four individuals: two African American female graduate students, a white male graduate student, and the African American male faculty collaborator on the project.

59. Not all youth had come to the attention of other authorities, however. Though all of the youths we spoke to reported having engaged in at least minor delinquency, just 50 percent of the young men and 37 percent of the young

women reported having been arrested in the last year (65 percent and 51 percent, respectively, reported having ever been arrested).

60. The survey was a modified version of the instrument used in my study of girls in gangs (Miller, 2001). That survey was a variation of several widely used survey instruments: Maxson and Klein's Gang Membership Resistance Survey, the Rochester Youth Development Study, and the Denver Youth Survey. I eliminated some questions more tangential to this second study and I added questions to provide information on youths' and their peers' attitudes toward and experiences with various forms of violence against women. Our use of these instruments is not survey research, however, given the purposive sampling and comparatively small sample.

61. Specifically, we asked young women whether any of the boys they know had called them names or said things to make them feel bad about themselves, had made sexual comments that made them feel uncomfortable, or had grabbed or touched them in ways that made them feel uncomfortable. We also asked who had done it and where (e.g., home, neighborhood, school, other) the incident(s) had occurred. We asked young men whether they and their friends had engaged in these same behaviors.

62. We asked young women the following questions, and then asked follow-up questions (when and where it happened, who did it) when they answered affirmatively: Have you been sexually assaulted, molested, or raped? Has anyone ever tried to sexually assault, molest, or rape you? Has anyone ever pressured you to have sex when you didn't want to? Has anyone ever had sex with you when you didn't want to, but you were unable to stop them because you were drunk or high? Has anyone ever pressured you into having sex when you didn't want to by using his position of authority (e.g., teacher, police officer, gang leader)? Has anyone ever tried to pressure you into having sex when you didn't want to by using his position of authority? Has a group of men or boys made you have sex with them when you didn't want to but felt like you didn't have a choice or couldn't say no? Have you seen someone else get sexually assaulted, molested, or raped? Have you seen someone else make a girl have sex when she didn't want to, but she was unable to stop them because she was high or drunk? We also asked young women whether they had been sexually abused by a member of their family, whether any of their friends have had men use physical force to get them to have sex with them, and about sexual coercion in dating relationships.

Of young men, we asked: Have you ever physically hurt or threatened to hurt someone to get them to have sex with you? Have you ever had sex with someone when she was too drunk or high to resist? Have you ever helped another person have sex with someone against their will? Have you and your friends ever run a train on a girl? We also asked young men whether they had been sexually abused by a member of their family; whether they had ever been sexually assaulted, molested, or raped; and whether they had seen someone else get sexually assaulted, molested, or raped. Again, we asked follow-up questions to collect more information if they answered affirmatively to any question.

63. The Conflict Tactics Scale (CTS) (Straus, 1979) is a controversial scale that is used to examine intimate partner violence. The controversy lies in its narrow focus on measuring acts of violence, divorced from information on the physical and psychological consequences of violence; "actors' interpretations, motivations and intentions"; and "the contexts of violence, the events precipitating it, and the sequence of events by which it progresses" (Dobash et al., 1992, p. 76; see also DeKeseredy and Schwartz, 1998). I discuss these issues in greater detail in chapter 5. Our group chose to use the CTS because it provided baseline information that could be compared with previous research and because our multimethod approach meant that we collected our primary data about dating violence during the in-depth interviews and focused on those issues absent from the CTS.

For young women, we used the CTS to measure victimization in their current, last, and any dating relationship. We added three questions at the end to examine sexual violence: Did [your boyfriend] ever pressure you into having sex with him when you didn't want to? Did he ever make you have sex with him when you didn't want to? Did he ever use physical force to make you have sex with him? We also asked young women how many of their female friends had ever had boyfriends who used physical force to resolve conflicts with them. We asked young men about their current or most recent relationship and about both perpetration and victimization. However, we did not ask young men whether they had been sexually victimized in a dating relationship, since research consistently finds that sexual violence in relationships is almost exclusively a male-perpetrated phenomenon (e.g., Bachman and Saltzman, 1995; Tjaden and Thoennes, 2000).

64. Research points to the significance of male peer support in facilitating violence against women (e.g., DeKeseredy and Schwartz, 1997; Schwartz and DeKeseredy, 1997). Thus, we asked both males and females how many of their male friends had used physical force to have sex with a young woman; how many had used physical force, like hitting, slapping, or beating, to resolve conflicts with their girlfriends; and how many had gotten girls drunk or high in order to have sex with them. We also asked youths whether their friends approve of a man slapping or hitting his girlfriend when she won't do what he tells her to do, she insults him when they are alone together, she insults him in front of other people, she gets drunk or high, she is crying hysterically, or she won't have sex with him. We then asked youths their own beliefs about the appropriateness of boys using violence in these situations.

Of young men, we also asked the following: Have any of your male friends ever told you that you should respond to your girlfriend's challenges to your authority by using physical force like hitting or slapping them? Have any of your male friends ever told you that it is all right for a man to hit his girlfriend in certain situations (if yes, in what situations)? Have any of your male friends ever told you that your dates or girlfriends should have sex with you when you want it? Have any of your male friends told you that if a man spends money on a date, she should have sex with him in return? Have any of your male friends ever told you that if your date or girlfriend doesn't want to have sex, you should use physical force to obtain sex? Have any of your male friends ever told you that it is all right for a man to physically force a woman to have sex with him in certain situations (if yes, in what situations)?

65. The survey allowed us to collect baseline information that could be tabulated to examine patterns in the data and provided a means to triangulate findings from the in-depth interviews. The use of multiple data sources allows for more systematic and rigorous analyses and increases confidence in the validity and reliability of research findings (Marshall and Rossman, 1989).

66. Although we also collected data on female-on-female conflicts and male-on-male conflicts, these are not included in the analysis here (but see Miller and Mullins, 2006).

67. Successfully capturing these aspects of youths' social worlds is not a straightforward task. For a variety of reasons, youths may be circumspect about the nature of their activities and experiences, and they may choose to conceal elements of their lives that they consider incriminating, embarrassing, shameful, or simply private. This is an unavoidable aspect of any social research and must be taken into account. For example, while many young women spoke openly with us about their victimization experiences, it is likely that others chose to conceal these incidents, and thus the rates of victimization we report are likely underestimates. In several cases, young women answered affirmatively in the survey about victimization experiences but then chose not to discuss these further in the in-depth interview. It is also probable that young men underreported their personal involvement in the victimization of young women. This is likely tied to both their concerns with presentation of self and their interpretations of what actually constitutes violence against young women. I explore this issue in greater detail in chapters 4 and 5.

In addition, some scholars believe that social distances between the researcher and research participant can result in suspicion and lack of trust, and this can affect the process of disclosure (e.g., DeVault, 1995; Taylor et al., 1995). Evidence of this is somewhat mixed, however. For instance, social distances can sometimes be beneficial in the interview setting, particularly because they "may elicit explanations that are assumed to be known to someone with insider status" (Taylor et al., 1995, p. 32; see also Currie and MacLean, 1997; Miller, 2001; Miller and Glassner, 2004). Moreover, it is extremely difficult to "match" interviewers and interviewees on social characteristics. In the current study, for instance, three of the four interviewers were African American, but one of these was an older college professor, one was a Ph.D. student (though from the same community), and one was an older woman with experience working in social agencies. Though matched on race, other social distances still remained. The fourth interviewer was a white male Ph.D. student who was distanced further because he was European rather than American.

Though we did not find variations in the kinds of information youth provided, there did appear to be some differences in the ability of the interviewers to establish good rapport with the youth they interviewed. On the whole, the most detailed interviews were those completed by the African American professor and the African American female Ph.D. student. In contrast, particularly when he interviewed young men, the white male's interviews were not as rich as the others. It is difficult to know the extent to which this was the result of social distances or the result of his interviewing style and interests. For example, the in-depth interviews were designed to allow for deviation into topics that arose spontaneously during the course of the conversation. However, when talking with young men, this particular interviewer sometimes discussed issues he was personally interested in but that were more tangential to the research questions we were interested in pursuing. Thus, he did not always ask as many follow-up questions as the other interviewers about the primary topics of the investigation. In addition, a couple of youth clearly responded to him with disinterest or even amused hostility, and this response was tied to social distances. The following conversation with Carlos is the most blatant example (and emanates from the interviewer pursuing his own line of questions):

Interviewer: I'm like, like me as a European, if I would come live in your neighborhood and wanting to join your gang, what would I have to do?

Carlos: Gotta get your ass beat, and then you gonna be in the gang. Then you gonna help beat somebody else up. Then if you don't help, probably gonna get kilt and you gonna be in a dumpster somewhere.

Intervewer: That's how it works?

Carlos: That's how it gonna work.

Interviewer: I'm not saying, I mean I don't live in your neighborhood, so. But that's how it would work?

Carlos: That's how it gonna work.

Interviewer: How what is gonna work?

Carlos: What I just said.

Interviewer: What?

Carlos: Huh?

Interviewer: What?

Carlos: Nuttin', nuttin'.

Interviewer: Yeah. Were you threatening me?

Carlos: Who me?

Interviewer: Yeah.

Carlos: No, I wasn't threatening you.

Interviewer: Okay, that's cool. 'Cause that wouldn't be cool.

Carlos: (laughing) Come on, man, ask me more questions.

Later in the interview, Carlos began rapping into the tape recorder and playing with it, and disengaged from providing meaningful answers to most of the questions posed. Nonetheless, during the periods of the interview in which Carlos was engaged, his account was quite similar to those provided by other youth. One additional young woman, interviewed by the African American M.A. student, also yielded thin results. Bridget answered most questions with one-word to three-word answers and did not respond favorably to attempts to probe for additional information. Again, her brief responses did not deviate from the accounts provided by other young women, despite the lack of depth in her answers.

Research of this sort invariably results in a handful of participants who choose not to open up during the in-depth interview. What is more striking, however, is that the vast majority of youth did provide detailed accounts about many of their experiences and beliefs. I believe that there are several reasons for this outcome. In research of this type, it is necessary to build rapport, show genuine interest, ensure confidentiality, and establish familiarity and trust (Glassner and Loughlin, 1987). In fact, we designed the data-collection steps to help facilitate this process. For instance, we began with the survey interview because it allowed each interview to start with relatively innocuous questions (demographics, living arrangements, attitudes toward school) and then slowly move toward more sensitive questions about delinquency and victimization. In addition, completing the survey first allowed the interviewers to establish some relationship with each participant, so that when they moved on to the in-depth interview, a level of familiarity was already established. The interviewers were trained to respond to youths' accounts in a nonjudgmental manner, and this provided a layer of understanding that facilitated frank discussions when these issues were revisited during the in-depth interviews.

Most significant for the success of such research, however, is that the in-depth interview provides youth with the opportunity to recognize themselves as experts and act as teachers. This can be both empowering and illuminating, because it provides a context in which they can reflect on and speak about their lives in ways not often available. This tends to give them some stake in the research process and is particularly important for youth who often find themselves stereotyped and devalued by the larger culture, and who are routinely denied the opportunity to be heard and have their perspectives taken seriously (e.g., Miller and Glassner, 2004).

68. Orbuch, 1997, p. 455; see also Spradley, 1979.

69. For a fuller discussion, see Miller and Glassner, 2004.

70. The most obvious set of contradictions in this study is that many young women have faced violence at the hands of young men, and even more have witnessed such incidents. Nonetheless, most still hold virulent victim-blaming attitudes about violence against women, including those who have been victimized themselves. Making sense of this complex reality is one of the primary goals of this book.

71. The research design and research questions provided a priori categories for the initial sorting of data. Thus, I began by separating the data from each interview into merged files that included the following: neighborhood-based accounts, sexual harassment and other female/male conflicts, sexual assault, gang rape, dating relationships and relationship violence, female-on-female conflicts, male-on-male conflicts, and recommendations for change. Narrative accounts that were relevant to multiple categories were duplicated in each relevant file. In addition, I created separate files for each category by gender, to facilitate comparative analysis. The next step in data analysis was to examine each newly created dataset for thematic patterns, making note of how frequently each theme occurred as well as documenting contradictory reports. For each basic category, I conducted my initial analysis of girls' and boys' accounts separately and then compared them for overlaps and divergences. To complete the analysis, I then refined the basic themes by examining how they fit together, probing the relationships between youths' descriptions and their explanations, and making theoretical sense of these relationships. The final step in the analysis involved carefully checking the validity of the analysis. This involved ensuring that the events and processes I drew from for analysis were representative of the broad patterns uncovered in the data, ensuring that messy complexities were accounted for and not discounted, searching for and explicating deviant cases and patterns, and, occasionally, drawing from atypical events that provide insight into broader patterns.

Data analysis is often the "black box" of qualitative inquiry because researchers often do not provide systematic descriptions of the analysis process, and its rigors remain misunderstood by many quantitative scholars (Ragin et al., 2004). However, there are a number of useful texts that provide detailed descriptions of the data analysis process and give insight into the basic analysis procedures I have described. For basic overviews, see Lofland and Lofland, 1984; Miles and Huberman, 1984; Spradley, 1979; Strauss, 1987.

This also seems the appropriate time to comment on my use of terms that indicate the strengths of the patterns I uncovered in data analysis. Quantitative researchers are often skeptical of such seemingly loose language as "many" or "a number of"—terms that are frequently used in qualitative writing. I use the words "the vast majority" to indicate approximately three-quarters or more; "most" or "the majority" to indicate more than one-half; "many" to indicate a sizeable minority (over one-third); and "a number" to indicate roughly one-quarter or more. I use "several" or "a few" to highlight themes mentioned by a small number of youth, but more than two.

72. Bursik and Grasmick, 1993; Wilson, 1996.

73. To ensure anonymity, census data for youths' neighborhoods were not obtained with the precision that would have come from using their addresses. Instead, we asked youths to provide the names of two cross streets near where they lived, and the data in table 1-1 come from census block data from these cross streets. This is not a precise measure but does provide a rough match for their neighborhoods. We also were unable to use the information provided by nine youths (four young men and five young women), because the street names they gave us ran parallel with one another. Fortunately, in all but three cases, we were able to narrow the location down to a given zip code, and these zip code–level census data were compared to the block-level data we obtained for the other 66 youths. These data are not included in the calculations presented in table 1-1, but they indicate that these youths lived in comparable neighborhood conditions. Notably, separate calculations for girls and boys yielded nearly identical neighborhood indicators, so these data were combined in the table. One additional note: unlike most U.S. cities, St. Louis City is not part of St. Louis County but makes up its own county. Thus, the figures shown for St. Louis County do not include St. Louis City.

74. Figures for the 1950s come from Decker and Van Winkle, 1996. Figures for 1990 and 2000 come from the U.S. Census for those years.

75. Baybeck and Jones, 2004. For a general discussion of the harms caused to city residents by deindustrialization, see Wilson, 1996.

76. Rusk, 1995, p. 30.

77. In 2000, the census changed its measurement of race, allowing individuals to identify themselves as biracial or multiracial. Thus, while a precise comparison between 1990 and 2000 is not possible, there is evidence that the impact of this change on these figures is minimal. Fewer than 0.01 percent of the city's residents, or approximately 6,500 people, described themselves as multiracial in 2000 (Planning and Urban Design Agency, 2001a).

78. St. Charles County, for example, borders St. Louis County to the northwest and experienced tremendous population growth in the 1990s. Considered one of the region's up and coming communities, and benefiting from considerable investments, in 2000, St. Charles County had a median family income more than $2,500 higher than St. Louis County, poverty rates more than 40 percent lower, lower rates of unemployment, and fewer female-headed families. Yet only 2.4 percent of its population was African American (U.S. Census, 2000). Thus, it's not just St. Louis City itself that has extreme problems with racial segregation but the entire St. Louis region. For a more detailed account of

demographic and socioeconomic trends in the metropolitan area, see Baybeck and Jones, 2004.

79. St. Louis remains almost exclusively African American and white in racial/ethnic composition. In 2000, approximately 2 percent of the population was Asian, and just 0.02 percent of the population categorized themselves as Hispanic or Latino (U.S. Census, 2000).

80. For a detailed account of these changes, see Planning and Urban Design Agency, 2001b.

81. In addition, these figures could overestimate the proportion of white residents in some of the youths' communities, because of our imprecise measure of youths' neighborhoods (see note 73 above). In several cases, the cross streets they identified as close to their homes led us to identify recently gentrified areas. In addition, some of St. Louis' public housing is located in disproportionately white areas of the city, though most of the public housing residents are African American. Several of the youths whose census data placed them in predominantly white areas gave cross streets quite close to such housing.

82. Specifically, 52 youths lived in neighborhoods that were more than 90 percent African American; 18 youths lived in neighborhoods that were approximately 50 percent African American; and 5 youths lived in neighborhoods that were between 80 and 90 percent African American.

83. Sampson and Wilson, 1995, p. 42 (my emphases). This is certainly the case for St. Louis. Of the predominantly white neighborhoods in St. Louis City, only one is below the city median on socioeconomic indicators. Moreover, this neighborhood still has much lower rates of poverty and unemployment than the averages found in our respondents' neighborhoods (Brunson, 2005).

84. While it may seem inconsistent for disadvantaged neighborhood residents to complain of *both* underpolicing and overpolicing, in fact, these can operate simultaneously. The police may be slow to respond to citizens' calls yet also engage in indiscriminate aggressive policing strategies against community residents. Both of these problems have been found in disadvantaged urban communities (Klinger, 1997; Weitzer, 1999). Although I do not examine police/youth relations in detail here, for analyses of these problems among the youth in this study, see Brunson and Miller, 2006a, 2006b.

85. Sampson et al., 2002, p. 457; see also McNulty and Bellair, 2003; Sampson et al., 1997, 1999.

86. Brunson and Miller, 2006a, 2006b; Sampson and Bartusch, 1998; Weitzer, 1999. This is not to say that police interventions were seen as wholly ineffective, however. While many youths were critical of police harassment in their neighborhoods, some reported positive neighborhood changes that resulted from police crackdowns in their communities, particularly when offender networks were disrupted and persistent criminals were incarcerated.

87. Krivo and Peterson, 1996, p. 639.

88. Sampson et al., 1999, p. 656.

89. Such accounts are confirmed by youths' survey responses. For example, during the survey, youths were asked whether there was "a lot of gang activity" in their neighborhoods, whether there were gang members living on their streets, and whether there were rival gangs close by. Two-thirds answered affirmatively to the first question, and nine out of ten answered "yes" to at least one of these questions.

90. In addition to using pseudonyms, I have changed the names of all streets, gangs, and other identifiable locations in this report. This is to ensure that youths and their neighborhoods remain anonymous.

91. Another notable gender difference was young men's greater likelihood to emphasize temporal variations in neighborhood crime. Both boys and girls described the nighttime as particularly treacherous, and girls described feeling particularly vulnerable to sexual violence if they were outside late at night (see chapter 2). But only young men provided nuanced accounts of how neighborhood activities escalated in the night, and they also described seasonal variations (e.g., summertime versus winter) in detail. These gender differences in youths' accounts provide further evidence of young men's greater embeddedness in neighborhood networks. They were likely more knowledgeable about the shifting nature of neighborhood activities because they were more often participants in such action.

92. Serious delinquency included the following self-report survey items: stealing over $50, stealing a motor vehicle, attacking someone with a weapon or with the intent to seriously hurt them, or committing a robbery. Though we asked youths whether they had carried a hidden weapon, and this item is typically included as serious delinquency, I have not included it in the percentages presented here. Because so many youths lived in dangerous neighborhoods, this item likely confounds delinquent activities with actions taken for protection. When carrying a hidden weapon was included, 75 percent of boys (versus 60 percent) and 77 percent of girls (versus 51 percent) would be classified as having engaged in serious delinquency. Similar increases occur for incidents in the last six months: 40 percent of boys (versus 30 percent) and 51 percent of girls (versus 34 percent) would be classified as serious delinquents. When drug sales were combined with serious delinquency, youths' participation rates were as follows: 23 girls (66 percent) reported ever having engaged in serious delinquency and/ or drug sales, including 15 (43 percent) in the last six months; and 29 boys (73 percent) had done so, including 16 (40 percent) in the last six months. From here onward, when I examine the relationship between serious delinquency and victimization or perpetration of violence against girls, I refer to these combined figures. I do so because of the association between participation in drug sales and greater participation in street activities and exposure to violence.

93. It may be that our survey measures, because they captured prevalence rather than frequency of delinquent involvement, overestimated young women's delinquency and thus were not good indicators of girls' participation in neighborhood street networks. Alternatively, it could be that girls' delinquency was less likely to occur within neighborhood contexts and thus was less tied to their integration into street networks. For instance, many fights between girls took place at school (Miller and Mullins, 2006), suggesting that locales aside from neighborhoods were important sites for girls' delinquency. Finally, it is also the case that youths' discussion of gangs and gang conflicts were quite gender-specific. Only one girl said she was a current gang member, with six additional girls reporting that they claimed or hung out with a gang. In contrast, ten boys (25 percent) reported that they were active gang members, with three more reporting that their friends were a gang. Likewise, gang fights were almost uniformly described by both boys and girls as the purview of young men, suggesting that those few young women involved with gangs were engaged more in their social activities than in gang and territorial defense.

94. Pattillo, 1998, p. 747.

95. Sampson et al., 1999.

96. Sampson et al., 2002, p. 469.

97. Sampson et al., 2002, p. 470.

98. Anderson, 1999; Benson et al., 2003; Bourgois, 1995; Lauritsen and Shaum, 2004; Maher, 1997; Miles-Doan, 1998; Miller, 2001; Steffensmeier, 1983; Steffensmeier and Terry, 1986; Wilson, 1996.

99. Gottfredson, 2001; Laub and Lauritsen, 1998.

NOTES TO CHAPTER 2

1. For example, Anderson, 1999; Bourgois, 1995; Maher, 1997; Miller, 2001; Steffensmeier, 1983; Steffensmeier and Terry, 1986; Wilson, 1996.

2. Lauritsen, 2003.

3. Sampson, 1997, p. 42.

4. As noted in chapter 1, youths' action spaces included both their own neighborhoods, neighborhoods they had recently moved out of, and the neighborhoods of relatives and friends. Except where specifically relevant to the story at hand, I do not make distinctions between youths' activities across these arenas and refer to them generally as youths' neighborhood contexts.

5. The totals in table 2-1 represent all reports of exposure to physical violence, not differentiated by locale (neighborhood, school, home). However, as I detail in this section, most of the reports, particularly of more serious violence, occurred in neighborhood contexts, including youths' own neighborhoods and those they spent time in.

6. Both incidents occurred in respondents' homes.

7. In fact, the extent of violence witnessed by these young people is likely underestimated here, because youths were not asked how many violent incidents they had witnessed, only whether they had and where the most recent incident had occurred. In all likelihood, most youths had witnessed multiple violent events. On the difficulties in measuring exposure to chronic community violence, see Wolfer, 1999.

8. Studies that have linked violence exposure to increased aggression include Durant et al., 1994; Farrell and Bruce, 1997; and Fitzpatrick, 1997. For research on emotional and psychological stressors associated with exposure to violence, see Richters and Martinez, 1993; Shakoor and Chalmers, 1991 (but see Farrell and Bruce, 1997). Brown and Gourdine, 2001, document the heightened sense of vigilance among girls exposed to community violence. Lauritsen et al., 1992, and Sampson and Lauritsen, 1990, emphasize the significance of ecological proximity to violence as a risk for victimization.

9. Farrell and Bruce, 1997, p. 3; see also Garbarino et al., 1991.

10. Graham-Bermann and Edleson, 2001. Though it is beyond the scope of my focus here, it is worth noting that about 50 percent of the youths in this study had witnessed domestic violence. A sizeable portion also reported having been abused by family members: 31 percent of girls and 28 percent of boys reported physical abuse, and 14 percent of girls reported having been sexually abused by a family member. In all, 66 percent of girls and 63 percent of boys reported some exposure to family violence—as witnesses, victims, or both.

11. This was the case even for the survey items I report here. During the survey, we did not ask youths specifically whether the incidents of physical violence they witnessed involved men using violence against women. However, in the in-depth interview, these issues were examined, as discussed in the next section.

12. Some youths also noted that males faced more dangers at the hands of the police (Brunson and Miller, 2006b). In contrast, several youths highlighted risks posed to girls who were involved in gangs and drug sales. If young women were visible players in offender networks within their neighborhood, they were believed to also be at risk for crime-related violence. For instance, Gail said gender "really don't matter, 'cause in my neighborhood the girls [are] tough as . . . the boys." And Katie noted, "some girls that live on the block, some of 'em are in gangs, they be doin' the same things the boys do. Try to fit in with the boys." Marvin said girls face "the same things as the boys face. 'Cause I mean, girls can be like boys too. They can do the same stuff as we can." Likewise, Rennesha said the risks were "about equal," explaining, " 'cause we have some females in the neighborhood that is gang related, they call them thug queens of they block and stuff like that." She said conflicts typically involved "like girls on girls, and the guys on the guys." This was not a predominant theme in the interviews but is noteworthy nonetheless.

13. On fear and risk among urban women, see Carvalho and Lewis, 2003.

14. Though a number of youths specifically mentioned that girls were "easy" targets for robbery, their survey responses did not correspond with these gender-based beliefs. In all, 65 percent of the young men, but only 14 percent of the young women, said they had been the victim of a robbery. Their rates of personal victimization were more comparable for other forms of physical violence, including being hit by someone (75 percent and 71 percent, respectively, for boys and girls), having been jumped or beaten up (68 percent and 57 percent, respectively), and having been stabbed (10 percent and 14 percent, respectively). Nevertheless, young men were more likely to have been threatened with a weapon (58 percent, versus 26 percent for girls) and to have been shot (15 percent, versus 3 percent).

15. For a discussion of women as situationally disadvantaged in public spaces, see Gardner, 1995. For an analysis of how gender is constructed through conversations about vulnerability to violence, see Hollander, 2001.

16. In addition, though not a common theme in girls' interviews when discussing their neighborhoods, some young men focused on dangers they believed young women created for themselves because of "their mouths." For instance, several young men said girls "talk too much" and thus "deserved" to be hit. These themes do come up in girls' discussions as well, primarily in their accounts of dating violence (see chapter 5) and conflicts with other girls (Miller and Mullins, 2006). Because young women did not describe these problems as specific dangers they felt within their neighborhoods, I examine the issues in greater detail in these subsequent chapters.

17. Benson et al., 2003, p. 227; see also Lauritsen and Schaum, 2004; Miles-Doan, 1998.

18. Bourgois, 1995; Joe-Laidler and Hunt, 1997; Maher, 1997; Miller, 2001.

19. School-based sexual harassment, as distinct from neighborhood harassment, is the focus of chapter 3. Because the sexual assault of young women is analyzed extensively in chapter 4, the discussion here is truncated.

20. An oversight in the in-depth interview guides meant that only young women were asked this question. In all, 43 percent described witnessing such incidents. Because we were interested in examining male peer support for violence against women, young men were asked only whether any of their friends engaged in such behaviors. Thus, broad accounts of violence against women in neighborhoods were not solicited from the young men. In hindsight, this was a disappointing omission.

21. The research literature on sexual harassment in schools is discussed in chapter 3. On harassment in public places, see Gardner, 1995; MacMillan et al., 2000. In fact, MacMillan and his colleagues suggest that street harassment has profound consequences for women's fear of sexual victimization.

22. While "sexual harassment" refers to unwanted sexual attention, the term "gender harassment" refers to hostile treatment toward women that includes sexist or degrading remarks or behavior. For a discussion, see Larkin, 1994.

In all, 51 percent of the girls described incidents of gender harassment, 71 percent reported sexual comments that made them uncomfortable, and 49 percent described unwanted sexual touching or grabbing. Of the 18 girls who reported gender harassment, 67 percent described incidents that occurred in school, and 55 percent described incidents in neighborhoods. Likewise with sexual comments: 60 percent reported school incidents, and 48 percent reported neighborhood incidents. The largest disparity between sites was for unwanted touching or grabbing: of the 17 girls who reported such incidents, 65 percent described them occurring at school, and 35 percent in the neighborhood. These numbers do not include incidents of sexual assault.

Young men were also asked whether they had engaged in sexual or gender harassment toward girls, but they were not asked to distinguish where the incidents took place. In all, 70 percent of the boys said they had called girls names or said things to put them down; 48 percent said they had made sexual comments to girls that made them uncomfortable; and 38 percent reported having grabbed or touched girls in ways that made them uncomfortable.

23. Youths used the term "dog" or "dogging" to refer generally to disrespectful treatment of those considered subordinate. In this instance, the term is used to suggest the man is attempting to manipulate the young woman for sexual gain.

24. Consider, for example, that Mary Koss and her colleagues' (1987) groundbreaking self-report studies of sexual assault among college students found that 12 percent of college women reported having been raped. The adolescent girls in our study report a rate more than double this figure.

25. Youths used the term "running train" to refer to "gang bangs" or gang rapes. As I discuss in chapter 4, nearly one-half of the young men interviewed reported having engaged in such behavior. Notably, they did not consider such incidents rape, though the three young women in our sample who had been victimized in this way did define what happened to them as a sexual assault.

26. An important part of this early sexualization for some girls is childhood sexual abuse. For instance, 20 percent of the girls in our study reported being victims of child sexual abuse. One of the subsequent outcomes of this is increased vulnerability to additional sexual coercion. I return to these issues in more detail in chapter 4.

27. Scully, 1990.

28. These strategies are not surprising, as they are in keeping with young men's accounts of the gang and drug-related risks they see as part and parcel of their negotiation of neighborhood and community spaces. What's notable, how-

ever, is the striking contrast to young women's more socially isolating approaches (Cobbina et al., 2007).

29. Koss et al., 1987; Lauritsen, 2003; Marciniak, 1998; Warshaw, 1988.

30. Pain, 1991; Stanko, 1990.

31. Miller, 2001.

32. Anderson, 1999.

NOTES TO CHAPTER 3

1. Gottfredson, 2001, p. 83.

2. Gottfredson, 2001, p. 65.

3. Cited in sequence: Carroll, 1998a; "Editorial," 1998; Pierce, 1998; Dobbs, 2004; Giegerich, 2006b; Giegerich, 2006a.

4. Franck, 2004. The accreditation score is based on an evaluation of three areas of performance: (1) the availability of basic resources such as course offerings, teacher certification, and maximum class sizes; (2) facilities, safety, libraries and guidance counselors; and (3) student performance. It is in the third area that St. Louis Public Schools are most deficient. Performance includes five measures of student testing (across elementary, middle, and high schools), dropout rates, attendance rates, vocational student program completion, ACT scores, students in college preparatory or advanced courses, and vocational student job placement. In 1999, the district failed to make the state standard in all but the final three of these criteria (Pierce, 1999e). Due to provisions in the settlement of a longstanding desegregation case against the city and state, the St. Louis Public School District was not immediately stripped of its accreditation; in 2000, it received "provisional accreditation," a status it still retained as of this writing (Franck, 2004). After its low score of 23 in 1999, the district's performance scores ranged from a high of 64 in 2003 to a low of 41 in 2004 (Howard, 2004). As recently as 2005, "only 6 percent of [St. Louis] high school graduates [were] proficient in English, only 3 percent [were] proficient in math, and only 2 percent [were] proficient in science" (Hughey, 2006).

5. The St. Louis Public School District had more than 115,000 students in 1967; by 2004 this number had dropped to approximately 37,000. While part of this is attributable to overall population decline in the city (see chapter 1), there is evidence that falling enrollments have "outpaced the overall decline in the city's population" (Howard and Kumar, 2004). Also troubling is that since the desegregation agreement of 1999, city students' participation in voluntary transfer programs to county schools has declined. Some county school districts have made fewer slots available under the voluntary program, and new zoning requirements have restricted student transfer choices (Hacker, 1999).

6. Pierce, 1999a; Carroll, 1998c.

7. Pierce, 1999c; see also Carroll, 1998c.

8. "St. Louis Post-Dispatch Gateway Guide," 2003, p. 14. This dropout rate is startling, even by St. Louis Public School standards. In 1999, the district's average dropout rate was 16.2 percent, compared with the state average of 5.3 percent (Pierce, 1999b).

The alternative schools were among a large number of St. Louis public schools closed down in 2003 as part of a reorganization effort to address a $90 million deficit. In fact, the specifics of this reorganization are a microcosm of the ongoing struggles of the school district. In a controversial move, the newly elected school board at that time paid a private consulting firm from New York —without expertise in educational reform—an estimated $5 million to complete a fiscal overhaul of the school district. The majority members of the board, elected on a slate heavily promoted by the white city mayor, approved the firm's decision to close 16 schools, 12 of which were located in North St. Louis, which is almost exclusively African American (see chapter 1). In addition, they eliminated over 1,000 jobs in the school district, which is one of the largest employers of African Americans in the region. The school board made these decisions quite rapidly and did so without making a concerted effort to include community members in the decision-making process or inform them about the bases for their decisions. Given a "legacy of racial mistrust" regarding city governance (Harris, 2003a), the result of the school board's actions was an unprecedented protest within St. Louis's Black community, with virulent accusations that "racism and a continued history of neglect" were behind the decisions (Harris, 2003b). For an excellent analysis of this incident and its links to racism, race relations, and politics in St. Louis, see Ron Harris's two-part series in the *St. Louis Post-Dispatch* (2003a, 2003b).

9. Carroll, 1998a.

10. Carroll, 1998b.

11. The majority of these ten were in a St. Louis public high school that was 100 percent African American and 99 percent low income, with a dropout rate of 7.5 percent and a graduation rate of 43 percent. Another attended a St. Louis public middle school that was 68 percent African American and 95 percent low income. The proportion of youths in these schools performing at or above the state testing standards was 0 to 3 percent at the high school and 0 to 8 percent at the middle school. St. Louis City schools have among the largest proportion of impoverished pupils in the region, with 82 percent enrolled in the federal lunch program in the 2001–2002 academic year ("St. Louis Post-Dispatch Gateway Guide," 2003, p. 14). According to 2000 U.S. Census data, the average neighborhood characteristics of the schools that youths in our sample attended were 93.7 percent African American, with median family incomes of $17,307 and poverty rates averaging 53.2 percent.

12. Hinman, 2006. In fact, a recent investigation revealed that a large number of students at this school who were not in attendance for anywhere from one-third to three-quarters of class days still received passing grades in many of their classes, including A's and B's (Hinman, 2006).

13. Gottfredson et al., 2005, p. 413.

14. Gottfredson et al., 2005, p. 413.

15. Gottfredson, 2001, p. 63.

16. Clubb, 2006; Howard and Shinkle, 2005.

17. Pierce, 1999d.

18. Increased research attention to the issue of school violence was spurred by the upsurge in youth violence in the late 1980s and early 1990s (Cook and Laub, 2002), while popular interest was galvanized by incidents like the infamous 1999 Columbine shootings. However, very little criminological research has examined male-on-female violence in schools. In fact, even analyses of the Columbine and Virginia Tech incidents and similar attacks have failed to notice both the disproportionate targeting of young women and the relevance of masculinity challenges as a driving force behind the incidents (for discussion, see Kimmel and Mahler, 2003; Klein and Chancer, 2000). There has been some research attention to young women's conflicts with other girls, including in schools, though much of this work has been done by psychologists rather than criminologists.

19. Stein et al., 2002, pp. 40–41.

20. AAUW Educational Foundation, 2001; Hand and Sanchez, 2000; Lahelma, 2002. A number of studies have also compared girls' and boys' experiences with sexual harassment. These consistently conclude that girls experience more severe forms of harassment, and suffer more severe consequences as a result of harassment, than boys. This is unsurprising, given that sexual labeling has different consequences for males and females (e.g., Quinn, 2002).

21. The limited research available is somewhat mixed. The AAUW Educational Foundation's (2001) adolescent survey did not find dramatic differences across race or across urban versus suburban or rural schools in students' reports of the prevalence of sexual harassment. However, prevalence measures tell us little about the nature, context, and broader consequences of sexual harassment, particularly—as I detail later—when such behaviors bridge both school and neighborhood peer settings. The AAUW data also suggest that African American girls reported less-severe negative emotional outcomes than white girls (AAUW Educational Foundation, 2001; Hand and Sanchez, 2000).

In contrast, Graham and Juvonen's (2002) study of sexual harassment among middle school students found that African American girls faced more peer rejection after incidents of sexual harassment than did girls from other racial groups. The authors attribute this finding to students' stereotyped expectations that African American youths are more aggressive than their peers in other racial groups, thus leading to the greater stigmatization of Black girls who are seen as failing to adequately stand up for themselves.

Studies of college students and adult women also suggest that Black women report more sexual harassment and more severe experiences with sexual harassment than white women, both in the workplace and in social settings (Wyatt and Riederle, 1995). This research also highlights the detrimental effect of gendered racial stereotypes that shape the sexual harassment of Black women (Mecca and Rubin, 1999), as well as the unique barriers Black women face in addressing sexual harassment (Adams, 1997).

22. As I mention in chapter 2, scholars typically make a distinction between sexual and gender harassment. The former refers to a variety of forms of unwanted sexual attention, whereas the latter refers to hostile treatment toward women that includes sexist or degrading remarks or behavior. Harassment has been further differentiated to distinguish between verbal, physical, and visual forms. Some of these can be differentiated further still. For example, verbal harassment can include making sexual comments, sexual propositions, or sexual threats; comments that are intended to ridicule a girl's appearance and sexual attractiveness; and spreading rumors or taunting a girl about her alleged or actual sexual activities. Likewise, physical harassment includes touching, grabbing, "hugging on," or rubbing, and can be more or less forceful or coercive. Finally, visual forms can include behaviors such as leering, sexual gesturing, and public exhibition of pornography, as well as distribution of sexually explicit images of girls themselves (Larkin, 1994).

23. Girls were asked specifically whether incidents had occurred at home, in school, in the neighborhood, or elsewhere and could respond affirmatively to multiple sites. For a more detailed breakdown, refer to note 22 in chapter 2.

24. In fact, there is evidence that young men are more likely than young women to perceive situations, behaviors, and interactions as more sexual (Foulis and McCabe, 1997; Perry et al., 1998). However, at least one study found that male sexualization of female intent was not related to the likelihood of engaging in or condoning sexual harassment (Saal, 1996). I return to these interpretive issues later in the chapter.

25. Shelton and Chavous, 1999, p. 594.

26. "Scrub" is a term originating from rap music, to refer to a man without economic resources; "pigeon" is a term used to describe women who are out to get men for their money.

27. Cleveland and Kerst, 1993; Duncan, 1999; Timmerman, 2003.

28. Hand and Sanchez, 2000, p. 719.

29. In fact, there has been a great deal more research on sexual harassment in the workplace than in school, though some of this work addresses issues of less-specific relevance for understanding peer harassment. For instance, important

dimensions of workplace sexual harassment include what Till (1980, quoted in Shelton and Chavous, 1999, p. 595) classifies as sexual bribery and sexual threat: "the promise of reward for the solicitation of sexual activity or other sex-related behavior" and "coercion of sexual activity by threats of punishment," respectively. Certainly, we can imagine circumstances in which social rewards or penalties could be offered or withheld within peer groups, but, generally speaking, this type of harassment is reserved for individuals with formal or informal power within organizations. In schools, such power is concentrated among adults.

30. Fineran and Bennett, 1999; Foulis and McCabe, 1997; Hand and Sanchez, 2000. Of course, this finding is not terribly surprising, since research also consistently finds that sexual harassment has more harmful consequences for females than males (see note 20).

31. Loe, 1996, p. 418. On the role of humor in sexual harassment, see Kehily and Nayak, 1997; Larkin, 1994; Quinn, 2000, 2002.

32. Quinn, 2002, p. 400.

33. Finkelhor and Asdigian, 1996; Lauritsen and Quinet, 1995.

34. Houston and Hwang, 1996, p. 190.

35. For a discussion of the dangers of the labeling process, see Duncan 1999, p. 60; see also Lauritsen and Quinet, 1995.

36. Lauritsen and Quinet, 1995, p. 147.

37. In fact, such connections are readily apparent. Researchers have consistently found that both (heterosexual) sexual activity and the denigration of women are effective methods for young men to demonstrate masculinity and gain status and respect within their male peer groups (Duncan, 1999; Kehily, 2001). Studies have also shown that adherence to hegemonic masculine identities, adversarial sexual beliefs, and rape myth acceptance are each correlated with greater tolerance for sexual harassment (Foulis and McCabe, 1997; Reilly et al., 1992). For similar examinations of these processes in the contexts of street gangs and college fraternities, respectively, see Miller, 2001; Stombler, 1994.

38. It is nonetheless worth briefly noting girls' descriptions of avoidance techniques. Several young women described staying away from young men, and others specifically said their means of avoiding any conflicts in school—with males or females—was, as Cleshay noted, to "stay to myself." Dawanna explained, "at school I keep to myself most of the time."

Yvonne focused on how she dressed as a means of avoiding unwanted attention: "I mean, I wear stuff that's kind of like revealing, but not too revealing, 'cause I don't want to draw no attention towards me now, whatsoever, like that." She situated this decision in an attempted sexual assault that "affected me a lot," shattered her sense of safety, and made her especially distrustful of—and confrontational with—young men. Her attempts to avoid male attention were thus partly an effort to keep herself out of trouble, since she knew she would aggressively confront young men's untoward behaviors.

39. In fact, there is some evidence to suggest that this process is especially profound for African American girls. As described in note 21 above, Graham and Juvonen (2002) found that Black girls faced greater peer rejection as a result of sexual harassment than other girls, a finding they link to the stronger expectation in African American communities that individuals stand up for themselves.

40. I use the term "worked" here loosely. Individual confrontations did not pose a serious challenge to sexual harassment or the cultural support it received. On occasion, confrontation did bring the incident to an end without further escalation, and thus it "worked" for the girl in that moment.

41. Yvonne reported multiple experiences with sexual violence, both as a victim and a witness. She described several attempted rapes, had been pressured into unwanted sex, and had seen multiple sexual assaults in her neighborhood.

42. It may well be that such incidents were for show as much as anything, and young men threatened violence believing that school personnel would intervene before they had to use it. In this manner, they could sanction the young woman's "disrespect" while avoiding violating the public norm discouraging male violence against women.

43. This rebuttal was significant in and of itself. By telling the young woman not to be "frontin'" him, he was specifically implying that she had behaved otherwise with him previously—that is, she had allowed him sexual access and was denying it in front of others. Thus, his response was a public challenge to her sexual reputation. Anishika also described witnessing such a strategy when a young man tried to hug a girl and she refused. According to Anishika, he replied, "aw, man, you just shady. Alright then. I don't know why you frontin' *now* for." Again, the implication was that the young woman had allowed the young man to touch her previously.

44. In fact, numerous girls described either themselves or other girls threatening to call a male relative or boyfriend to intervene when they had conflicts with young men.

45. Some young men concurred. For instance, Leon said that "some of the teachers, they don't care. They might know but [don't take action]." One problem with such indifference is that it "communicates to students that such behavior is acceptable" rather than recognizing it as a powerful form of gendered social control (Lahelma, 2002, p. 303). Unfortunately, a limitation of our data collection was that we failed to ask youths whether there were gender differences in the responsiveness of school staff and administrators to the problem of sexual harassment. However, it is striking that most of the descriptions we came across—particularly when teachers failed to take effective action—were in reference to male staff specifically.

46. Youths also reported that security personnel and staffing were often inadequate to respond to conflicts. Raymond said his school "only got one security guard, so he don't be knowing what really going on 'til he hear about it on his speaker phone or by students or something. . . . [He] just watch the front door, that's all he do." Likewise, Dawanna said that "most of the time, [security guards] ain't nowhere to be found. They probably with somebody else in another classroom fight or something like that." And Leon noted that security would "get there, but they won't get there 'til the last minute."

47. See notes 19 to 21 above.

48. William also noted that "if the guards hear the dude cursing a girl out or the girl cursing a dude out, they get suspended, but if the guard don't hear it [for himself], nothing happens."

49. Lisa's case was somewhat different, in that she was not the target of the harassment in question. She explained, "I mean, he wasn't tellin' people he had sex with me. He was tellin' people he had sex with the other girl. So they figured I didn't have anything to do with it."

50. Kehily and Nayak, 1997; Quinn, 2002.

51. For an overview, see Yoder and Aniakudo, 1995.

52. Yoder and Aniakudo, 1995.

53. Quinn, 2000.

54. Marin and Guadagno (1999) also highlight the negative consequences for women of reporting sexual harassment. They employed sexual harassment scenarios to examine how individuals respond to women who label incidents as sexual harassment and report these behaviors. In both cases, they found that such women were viewed as less trustworthy and less feminine.

55. Fineran and Bennett, 1999, p. 57.

56. According to Kopels and Dupper (1999, p. 449), while the Supreme Court ruling allows students to sue school districts for failures to respond to sexual harassment, "the Court established that Title IX funding recipients may be held liable only 'where they are deliberately indifferent to sexual harassment, of which they have actual knowledge, that is so severe, pervasive, and objectively offensive that it can be said to deprive the victims of access to the educational opportunities or benefits provided by the schools.' " Thus, "all that is necessary is that school officials respond to known peer harassment in a manner that is not clearly unreasonable" (p. 451). In addition, the Court noted that because "students are still learning how to interact appropriately with their peers," they "often engage in insults, banter, teasing, shoving, pushing, and other gender-related conduct that is upsetting to the students who are subjected to these behaviors" (p. 449). Thus, the standard for what constitutes "severe, pervasive, and objectively offensive" behaviors is even more stringent than for employment discrimination law.

57. Kopels and Dupper, 1999, p. 454. Given the pervasiveness of harassment

perpetration and victimization, a case-by-case, individualistic approach is untenable, as it fails to address both the culture and the institutional setting in which these acts are embedded (Cleveland and McNamara, 1996; Lee et al., 1996).

58. Ferguson, 2001.

59. Kopels and Dupper, 1999, p. 454.

60. Anderson, 1999; Benson et al., 2003; Bourgois, 1995; Lauritsen and Shaum, 2004; Maher, 1997; Miles-Doan, 1998; Miller, 2001; Steffensmeier, 1983; Steffensmeier and Terry, 1986; Wilson, 1996.

61. AAUW Educational Foundation, 2001.

62. Tolman et al., 2003b, pp. 160, 162. The denial and denigration of female sexual agency is a particularly insidious facet of the forms of sexual mistreatment and labeling documented here and in chapters 2 and 4. For further discussion, see Fine, 1988; Tolman, 1994. I return to the issue in chapter 6.

NOTES TO CHAPTER 4

1. I use the term "acquiesce" here not to deny young women's sexual agency (e.g., Fine, 1988; Tolman, 1994) but because the types of sexual incidents I examine here and the ways in which young women are identified for participation are strongly suggestive of coercive techniques. I further distinguish in the analyses, to the extent possible, some of the differences between sexual coercion and sexual assault. While I examine these behaviors on a continuum, there is evidence to suggest that coercion and assault are qualitatively different phenomena with distinct risk factors (Testa and Dermen, 1999), each of which implicate normative constructions of heterosexual sex (for discussion, see Gavey, 1999).

2. "Running trains" is the terminology youths used to describe incidents of gang rape, or coercive group sex with a single girl. Young men—but not the young women in our sample to whom it had happened—typically defined such incidents as consensual. This is an issue I return to in detail later in this chapter.

3. To more accurately arrive at this figure, I used follow-up questions to identify duplicate answers. During the survey portion of the interview, we asked follow-up questions for affirmative answers that included how many times it happened, who did it, and where. We asked additional follow-up questions in the in-depth interviews. Thus, I was able to account for duplicate answers in the survey responses. For example, of the 9 young women who reported having been sexually assaulted, molested, or raped, 5 of these were incidents involving family members; 2 involved boyfriends, though one of these also reported a stranger rape. Likewise, of 13 girls who reported being pressured into unwanted sex, 9 of these were incidents by boyfriends. In reporting girls' experiences with multiple victimizations, I have counted duplicate answers only once, except when young women describe multiple incidents in a single category. Since childhood sexual abuse and incest often involve ongoing incidents by the same per-

petrator, these were also counted only once (none described multiple offenders), as were multiple incidents in which the same boyfriend pressured a girl into unwanted sex.

4. For a discussion, see Lauritsen and Rennison, 2006. Interestingly, however, Kalof's (2000) study of undergraduate women found that Black females reported significantly higher rates of sexual *coercion* than white, Hispanic, or Asian females, but white females reported the highest rates of rape. Urquiza and Goodlin-Jones (1994), in a sample of community college students, report that African American women had higher rates of rape victimization and revictimization than other groups. In contrast, Kalof's (1995) study of middle-class adolescent youth revealed that Black girls reported lower rates of participation in unwanted sex than white girls, as well as boys of both races. Each of these studies suggest a complex relationship between race, class, and sexual victimization that merits careful contextual examination.

5. Lauritsen, 2003; Lauritsen and Schaum, 2004. For a similar analysis of how neighborhood characteristics shape race differences in sexual activity among adolescent girls, see Brewster, 1994.

6. Bureau of Justice Statistics, 1992, 2005.

7. Lauritsen et al., 1992; Sanders and Moore, 1999.

8. Collins, 1998; Grauerholz, 2000; West et al., 2000.

9. Research has shown that participation in delinquency and other interpersonal violence is correlated with participation in sexual violence for young men (Calhoun et al., 1997; Malamuth, 1981; Marciniak, 1998).

10. Nykeshia reported that she had to move out of her mother's house and in with her father and stepmother for a period after the rape. Charges were pressed against the man, and he served a short sentence. Nykeshia reported that, after his release, "he wasn't even out a good two weeks" before he was picked up for burglarizing a store and returned to prison.

11. Chesney-Lind and Pasko, 2004; Miller, 2001.

12. For example, Chandy et al. (1996) found that adolescent girls with a history of sexual abuse had more adverse outcomes when they faced additional family stressors; see also Sanders and Moore, 1999.

13. Regarding the relationship between sexual abuse and additional sexual revictimization, see Collins, 1998; Mayall and Gold, 1995; Urquiza and Goodlin-Jones, 1994; and West et al., 2000. In fact, Irwin (1999) found that childhood sexual abuse was linked not just to sexual revictimization but to other forms of both violent and nonviolent victimization for adult women.

14. Finkelhor and Brown, 1985; Mayall and Gold, 1995.

15. Grauerholz, 2000.

16. Grauerholz, 2000; Mayall and Gold, 1995. Though their research does not examine sexual revictimization, Lauritsen and Quinet (1995) provide a detailed discussion of the various state-dependent factors that can contribute to

revictimization. Finkelhor and Asdigian (1996) also describe facets of vulnerability that are congruent with the motives and needs of offenders.

17. Because of my focus here on peer violence, I do not discuss girls' experiences with childhood sexual abuse and incest. LaSondra was the only young woman who described being the victim of a stranger rape involving an adult man, and I discuss her experience in chapter 2.

18. Gavey, 1999; Warshaw, 1988.

19. Crawford and Popp, 2003.

20. Truman et al., 1996; Vass and Gold, 1995.

21. Bourgois, 1996; Messerschmidt, 1993; Mullins, 2006. For research specific to the role of male peer support, see Schwartz and DeKeseredy, 1997.

22. The classic research on this issue is Diana Scully's (1990) *Understanding Sexual Violence.* A large proportion of the convicted rapists she interviewed were what she calls "deniers." Drawing from rape myths prominent in U.S. culture, these men characterized even brutal acts of sexual violence as consensual.

23. King, 2003.

24. Some researchers have suggested that African American men, in particular, may resist viewing sexually coercive or violent actions as rape specifically because of the legacy of the "myth of the Black rapist." Marciniak (1998, p. 297), for example, argues that African American males may be "more likely to point to victims' behavior to lessen a heightened sense of vulnerability to rape accusations that stems from a stereotypic image of the 'rapist'" (see also Lefley et al., 1993). Thus, Kalof and Wade's (1995) study of college students found significantly greater gender disparity among African American than among white women and men in the likelihood of adhering to rape myths, gender stereotypes, and adversarial sexual beliefs.

25. Part of Bobby's ambivalence in labeling the young woman a "rat" was that he continued to date her afterward. As discussed in chapter 5, he was also ambivalent about whether to call her his "girlfriend" because he believed she acquiesced to his sexual pressure too readily. In fact, Crawford and Popp (2003) found that men judge women's sexual behaviors more harshly when considering them as potential romantic partners.

26. Testa and Dermen, 1999. In keeping with the conceptualization of sexual violence as a continuum of behaviors, some researchers, instead, distinguish between different types of coercion, including physical coercion (Basile, 1999; Koss et al., 1987).

27. Struckman-Johnson et al., 2003.

28. Gavey, 1999. For a thorough treatment of sexual compliance, see Impett and Peplau, 2003.

29. As described in note 3 above, the majority of affirmative survey responses to this question referred to boyfriends. Unfortunately, an oversight in the in-depth interview guide was that during the portion that asked questions about

relationship conflict and violence, we did not ask specific follow-up questions about sexual coercion. Thus, unless girls raised the issue again themselves, we failed to collect detailed information about these incidents.

30. Psychologists Zoë Peterson and Charlene Muehlenhard (2007) have examined the extent of such ambivalence surrounding the issue of "wantedness" in both consensual and nonconsensual sex. They argue that, regardless of whether a woman had some reasons to "want" sex, this is conceptually distinct from the issue of whether they *consented* to sex. In Sheron's case, for example, she expressed some ambivalence about "wanting" to have sex with her former boyfriend because she "still had feelings" for him. However, she also described not consenting. She acquiesced because she felt she "ain't have no choice." Peterson and Muehlenhard argue that blurring the distinction between "wanting" and "consenting" is detrimental to rape victims. It leads to victim-blaming and decreases the likelihood that incidents of nonconsensual sex will be recognized as rape.

31. Basile, 1999; Cleveland, et al., 1999; Impett and Peplau, 2003.

32. Crosby et al., 2000. An additional troubling facet of this research is that these events are significantly less likely to involve condom use.

33. In all, 24 of the girls we interviewed (71 percent) reported they were sexually active. Their average age of first sexual intercourse was 14. Of these 24 girls, one-third (8 girls) reported having had one sexual partner, one-quarter (6 girls) reported two sexual partners, and almost one-half (the remaining 10 girls) had three or more sexual partners. In contrast, all but two young men (95 percent) in our sample said they were sexually active, with a mean age of first sexual intercourse just under age 13. Just two young men reported only one sexual partner, with an additional seven describing two sexual partners. In all, 58 percent of young men reported five or more sexual partners, and over 33 percent reported more than ten.

34. Since Mary Koss's groundbreaking research in the 1980s, feminist scholars have dealt with the conundrum that many women who experience sexual violence that meets legal definitions of rape do not define their experiences as such (Koss et al., 1987). There is strong evidence that the internalization of rape myths plays a role in this process (Peterson and Muehlenhard, 2004). Thus, rather than labeling the incidents as rape for them, my goal in this chapter is to "offer analyses and critiques that help make sense of [young] women's experiences as they are shaped and constrained by power relations in social contexts" (Gavey, 1999, p. 68).

35. Marciniak, 1998.

36. Cleveland, et al., 1999.

37. Mustaine and Tewksbury, 1998; Sanday, 1990; Schwartz and DeKeseredy, 1997; Tyler et al., 1998.

38. Boswell and Spade, 1996, p. 143.

39. Boswell and Spade, 1996, p. 137.

40. Martin and Hummer, 1989.

41. Cleveland et al., 1999, p. 533.

42. In fact, a number of girls believed that either how they carried themselves or their ties to boyfriends or male peers would insulate them from sexual victimization. Unfortunately, a few learned the hard way that "respecting" themselves was insufficient to protect them when they inadvertently became too intoxicated. Even when they weren't intoxicated, relationships with young men did not and could not always protect them. Nicole, for instance, had a friend who was raped at a party by a young man who followed her into the bathroom and held a rag over her mouth while her boyfriend was in the next room. As La-Sondra explained, "I hate people who say 'this ain't ever gonna happen to me.' You never know. You should never say never."

43. Ratner, 1993.

44. Testa and Dermen, 1999.

45. Cisco is a high-proof alcohol that comes in fruit flavors and is known for getting its consumers rapidly intoxicated. It has been widely touted by some rap artists. In fact, in the 1990s the producers of Cisco were censured by the federal government for misleading labeling and were required to change their marketing strategies. For further information, see http://www.dallasobserver.com/1994-11-17/news/wine-punch.

46. This was nearly one-half (48 percent) of all delinquent boys, compared with just over one-third (36 percent) of boys who hadn't engaged in serious delinquency.

47. On face value, it may seem contradictory that 18 boys reported having run trains on girls but only three girls reported having been victims of gang rape. It may be that because this kind of sexual victimization is especially stigmatizing for young women, these events were underreported by girls in our sample. This has been found with other stigmatizing sexual behaviors, such as sexual initiation practices for girls in gangs (Miller, 2001) and sex-for-crack exchanges among female drug users (Maher, 1997). However, these numbers may also be close to accurate. By definition, these events involve multiple perpetrators and a single victim. So, for example, if on average six young men participate in a train on a single girl, the ratio of perpetrators to offenders is 6 to 1. This is the ratio of reported perpetration and victimization we found in our sample.

48. Wood, 2005, p. 306; see also Bourgois, 1996.

49. Franklin, 2004, p. 35.

50. Franklin, 2004; Sanday, 1990.

51. Sanday, 1990, p. 181.

52. Franklin, 2004, p. 29.

53. Ullman, 1999.

54. This appears to be a fairly consistent finding in research on gang rape (Sanday, 1990; Wood, 2005). Wood's research on gang rape among disadvantaged men in South Africa, for example, examined the ways in which young men legitimized group sexual assaults. Young men argued that such incidents were not rape, because they typically involved trickery or coercion rather than outright physical violence and because the victims "failed" to resist. When pressed, however, a few admitted that the young women were "fearful, outnumbered, and had 'nowhere to run'" (Wood, 2005, p. 312).

55. The noises Frank made into the tape recorder were not those suggestive of sexual pleasure, thus the reason he asked the girl, "What's wrong with you?" Because he defined the girl as a "freak" and the incident as consensual, it didn't occur to him to interpret her "noises" as pain or discomfort. Of course, her pain is not a guarantee that the event was nonconsensual, but it is certainly suggestive. There were similar clues in other young men's accounts, described later.

56. In fact, these differences in young men's accounts were shaped by who they were interviewed by. Lamont's, Frank's, and Robert's accounts, in which they were adamant that the young women involved were willing, even eager participants, were conducted by the white male interviewer. They depicted themselves as without culpability, and their descriptions were graphic, focusing specific attention to the details of their sexual performances. This appears to be masculinity at play in the interview context. In contrast, the two cases discussed next—Terence's and Tyrell's—were drawn from interviews conducted by the African American female Ph.D. student. Their descriptions are not sexually graphic, and, though both young men still perceived the incidents as consensual, they were much more forthcoming about details that suggested otherwise.

57. Tyrell, his friend, and the girl all worked at a local community center that gave jobs to youths in the community. Thus the reason they were able to watch movies while at work.

58. This interpretation is consistent with Willan and Pollard's (2003) research on acquaintance rape. They found that men at risk for such behavior "misperceive" women's sexual intentions by reading sexual cues into a range of interactions. For instance, agreeing to go to a party with them or agreeing to come to their house is read as evidence that the woman will let the man engage in sex. Her refusal to have sex when they are alone together is then read as reneging on a previously agreed-on offer. Again, this is consistent with King's (2003) position that men's definitions of women's consent are based on notions of male entitlement and ignore women's definitions of both the meanings behind what they view as innocuous interactions with men and their actual desires in potential sexual interactions.

59. Bourgois (1996) makes this point as well, based on his ethnography of Puerto Rican drug dealers in East Harlem.

60. Nurius et al., 1992; Santello and Leitenberg, 1993.

61. Brunson and Miller, 2006a; Neville and Pugh, 1997; Wyatt, 1992.
62. Sullivan and Rumptz, 1994.

NOTES TO CHAPTER 5

1. Graham-Bermann and Edleson, 2001.
2. Straus and Gelles, 1990. Studies that find similar rates of physical relationship violence across gender typically use a version of Straus's (1979) Conflict Tactics Scale (CTS). Importantly, this research does not find gender parity with regard to sexual violence in relationships, which is almost exclusively a male-perpetrated phenomenon. As an approach for measuring relationship violence, the Conflict Tactics Scale has met with numerous critiques. Most important among these are the fact that this scale provides a count of violence but does not examine the contexts in which such acts take place (for instance, whether the violence was in self-defense), violent events are not operationalized sufficiently to determine the severity of incidents, and the consequences of violence, including injury, are not taken into account (DeKeseredy and Schwartz, 1998; Dobash et al., 1992). In fact, recent research with primarily adult populations contradicts findings of gender symmetry. Drawing from the National Crime Victimization Survey, this research suggests that women are "about six times more likely than men to experience violence committed by an intimate" (Backman and Saltzman, 1995, p. 1; see also Tjaden and Thoennes, 2000).
3. Gray and Foshee, 1997; Molidor and Tolman, 1998; Morse, 1995; O'-Keefe, 1997; O'Keefe and Treister, 1998. Morse (1995), for example, used National Youth Survey data and found that girls were more likely than boys to report engaging in partner violence and were also twice as likely to describe such violence as nonreciprocal. Nonetheless, she found that girls suffered more negative consequences from partner violence when they were victimized. Molidor and Tolman (1998) found that adolescent boys were significantly more likely to report less-severe or moderate forms of physical victimization, while girls were significantly more likely to experience severe violence, including sexual violence. Like Morse, they found that girls were significantly more likely to report having experienced physical injury as a result of a violent victimization. O'Keefe (1997) suggests that African American youths report more dating violence perpetration than youths in other racial groups, with African American girls reporting the highest levels. Such findings have not been replicated for adults.
4. Table 5-1 only includes those youths who described having had a boyfriend or girlfriend sometime in the past. The table combines youths' reports of relationship violence in their current and past relationships. The percentages in table 5-1 do not precisely match those in Miller and White (2003). For some items, this is due to our exclusion (at a reviewers' request) in the *Criminology*

article of two youths for whom we were unable to complete in-depth interviews. For one item (whether boys reported a girlfriend throwing, smashing, or kicking something), it was a function of author error, which, fortunately, did not change the substance of our analyses there. Finally, girls' and boys' reports in table 5-1 (but not in Miller and White, 2003) are not strictly comparable, because girls were asked about dating violence in their current and last relationships, as well as in any previous relationship. Boys were asked about their current and last relationships only. Thus, girls' higher reported prevalence of some dating victimization items here (compared with the data in the 2003 article) is due to the inclusion of their responses to whether they had been victimized in any previous relationship. For the strict comparisons, see Miller and White, 2003. Here I include all of the girls' reports, in keeping with the specific focus of my analysis of the extent and context of girls' experiences of gender-based violence.

5. In all, 24 girls (69 percent) described currently having a boyfriend when they were interviewed, nine (26 percent) did not have a current boyfriend but reported having had one in the past, and two (6 percent) (Kendall and Nykeshia) described never having had a boyfriend. By comparison, 80 percent of the boys we interviewed described having a current girlfriend. Only one—Larry—described never having had a girlfriend, though he reported more than 20 sexual partners, had run trains on girls, and described having sex with a girl when she was too drunk to consent. Most youths who described being in a current relationship said they were sexually active in that relationship (50 percent of girls and 69 percent of boys). While nine girls (26 percent) reported pregnancies, including two girls who were pregnant at the time of their interviews and three who reported multiple pregnancies, only five (14 percent) had children. Three girls described having had miscarriages, and one reported that she had had an abortion. Unfortunately, we did not ask young men whether they had children.

6. Jackson et al., 2000; Molidor and Tolman, 1998; Morse, 1995; Tjaden and Thoennes, 2000; Vivan and Langhinrichsen-Rohling, 1994.

7. Dobash et al., 1992, p. 76.

8. For a discussion of the problems of distinguishing severe assaults from less-serious acts of violence using CTS-based measures, see DeKeseredy and Schwartz, 1998.

9. Figures presented here do not include questions from table 5-1 that are not explicitly physically violent (e.g., verbal abuse, as well as threats or throwing, smashing, or kicking something). It does include two items not listed in table 5-1 because they were asked of girls but not boys: being "beaten up" by a boyfriend (two girls, or 6 percent), or being choked by a boyfriend (seven girls, or 21 percent). Percentages are calculated from a base of 33, since two girls reported never having had a boyfriend.

10. Because sexual violence in relationships has consistently been found to be primarily a male-perpetrated phenomenon, we did not ask young men about their experiences with sexual coercion or violence.

11. Thorne, 1993, p. 135.

12. My use of the term "hegemonic" here is not precisely in keeping with Connell's (2002). While hegemonic masculinities typically refer to those lauded in the broader culture, I use the term here to refer specifically to those facets of masculinity that were dominant—or hegemonic—in the urban youth culture under investigation.

13. Young women also described the impact of males' playa' behaviors on girls' safety and reputations (as discussed in previous chapters), as well as on their dating relationships. An additional consequence of playa' behavior for girls was its contribution to female-on-female conflicts. For a discussion, see Miller and Mullins, 2006.

14. A minority of young men—primarily those in lengthier committed relationships—did not engage in sex talk specifically about their girlfriends. Instead, they kept all of the details of their relationship (sexual and otherwise) to themselves, defining it as "private."

15. Majors and Billson, 1992.

16. See also Eyre et al., 1998.

17. Ford et al., 2002.

18. Molidor and Tolman (1998) found that nearly one-half of the violent incidents youths in their high school sample reported occurred in the presence of others, and many occurred on school grounds.

19. See also Bethke and DeJoy, 1993.

20. In their narrative descriptions of their own experiences, about one-third of the youths we talked to described incidents of what they deemed "play" violence—teasing and play arguments (about such things as who was going to eat the last cookie or who had the TV remote) that included a physical element. I do not focus on play violence in the analysis here, though it is worth noting that such physicality in play sometimes created a pattern of interaction that could result in the use of violence in angry encounters, and there were occasions when play violence escalated into serious conflict.

21. There remains considerable debate about the validity and reliability of using victim versus perpetrator accounts of partner violence, as well as concern about how gender affects the reporting of partner violence (Moffitt et al., 1997; Sugarman and Hotaling, 1997). In particular, there is some evidence that males are more likely to minimize their role in such violence (Dobash et al., 1998; Gray and Foshee, 1997; but see Morse, 1995). Based on their comparative analysis of couples' accounts of violence, Hanley and O'Neill (1997, pp. 700–701) conclude that research should not assume "one person is 'telling the truth' or

has a better memory. . . . Men and women may think differently about aggression and may systematically label acts differently."

22. Kimmel, 2002; O'Keefe, 1997; O'Keefe and Treister, 1998.

23. In fact, during the survey, youths were asked if it was appropriate for a young man to hit his girlfriend when she hit him first. In all, 10 girls (29 percent) and 16 boys (40 percent) answered affirmatively. See also Kimmel, 2002; O'Keefe and Treister, 1998.

24. Several studies are of note in this regard. O'Keefe (1997, p. 565) reports that the "seriousness of the relationship [is] a significant predictor [of dating violence perpetration] for females but not males, suggesting that male dating violence may be less tied to their level of emotional commitment to their partners or that they evaluate their dating relationships less seriously than females." Likewise, in a couples study of dating violence, Hanley and O'Neill (1997, p. 699) found that "although more emotional commitment is reported by violent couples, there is much more disagreement between the partners about commitment issues." Specifically, they found that women have greater emotional commitment than men, but they also perceive their partners as more committed than the partners report. These authors conclude that incongruence in perceived commitment "may indicate greater insecurity in the relationship, a stronger tendency toward jealousy, and difficulty in establishing mutual expectations and trust" (p. 700).

25. While studies of adolescent dating violence find that boys and girls both rank consistently high for describing anger and jealousy as motives for violence, significant gender differences emerge with regard to the issue of control. O'Keefe (1997) reports that anger was the most frequent motive mentioned by both groups, followed by self-defense for girls, and the desire to get control over their partners for boys, with jealousy the third most cited motive for both genders.

26. In fact, Felson and Messner's (2000) examination of assault found that the control motive is significantly more likely to occur in male-to-female intimate partner assaults than any other kind of violence. Importantly, they also argue that the control motive is linked—not just to an individual's desire to exert influence within the relationship but to their relative coercive power (see also O'Keefe and Treister, 1998). This is where the most significant gender difference may lie: "A threat delivered by the less powerful party is likely to lack credibility, and it may lead to retaliation rather than to fear and compliance (Felson and Messner, 2000, p. 87; see also Follingstad et al., 1999).

27. Molidor and Tolman (1998) found that one-half of the adolescent boys in their study described laughing when they were victims of partner violence, and one-third described ignoring it. In contrast, a larger proportion of girls reported fighting back, obeying their partner, or trying to talk to him. Similarly, male

students in O'Keefe and Treister's (1998) study reported that their most common reactions to relationship victimization were amusement or anger, while girls reported fear and emotional hurt as their most common reactions. See also Anderson and Umberson (2001, p. 375), who argue that men's minimization of women's violence functions to "naturalize a binary and hierarchical gender system."

28. Alhough attitudinal studies consistently find that female-perpetrated violence is generally viewed as more acceptable than male-perpetrated violence, these studies also report that males indicate greater acceptance of male-perpetrated violence than do females (O'Keefe and Treister, 1998) and that respondents of both genders are more tolerant of male violence when the relationship is serious rather than casual (Bethke and Dejoy, 1993).

29. Group processes play a facilitative role in such violence (e.g., DeKeseredy and Schwartz, 1997). But perhaps it's an encouraging sign for policy and practice that many youths perceive themselves as opposing violence against women more than their peers.

30. Osthoff, 2002, p. 1522.

31. That her mother's interventions were not more swiftly forthcoming (the relationship lasted for a year) may be a function of LaSondra's chaotic home life. She described mostly being raised by her grandmother, but she was living with her mother, her mother's husband, and an adult cousin. LaSondra's mother was herself in an abusive relationship with a husband who was a heavy alcohol and drug user.

32. This is in contrast to the discussion in chapter 2 regarding violence against women in their neighborhoods. Recall that youths routinely witnessed such violence but did not make efforts to intervene, particularly when the incidents involved adults or casual acquaintances. However, it is in keeping with girls' descriptions in chapter 4 about their attempts to intervene to protect friends and family members from sexual aggression.

33. See also Hamberger and Guse, 2002, p. 1319.

34. In fact, recent research documents individual-level gender similarity in the correlates of partner violence perpetration, including participation in delinquency and an "angry self concept" (Giordano et al., 1999; Moffitt et al., 2000, 2001). This research highlights the importance of analyzing the social contexts that shape partner violence. It is not categorical differences between women and men that predispose them to use violence. Instead, gender inequality, as it operates simultaneously at the structural, situational, and normative levels, is what shapes the nature and consequences of partner violence to the detriment of young women.

35. Anderson, 1999; Hill and Crawford, 1990; Majors and Billson, 1992; Wilson, 1996.

NOTES TO CHAPTER 6

1. Bursik and Grasmick, 1993; Gibbs, 1990; Krivo and Peterson, 1996; McNulty and Bellair, 2003; Sampson and Wilson, 1995; Sampson et al., 1997, 1999, 2002; Wilson, 1996.

2. Maher, 1997; Miller, 2001; Richie, 1996.

3. Brunson and Miller, 2006b; Davis, 1981; Ferguson, 2001; Quillian and Pager, 2001.

4. Anderson, 1999; Bourgois, 1996.

5. Benson et al., 2003; Dugan and Castro, 2006; Lauritsen and Schaum, 2004.

6. While the primary focus of the analysis here is on how gender structures risks for young women, young men's risks are also gendered. For a discussion from this same study, see Cobbina et al., 2007.

7. For a detailed discussion of girls' perceptions of and experiences with the police, see Brunson and Miller, 2006a.

8. Pain, 1991; Stanko, 1990.

9. On African American girls' risks, see Lauritsen, 2003. On patterns of sexual violence against women, see Koss et al., 1987; Warshaw, 1988.

10. Tolman et al., 2003b, p. 162. See also AAUW Educational Foundation, 2001; Hand and Sanchez, 2000; Stein et al., 2002.

11. Bureau of Justice Statistics, 1992, 2005; Koss et al., 1987.

12. Anderson, 1999; see also Bourgois, 1996.

13. Anderson, 1999; Majors and Billson, 1992; McCall, 1994; Messerschmidt, 1993.

14. Sampson and Lauritsen, 1994, p. 89.

15. Sampson and Lauritsen, 1994; Wilson, 1996.

16. McNulty and Bellair, 2003; Sampson et al., 1997, 1999, 2002.

17. Brown and Gourdine, 2001, p. 294.

18. For detailed analyses of youths' perceptions of and experiences with the police, see Brunson, 2007; Brunson and Miller, 2006a, 2006b. While it may seem inconsistent for complaints to include both underresponsive policing and aggressiveness, both are grounded in concerns about the lack of responsiveness to community members' needs and desires. Aggressive policing strategies are often proactive in nature, based on police definitions of the situation, and cast a wide net of suspicion over neighborhood residents. This often occurs concurrently with underresponsive policing, when officers are slow to respond to calls for service and define and treat victims as suspect and thus deserving.

19. Fagan and Davies, 2000; Jacobs and O'Brien, 1998; Kane, 2002; Mastrofski et al., 2002; Smith and Holmes, 2003; Terrill and Reisig, 2003; Terrill et al., 2003.

20. Klinger, 1997.

21. Kane, 2002; Mastrofski et al., 2002; Terrill and Reisig, 2003.

22. Sampson and Bartusch, 1998; Weitzer and Tuch, 2002.

23. Robinson and Chandek, 2000. For an overview of the problem of differential police response to violence against women, as well as recent policy innovations, see Eigenberg et al., 1996; Iovanni and Miller, 2001; Jones and Belknap, 1999; Valente et al., 2001.

24. Kraska and Kappeler, 1995; see also Fine et al., 2003; Maher, 2003.

25. Neville and Pugh, 1997; see also Robinson and Chandek, 2000; Wyatt, 1992.

26. Sampson and Bartusch, 1998.

27. Gottfredson, 2001, p. 83; see also Ferguson, 2001.

28. Gottfredson, 2001, p. 65.

29. Gottfredson, 2001, p. 65.

30. Ferguson, 2001; Thorne, 1993.

31. Stein et al., 2002.

32. Lee et al., 1996, p. 409.

33. Lee et al., 1996,, p. 410; see also Quinn, 2002.

34. Jones, 1985, p. 35.

35. Kenway and Fitzclarence, 1997, p. 126.

36. Kopels and Dupper, 1999, p. 454.

37. April's interviewer was Toya Like, the African American Ph.D. student I described in chapter 1 as having established meaningful rapport with the young people she interviewed. She was approximately 10 years older than the youths she interviewed but grew up in North St. Louis herself. Youths seemed to know she understood where they were coming from and recognized her authentic concern for their well-being.

38. Freudenberg et al., 1999, p. 801.

39. Foshee and Linder, 1997, p. 660. This same research did find, however, that female and African American service providers were more likely to report a willingness to help than male and white providers. The authors did not report comparisons within gender across race.

40. Sullivan and Rumptz, 1994; Wyatt, 1992.

41. Nurius et al., 1992; Santello and Leitenberg, 1993.

42. Lefley et al., 1993; Wyatt, 1992.

43. In order, these were comments made by Kristy, Sharmi, Rennesha, Alicia, Jamellah, Gail, and Tisha.

44. Breitenbecher et al., 1999; Lavoie et al., 1995.

45. Daiute et al., 2003; MacMahon and Washburn, 2003; Wyatt, 1992.

46. Testa and Dermen, 1999; Warshaw, 1988.

47. Gordon and Riger, 1989; Madriz, 1997; Pain, 1991; Stanko, 1990. In

fact, this was striking when we asked young men what could be done to address violence against young women in their communities. Like girls, the boys focused on changing girls' behavior and demeanor (e.g., their dress, standing up for themselves), but several young men focused on restricting their community activities further. Cooper said girls should "have they parents with 'em at all times," and Wayne suggested, "maybe an earlier curfew for girls or something like that. Maybe that would keep them off the streets at night."

48. King, 2003; Scully, 1990. King points out that "the rape prevention tactic of encouraging women to be more clear, while sensible, suggests that women's lack of clarity is part of the problem, even though men can interpret virtually anything that women do as signs of desire" (p. 874). This is a primary reason that rape-education programs are often successful in increasing women's understanding of the problem but not in decreasing their risks for sexual assault (e.g., Breitenbecher and Scarce, 1999).

49. Schwalbe and Mason-Schrock, 1996, p. 141. These authors describe oppositional identity work as those group processes that allow "subordinated groups [to] not only resist their devaluation at the hands of the dominant group, [but] create themselves as people, individually and collectively" (p. 141). In fact, many have argued that young men's strategies in disadvantaged communities—including the adoption of what Anderson (1999) calls the "code of the streets," or Majors and Billson's (1992) "cool pose"—are forms of oppositional identity work. These efforts to "resist the stigma imposed by a dominant group" (Shwalbe and Mason-Schrock, 1996, p. 141) can themselves sometimes result in greater harm.

50. Tolman et al., 2005, p. 15.

51. Tolman et al., 2005, p. 11; see also Fine, 1988; Oriel, 2005.

52. Tolman et al., 2005, p. 15.

53. Kenway and Fitzclarence, 1997, p. 129.

54. Collins, 1990; hooks, 1981.

55. Wyatt, 1992.

56. MacMahon and Washburn, 2003; MacMahon and Watts, 2002.

57. Way, 1995.

58. Brown and Gourdine, 2001, p. 295.

59. Calhoun et al. 1997; Malamuth, 1981; Marciniak, 1998; Truman et al., 1996; Vass and Gold, 1995; Willan and Pollard, 2003.

60. Sanday, 1990.

61. DeKeseredy and Schwartz, 1997.

62. Lisak and Ivan, 1995, p. 305; see also Pithers, 1999, p. 269; Schewe and O'Donohue, 1993; Scully, 1990.

63. Pithers, 1999, p. 265; see also King, 2003.

64. Pithers, 1999, p. 270.

65. Winkel and de Kleuver, 1997.
66. Winkel and de Kleuver, 1997, p. 525; see also Day, 2001; Hollander, 2001.
67. Truman et al., 1996, p. 559.
68. Truman et al., 1996, p. 559.
69. Tolman et al., 2003a, p. 11.
70. MacMahon and Washburn, 2003, p. 59.
71. Eder, 1995, p. 10.
72. Kalof, 1995.
73. Truman et al., 1996, p. 560.

References

AAUW Educational Foundation. 2001. *Hostile Hallways: Bullying, Teasing, and Sexual Harassment in School.* New York: AAUW Educational Foundation.

Adams, Jann H. 1997. "Sexual Harassment and Black Women: A Historical Perspective." Pp. 213–224 in *Sexual Harassment: Theory, Research and Treatment*, edited by W. O. Donahue. Boston: Allyn and Bacon.

Alder, Christine, and Anne Worrall, eds. 2004. *Girls Violence?* New York: SUNY Press.

Anderson, Elijah. 1999. *Code of the Street.* New York: Norton.

Anderson, Kristin L., and Debra Umberson. 2001. "Gendering Violence: Masculinity and Power in Men's Accounts of Domestic Violence." *Gender and Society* 15: 358–380.

Bachman, Ronet, and Linda E. Saltzman. 1995. *Violence against Women: Estimates from the Redesigned Survey, August 1995.* NCJ 154348 Special Report. Washington, D.C.: Bureau of Justice Statistics.

Basile, Kathleen C. 1999. "Rape by Acquiescence: The Ways in Which Women 'Give In' to Unwanted Sex with Their Husbands." *Violence against Women* 5: 1036–1058.

Baumer, Eric P., Richard B. Felson, and Steven F. Messner. 2003. "Changes in Police Notification for Rape, 1973–2000." *Criminology* 41: 841–872.

Baybeck, Brady, and E. Terrence Jones, eds. 2004. *St. Louis Metromorphosis: Past Trends and Future Directions.* St. Louis: Missouri Historical Society Press.

Benson, Michael L., Greer L. Fox, Alfred DeMaris, and Judy Van Wyk. 2003. "Neighborhood Disadvantage, Individual Economic Distress and Violence against Women in Intimate Relationships." *Journal of Quantitative Criminology* 19: 207–235.

Bethke, Teresa M., and David M. DeJoy. 1993. "An Experimental Study of Factors Influencing the Acceptability of Dating Violence." *Journal of Interpersonal Violence* 8: 36–51.

Boswell, A. Ayres, and Joan Z. Spade. 1996. "Fraternities and Collegiate Rape Culture: Why Are Some Fraternities More Dangerous Places for Women?" *Gender and Society* 10: 133–147.

Bourgois, Philippe. 1995. *In Search of Respect: Selling Crack in El Barrio.* Cambridge: Cambridge University Press.

Bourgois, Philippe. 1996. "In Search of Masculinity." *British Journal of Criminology* 36: 412–427.

Bourgois, Philippe, and Eloise Dunlap. 1993. "Exorcising Sex-for-Crack: An Ethnographic Perspective from Harlem." Pp. 97–132 in *Crack Pipe as Pimp: An Ethnographic Investigation of Sex-for-Crack Exchanges,* edited by Mitchell S. Ratner. New York: Lexington.

Boyle, Douglas J., and Dina Vivian. 1996. "Generalized versus Spouse-Specific Anger/Hostility in Men's Violence against Intimates." *Violence and Victims* 11: 293–317.

Breitenbecher, Kimberly Hanson, and Michael Scarce. 1999. "A Longitudinal Evaluation of the Effectiveness of a Sexual Assault Education Program." *Journal of Interpersonal Violence* 14: 459–478.

Brewster, Karin L. 1994. "Race Differences in Sexual Activity among Adolescent Women: The Role of Neighborhood Characteristics." *American Sociological Review* 59: 408–424.

Britton, Dana M. 2000. "Feminism in Criminology: Engendering the Outlaw." *Annals of the American Academy of Political and Social Science* 571: 57–76.

Brown, Annie Woodley, and Ruby Gourdine. 2001. "Black Adolescent Females: An Examination of the Impact of Violence on Their Lives and Perceptions of Environmental Supports." *Journal of Human Behavior in the Social Environment* 4: 275–298.

Brownmiller, Susan. 1975. *Against Our Will: Men, Women and Rape.* New York: Simon and Schuster.

Brunson, Rod K. 2005. "Race, Neighborhood and Police/Youth Interactions." Unpublished ms., University of Alabama–Birmingham.

Brunson, Rod K. 2007. " 'Police Don't Like Black People': African American Young Men's Accumulated Police Experiences." *Criminology and Public Policy* 6: 71–102.

Brunson, Rod K., and Jody Miller. 2006a. "Gender, Race, and Urban Policing: The Experience of African American Youths." *Gender and Society* 20: 531–552.

Brunson, Rod K., and Jody Miller. 2006b. "Young Black Men and Urban Policing in the United States." *British Journal of Criminology* 46: 613–640.

Bureau of Justice Statistics. 1992. *Criminal Victimization in the United States.* Washington, D.C.: U.S. Department of Justice.

Bureau of Justice Statistics. 2005. *Criminal Victimization in the United States.* Washington, D.C.: U.S. Department of Justice.

Bursik, Robert J., Jr., and Harold G. Grasmick. 1993. *Neighborhoods and Crime: The Dimensions of Effective Community Control.* New York: Lexington.

Burt, Martha R., Lisa C. Newmark, Krista K. Olson, Laudan Y. Aron, and Adele V. Harrell. 1997. *1997 Report: Evaluation of the STOP Formula Grants under the Violence against Women Act of 1994.* Washington, D.C.: Urban Institute.

Calhoun, Karen S., Jeffrey A. Bernat, Gretchen A. Clum, and Cynthia L. Frame. 1997. "Sexual Coercion and Attraction to Sexual Aggression in a Community Sample of Young Men." *Journal of Interpersonal Violence* 12: 392–406.

Carroll, Colleen. 1998a. "Mayor Backs $51 Million Bond Issue to Rebuild, Restore Crumbling Schools." *St. Louis Post-Dispatch,* March 21, p. 12.

Carroll, Colleen. 1998b. "4 Acting Principals in City Lose Posts over Credentials." *St. Louis Post-Dispatch,* May 12, p. B1.

Carroll, Colleen. 1998c. "City Schools Are Short 270 Teachers as Year Begins." *St. Louis Post-Dispatch,* August 24, p. A1.

Carvalho, Irene, and Dan A. Lewis. 2003. "Beyond Community: Reactions to Crime and Disorder among Inner-City Residents." *Criminology* 41: 779–812.

Chandy, Joseph M., Robert W. Blum, and Michael D. Resnick. 1996. "Female Adolescents with a History of Sexual Abuse: Risk Outcome and Protective Factors." *Journal of Interpersonal Violence* 11: 503–518.

Chesney-Lind, Meda. 1993. "Girls, Gangs and Violence: Anatomy of a Backlash." *Humanity and Society* 17: 321–344.

Chesney-Lind, Meda, and Lisa Pasko. 2004. *The Female Offender.* 2nd ed. Thousand Oaks, Calif.: Sage.

Cleveland, H. Harrington, Mary P. Koss, and James Lyons. 1999. "Rape Tactics from the Survivor's Perspective: Contextual Dependence and Within-Event Independence." *Journal of Interpersonal Violence* 14: 532–547.

Cleveland, Jeanette N., and Melinda E. Kerst. 1993. "Sexual Harassment and Perceptions of Power: An Under-Articulated Relationship." *Journal of Vocational Behavior* 42: 49–67.

Cleveland, Jeanette N., and Kathleen McNamara. 1996. "Understanding Sexual Harassment: Contributions from Research on Domestic Violence and Organizational Change." Pp. 217–240 in *Sexual Harassment in the Workplace: Perspectives, Frontiers, and Response Strategies,* edited by Margaret S. Stockdale. Thousand Oaks, Calif.: Sage.

Clubb, Shawn. 2006. "Stopping School Violence Priority for New Board Members." *St. Louis Post-Dispatch,* April 12, p. A1.

Cobbina, Jennifer E., Jody Miller, and Rod K. Brunson. 2007. "Gender, Neighborhood Danger, and Risk-Avoidance Strategies among Urban African American Youth." Unpublished ms., University of Missouri–St. Louis.

Collins, Mary Elizabeth. 1998. "Factors Influencing Sexual Victimization and Revictimization in a Sample of Adolescent Mothers." *Journal of Interpersonal Violence* 13: 3–24.

268 | *References*

Collins, Patricia Hill. 1990. *Black Feminist Thought.* Boston: Unwin Hyman.

Connell, R. W. 2002. *Gender.* Cambridge: Polity.

Cook, Phillip J., and John H. Laub. 2002. "After the Epidemic: Recent Trends in Youth Violence in the United States." Pp. 1–17 in *Crime and Justice,* vol. 24, edited by M. Tonry and M. Moore. Chicago: University of Chicago Press.

Crawford, Mary, and Danielle Popp. 2003. "Sexual Double Standards: A Review and Methodological Critique of Two Decades of Research." *Journal of Sex Research* 40: 13–26.

Crosby, Richard A., Ralph J. DiClemente, Gina M. Wingood, Catlainn Sionean, Brenda K. Cobb, and Kathy Harrington. 2000. "Correlates of Unprotected Vaginal Sex among African American Female Adolescents." *Archive of Pediatric Adolescent Medicine* 154: 893–899.

Currie, Dawn H., and Brian D. MacLean. 1997. "Measuring Violence against Women: The Interview as a Gendered Social Encounter." Pp. 157–178 in *Researching Sexual Violence against Women: Methodological and Personal Perspectives,* edited by Martin D. Schwartz. Thousand Oaks, Calif.: Sage.

Daiute, Colette, Rebecca Stern, and Corina Lelutiu-Weinberger. 2003. "Negotiating Violence Prevention." *Journal of Social Issues* 59: 83–101.

Daly, Kathleen, and Meda Chesney-Lind. 1988. "Feminism and Criminology." *Justice Quarterly* 5: 497–538.

Davis, Angela. 1981. *Women, Race and Class.* New York: Vintage.

Day, Kristen. 2001. "Constructing Masculinity and Women's Fear in Public Space in Irvine, California." *Gender, Place and Culture* 8: 109–127.

Decker, Scott H., and Barrik Van Winkle. 1996. *Life in the Gang.* Cambridge: Cambridge University Press.

DeKeseredy, Walter S., and Martin D. Schwartz. 1997. *Woman Abuse on the College Campus: Results from the Canadian National Survey.* Thousand Oaks, Calif.: Sage.

DeKeseredy, Walter S., and Martin D. Schwartz. 1998. *Measuring the Extent of Woman Abuse in Intimate Heterosexual Relationships: A Critique of the Conflict Tactics Scale.* Washington, D.C.: U.S. Department of Justice.

DeVault, Marjorie L. 1995. "Ethnicity and Expertise: Racial-Ethnic Knowledge in Sociological Research." *Gender and Society* 9: 612–631.

Dobash, Russell P., R. Emerson Dobash, Margo Wilson, and Martin Daly. 1992. "The Myth of Sexual Symmetry in Marital Violence." *Social Problems* 39: 71–91.

Dobash, Russell P., R. Emerson Dobash, Kate Cavanagh, and Ruth Lewis. 1998. "Separate and Intersecting Realities: A Comparison of Men's and Women's Accounts of Violence against Women." *Violence against Women* 4: 382–414.

Dobbs, Michael. 2004. "Corporate Model Proves Imperfect Fit for School System." *Washington Post,* December 5, p. A3.

Dugan, Laura, and Robert Apel. 2003. "An Exploratory Study of the Violent

Victimization of Women: Race/Ethnicity and Situational Context." *Criminology* 41: 959–980.

Dugan, Laura, and Jennifer L. Castro. 2006. "Predictors of Violent Victimization: National Crime Victimization Survey Women and Jailed Women." Pp. 171–194 in *Gender and Crime: Patterns of Victimization and Offending*, edited by Karen Heimer and Candace Kruttschnitt. New York: New York University Press.

Duncan, Neil. 1999. *Sexual Bullying: Gender Conflict and Pupil Culture in Secondary Schools.* New York: Routledge.

Durant, Robert, Chris Cadenhead, Robert A. Pandergrast, Greg Slavens, and Charles W. Linder. 1994. "Factors Associated with the Use of Violence among Urban Black Adolescents." *American Journal of Public Health* 84: 612–617.

Eder, Donna. 1995. *School Talk: Gender and Adolescent Culture*. New Brunswick, N.J.: Rutgers University Press.

"Editorial: State of Emergency." 1998. *St. Louis Post-Dispatch*, November 20, p. C20.

Eigenberg, Helen M., Kathryn E. Scarborough, and Victor E. Kappeler. 1996. "Contributory Factors Affecting Arrest in Domestic and Non-Domestic Assaults." *American Journal of Police* 15: 27–54.

Estrich, Susan. 1987. *Real Rape: How the Legal System Victimizes Women Who Say No*. Cambridge: Harvard University Press.

Eyre, Stephen, Colette Auerswald, Valerie Hoffman, and Susan G. Millstein. 1998. "Fidelity Management: African-American Adolescents' Attempts to Control the Sexual Behaviors of Their Partners." *Journal of Health Psychology* 3:393–406.

Fagan, Jeffrey, and Garth Davies. 2000. "Street Stops and Broken Windows: Terry, Race and Disorder in New York City." *Fordham Urban Law Journal* 28: 457–504.

Farrell, Albert D., and Steven E. Bruce. 1997. "Impact of Exposure to Community Violence on Violent Behavior and Emotional Distress among Urban Adolescents." *Journal of Clinical Child Psychology* 26: 2–14.

Felson, Richard B. 2002. *Violence and Gender Reexamined*. Washington, D.C.: American Psychological Association.

Felson, Richard B., and Steven F. Messner. 2000. "The Control Motive in Intimate Partner Violence." *Social Psychology Quarterly* 63: 86–94.

Ferguson, Ann Arnett. 2001. *Bad Boys: Public Schools in the Making of Black Masculinity*. Ann Arbor: University of Michigan Press.

Fine, Michelle. 1988. "Sexuality, Schooling and Adolescent Females: The Missing Discourse of Desire." *Harvard Educational Review* 58: 29–53.

Fine, Michelle, Nick Freudenberg, Yasser Payne, Tiffany Perkins, Kersha Smith, and Katya Wanzer. 2003. " 'Anything Can Happen with Police Around':

Urban Youth Evaluate Strategies of Surveillance in Public Places." *Journal of Social Issues* 59: 141–158.

Fineran, Susan, and Larry Bennett. 1999. "Gender and Power Issues of Peer Sexual Harassment among Teenagers." *Journal of Interpersonal Violence* 14: 626–641.

Finkelhor, David, and Nancy L. Asdigian. 1996. "Risk Factors for Youth Victimization: Beyond a Lifestyles/Routine Activities Theory Approach." *Violence and Victims* 11: 3–19.

Finkelhor, David, and Angela Browne. 1985. "The Traumatic Impact of Child Sexual Abuse: A Conceptualization." *American Journal of Orthopsychiatry* 55: 530–541.

Fitzpatrick, Kevin M. 1997. "Aggression and Environmental Risk among Low-Income African-American Youth." *Journal of Adolescent Health* 21: 172–178.

Fleisher, Mark S. 1998. *Dead End Kids: Gang Girls and the Boys They Know.* Madison: Wisconsin University Press.

Follingstad, Diane R., Rebekah G. Bradley, James E. Laughlin, and Leslie Burke. 1999. "Risk Factors and Correlates of Dating Violence: The Relevance of Examining Frequency and Severity Levels in a College Sample." *Violence and Victims* 14: 365–380.

Ford, Kathleen, Woosung Sohn, and James Lepkowiski. 2002. "American Adolescents: Sexual Mixing Patterns, Bridge Partners, and Concurrency." *Sexually Transmitted Diseases* 29: 13–19.

Foshee, Vangie, and G. Fletcher Linder. 1997. "Factors Influencing Service Provider Motivation to Help Adolescent Victims of Partner Violence." *Journal of Interpersonal Violence* 12: 648–664.

Foulis, Danielle, and Marita P. McCabe. 1997. "Sexual Harassment: Factors Affecting Attitudes and Perceptions." *Sex Roles* 37: 773–798.

Franck, Matthew. 2004. "City School Officials Stress the Positive to State Board." *St. Louis Post-Dispatch,* October 8, p. B6.

Franklin, Karen. 2004. "Enacting Masculinity: Antigay Violence and Group Rape as Participatory Theater." *Sexuality Research and Social Policy* 1: 25–40.

Freudenberg, Nicholas, Lynn Roberts, Beth E. Richie, Robert T. Taylor, Kim McGillicuddy, and Michael B. Greene. 1999. "Coming up in the Boogie Down: The Role of Violence in the Lives of Adolescents in the South Bronx." *Health Education and Behavior* 26: 788–805.

Garbarino, James, Kathleen Kostelney, and Nancy Dubrow. 1991. "What Children Can Tell Us about Living in Danger." *American Psychologist* 46: 376–383.

Gardner, Carol B. 1995. *Passing By: Gender and Public Harassment.* Berkeley: University of California Press.

Gavey, Nicola. 1999. " 'I Wasn't Raped, But . . .': Revisiting Definitional Problems in Sexual Victimization." Pp. 57–81 in *New Versions of Victims,* edited by Sharon Lamb. New York: New York University Press.

Gibbs, Jewelle Taylor. 1990. "Mental Health Issues of Black Adolescents: Implications for Policy and Practice." Pp. 21–52 in *Ethnic Issues in Adolescent Mental Health,* edited by Arlene Rubin Stiffman and Larry E. Davis. Newbury Park, Calif.: Sage.

Giegerich, Steve. 2006a. "All Vashon Freshman, 65 Seniors to Be Moved." *St. Louis Post-Dispatch,* January 12, p. A1.

Giegerich, Steve. 2006b. "Donors to St. Louis Public Schools Are Thinking Twice." *St. Louis Post-Dispatch,* September 3, p. C4.

Gilfus, Mary E. 1992. "From Victims to Survivors to Offenders: Women's Routes of Entry and Immersion into Street Crime." *Women and Criminal Justice* 4: 63–89.

Giordano, Peggy C., Toni J. Millhollin, Stephen A. Cernkovich, M. D. Pugh, and Jennifer L. Rudolph. 1999. "Delinquency, Identity, and Women's Involvement in Relationship Violence." *Criminology* 37: 17–37.

Glassner, Barry, and Julia Loughlin. 1987. *Drugs in Adolescent Worlds: Burnouts to Straights.* New York: St. Martin's.

Gordon, Margaret T., and Stephanie Riger. 1989. *The Female Fear.* New York: Free Press.

Gottfredson, Denise C. 2001. *Schools and Delinquency.* Cambridge: Cambridge University Press.

Gottfredson, Gary D., Denise C. Gottfredson, Allison Ann Payne, and Nisha C. Gottfredson. 2005. "School Climate Predictors of School Disorder: Results from a National Study of Delinquency Prevention in Schools." *Journal of Research in Crime and Delinquency* 42: 412–444.

Graham, Sandra, and Jaana Juvonen. 2002. "Ethnicity, Peer Harassment, and Adjustment in Middle School: An Exploratory Study." *Journal of Early Adolescence* 22: 173–199.

Graham-Bermann, S. A., and J. L. Edleson, eds. 2001. *Domestic Violence in the Lives of Children: The Future of Research, Intervention, and Social Policy.* Washington, D.C.: American Psychological Association.

Grauerholz, Liz. 2000. "An Ecological Approach to Understanding Sexual Revictimization: Linking Personal, Interpersonal, and Sociocultural Factors and Processes." *Child Maltreatment* 5: 5–17.

Gray, Heather M., and Vangie Foshee. 1997. "Adolescent Dating Violence: Differences between One-Sided and Mutually Violent Profiles." *Journal of Interpersonal Violence* 12: 126–141.

Hacker, Holly K. 1999. "Desegregation Busing System Is Changing." *St. Louis Post-Dispatch,* November 26, p. C5.

Hagan, John, and Bill McCarthy. 1997. *Mean Streets: Youth Crime and Homelessness.* Cambridge: Cambridge University Press.

Hamberger, Kevin L., and Clare E. Guse. 2002. "Men's and Women's Use of Intimate Partner Violence in Clinical Samples." *Violence against Women* 8: 1301–1331.

Hand, Jeanne Z., and Laura Sanchez. 2000. "Badgering or Bantering? Gender Differences in Experiences of, and Reactions to, Sexual Harassment among U.S. High School Students." *Gender and Society* 14: 718–746.

Hanley, M. Joan, and Patrick O'Neill. 1997. "Violence and Commitment: A Study of Dating Couples." *Journal of Interpersonal Violence* 12: 685–703.

Harris, Ron. 2003a. "Power, Race and Trust: Part 1 of 2." *St. Louis Post-Dispatch,* September 7, p. A1.

Harris, Ron. 2003b. "Power, Race and Trust: Part 2 of 2." *St. Louis Post-Dispatch,* September 8, p. A1.

Heimer, Karen, and Candace Kruttschnitt, eds. 2005. *Gender and Crime: Patterns of Victimization and Offending.* New York: New York University Press.

Helliwell, Christine. 2000. " 'It's Only a Penis': Rape, Feminism and Difference." *Signs* 25: 789–816.

Hiese, Lori L. 1998. "Violence against Women: An Integrated Ecological Framework." *Violence against Women* 4: 262–290.

Hill, Gary D., and Elizabeth M. Crawford. 1990. "Women, Race, and Crime." *Criminology* 28: 601–623.

Hinman, Kristen. 2006. "An Incomplete Education." *Riverfront Times,* May 17, http://www.riverfronttimes.com/2006-05-17/news/an-incomplete-education.

Hollander, Jocelyn A. 2001. "Vulnerability and Dangerousness: The Construction of Gender through Conversation about Violence." *Gender and Society* 15: 83–109.

hooks, bell. 1981. *Ain't I a Woman.* Boston: South End.

Houston, Sandra, and Naomi Hwang. 1996. "Correlates of Objective and Subjective Experiences of Sexual Harassment in High School." *Sex Roles* 34: 189–204.

Howard, Trisha L. 2004. "St. Louis Schools Get Bad State Grade." *St. Louis Post-Dispatch,* October 27, p. D2.

Howard, Trisha L., and Kavita Kumar. 2004. "Charters, Suburban Districts Lure City Students." *St. Louis Post-Dispatch,* September 20, p. B1.

Howard, Trisha L., and Peter Shinkle. 2005. "Schools Try to Reduce 'Official Hooky.' " *St. Louis Post-Dispatch,* May 24, p. B1.

Hughey, Gary H. 2006. "The Critical Mission of Educating Our Kids Is Absolutely Essential." *St. Louis Post-Dispatch,* January 22, p. B3.

Hunt, Geoffrey, and Karen Joe-Laidler. 2001. "Situations of Violence in the Lives of Girl Gang Members." *Health Care for Women International* 22: 363–384.

Impett, Emily A., and Letitia A. Peplau. 2003. "Sexual Compliance: Gender,

Motivational, and Relationship Perspectives." *Journal of Sex Research* 40: 87–100.

Iovanni, LeeAnn, and Susan L. Miller. 2001. "Criminal Justice Responses to Domestic Violence: Law Enforcement and the Courts." Pp. 303–328 in *Sourcebook on Violence against Women,* edited by Claire Renzetti, Jeff Edelsen, and Rachel Bergen. Thousand Oaks, Calif.: Sage.

Irwin, Harvey J. 1999. "Violent and Nonviolent Revictimization of Women Abused in Childhood." *Journal of Interpersonal Violence* 14: 1095–1110.

Jackson, Susan M., Fiona Cram, and Fred W. Seymour. 2000. "Violence and Sexual Coercion in High School Students' Dating Relationships." *Journal of Family Violence* 15: 23–36.

Jacobs, David, and Robert M. O'Brien. 1998. "The Determinants of Deadly Force: A Structural Analysis of Police Violence." *American Journal of Sociology* 103: 837–862.

Joe-Laidler, Karen A., and Geoffrey Hunt. 1997. "Violence and Social Organization in Female Gangs." *Social Justice* 24: 148–169.

Jones, Carol. 1985. "Sexual Tyranny: Male Violence in a Mixed Secondary School." Pp. 26–39 in *Just a Bunch of Girls: Feminist Approaches to Schooling,* edited by Gaby Weiner. Berkshire, U.K.: Open University Press.

Jones, Dana A., and Joanna Belknap. 1999. "Police Responses to Battering in a Progressive Pro-Arrest Jurisdiction." *Justice Quarterly* 16: 249–273.

Kalof, Linda. 1995. "Sex, Power and Dependency: The Politics of Adolescent Sexuality." *Journal of Youth and Adolescence* 24: 229–249.

Kalof, Linda. 2000. "Ethnic Differences in Female Sexual Victimization." *Sexuality and Culture* 4: 75–91.

Kalof, Linda, and Bruce H. Wade. 1995. "Sexual Attitudes and Experiences with Sexual Coercion: Exploring the Influence of Race and Gender." *Journal of Black Psychology* 21: 224–238.

Kane, Robert J. 2002. "The Social Ecology of Police Misconduct." *Criminology* 40: 867–896.

Kehily, Mary. 2001. "Bodies in School: Young Men, Embodiment, and Heterosexual Masculinities." *Men and Masculinities* 4: 173–185.

Kehily, Mary Jane, and Anoop Nayak. 1997. " 'Lads and Laughter': Humour and the Production of Heterosexual Hierarchies." *Gender and Education* 9: 69–87.

Kenway, Jane, and Lindsay Fitzclarence. 1997. "Masculinity, Violence and Schooling: Challenging 'Poisonous Pedagogies.' " *Gender and Education* 9: 117–133.

Kimmel, Michael. 2002. " 'Gender Symmetry' in Domestic Violence: A Substantive and Methodological Research Review." *Violence against Women* 8: 1332–1363.

Kimmel, Michael, and Matthew Mahler. 2003. "Adolescent Masculinity, Homophobia, and Violence." *American Behavioral Scientist* 46: 1439–1458.

King, Neal. 2003. "Knowing Women: Straight Men and Sexual Certainty." *Gender and Society* 17: 861–877.

Klein, Jessie, and Lynn S. Chancer. 2000. "Masculinity Matters: The Omission of Gender from High Profile School Violence Cases." Pp. 129–162 in *Smoke and Mirrors: The Hidden Context of Violence in Schools and Society*, edited by Stephanie Urso Spina. Lanham, Md.: Rowman and Littlefield.

Klinger, David A. 1997. "Negotiating Order in Patrol Work: An Ecological Theory of Police Response to Deviance." *Criminology* 35: 277–306.

Kopels, Sandra, and David R. Dupper. 1999. "School-Based Peer Sexual Harassment." *Child Welfare* 78: 435–460.

Koss, Mary P., C.A. Gidycz, and W. Wisniewski. 1987. "The Scope of Rape: Incidence and Prevalence of Sexual Aggression and Victimization in a National Sample of Higher Education Students." *Journal of Consulting and Clinical Psychology* 55: 162–170.

Kraska, Peter B., and Victor E. Kappeler. 1995. "To Serve and Pursue: Exploring Police Sexual Violence against Women." *Justice Quarterly* 12: 85–111.

Krivo, Lauren J., and Ruth D. Peterson. 1996. "Extremely Disadvantaged Neighborhoods and Urban Crime." *Social Forces* 75: 619–650.

Kruttschnitt, Candace. 2002. "Author-Meets-Reader: Violence and Gender Reexamined." Paper presented at the Annual Meetings of the American Society of Criminology, Chicago.

Lahelma, Elina. 2002. "Gendered Conflicts in Secondary School: Fun or Enactment of Power?" *Gender and Education* 14: 295–306.

Larkin, June. 1994. "Walking through Walls: The Sexual Harassment of High School Girls." *Gender and Education* 6: 263–280.

Laub John H., and Janet L. Lauritsen. 1998. "The Interdependence of School Violence with Neighborhood and Family Conditions." Pp. 127–155 in Delbert S. Elliott, Beatrix A. Hamburg, and Kirk R. Williams, eds., *Violence in American Schools*. Cambridge: Cambridge University Press.

Lauritsen, Janet L. 2003. *How Families and Communities Influence Youth Victimization*. Juvenile Justice Bulletin. Washington, D.C.: U.S. Department of Justice.

Lauritsen, Janet L., and Kenna F. Davis Quinet. 1995. "Repeat Victimization among Adolescents and Young Adults." *Journal of Quantitative Criminology* 11: 143–166.

Lauritsen, Janet L., and Callie Marie Rennison. 2006. "The Role of Race and Ethnicity in Violence against Women." Pp. 303–322 in *Gender and Crime*, edited by Karen Heimer and Candace Kruttschnitt. New York: New York University Press.

Lauritsen, Janet L., and Robin J. Schaum. 2004. "The Social Ecology of Violence against Women." *Criminology* 42: 323–357.

Lauritsen, Janet L., and Norman A. White. 2001. "Putting Violence in Its Place: The Influence of Race, Ethnicity, Gender and Place on the Risk for Violence." *Criminology and Public Policy* 1: 37–59.

Lauritsen, Janet L., Robert J. Sampson, and John H. Laub. 1991. "The Link between Offending and Victimization among Adolescents." *Criminology* 29: 265–292.

Lauritsen, Janet L., John H. Laub, and Robert J. Sampson. 1992. "Conventional and Delinquent Activities: Implications for the Prevention of Violent Victimization among Adolescents." *Violence and Victims* 7: 91–108.

Lavoie, Francine, Lucie Véniza, Christiane Piché, and Michel Boivin. 1995. "Evaluation of a Prevention Program for Violence in Teen Dating Relationships." *Journal of Interpersonal Violence* 10: 516–524.

Leadbeater, Bonnie J. Ross, and Niobe Way, eds. 1996. *Urban Girls: Resisting Stereotypes, Creating Identities.* New York: New York University Press.

Lee, Valerie E., Robert G. Croninger, Eleanor Linn, and Xianglei Chen. 1996. "The Culture of Sexual Harassment in Secondary Schools." *American Educational Research Journal* 33: 383–417.

Lees, Sue. 1993. *Sugar and Spice: Sexuality and Adolescent Girls.* New York: Penguin.

Lefkowitz, Bernard. 1997. *Our Guys.* Berkeley: University of California Press.

Lefley, Harriet P., Clarissa S. Scott, Maria Llabre, and Dorothy Hicks. 1993. "Cultural Beliefs about Rape and Victims' Response in Three Ethnic Groups." *American Journal of Orthopsychiatry* 63: 623–632.

Levy, Barrie, ed. 1991. *Dating Violence: Young Women in Danger.* Seattle: Seal.

Lisak, David, and Carol Ivan. 1995. "Deficits in Intimacy and Empathy in Sexually Aggressive Men." *Journal of Interpersonal Violence* 10: 296–308.

Loe, Meika. 1996. "Working for Men: At the Intersection of Power, Gender and Sexuality." *Sociological Inquiry* 66: 399–421.

Lofland, John, and Lyn H. Lofland. 1984. *Analyzing Social Settings: A Guide to Qualitative Observation and Analysis.* Belmont, Calif.: Wadsworth.

MacMahon, Susan D., and Jason J. Washburn. 2003. "Violence Prevention: An Evaluation of Program Effects with Urban African American Students." *Journal of Primary Prevention* 24: 43–62.

MacMahon, Susan D., and Roderick J. Watts. 2002. "Ethnic Identity in Urban African American Youth: Exploring Links with Self-Worth, Aggression, and Other Psycho-Social Variables." *Journal of Community Psychology* 30: 411–431.

MacMillan, Ross, Annette Nierobisz, and Sandy Welsh. 2000. "Experiencing the Streets: Harassment and Perceptions of Safety among Women." *Journal of Research in Crime and Delinquency* 37: 306–322.

Madriz, Esther. 1997. *Nothing Bad Happens to Good Girls: Fear of Crime in Women's Lives*. Berkeley: University of California Press.

Maher, Lisa. 1997. *Sexed Work: Gender, Race and Resistance in a Brooklyn Drug Market*. Oxford: Clarendon.

Maher, Timothy M. 2003. "Police Sexual Misconduct: Officers' Perceptions of Its Extent and Causality." *Criminal Justice Review* 29: 355–381.

Majors, Richard, and Janet Mancini Billson. 1992. *Cool Pose: The Dilemma of Black Manhood in America*. New York: Lexington.

Malamuth, N. M. 1981. "Rape Proclivity among Males." *Journal of Social Issues* 37: 138–157.

Mann, Coramae Richey, and Marjorie Zatz, eds. 2002. *Images of Color/Images of Crime*. Los Angeles: Roxbury.

Marciniak, Liz Marie. 1998. "Adolescent Attitudes toward Victim Precipitation of Rape." *Violence and Victims* 13: 287–300.

Marin, Amy J., and Rosanna E. Guadagno. 1999. "Perceptions of Sexual Harassment Victims as a Function of Labeling and Reporting." *Sex Roles* 41: 921–940.

Marshall, Catherine, and Gretchen B. Rossman. 1989. *Designing Qualitative Research*. Newbury Park, Calif.: Sage.

Martin, Patricia Yancey, and Robert A. Hummer. 1989. "Fraternities and Rape on Campus." *Gender and Society* 3: 457–473.

Mastrofski, Stephen D., Michael D. Reisig, and John D. McCluskey. 2002. "Police Disrespect toward the Public: An Encounter-Based Analysis." *Criminology* 40: 515–551.

Matoesian, Gregory M. 1993. *Reproducing Rape: Domination through Talk in the Courtroom*. Chicago: University of Chicago Press.

Mayall, Alice, and Steven R. Gold. 1995. "Definitional Issues and Mediating Variables in the Sexual Revictimization of Women Sexually Abused as Children." *Journal of Interpersonal Violence* 10: 26–42.

McCall, Nathan. 1994. *Makes Me Wanna Holler: A Young Black Man in America*. New York: Vintage.

McNulty, Thomas L., and Paul E. Bellair. 2003. "Explaining Racial and Ethnic Differences in Serious Adolescent Violent Behavior." *Criminology* 41: 709–748.

Mecca, Susan J., and Linda J. Rubin. 1999. "Definitional Research on African American Students and Sexual Harassment." *Psychology of Women Quarterly* 23: 813–817.

Messerschmidt, James W. 1993. *Masculinities and Crime*. Lanham, Md.: Rowman and Littlefield.

Miles, Matthew B., and A. Michael Huberman. 1984. *Qualitative Data Analysis: A Sourcebook of New Methods*. Newbury Park, Calif.: Sage.

Miles-Doan, Rebecca. 1998. "Violence between Spouses and Intimates: Does Neighborhood Context Matter?" *Social Forces* 77: 623–645.

Miller, Jody. 2001. *One of the Guys: Girls, Gangs and Gender.* New York: Oxford University Press.

Miller, Jody, and Barry Glassner. 2004. "The 'Inside' and the 'Outside': Finding Realities in Interviews." Pp. 125–139 in *Qualitative Research,* 2nd ed., edited by David Silverman. London: Sage.

Miller, Jody, and Christopher W. Mullins. 2006. "Stuck Up, Telling Lies, and Talking Too Much: The Gendered Context of Young Women's Violence." Pp. 41–66 in *Gender and Crime: Patterns of Victimization and Offending,* edited by Karen Heimer and Candace Kruttschnitt. New York: New York University Press.

Miller, Jody, and Norman A. White. 2003. "Gender and Adolescent Relationship Violence: A Contextual Examination." *Criminology* 41: 1501–1541.

Moffitt, Terrie E., Avshalom Caspi, Robert F. Krueger, Lynn Magdol, Gayla Margolin, Phil A. Silva, and Ros Sydney. 1997. "Do Partners Agree about Abuse in Their Relationship? A Psychometric Evaluation of Interpartner Agreement." *Psychological Assessment* 9: 47–56.

Moffitt, Terrie E., Robert F. Krueger, Avshalom Caspi, and Jeff Fagan. 2000. "Partner Abuse and General Crime: How Are They the Same? How Are They Different?" *Criminology* 38: 199–232.

Moffitt, Terrie E., Richard W. Robins, and Avshalom Caspi. 2001. "A Couples Analysis of Partner Abuse with Implications for Abuse-Prevention Policy." *Criminology and Public Policy* 1: 5–36.

Molidor, Christian, and Richard M. Tolman. 1998. "Gender and Contextual Factors in Adolescent Dating Violence." *Violence against Women* 4: 180–194.

Morse, Barbara J. 1995. "Beyond the Conflict Tactics Scale: Assessing Gender Differences in Partner Violence." *Violence and Victims* 4: 251–272.

Mullins, Christopher W. 2006. *Holding Your Square: Masculinities, Streetlife and Violence.* Devon, U.K.: Willan.

Mustaine, Elizabeth Ehrhardt, and Richard Tewksbury. 1998. "Victimization Risks at Leisure: A Gender-Specific Analysis." *Violence and Victims* 13: 231–249.

Neville, Helen A., and Aalece O. Pugh. 1997. "General and Culture-Specific Factors Influencing African American Women's Reporting Patterns and Perceived Social Support following Sexual Assault." *Violence against Women* 3: 361–381.

Nurius, Paula S., Jacqueline Furrey, and Lucy Berliner. 1992. "Coping Capacity among Women with Abusive Partners." *Violence and Victims* 7: 229–243.

O'Keefe, Maura. 1997. "Predictors of Dating Violence among High School Students." *Journal of Interpersonal Violence* 12:546–568.

O'Keefe, Maura, and Laura Treister. 1998. "Victims of Dating Violence among High School Students: Are the Predictors Different for Males and Females?" *Violence against Women* 4: 195–223.

Oliver, William. 1994. *The Violent Social World of Black Men*. New York: Lexington.

Orbuch, Terri L. 1997. "People's Accounts Count: The Sociology of Accounts." *Annual Review of Sociology* 23: 455–478.

Oriel, Jennifer. 2005. "Sexual Pleasure as a Human Right: Harmful or Helpful to Women in the Context of HIV/AIDS?" *Women's Studies International Forum* 28: 392–404.

Osthoff, Sue. 2002. " But, Gertrude, I Beg to Differ, A Hit Is Not a Hit Is Not a Hit: When Battered Women Are Arrested for Assaulting Their Partners." *Violence against Women* 8: 1521–1544.

Pain, Rachel. 1991. "Space, Sexual Violence, and Social Control: Integrating Geographical and Feminist Analyses of Women's Fear of Crime." *Progress in Human Geography* 15: 415–431.

Pattillo, Mary E. 1998. "Sweet Mothers and Gangbangers: Managing Crime in a Black Middle-Class Neighborhood." *Social Forces* 76: 747–774.

Perry, Elissa L., James M. Schmidtke, and Carol T. Kulik. 1998. "Propensity to Sexually Harass: An Exploration of Gender Differences." *Sex Roles* 38: 443–460.

Peterson, Dana, Jody Miller, and Finn-Aage Esbensen. 2001. "The Impact of Sex Composition on Gangs and Gang Member Delinquency." *Criminology* 39: 411–439.

Peterson, Ruth, and William C. Bailey. 1992. "Rape and Dimensions of Gender Socioeconomic Inequality in U.S. Metropolitan Areas." *Journal of Research in Crime and Delinquency* 29: 162–177.

Peterson, Zoë, and Charlene L. Muehlenhard. 2004. "Was It Rape? The Function of Women's Rape Myth Acceptance and Definitions of Sex in Labeling Their Own Experiences." *Sex Roles* 51: 129–144.

Peterson, Zoë, and Charlene L. Muehlenhard. 2007. "Conceptualizing the 'Wantedness' of Women's Consensual and Nonconsensual Sexual Experiences: Implications for How Women Label Their Experiences with Rape." *Journal of Sex Research* 14: 72–88.

Pierce, Rick. 1998. "Harmon Lambasts City School System." *St. Louis Post-Dispatch*, November 24, p. B1.

Pierce, Rick. 1999a. "City Schools Pass 1st Part of Accreditation Test." *St. Louis Post-Dispatch*, April 14, p. B3.

Pierce, Rick. 1999b. "40 St. Louis Schools Are Put on Notice." *St. Louis Post-Dispatch*, May 26, p. A1.

Pierce, Rick. 1999c. "St. Louis Schools Are Crafting Plan to Hold Teachers Accountable." *St. Louis Post-Dispatch,* August 26, p. A1.

Pierce, Rick. 1999d. "Report: Safety Violations Are Down at City Schools, But Number of Weapons Used, Assault Cases Increase." *St. Louis Post-Dispatch,* September 16, p. B1.

Pierce, Rick. 1999e. "City Schools Likely Will Lose Accreditation." *St. Louis Post-Dispatch,* October 14, p. A1.

Pierce, Rick. 2000. "Offenses in St. Louis Public Schools Drop." *St. Louis Post-Dispatch,* November 29, p. B1.

Pithers, William D. 1999. "Empathy: Definition, Enhancement, and Relevance to the Treatment of Sexual Abusers." *Journal of Interpersonal Violence* 14: 257–284.

Planning and Urban Design Agency. 2001a. *Census St. Louis: Working Paper No 1.* St. Louis: City of St. Louis (http://stlcin.missouri.org/census).

Planning and Urban Design Agency. 2001b. *Census St. Louis: Working Paper No 2.* St. Louis: City of St. Louis (http://stlcin.missouri.org/census).

Quillian, Lincoln, and Devah Pager. 2001. "Black Neighbors, Higher Crime? The Role of Racial Stereotypes in Evaluations of Neighborhood Crime." *American Journal of Sociology* 106: 717–767.

Quinn, Beth A. 2000. "The Paradox of Complaining: Law, Humor and Harassment in the Everyday Work World." *Law and Social Inquiry* 25: 1151–1185.

Quinn, Beth A. 2002. "Sexual Harassment and Masculinity: The Power and Meaning of 'Girl Watching.' " *Gender and Society* 16: 386–402.

Ragin, Charles C., Joane Nagel, and Patricia White. 2004. *Workshop on Scientific Foundations of Qualitative Research.* Washington, D.C.: National Science Foundation.

Raphael, Jody. 2004. *Listening to Olivia: Violence, Poverty and Prostitution.* Boston: Northeastern University Press.

Ratner, Mitchell S, ed. 1993. *Crack Pipe as Pimp: An Ethnographic Investigation of Sex-for-Crack Exchanges.* New York: Lexington.

Reilly, M.E., B. Lott, D. Caldwell, and L. DeLuca. 1992. "Tolerance for Sexual Harassment Related to Self-Reported Sexual Victimization." *Gender and Society* 6: 122–138.

Renzetti, Claire, Jeff Edelsen, and Rachel Bergen, eds. 2001. *Sourcebook on Violence against Women.* Thousand Oaks, Calif.: Sage.

Richie, Beth E. 1996. *Compelled to Crime: The Gender Entrapment of Battered Black Women.* New York: Routledge.

Richters, John E., and Pedro Martinez. 1993. "The NIMH Community Violence Project: Children as Victims of and Witnesses to Violence." *Psychiatry* 56: 7–35.

Robinson, Amanda L., and Meghan S. Chandek. 2000. "Differential Police

Response to Black Battered Women." *Women and Criminal Justice* 12: 29–61.

Rodriguez, Luis J. 1993. *Always Running: La Vida Loca—Gang Days in L.A.* New York: Touchstone.

Rusk, David. 1995. *Cities without Suburbs,* 2nd ed. Washington, D.C.: Woodrow Wilson Center Press.

Saal, Frank E. 1996. "Men's Misperceptions of Women's Interpersonal Behaviors and Sexual Harassment." Pp. 67–84 in *Sexual Harassment in the Workplace: Perspectives, Frontiers, and Response Strategies,* edited by Margaret S. Stockdale. Thousand Oaks, Calif.: Sage.

Sampson, Robert J. 1997. "The Embeddedness of Child and Adolescent Development: A Community-Level Perspective on Urban Violence." Pp. 31–77 in *Violence and Childhood in the Inner City,* edited by Joan McCord. Cambridge: Cambridge University Press.

Sampson, Robert J., and Dawn Jeglum Bartusch. 1998. "Legal Cynicism and (Subcultural?) Tolerance of Deviance: The Neighborhood Context of Racial Differences." *Law and Society Review* 32: 777–804.

Sampson, Robert J., and Janet L. Lauritsen. 1990. "Deviant Lifestyles, Proximity to Crime, and the Offender-Victim Link in Personal Violence." *Journal of Research in Crime and Delinquency* 27: 110–139.

Sampson, Robert J., and Janet L. Lauritsen. 1994. "Violent Victimization and Offending: Individual-, Situational-, and Community-Level Risk Factors." Pp. 1–114 in *Understanding and Preventing Violence,* vol. 3, edited by Albert J. Reiss and Jeffrey A. Roth. Washington, D.C.: National Research Council, National Academy Press.

Sampson, Robert J., and William Julius Wilson. 1995. "Toward a Theory of Race, Crime and Urban Inequality." Pp. 37–54 in *Crime and Inequality,* edited by John Hagan and Ruth D. Peterson. Stanford, Calif.: Stanford University Press.

Sampson, Robert J., Stephen W. Raudenbush, and Felton Earls. 1997. "Neighborhoods and Violent Crime: A Multilevel Study of Collective Efficacy." *Science* 277: 918–924.

Sampson, Robert J., Jeffrey D. Morenoff, and Felton Earls. 1999. "Beyond Social Capital: Spatial Dynamics of Collective Efficacy for Children." *American Sociological Review* 64: 633–660.

Sampson, Robert J., Jeffrey D. Morenoff, and Thomas Gannon-Rowley. 2002. "Assessing 'Neighborhood Effects': Social Processes and New Directions in Research." *Annual Review of Sociology* 28: 443–478.

Sanday, Peggy Reeves. 1981. "The Socio-Cultural Context of Rape: A Cross-Cultural Study." *Journal of Social Issues* 37: 5–27.

Sanday, Peggy Reeves. 1990. *Fraternity Gang Rape: Sex, Brotherhood, and Privilege on Campus.* New York: New York University Press.

Sanders, Barbara, and Dina L. Moore. 1999. "Childhood Maltreatment and Date Rape." *Journal of Interpersonal Violence* 14: 115–124.

Santello, Mark D., and Harold Leitenberg. 1993. "Sexual Aggression by an Acquaintance: Methods of Coping and Later Psychological Adjustment." *Violence and Victims* 8: 91–104.

Schewe, Paul A., and William O'Donohue. 1993. "Sexual Abuse Prevention with High-Risk Males: The Roles of Victim Empathy and Rape Myths." *Violence and Victims* 8: 339–351.

Schwalbe, Michael L., and Douglas Mason-Schrock. 1996. "Identity Work as Group Process." *Advances in Group Processes* 13: 113–147.

Schwartz, Martin D. 1997. "Doing Research on Violence against Women." Pp. 129–130 in *Researching Sexual Violence against Women: Methodological and Personal Perspectives*, edited by Martin D. Schwartz. Thousand Oaks, Calif.: Sage.

Schwartz, Martin D., and Walter S. DeKeseredy. 1997. *Sexual Assault on the College Campus: The Role of Male Peer Support*. Thousand Oaks, Calif.: Sage.

Scully, Diana. 1990. *Understanding Sexual Violence*. Boston: Unwin Hyman.

Shakoor, Bambade H., and Deborah Chalmers. 1991. "Covictimization of African-American Children Who Witness Violence and the Theoretical Implications of Its Effects on Their Cognitive, Emotional and Behavioral Development." *Journal of the National Medical Association* 83: 233–238.

Shelton, J. Nicole, and Tabbye M. Chavous. 1999. "Black and White College Women's Perceptions of Sexual Harassment." *Sex Roles* 40: 593–615.

Short, James F. 1998. "The Level of Explanation Problem Revisited: The American Society of Criminology 1997 Presidential Address." *Criminology* 36: 3–36.

Simmons, Rachel. 2003. *Odd Girl Out: The Hidden Culture of Aggression in Girls*. New York: Harvest.

Simpson, Sally. 2002. "Author-Meets-Reader: Violence and Gender Reexamined." Paper presented at the Annual Meetings of the American Society of Criminology, Chicago.

Smart, Carol. 1976. *Women, Crime and Criminology: A Feminist Critique*. London: Routledge and Kegan Paul.

Smith, Brad W., and Malcolm D. Holmes. 2003. "Community Accountability, Minority Threat, and Police Brutality: An Examination of Civil Rights Criminal Complaints." *Criminology* 41: 1035–1064.

Snyder, Howard N., and Melissa Sickmund. 1999. *Juvenile Offenders and Victims: 1999 National Report*. Washington, D.C.: U.S. Department of Justice, Office of Juvenile Justice and Delinquency Prevention.

Spelman, Elizabeth. 1989. *Inessential Woman*. Boston: Unwin Hyman.

Spradley, James. 1979. *The Ethnographic Interview*. New York: Holt.

Stanko, Elizabeth A. 1990. *Everyday Violence: How Women and Men Experience Sexual and Physical Danger.* London: Pandora.

Steffensmeier, Darrell J. 1983. "Organizational Properties and Sex-Segregation in the Underworld: Building a Sociological Theory of Sex Differences in Crime." *Social Forces* 61: 1010–1032.

Steffensmeier, Darrell J., and Robert Terry. 1986. "Institutional Sexism in the Underworld: A View from the Inside." *Sociological Inquiry* 56: 304–323.

Stein, Nan, Deborah L. Tolman, Michelle V. Porche, and Renee Spencer. 2002. "Gender Safety: A New Concept for Safer and More Equitable Schools." *Journal of School Violence* 1: 35–50.

"St. Louis Post-Dispatch Gateway Guide to Missouri Public Schools." 2003. *St. Louis Post-Dispatch,* May 15, insert, pp. 1–23.

Stombler, Mindy. 1994. " 'Buddies' or 'Slutties': The Collective Sexual Reputation of Fraternity Little Sisters." *Gender and Society* 8: 297–323.

Straus, Murray A. 1979. "Measuring Intrafamily Conflict and Violence: The Conflict Tactics (CT) Scales." *Journal of Marriage and the Family* 41: 75–88.

Straus, Murray A., and Richard J. Gelles, eds. 1990. *Physical Violence in American Families.* New Brunswick, N.J.: Transaction.

Strauss, Anselm L. 1987. *Qualitative Analysis for Social Scientists.* Cambridge: Cambridge University Press.

Struckman-Johnson, Cindy, David Struckman-Johnson, and Peter B. Anderson. 2003. "Tactics of Sexual Coercion: When Men and Women Won't Take No for an Answer." *Journal of Sex Research* 40: 76–86.

Sugarman, David B., and Gerald T. Hotaling. 1997. "Intimate Violence and Social Desirability: A Meta-Analytic Review." *Journal of Interpersonal Violence* 12: 275–290.

Sullivan, Cris M., and Maureen H. Rumptz. 1994. "Adjustment and Needs of African-American Women Who Utilized a Domestic Violence Shelter." *Violence and Victims* 9: 275–286.

Taylor, Jill McLean, Carol Gilligan, and Amy M. Sullivan. 1995. *Between Voice and Silence: Women and Girls, Race and Relationship.* Cambridge: Harvard University Press.

Terrill, William, and Michael D. Reisig. 2003. "Neighborhood Context and Police Use of Force." *Journal of Research in Crime and Delinquency* 40: 291–321.

Terrill, William, Eugene A. Paoline III, and Peter K. Manning. 2003. "Police Culture and Coercion." *Criminology* 41: 1003–1034.

Testa, Maria, and Kurt H. Dermen. 1999. "The Differential Correlates of Sexual Coercion and Rape." *Journal of Interpersonal Violence* 14: 548–561.

Thorne, Barrie. 1993. *Gender Play: Girls and Boys in School.* New Brunswick, N.J.: Rutgers University Press.

Timmerman, Greetje. 2003. "Sexual Harassment of Adolescents Perpetrated by

Teachers and by Peers: An Exploration of the Dynamics of Power, Culture, and Gender in Secondary Schools." *Sex Roles* 44: 231–245.

Tjaden, Patricia, and Nancy Thoennes. 2000. "Prevalence and Consequences of Male-to-Female and Female-to-Male Intimate Partner Violence as Measured by the National Violence against Women Survey." *Violence against Women* 6: 142–161.

Tolman, Deborah L. 1994. "Doing Desire: Adolescent Girls' Struggles for/with Sexuality." *Gender and Society* 8: 324–342.

Tolman, Deborah L., Meg I. Striepe, and Tricia Harmon. 2003a. "Gender Matters: Constructing a Model of Adolescent Sexual Health." *Journal of Sex Research* 40: 4–12.

Tolman, Deborah L., Renee Spencer, Myra Rosen-Reynoso, and Michelle V. Porche. 2003b. "Sowing the Seeds of Violence in Heterosexual Relationships: Early Adolescents Narrate Compulsory Heterosexuality." *Journal of Social Issues* 59: 159–178.

Tolman, Deborah L., Celeste Hirschman, and Emily A. Impett. 2005. "There Is More to the Story: The Place of Qualitative Research on Female Adolescent Sexuality in Policy Making." *Sexuality Research and Social Policy* 2: 4–17.

Truman, Dana M., David M. Tokar, and Ann R. Fischer. 1996. "Dimensions of Masculinity: Relations to Date Rape Supportive Attitudes and Sexual Aggression in Dating Situations." *Journal of Counseling and Development* 74: 555–562.

Tyler, Kimberly A., Danny R. Hoyt, and Les B. Whitbeck. 1998. "Coercive Sexual Strategies." *Violence and Victims* 13: 47–61.

Ullman, Sarah. E. 1999. "A Comparison of Gang and Individual Rape Incidents." *Violence and Victims* 14: 123–133.

Urquiza, Anthony J., and Beth L. Goodlin-Jones. 1994. "Child Sexual Abuse and Adult Revictimization with Women of Color." *Violence and Victims* 9: 223–232.

Valdez, Avelardo. 2007. *Mexican American Girls and Gang Violence.* New York: Palgrave Macmillan.

Valente, Roberta L., Barbara J. Hart, Seema Zeya, and Mary Malefyt. 2001. "The Violence against Women Act of 1994: The Federal Commitment to Ending Domestic Violence, Sexual Assault, Stalking, and Gender-Based Crimes of Violence." Pp. 279–302 in *Sourcebook on Violence against Women,* edited by Claire Renzetti, Jeff Edelsen, and Rachel Bergen. Thousand Oaks, Calif.: Sage.

Vass, Jason S., and Steven R. Gold. 1995. "Effects of Feedback on Emotion in Hypermasculine Males." *Violence and Victims* 10: 217–228.

Vivan, Dina, and Jennifer Langhinrichsen-Rohling. 1994. "Are Bi-directionally Violent Couples Mutually Victimized? A Gender-Sensitive Comparison." *Violence and Victims* 9: 107–124.

Walsh, Anthony. 1987. "The Sexual Stratification Hypothesis and Sexual Assault in Light of the Changing Conceptions of Race." *Criminology* 25: 153–174.

Warshaw, Robin. 1988. *I Never Called It Rape*. New York: Harper and Row.

Way, Niobe. 1995. " 'Can't You See the Courage, the Strength That I Have?': Listening to Urban Adolescent Girls Speak about Their Relationships." *Psychology of Women Quarterly* 19: 107–128.

Weitzer, Ronald. 1999. "Citizen Perceptions of Police Misconduct: Race and Neighborhood Context." *Justice Quarterly* 16: 819–846.

Weitzer, Ronald, and Steven A. Tuch. 2002. "Perceptions of Racial Profiling: Race, Class and Personal Experience." *Criminology* 40: 435–457.

West, Carolyn M., Linda M. Williams, and Jane A. Siegel. 2000. "Adult Sexual Revictimization among Black Women Sexually Abused in Childhood: A Prospective Examination of Serious Consequences of Abuse." *Child Maltreatment* 5: 49–57.

Whaley, Rachel Bridges. 2001. "The Paradoxical Relationship between Gender Inequality and Rape: Toward a Refined Theory." *Gender and Society* 15: 531–555.

Willan, V. J., and Paul Pollard. 2003. "Likelihood of Acquaintance Rape as a Function of Males' Sexual Expectations, Disappointment, and Adherence to Rape-Conducive Attitudes." *Journal of Social and Personal Relationships* 20: 637–661.

Wilson, William Julius. 1996. *When Work Disappears: The World of the New Urban Poor*. New York: Knopf.

Winkel, Frans Willem, and Esther de Kleuver. 1997. "Communication Aimed at Changing Cognitions about Sexual Intimidation: Comparing the Impact of a Perpetrator-Focused versus a Victim-Focused Persuasive Strategy." *Journal of Interpersonal Violence* 12: 513–529.

Wiseman, Rosalind. 2002. *Queen Bees and Wannabes*. New York: Crown.

Wolfer, Terry A. 1999. " 'It Happens All the Time': Overcoming the Limits of Memory and Method for Chronic Community Violence Experience." *Journal of Interpersonal Violence* 14: 1070–1094.

Wood, Kate. 2005. "Contextualizing Group Rape in Post-Apartheid South Africa." *Culture, Health and Sexuality* 7: 303–317.

Wyatt, Gail E. 1992. "The Sociocultural Context of African American and White American Women's Rape." *Journal of Social Issues* 48: 77–91.

Wyatt, Gail E., and Monika Rierderle. 1995. "The Prevalence and Context of Sexual Harassment among African American and White American Women." *Journal of Interpersonal Violence* 10: 309–321.

Yoder, Janice D., and Patricia Aniakudo. 1995. "The Responses of African American Women Firefighters to Gender Harassment at Work." *Sex Roles* 32: 125–137.

Index

Adolescence
 action spaces and, 29–30, 239n4
 dating violence and, 151, 256n3,
  258n18, 259n25
 gendered violence and, 7–8
 in disadvantaged neighborhoods, 7–8,
  32
 sexual victimization and, 195
 See also African American girls
Adult men
 girls' apprehension of, 52–57
 sexual assault and, 124–127
African American girls
 empowerment of, 216–217, 263n49
 rates of victimization, 8, 33
 scholarly neglect of, ix, xiii, 2–3, 11,
  191, 225n11, 228n53
 victimization of, ix–x
Alcohol and drugs, 7–8
 sexual activity and, 129–134
 sexual aggression and, 56, 57, 59, 126–
  134, 195, 196
Anderson, Elijah, 5, 195, 226n23
Anderson, Kristin L., 260n27
Androcentrism in criminology, 2, 41, 69–
  70, 191, 245n18
Aniakudo, Patricia, 111
Asdigian, Nancy L., 252n16

Benson, Michael L., 6, 41
Billson, Janet M., 158
"Blurred boundaries" of girls' victimiza-
  tion and offending, 3, 9
 See also Delinquency
Boswell, A. Ayres, 127
Brown, Annie W., 202

Caring adults, 208, 210–211, 212

Chandy, Joseph M., 251n12
Chavous, Tabbye M., 73
Cisco, 131, 254n45
Cleveland, H. Harrington, 127
Collective efficacy, 6–7, 20, 41, 195, 198–
  199
Community agencies, 201, 209–213, 215
Community programs
 need for, 199–201, 211–213
Conflict Tactics Scale, 14
 critiques of, 231n63, 256n2
Controlling behavior. *See* Dating relation-
  ships; Dating violence
Cool pose, 158–160, 161, 166–168, 173,
  175, 188–189

Dating relationships, 257n5
 conflicts in, 153, 160–171
 control in, 161, 166–171
 cool pose and, 158–159, 161, 166–168,
  171
 girls as "emotionally out of control" in,
  168–169, 189
 infidelity in, 153, 162–166
 insecurity in, 160, 164
 jealousy in, 160–166, 169, 171, 173–
  174
 Playa' climate and, 156–158, 160–161,
  164, 166
 positive features of, 158
Dating violence
 attitudes about, 178–179
 chronic battering, 183–185
 control and, 183–186, 259n25–26
 distinctive features of adolescent, 151,
  256n3, 258n18, 259n25
 emotional detachment and, 175–177,
  182

Dating violence (*continued*)
female-perpetrated, 172, 173–177
gender and interpretations of, 172, 173,
177, 180, 182–183, 186–188,
259n27, 260n28
gendered consequences of, 152, 260n34
gendered patterns of, 153, 171–188,
189–190, 196, 256n3, 260n34
gender parity in rates of, 152, 256n2
intervening on, 185, 187–188, 260n32
male-perpetrated, 172, 177–188
measurement issues, 258n21. *See also*
Conflict tactics scale
minimization of girls', 177
non-reciprocal male, 172, 183–188
perceived infidelity and, 174, 175–176,
178
"play" violence, 172, 258n20
rates among sample, 151–152, 153,
172, 185
triggers for, 153
See also Intimate partner violence
Delinquency
participation in, 25, 116, 238n92
risks for victimization and, 3, 8, 9, 35,
36, 116–119, 201
sexual aggression and, 251n251
Derman, Kurt H., 121
Disadvantaged neighborhoods
crime in, 19–20,
cultural structure of, 33
drug trade in, 21–22, 55–56. *See also*
Drug trade
gangs in, 22–23, 35. *See also* Gangs
policing and police distrust in, 21, 45–
46, 47, 53, 60, 63, 150, 202–205,
237n84, 237n86, 261n18
violence against girls in, xi, 1, 57–61,
218
violence against women in, 41–48. *See
also* Violence against women
See also Urban disadvantage
Double binds, 52, 87, 92, 99, 102–103,
111, 193–194
Drug trade
disadvantaged neighborhoods and, 21–
22, 25, 35, 129, 192
harassment and, 22
participation in drug sales, 25, 238n92
sexual harassment and, 55–56
sexual mistreatment and, 56

Drug use. *See* Alcohol and drugs
Dupper, David R., 207, 249n56

Emotional disengagement. *See* Cool pose;
Dating relationships; Dating violence
Exposure to violence
delinquency as a predictor of, 8, 116
family, 116–118
neighborhood context and, 22–23, 25,
28, 30, 33–34, 35
personal victimization among sample,
241n14
See also Neighborhood risks; Violence
against women; Witnessing violence

Family problems
risks for victimization and, 116–118
sexual abuse, 116, 122, 123, 240n10,
250n3
violence, 116–118, 123
Felson, Richard B., 259n26
Finkelhor, David, 252n16
Fitzclarence, Lindsay, 207
Franklin, Karen, 135
Freudenberg, Nicholas, 212

Gang rape
characteristics of, 136
group processes and, 135–136
masculinity and, 135
party context and, 141–143
use of drugs in, 141
See also Running trains
Gangs, 22–24, 35–36, 56, 134–135,
238n89, 239n93
gender inequality and, xv, 9
risk exposure and, 35
violence against girls and, 6, 9, 135
violence and, 22
Gavey, Nicola, 121
Gender harassment
definitions of, 73, 74, 242n22, 246n22
in schools, xi, 71–75, 106, 111
relationship with sexual harassment, 51,
94
See also Sexual harassment
Gibbs, Jewelle Taylor, 7
Goodlin-Jones, Beth L., 251n4
Gottfredson, Denise C., 67, 205
Gourdine, Ruby, 202
Graham, Sandra, 245n21, 248n39

Grauerholz, Liz, 118, 197
Guadagno, Rosanna E., 249n54

Hagan, John, 9
Hanley, M. Joan, 258n21, 259n24
Hiese, Lori L., 197
Houston, Sandra, 91
Hummer, Robert A., 4–5, 127
Humor
  functions of, 48, 84, 94
Hwang, Naomi, 91

Infidelity. *See* Dating relationships; Dating
  violence
Institutional accountability. *See* Police;
  Policy recommendations; Schools
Intimate partner violence, 41–47, 151
  male peer support and, 6, 179–180
  predictors of, 259n24
  urban inequality and, 6–7, 41, 190
  See also Dating violence
Irwin, Harvey J., 251n13

Jealousy. *See* Dating relationships
Juvonen, Jaana, 245n21, 248n39

Kalof, Linda, 251n4, 252n24
Kenway, Jane, 207
King, Neal, 119, 255n58
Kleuver, Esther, 219
Klinger, David A., 202
Kopels, Sandra, 207, 249n56
Koss, Mary P., 242n24, 253n34
Krivo, Lauren J., 21

Lauritsen, Janet L., 8, 33, 197–198,
  251n16
Lee, Valerie E., 207
Loe, Meika, 84

Majors, Richard, 158
Male peer support
  of violence against women and girls, 5,
  6, 59, 83, 87, 95, 100–101, 119, 155,
  179–180, 231n64
  See also Masculinity
Marciniak, Liz M., 252n24
Marin, Amy J., 249n54
Martin, Patricia Y., 4, 4–5, 127
Masculinity
  gender relations and, 154–160

relationship conflicts and, 153, 160–171
structural dislocation and, 5, 119, 128,
  197, 218
violence against women and, 5, 59, 119,
  127–128, 197, 218, 226n24, 247n37,
  255n58
See also Cool pose; Male peer support;
  Normative heterosexuality; Playa'
  climate
Mason-Schrock, Douglas, 263n49
McCall, Nathan, 1
McCarthy, Bill, 9
Messner, Steven F., 259n26
Methodology. *See* Study methodology
Miller, Jody, 256n4
Molider, Christian, 256n3, 258n18,
  259n27
Morse, Barbara J., 256n3
Muehlenhard, Charlene, 253n30
Myth of the Black rapist, 2, 252n24

National Crime Victimization Survey, 8,
  33, 69, 256n2
Neighborhood context. *See* Disadvantaged
  neighborhoods; Neighborhood risks;
  Racially heterogenous neighborhoods;
  Residential instability; St. Louis City;
  Study setting; Urban disadvantage
Neighborhood peer networks, 57, 62, 63–
  64, 119, 162
  delinquency and, 8
  sexual aggression and, 48, 57, 59, 135,
  194, 195
  victimization risk and, 8, 118
  See also Male peer support
Neighborhood risks, 192
  exposure to community violence, 33–
  34, 240n7
  gang-related, 35
  gendered perceptions of, 33–41,
  240n12, 241n14
  girls' behavior/dress and, 39–40, 51,
  214n16
  neighborhood geography and, 36–37
  nighttime and, 36–37
  perceptions of girls as weak and, 38–39
  sexualized, 36, 37–38
Non-intervention norms, 43–44, 46–47,
  61, 66, 100, 113, 143, 145, 185, 188,
  189, 195, 196, 249n49
  consequences of, 108, 112

Non-intervention norms (*continued*)
  gender and, 47–48
  See also Disadvantaged neighborhoods;
    Risk-avoidance strategies
Normative heterosexuality
  sexual aggression and, 119, 120, 195,
    220, 250n1, 255n58
  See also Male peer support; Sexual
    double standard
Norms against male violence, 172, 173–
    174, 248n42
  contingent nature of, 97, 177–180,
    181–182, 185, 259n23

O'Keefe, Maura, 256n3, 258n18, 259n27
O'Neil, Patrick, 258n21, 259n24

Patillo, Mary E., 26
Peterson, Ruth, 21
Peterson, Zöe, 253n30
Playa' climate, 154–157, 160–161, 166,
    170, 174, 188–189, 258n13
"Play" claims, 49, 82–87
  contested nature of, 83–84
Police
  distrust of, 21, 47, 150, 202–205,
    237n84, 237n86, 261n18
  lack of responsiveness, 45–46, 53, 60,
    203, 261n18
  sexual misconduct by, 53, 203
  See also Policy recommendations
Policy recommendations
  bridging the gender divide, 218–221
  building solidarity among girls, 214–
    217
  challenging gender inequality, 214–221
  challenging street masculinities, 218–
    221
  enhancing efficacy among girls, 214–
    217
  facilitating relationships with caring
    adults, 208–214
  improving neighborhoods, 197–201
  increasing institutional accountability,
    201–202
  police accountability, 202–205
  school accountability, 205–208
  stabilizing community agencies, 208–
    214
Pollard, Paul, 255n58

Public space
  male control of, xi, xii, 39, 41, 65, 195

Quinet, Kenna F. Davis, 251n16

Racially heterogeneous neighborhoods,
    27–28
Racial segregation, 17–18
  See also Disadvantaged neighborhoods;
    St. Louis City; Study setting; Urban
    disadvantage
Rape, 60–61
  alcohol, drugs and, 132–133
  culture, 4
  fear of reporting, 61
  intraracial patterns of, 3
  isolation strategies and acquaintance,
    127
  male peer support and, 5, 59, 119
  social context and, 4
  structural gender inequality and, 4,
    226n16
  See also Gang rape; Running trains; Sex-
    ual aggression; Sexual assault; Sexual
    coercion; Sexual victimization
Rape myths
  correlates of acceptance of, 252n24
  sexual violence and, 252n22, 253n34
Rape prevention programming, 215–216,
    219–220, 263n48
Relationship violence. *See* Dating violence;
    Intimate partner violence
Repeat victimization, 91, 114–115, 122–
    123
  risks for, 116–118, 123, 251n13,
    251n16
Residential instability, 28–29, 64
  See also Disadvantaged neighborhoods;
    Policy recommendations
Resistance strategies
  for addressing sexual aggression, 143–
    149
  in addressing sexual harassment, 92–99,
    111
  See also Retaliation; Risk-avoidance
    strategies Self-help strategies; Standing
    up for oneself
Retaliation
  for sexual violence, 133, 141
Re-victimization. *See* repeat victimization

Risk-avoidance strategies
  community ties and, 62–64
  for sexual violence, 143–149, 254n42
  gender and, 61–62, 242n28
  in neighborhoods, 61–65, 145, 192–
    193
  limitations of, 192–193, 216
  public space and, 62, 65
  See also Retaliation; Resistance strate-
    gies; Self-help strategies, Standing up
    for oneself
Rodriguez, Luis J., 1
Running game, 160
  See also Playa' climate
Running trains, 58, 134–143, 242n25
  perceptions of consent and, 136–140,
    255n54–56
  rates of, 120, 134–135, 254n47
  serious delinquency and, 135, 254n46
  urban disadvantage and, 1, 149
  See also Gang Rape

Sample characteristics, 12–13
  age range, 228n56
  alcohol and drug use, 128
  arrests, 229n59
  attitudes about dating violence, 178–
    179, 259n23
  childhood sexual abuse, 242n26
  dating relationships, 257n5
  dating violence, 151–152, 153, 172, 185
  exposure to community violence, 33–
    34, 240n7
  exposure to gangs, 238n89, 239n93
  family problems, 116–117
  family violence, 116, 240n10
  gender harassment, 242n22
  participation in drug sales, 25, 238n92
  participation in serious delinquency, 25,
    116, 238n92
  personal victimization, 241n14
  residential mobility, 28
  running trains, 134–135
  sexual activity, 253n33
  sexual harassment, 48, 71, 242n22
  sexual victimization, 57, 114–118, 149,
    250n3
  sexual violence perpetration, 119–120
Sampson, Robert J., 18, 29, 33, 197–198
Sanday, Peggy Reeves, 4, 135, 218

Schools
  gender harassment in, xi, 73–75
  responsiveness to harassment, 103–110,
    112–113, 194, 205–208, 248n45,
    249n46
  sexual harassment in, xi, 70, 71–73,
    75–82, 193–194
  urban disadvantage and, 67–69, 112–
    113
  violence in, 67, 68–70, 91, 95, 193
  See also Policy recommendations; St.
    Louis Public Schools
Schwalbe, Michael L. 263n49
Scully, Diana, 10, 252n22
Self-help strategies
  victimization and, xi
  See also Resistance strategies; Retalia-
    tion; Risk-avoidance strategies
Sexual aggression
  alcohol, drugs and, 57, 59, 127–134,
    195–196
  contextual features of, 119–143, 149,
    195
  degradation of women and, 133–134
  interpretations of, 128–130, 131, 144
  intervening on, 147–148
  normative heterosexuality and, 119,
    120, 195, 220, 250n1, 255n58
  rates among sample, 119–120
  See also Rape; Sexual assault; Sexual co-
    ercion Sexual victimization
Sexual assault
  adult men and, 124–127
  alcohol, drugs and, 57, 59, 128
  in neighborhoods, 57–61
  See also Rape; Sexual aggression; Sexual
    coercion; Sexual victimization
Sexual coercion, 250n1
  alcohol, drugs and, 57, 59, 128, 130,
    132
  in neighborhoods, 57–61
  risks for, 121, 123, 130
  sexual compliance and, 119–123
  targeting vulnerable girls for, 58–59,
    121–122
  See also Rape; Sexual aggression; Sexual
    assault; Sexual victimization
Sexual double standard, xvi, 119, 154,
    155–156, 166, 170, 188, 196,
    252n25

Sexual double standard (*continued*)
  dating conflict and, 188
  girls sexual agency and, 250n62
  girls' sexual reputation and, 79, 87,
    248n43
  See also Normative heterosexuality
Sexual harassment
  ambivalence about, 48–49
  boundary testing and, 89–90
  by adolescent peers, 48–52
  by adult men, 52–57
  definitions of, 75, 242n22, 246n22,
    246n29
  drug trade and, 55–56
  escalations of, 51, 87, 94–99
  harmful effects of, 70, 110, 112,
    245n20
  in neighborhoods, 48–57
  in schools, xi, 70, 71–73, 75–82, 193–
    194
  interpretations of, 50, 51, 82–92,
    246n24
  intervening on, 50, 53–54, 55, 101–
    102, 108, 112, 248n44
  limits of reactive remedies for, 107, 112,
    207, 249n57
  male peer support and, 83, 87, 95, 100–
    101
  motives for, 84–85, 86
  physical, 80–82
  public nature of, 95
  race and, 245n21
  rates among sample, 48, 71, 242n22
  relationship to sexual violence, 57, 91–
    92, 95, 113, 114, 118, 194, 247n38
  responses to, 52, 92–99, 111, 247n38,
    249n54
  retaliatory violence and, 95–99
  role of peers in, 99–103
  school/neighborhood overlaps in, 80,
    113
  school responsiveness to, 103–110,
    112–113, 205–208, 248n45, 249n46
  selective targeting for, 87–92
  sexual rumors, 75–80
  systemic nature of, 71–73, 110
  U.S. Supreme Court ruling on, 112, 205,
    249n56
  verbal, 75–80, 94–95
  See also Gender harassment

Sexual victimization
  coping with, 150, 196, 208, 213
  perceptions of consent and, 253n30
  race and, 251n4
  rates among sample, 57, 114–118, 149,
    250n3
  risks for, 6–7, 39–41, 57, 59, 116–118,
    130, 141, 154, 214
  sexual harassment and, 57, 91–92, 95,
    113, 114, 118, 247n38
  See also Rape; Sexual aggression; Sexual
    assault; Sexual coercion
Shelton, J. Nicole, 73
Social isolation, 6
  racially heterogeneous neighborhoods
    and, 30
  sexual harassment and, 92, 103, 248n39
  victimization and, x
  See also Policy recommendations; Self-
    help strategies
Spade, Joan Z., 127
Standing up for oneself
  importance of, 52, 66, 93, 145–146,
    194, 248n39
  See also Resistance strategies; Risk-
    avoidance strategies
Stein, Nan, 70
St. Louis City
  population decline, 17, 236n78
  racial segregation and racial inequality,
    17–18, 236n77, 237n79, 237n83
  socioeconomic characteristics, 17
  See also Study setting
St. Louis Public Schools, 67–69, 103, 205,
    243n5
  performance scores, 243n4, 244n11
  racial distrust and, 244n8
  rates of crime in, 69
  See also Schools
Strategies to gain sexual compliance, 119–
    123, 128, 129, 131–133, 154, 196
  See also Sexual coercion
Strategies to stay safe, 61–65, 92–95,
    143–150, 192
  See also Resistance strategies; Risk-
    avoidance strategies
Strauss, Murray A., 256n2
Study methodology, 8–16
  comparative design, xii, 10–11, 228n50,
    228n54

data analysis procedures, 235n71
human subjects protections, 12, 228n57, 238n90
interviewer characteristics and impact, 229n58, 232n67, 255n56
issues of validity and reliability, 232n65, 232n67
qualitative interview data, 10, 12, 14–16
sampling, 12–13, 25
survey data, 10, 12, 13–14, 230n60–62, 231n63–64
See also Sample characteristics; Study setting
Study setting, 16–30
gendered descriptions of, 23–25, 65, 238n91, 239n93
proximity to crime, 25–26, 238n89
youths' neighborhood characteristics, 17, 237n82
youths' neighborhood descriptions, 19–25
See also St. Louis City; St. Louis Public Schools

Testa, Maria, 121
Tolman, Deborah L., 220
Treister, Laura, 260n27
Truman, Dana M., 220

Umberson, Deborah, 260n27
Urban disadvantage
causes of, 197–198
ecological embeddedness of, 21, 26, 28–30
gendered dimensions of, 32–33, 119. *See also* Violence against women
neighborhood processes and, 20–21, 226n23
racial inequality and, xvi, 1, 18, 21
schools and, 67–69
See also Disadvantaged neighborhoods; St. Louis City; Study setting
Urquiza, Anthony, J., 251n4

Victim assistance. *See* Victim's service agencies
Victim blaming, x, 9, 39–41, 42, 51–52, 58, 59–61, 87–92, 93, 95, 102, 128–130, 134, 143, 155–156, 196

consequences of, xi, 47, 66, 92–93, 193, 214–215
dating violence and, 185–188, 189
reasons for girls', 214–215
sexual harassment and, 88, 90, 113
sexual violence and, 146, 253n30
See also Victim labeling
Victim labeling, 42, 91–95, 102, 110, 118, 123
See also Victim blaming
Victim's service agencies
skepticism of, 149–150, 209–210, 213
Violence against women
adolescence and, 7–8
as public spectacle, 43–45, 48, 66, 193
gender inequality and, 2
intervention into, 45–46, 147–148, 215
lack of police responsiveness, 45–46, 203
male dominated settings and, 4–5
male peer support and, 5, 6, 231n64.
See also Male peer support
masculinity and, 5, 59, 119, 127–128, 197, 218, 226n24, 247n37, 255n58
public nature of, 41–48, 56, 66, 142–143, 151
urban inequality and, xvi–xvii, 1, 6, 191, 221
witnessing, 34–35, 41–48, 241n20
See also Dating violence; Gang rape; Gender harassment; Intimate partner violence; Rape; Repeat victimization; Running trains; Sexual aggression, Sexual assault; Sexual coercion; Sexual harassment; Sexual victimization

Wade, Bruce H., 252n24
Way, Niobe, 217
Whaley, Rachel B., 226n16
White, Norman A., 256n4
Willan, V. J., 255n58
Wilson, William J., 18
Winkel, Frans Willem, 219
Witnessing violence, 33–34
against women, 34–35, 41–48, 241n20
impact of, 34, 47, 66, 151, 240n8
Wood, Kate, 255n54
Wyatt, Gail E., 217

Yoder, Janice D., 111

About the Author

Jody Miller is Associate Professor of Criminology at the University of Missouri–St. Louis. She is the author of *One of the Guys: Girls, Gangs, and Gender.*